LAMENT FOR A NOTION

LAMENT FOR A NOTION

The Life and Death of Canada's Bilingual Dream

SCOTT REID

ARSENAL PULP PRESS
Vancouver, Canada

LAMENT FOR A NOTION
Copyright © 1993 by Scott Reid

All rights reserved. No part of this book may be reproduced in any part by any means without the written permission of the publisher, except by a reviewer, who may use brief excerpts in a review.

ARSENAL PULP PRESS
100-1062 Homer Street
Vancouver, B.C.
Canada v6b 2w9

The publisher gratefully acknowledges the assistance of the Canada Council and the Cultural Services Branch, B.C. Ministry of Tourism and Minister Responsible for Culture.

Typeset by the Vancouver Desktop Publishing Centre
Printed and bound in Canada by Kromar Printing

CANADIAN CATALOGUING IN PUBLICATION DATA:

Reid, Scott, 1964-
  Lament for a notion

  Includes bibliographical references and index.
  ISBN 0-88978-269-5

  1. Canada—Languages—Law and legislation. 2. Bilingualism—Law and legislation—Canada. 3. Canada—Languages—Political aspects. I. Title.
KE4413.R44 1993   344.71'09   C93-091843-6
KF4483.B5R44 1993

Contents

	ACKNOWLEDGEMENTS	vii
	INTRODUCTION	9
1	Language and Justice	15
2	Linguistic Intolerance and Demographic Decline: A Canadian History	40
3	The Victory of Asymmetrical Bilingualism	63
4	The Limits of Language Policy	83
5	Assimilation and the Failure of Federal Action	100
6	Speaking in Tongues: The Delivery of Official Language Services	124
7	Passing the Buck: Legislating Language Use in the Private Sector	154
8	The Lord of the Files: The Bureaucracy of Language in the Federal Public Service	169
9	Language and Education	199
10	The Dollars and Sense of Official Bilingualism	222
	CONCLUSION	251
	APPENDIX A Federal Translation Costs: A Study in Waste	254
	FOOTNOTES	260
	NOTES ON FIGURES	299
	BIBLIOGRAPHY	301
	INDEX	315

Acknowledgements

I am grateful for the extraordinary support I received from many friends, colleagues, and family members throughout the two years that I spent researching and writing this book. They include:

Larry Thompson, my editorial assistant, who came as close as anyone ever will to convincing me of the truth of Isaac Babel's dictum that there is nothing so powerful as a well placed period.

Stephanie Mullen, my research assistant, who single-handedly filed three percent of all the federal access to information requests placed by the Canadian media last year, in her merciless pursuit of the data and documentation needed for the book. She also appears to have set some sort of Carleton University record for interlibrary loans.

Neil Morrison, who critiqued the manuscript, for his detailed review, his numerous corrections and suggestions, and particularly his recollections of his work on the B&B Commission and his observations on Bill 101 (on which subject we still disagree).

Tom Flanagan, to whom earlier versions of Chapters Six and Eight were submitted as background papers. It was this exercise that made me realize the need for this book.

Brian Lam, my editor, who patiently tolerated endless delays and rewrites.

My father, Gordon Reid, for his wisdom and support.

My mother, Leatrice Reid, for her patience and support.

Suzanne Fraser, for her proofreading prowess.

Richard Joy, for his help early on in the research process.

Tony Kondaks, for permission to quote from personal correspondence.

Ken Pack, for providing background information on the impact of Canada's packaging and labelling laws.

The helpful library staff at Carleton University and the National Library of Canada, where Stephanie did most of her research, and at the University of Ottawa, where I did most of mine.

A number of public servants who cannot be named.

And, as always, Poh Lan, to whom this book is dedicated.

Introduction

> Some forget that it wasn't bilingualism that made the country, that it cannot ensure its survival, and that it could even lead to its destruction.
> —*Christian Dufour (1990)*[1]

> ... the main goal of any language policy should be to promote linguistic justice.... [But] perhaps, at this point in our history, no single policy will be both fair and unifying.
> —*Leslie Green and Denise Réaume, Network on the Constitution (1991)*[2]

PICTURE the scene:

A sumptuously decorated room, dimly lit by a single Tiffany lamp suspended low over the polished surface of a conference table. One by one, sinister figures move out of the shadowy corners to take their places at the table. The stern and ominous faces of the conspirators are concealed by the darkness. Some are clothed in expensive suits, others wear judges' gowns and one is in the deep red robes of a cardinal of the Roman Catholic Church. As Canada's political, economic and social leaders begin their meeting, each one silently makes the sign of the fleur-de-lys. The Prime Minister bids his minions and ministers be seated. The conspiracy to Frenchify Canada is in session.

Any resemblance between this scene and reality is purely accidental. Unfortunately, two centuries of Canadian language policy have been built on cheap stereotypes and conspiracy theories only slightly less ridiculous than this one. There have been surprisingly few periods in our history in which there have not been large numbers of people in one or the other of the country's two main language groups thoroughly convinced that their language was about to be swept into oblivion by its rival. In consequence, there have only been a few brief interludes in which English Canadians have not been busily at work systematically suspending the language rights of French Canadians, or in which French Canadians have not been doing similar violence to the rights of those who speak English.

Invariably, the cause of such demographic fears has been ignorance. The sociology of language, the patterns of language demographics, and the economic factors at the root of assimilation are all immensely complex subjects. Their effects concern everybody, but they are understood by almost no one.

Faced with a few alarming statistics about dropping birthrates, rising immigration or rapid assimilation, people who don't have all the facts about all these subjects will naturally begin to speculate about the possibility that their language is in danger of decline or extinction.

Add to this sense of alarm the not-very-well-understood language policies of various levels of government who seem to be promoting the collective interests of one language group at the expense of the other, and the material exists for some pretty deep-seated fears. In this way, ignorance can breed suspicion, resentment, prejudice and, ultimately, hatred. These are not national characteristics that Canadians immediately recognize in themselves, but they are as much a part of this country as snowdrifts, hockey, and forgetting the words to the national anthem.

To a disturbing extent, the blame for Canadians' ignorance on matters of language, and thus their fears, must be laid at the foot of the body that governs our land. The federal government certainly is not engaged in the conspiracies imagined by perfervid critics like Jock Andrews, who in his book, *Bilingual Today, French Tomorrow*, warns that Ottawa is engaged in an elaborate plot to force all English-Canadians to assimilate into the French language. But in rejecting conspiracy theories and explanations that rely on elaborate Machiavellianism, I do not mean to suggest that federal language regulation is open, or honest, or just, or well-administered, or even internally consistent.

I do mean to suggest that federal language policy, which was intended to bring Canada long-needed justice and simultaneously to foster national unity, has in practice abandoned the first of these two goals whenever it clashes with the second. From a starting point of well-meaning idealism in the Pearson and early Trudeau years, the federal ship of state has drifted incrementally into a position where, in matters of federal jurisdiction, it continues to subsidize and support both the French-speaking minority outside Quebec and the English-speaking minority within the province, while in its interactions with the Quebec government it has been trapped into silently aiding in enforced French-only unilingualism. This self-contradictory stand was a source of silent agony for Pierre Trudeau; it seems to have posed less of a dilemma for his less principled successors and underlings, who have accepted the contradictions as facts of life or even embraced them as sources of bureaucratic or brokerage power.

Having been trapped into supporting mutually contradictory policies, various agencies in Ottawa have found it necessary to conceal, behind veils of bureaucratic obscurity and under mountains of deliberately misleading statistics, the information that Canadians need in order to gain an intelligent understanding of language policy. By not being open and honest about the manner in which Official Bilingualism is administered, the federal government has become its own worst enemy, and ultimately has found itself having to deal with ludicrous visions of itself, like the one sketched out above.

As things stand today, Ottawa is fully willing to sacrifice linguistic justice for the sake of national unity wherever and whenever necessary. Increasingly, it does so as a matter of course.

It is the slow and painful death of the notion that justice should be co-equal with unity as a policy objective, or even accorded superior status in Ottawa's language policy, that this book laments.

Perhaps the sacrifice of justice on the altar of unity was inevitable. Indeed, the logic of using language policy as an instrument of unity forces the federal government to embrace practices and policies that are unjust by any consistent set of standards. This is because both the francophones who form the majority in Quebec and the anglophones who form the majority in the rest of Canada are capable of unmaking the federation. So each group must be propitiated according to its own standards.

In order to be effective in deflecting separatism, federal politicians know that they must demonstrate to Quebec's francophone majority that the French language will be more strongly promoted within a united Canada than in an independent Quebec. If such a demonstration could be made, Ottawa would outflank the separatists as defenders of the French culture, Québécois separatism would lose its *raison d'être*, and Canadian unity would be guaranteed.

The Quebec government's language policies likewise seek to boost the prestige, historical status and assimilative power of the French language relative to English. This is done mostly by placing legal restrictions on the use of English in areas of provincial jurisdiction (education, the workplace, municipal services, etc.). To outflank the separatists, Ottawa must tolerate these actions. As well, it must promote the French language outside Quebec, while warning that such protection and subsidies as the francophones in other provinces presently enjoy would be swept away by Quebec independence.

But of course, there is a fundamental difference between the policies of the two governments. Quebec can promote its ends openly and without duplicity, while Ottawa must play both sides of the language fence. In order to avoid alienating English Canada completely, the federal government must take a stance completely incompatible with its policy of outdoing the *indépendantistes* as defenders of the French language. Thus, Ottawa asserts publicly that its goal is equal treatment for both official-language minorities, and insists that all its language policies are carried out in the name of this equality.

The practical result of this insistence on equality is that if any right or service is extended by the federal government to the francophone minority outside Quebec, it must also be extended to the English-speaking minority inside Quebec. Services and rights extended to francophones outside Quebec serve the goal of promoting unity, but when the reverse is done within Quebec, it only serves to provide an additional reminder to French-speaking Quebecers that English is an omnipresent cultural threat.

Faced with these contradictions, federal language policy has become inconsistent, confused and generally counterproductive. Quebec government policy, by contrast, may be bloody-minded but it is undeniably straightforward: the French language must be protected regardless of cost, and that is that.

So perverse is the present mismatched set of language laws governing Canada that:
- the federal government's official definition of "sufficient demand" for minority-language services is a dozen pages long and so convoluted that it is necessary to use Canada's Access to Information law to find out which parts of the country have been designated as eligible for these services;
- under the federal laws guaranteeing minority-language services, the twenty anglophones of Barkmere, Quebec qualify for federal services in English. Under the province of Quebec's minority-language services law, the 119,000 anglophones[3] of the city of Montreal are judged to be too insignificant a proportion of the municipal population to qualify for municipal services in English;
- the federal government is the chief financier of Quebec's Bill 101, as the result of a transfer payment policy designed to foster national unity;
- in order to boost French-speaking participation in the federal public service, the federal government has adopted a system of hiring and promotion that not only systematically discriminates against most anglophones, but also against two-thirds of Canada's francophones;
- a quarter of a century after the *Official Languages Act* was adopted in the hopes of discouraging Quebec separatism, Official Bilingualism has added nearly $50 billion to the federal debt, substantially reducing Quebec's financial incentive to remain in Canada. Moreover, the enormous cost of bilingualism has caused a backlash in English Canada that is so severe that many English Canadians are prepared, for the first time ever, to tolerate Quebec separation, or even to throw the province out of Confederation.

This book has three objectives. The first is to review Canada's ignoble history of intolerance and misunderstanding on matters of language, which is so much at odds with the otherwise open, generous, and tolerant nature of both French- and English-speaking Canadians. I will argue that the omnipresent fears that have always been at the source of Canadian language laws are such powerful political forces that they make it virtually impossible for politicians to successfully execute ambitious language policies of the sort that Pierre Trudeau introduced when he first came to office.

The second objective is to attack the myths and misunderstandings that underlie most of today's federal language policies. Not only are Ottawa's language policies ambitious in scope, the unproved assumptions upon which they were initially based are positively heroic. In particular, an amazing leap of faith was made regarding the ability of governments to control the processes of assimilation. This faith will be shown to have been badly misplaced.

Finally, I will examine the practical impact of the current language policies of the federal government. The pervasive and often destructive impact of Official Bilingualism, as it is presently practiced, on fields as diverse as education, public service hiring, and cross-border shopping will be put under the microscope. I will also provide a well-researched estimate of the annual cost of federal official languages programs, which is so often a source of dispute, and so rarely a subject of careful analysis.

A Note on the Title

Some readers will have noticed the similarity between the title of this book and that of another, published in 1965. In that year, Canadian philosopher George Grant published a slim volume titled *Lament for a Nation*. To lament, Grant explained, is to cry out in grief at the death of something loved. The book was his way of crying out at the death of the political culture and self-image of English-speaking Canada. He feared the apparent victory of a new continentalist self-image, which would cause Canadians to willingly assimilate into the ubiquitous and homogenizing cultural influence of international conformity. By contrast, Grant found Quebec's communal reaffirmation of its sense of collective identity to be invigorating and admirable (although he felt that in the long run Quebec was doomed to the same fate as English Canada).

It was at precisely this time that the Pearson government was conducting its experiments with reconstituting the federation. Within three years, Pierre Trudeau would take power with an eclectic and riveting vision of a new language policy that would be the rectification of past wrongs and the basis for a new pan-Canadian culture.

At the time it seemed that the dangers of which Grant had warned might, perhaps, be put off by this daring new approach. The nation whose death Grant had predicted might, in a sense, be replaced by this new post-nationalist ideal, or notion. Canada would not only survive, but would serve as a model of unity and linguistic justice to the rest of the world.

Unfortunately, Trudeau's city on the hill turned out to be based on little more than the half-thought-out contrivances of an idiosyncratic personal philosophy.

As Trudeau's language policies imposed increasingly heavy burdens but failed to deliver their predicted benefits, Canadians became increasingly alienated from their central national institutions. The failure of Brian Mulroney to address this alienation drove popular frustrations to new heights, as demonstrated by the results of the 1993 federal election. Language policy is not the only policy from which alienation is felt, but it is central to the frustration and anger felt by Canadians of both language groups.

My lament, therefore, is for the loss of faith, of confidence, and of a quarter century of precious time, while Canadian politics has been dominated by a language policy that provides no more than the chimera of the justice it promised, nor of the unity it was supposed to guarantee.

CHAPTER ONE

Language and Justice

> ...the main goal of any language policy should be to promote linguistic justice. Nothing in the conventional analysis even addresses this question.
> —Leslie Green and Denise Réaume,
> *Newsletter of The Network on the Constitution (July 1991)*[1]

FOR THIRTY YEARS, successive Canadian governments have wielded official languages policy as if it were nothing more than a weapon in the battle for national unity. But often English- and French-speaking Canadians have looked to federal policy with different objectives in mind. Rather than adopting a single policy which seems just and then holding to it firmly, the federal government has repeatedly wavered, trying to give each side what it wants, even when the two linguistic communities' visions clash and cancel one another out. Three decades of attempting to please everybody at once have created a vast, top-heavy edifice of language laws that are incoherent, contradictory, unjust and mostly self-defeating. It is not surprising, therefore, that Canada's language regime is on the verge of self-destruction.

Canadian politicians can always be counted on to talk at length of the importance of fair treatment for minorities, of the necessity for equal status between English and French, and of the value of respecting our founding cultures. But their words are often clouded in a haze of conceptual confusion, to say nothing of the usual layers of deception and vagueness that mask political rhetoric in all countries. Canada has no single, pithy, universally approved definition of linguistic justice that is accepted by all and sundry.

This oversight is not without its advantages for policy-makers. It means there is no clear, generally-accepted model of linguistic justice against which existing policies can be compared and found wanting. On the other hand, the absence of universal agreement on linguistic first principles is precisely why we have unity problems in the first place.

Historically, linguistically-mixed federations have based their language laws on one of two philosophies. The first is known as the principle of territorialism. Under this principle, language rights are non-portable; in other words, they do not cross borders. The territory in which each citizen lives determines the rights he or she will hold. As a rule, territorialism means in practice that the language of the majority in each province or state of the federation is the only language in which government services are offered, courts are administered, laws are published, and children are educated. Minorities have no right to use their own language outside of private transactions, and are expected simply to conform.

The second philosophy of language administration is known as the *personality* principle. Under this principle, place of residence has no bearing on individual language rights, which are fully portable. All services are available in all official languages throughout the federation, regardless of the language of the local majority.

The territorial principle is appropriate for federations where the linguistic minorities are very small, since it keeps the costs of servicing these minorities to a minimum. The personality principle increases these costs, but it is generally recognized as the best system for federations in which the minorities are large and evenly spread throughout the constituent units of the country.

Neither system by itself is well suited to Canada, with its large but scattered minorities. In order to be just, both to the minorities that benefit from broadly extended language rights, and to the majorities that must foot most of the bill, the policy used in this country would have to combine features of the two principles.

An alternative which would work well in Canada would be to apply the personality principle in parts of the country where the minorities are large and concentrated, and territoriality where they are thinly spread. This would keep costs low, but would still service most of the individuals who are members of minority communities. This policy has been called *territorial bilingualism* by some of its advocates, since it would extend institutional bilingualism only to certain territories within Canada.

Instead of adopting this policy, Ottawa has lurched unsystematically between outright advocacy of the personality principle and partial adaptation of a different form of compromise between the territorial and personality principles. This second form of compromise accomplishes almost the exact reverse of the ideal territorial bilingualism solution. It applies the territorial principle to Canada's most populous and geographically concentrated minority language grouping and extends the personality principle to thinly scattered populations. This policy was described as *asymmetrical bilingualism* by Lucien Bouchard when he first entered federal politics.[2] Official Ottawa does not use this name, but it has allowed elements of the concept to creep into its policies. In moving towards asymmetrical bilingualism, Canada has adopted a policy that extends minimal benefits at a high cost, both in dollars and in the inconveniences created for the majority communities.

As conceived by its advocates, asymmetrical bilingualism extends full and extensive rights to Canada's francophone minority—which is widely dispersed across nine provinces—and imposes strict limits on Quebec's English speakers, who are mostly located in a single city. This fact explains the 'asymmetry' label: full rights to speakers of French, second class status to speakers of English.

The federal government does not endorse this inherent ethnic discrimination, and practices it only reluctantly. But unpalatable as it may be, asymmetrical bilingualism does have a single virtue: so far, it has proved to be a politically feasible compromise that wins votes for the federal political parties advocating it. Asymmetrical bilingualism gives the Quebec government room to do as it will with its minorities. This wins votes in Quebec. Asymmetrical bilingualism also wins votes in English Canada because it holds out the chimerical hope that language policy really can guarantee national unity.

To the politicians and bureaucrats of Ottawa's National Unity industry, avoiding confrontation between French Canada and English Canada's irreconcilable visions of linguistic justice has become a key function. Asymmetrical bilingualism, as entrenched in federal policy, is an attempt to take a little of each culture's view on the subject and to mix them together into a brew that doesn't actually make anyone happy, but which puts off direct confrontation for a little while longer. The memoranda and directives fly around Ottawa, and Canada's execution is stayed for another day.

It is not so much memoranda that Ottawa's lords of obscurity have been spinning for the past two decades, as the rope with which we will eventually hang ourselves. Left to fester in some dark corner, the fundamental conflict of interests will eventually surface—after all, it continues on, in a muffled way, beneath the mountains of documentation. And when it does surface, it will be the fiercer for having fed on so many years of miscommunication.

Actually, piecing together a definition of linguistic justice that would be acceptable to most Canadians is probably not as difficult as our endless policy disputes might suggest. The source of contention between English and French Canadians is not a struggle over first principles. It is about how often, and to what extent, political realities require that we must violate our own concepts of linguistic justice, and who gets to be the victim. With a return to first principles, such conflicts could be avoided or at least reduced.

A much more desirable alternative than the present course of action would be a clearly defined concept of linguistic justice that could be defined and enshrined in law, where it would serve as the basis for a simple and readily comprehensible system of Canadian language legislation.

LANGUAGE AND JUSTICE

What is Language? Why is it Important?

[The] normal state between languages is that of war.
—*Jean Laponce*[3]

At first glance, the passion with which Canadians invest their language disputes seems grossly misplaced. In function, language is nothing more than a system of audible code. Even the greatest languages of human literature and commercial intercourse are not living things; they are inanimate systems of communication, as cold and dead as the binary codes that serve as languages for computers. Languages, unlike living things, can vanish from common use and survive only upon library shelves. Latin, for instance, exists today only in books and the halls of the Vatican. New languages can be invented, as was Esperanto. Extinct languages can even be revived and made once more the language of a nation, as Hebrew has been made the language of Israel. These are not the characteristics of living things.

Yet in their interactions, languages behave exactly like living things engaged in mortal competition. Like the organisms of Darwin's natural world, languages evolve to fit new circumstances and applications. They gain popularity and new speakers as they become more useful, just as individual species expand in numbers as they evolve to fill broader niches in the natural order. Each language attracts new adherents in proportion to its usefulness, versatility and the ease with which it may be learned. Viewed from one perspective, the history of language conflict in any country is the history of the struggle of these languages to win from each other the loyalties of the country's inhabitants. A byproduct of any individual language's success in this game is that it must wipe out any competing languages.

Naturally, this struggle for dominance has an impact upon the human beings involved in it. Human interests and emotions enter the war of languages because humans must invest their energies in learning one language or another. Once they are adults, most people cannot learn new languages without great effort. Yet whenever members of different cultures interact, members of one group or the other must make the investment in learning the language of the other culture.

In commercial transactions, this investment can add substantially to the cost of doing business.[4] As a result there is a strong financial incentive for each language group to force the other to use its language as the common tongue of the business world. Usually, one group is economically more powerful than the other, and it can use economic pressure to obtain this goal. However, occasionally the economically weaker group controls the political system, and can demand the passage of laws forcing the economically dominant group to be the one to make the shift. One may recognize shades of Quebec in this conflict.

Ernest Gellner, a Cambridge philosopher and well-known student of the phenomenon of nationalism, traces the roots of nationalism back to the conflict of interest over the cost incurred whenever languages meet:

> In industrial and industrializing society, work ceases to be manual and becomes semantic.... Work is communication, and communication between strangers. That has enormous implications which people haven't properly understood. It means, before this is possible, before one can be understood by a stranger, we have to observe certain rules, rules which ensure that the actual message is understood, irrespective of context.... This is not a skill which can be acquired on the job in the course of ordinary living, simply by the peer group, simply by the environment in the village or community. It can only be acquired by sustained formal education, and this means that the person's main investment in life—the main thing which really makes him employable, acceptable, marriageable, socially and politically and economically usable—is his mastery of that code. That code has to be in some language or other, and everything else falls from this. Cultural homogeneity and the culture in which one has the skill becomes a central feature of human beings. This, to my mind, is the underlying root of nationalism.[5]

Even if the necessary investment of time is made to learn a second language, and even if the speaker is one of those rare and gifted people who can eventually learn to speak without a trace of accent, all of that person's family and cultural connections remain caught up in the ancestral language. As Québécois language scholar Jacques Leclerc writes:

> Talk of language can never be reduced to talk of codes, for one must also discuss the speakers of each language, describe their history, their institutions, and their social and political struggles. Language must, therefore, be seen as a social institution; it surrounds the individual, who can neither use it nor modify it without putting communication itself in peril.... The ties that bind language and society are so close that it is difficult to talk of one without referring to the other. In fact, language and society are one indissoluble whole, because language is society's mirror image.[6]

It is for this reason that the war between languages is not just a passionless struggle between competing verbal codes with victory measured by the number of speakers that each language accumulates. Once they have made their commitment to a language, people become its passionate partisans. Its victories become their victories; its losses affect their wealth, their chances for advancement, and the sense of well-being shared by everyone in their community.

Linguistic Justice: The Ground Rules

> ... one expert (from Toronto) advanced a "moral" theory of language rights. Such sophisticated attempts to elevate self-interest into moral claims is nonsense on stilts. Language rights in Canada are not about individual rights. They are about self-interest, the collective self-interest of the two founding peoples. English and French Canadians both want to live and to work and to raise their families in their own languages, their own traditions.
>
> —*F.L. Morton (1989)*[7]

To settle the disputes that inevitably arise between the speakers of competing languages, it is necessary to have recourse to a coherent theory of language justice. Without a theory of justice to serve as society's guide, the only option in matters of language will be for the strong to dominate the weak, which is a course of action that civilized people have rejected ever since Plato began his *Republic* by refuting the claim that justice is nothing more than the personal interest of the powerful.

'Justice' is simply the word we use to describe the interaction of rights and obligations. A 'right' is the legitimate expectation that you will be treated in a certain manner by other persons or by institutions. An 'obligation' is the duty of an individual or institution to treat another individual or institution in this expected manner.

Negative Rights and Positive Rights

It is important to understand that the rights and obligations which are at the heart of the definition of justice are themselves divisible into two classes: 'negative' rights and obligations, and 'positive' rights and obligations.[8] A negative right is one which imposes a negative obligation on others, restraining them from causing harm, but requiring no actual effort to be taken on their part (aside from self-restraint). Thus, for example, each person's right to life, security of the person, freedom of movement and freedom of speech are the reflections of everybody else's negative obligations *not* to kill, assault, forcibly confine or to censor. To take an example familiar to everybody, the Ten Commandments from the Book of Exodus are mostly negative obligations: thou shalt *not* steal, kill, covet and so on.

A positive right is one which imposes a positive obligation upon others. In the case of the Ten Commandments, only the injunction to "honour thy mother, and thy father" can be considered a positive obligation, since it requires that a positive action be taken, rather than the simple exercise of restraint. The result of this obligation is that mothers and fathers have the positive right to be honoured, in addition to their negative rights not to be killed, to be stolen from or have their chattels coveted. In modern times, the rights to a public education, health care or a state pension all fall into the category of positive rights, since each of these rights involves the positive obligation of somebody else to pay taxes, in order that these relatively expensive rights can be exercised.

Positive obligations are as a rule considerably more burdensome than are negative obligations; most people are far more reluctant to pay their taxes, for example, than they are to restrain themselves from assaulting their neighbours. This is the reason why negative rights are not usually controversial, while most political disputes revolve around the extent to which specific positive rights ought to be extended.

Language rights, like any other set of rights, are divisible into the negative and positive categories. The right to express oneself in the language of one's choice is obviously a variation on the right to freedom of speech; it is a negative right. The right to educate one's children in one's own language is a positive right (unless one is paying for a private education out-of-pocket), since it is the community that must pay the cost of schooling, including any extra expenses that a minority-language education may entail. Similarly, the right to receive government services in the language of one's choice is a tax-subsidized positive right.

These positive language rights are nominally the obligation of the government to fulfill; in reality, they are the obligation of every taxpayer. If providing services in a minority language costs more money than providing them in the language of the majority, then the services become a burden on all taxpayers. A conflict of interests emerges between the minorities who are the beneficiaries of these services and the majority who pay most of the taxes and therefore foot most of the bills. In other words, my right to maintain my culture and language becomes your obligation to accept a somewhat lower standard of living. Of course, if the services were cut off, then I might suffer a drastically lower quality of life, and would blame you for having been ungenerous with your tax dollars. Herein lies the seed of language conflict. Determining the appropriate mix of majority obligation and minority right is the essence of searching out an appropriate definition of linguistic justice.

From this perspective, negative language rights such as the freedom to speak in one's language of choice (or to erect signs in that language) would seem to be deserving of iron-clad legal protection, since they impose no meaningful cost on anybody. Positive language rights would appear to be justified only when the amount of quantitatively-measured benefit generated outweighs the costs that the right is imposing on others.

THE FUNDAMENTALS: PERSONALITY VS. TERRITORIAL

The fundamental problem in applying the rule of linguistic justice to Canada is the fact that linguistic minorities and provincial boundaries do not coincide. If they did, there would be no need to discuss minority language rights in areas of provincial jurisdiction. Education would not be an issue, nor the provision of hospital and health services. Even most federal responsibilities would be a simple matter. Post offices and other federal services in Quebec would serve their customers in French; elsewhere they would be English.

In some countries, the frontiers between provinces and the frontiers between language regions coincide perfectly. In Canada they do not. This can be seen by following Quebec's borders with the other provinces and the United States. The language frontier between English and French runs fairly close to the interprovincial border in some spots, but it does not follow it perfectly at any point.

Starting in the northwest, areas of mostly French settlement extend far into Ontario, including towns like Kapuskasing (which lies 150 miles west of the border and is two-thirds French). As one moves south, the Ottawa River forms the interprovincial border. At this point, west of the city of Ottawa, the language frontier veers north-east onto Quebec soil. Pontiac county, located northwest of Ottawa, is Quebec's only English-majority county.

The frontier recrosses into Ontario just east of Parliament Hill; much of Ottawa's east end is French. The Ontario counties east of Ottawa are as solidly French as most parts of Quebec. But to the southeast, just as the interprovincial border intersects with the northern tip of New York state, the language frontier crosses back into Quebec. A few small townships that lie on the Quebec side of this part of the border are mostly English, as is the west end of Montreal. Travelling due east along the border with the New England states, the language frontier follows the international boundary fairly closely until the eastern tip of Quebec is reached. Here the area of French predominance extends into the northern tip of the state of Maine, and continues east to include most of northern New Brunswick. The language frontier now turns north and crosses and recrosses the unmarked saltwater boundaries between the Atlantic provinces in enough spots to touch on the territory of Quebec in three different places, and on each of the Atlantic provinces at least once.

Having landed on Quebec territory once more, the language frontier cuts across the northern part of the province, bisecting its southern half, where French predominates, from its north (where English and aboriginal languages are dominant) before rejoining the spot where the journey started.

Since the settlement patterns don't have much to do with the location of the formal borders of Quebec, a question naturally arises. Which is more important in determining how to treat these minority populations: the location of the people, or the location of the borders?

As mentioned above, the two opposing ways of dealing with this problem are the *territorial* principle of administration and the *personality* principle. All specific proposals for language policy in any country, including the four fundamental policy alternatives that have been advocated for Canada, are mixtures of elements taken from these two principles.

Figure 1.1:
The Language Frontier Between French and English

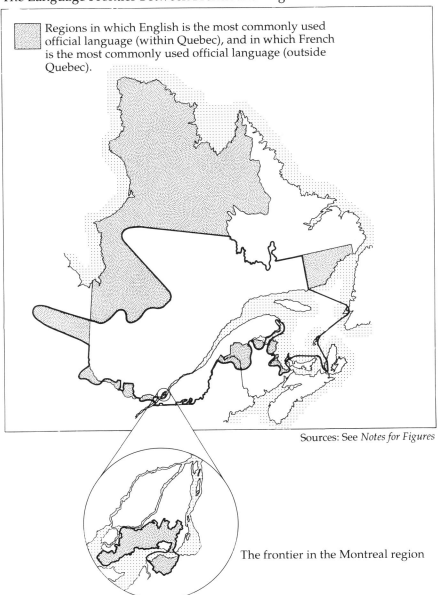

Regions in which English is the most commonly used official language (within Quebec), and in which French is the most commonly used official language (outside Quebec).

Sources: See *Notes for Figures*

The frontier in the Montreal region

Territoriality

Some federations, most notably Belgium and Switzerland, follow the administrative principle of *territoriality*. In such countries, language rights operate only on specific pieces of territory. In Switzerland, there are twenty-three cantons which are similar in status to Canadian provinces. None is obliged by federal law to provide services in any language other than that of the canton's majority, and the federal government offers almost no additional minority-language support. French, German and Italian are all Swiss national languages, but the speakers of each language have no legally-entrenched linguistic rights extending beyond the frontiers of the cantons in which their own language predominates. Most of the cantons are officially unilingual. Four cantons are exclusively French, fourteen are exclusively German, and one offers services only in Italian. The remaining four cantons are bilingual. Several of the unilingual cantons have language laws as restrictive as Ontario's infamous Regulation 17 or Quebec's Bill 101.

Personality

The inverse of the territorial administrative principle is the principle of *personality*. Countries that organize themselves on this basis treat language rights as being intrinsic to each individual. These rights therefore remain in effect in every part of the country, regardless of local demographics. All citizens

Figure 1.2
In Switzerland and some Canadian provinces, Territorialism serves the public interest, but in other provinces it would be unjust

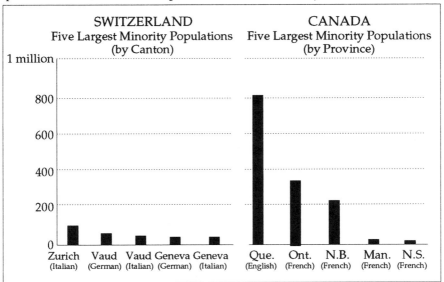

Sources: See *Notes for Figures*

have the ability to exercise not only all negative rights in all parts of the country, but a full range of positive rights as well.

In practice, this means that all government services must be provided everywhere in all official languages. The country that follows this principle most closely is South Africa, where all services are provided throughout the country in the two official languages of the white population: English and Afrikaans (speakers of the country's many native languages are out of luck, although this may soon change if the country's language laws are modified with the shift to majority rule).

This policy works well—at least for speakers of English and Afrikaans—because about two-thirds of the white population is already bilingual.[9] Few people are therefore inconvenienced by the requirement that most civil servants be bilingual, and the financial costs of minority-language services are relatively low, as compared to the numbers of beneficiaries, since fairly large minorities take advantage of bilingual services in every part of the country.

Each of the two principles has advantages and disadvantages. The personality principle has the virtue of extending both negative and positive rights as broadly as possible, but it imposes onerous and expensive positive obligations on all of society. The territorial principle virtually eliminates these obligations, but it strips minorities of even the most modest protections.

Figure 1.3
In South Africa, the Personality principle serves the public interest, but in Canada it would be unjust.

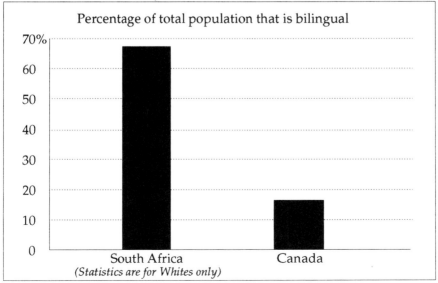

Source: See *Notes for Figures*

Different Strokes for Different Volks

In practice, the personality system is best suited to countries with a high level of geographic integration between language groups. South Africa fits this description, as does the quadrilingual city-state of Singapore. Canada, with 90.2 percent of its French-speaking population living inside Quebec and ninety-six percent of its English-speakers residing in the other nine provinces, clearly does not.

But Canada does not easily fit the territorial model either. In Switzerland, the total minority-language population of the unilingual cantons is less than 450,000. This total is fragmented between two minority language communities in each canton (French and Italian in the German cantons, German and Italian in the French cantons, etc.). These parallel minorities are then further divided twenty-three ways between the twenty-three cantons. As a result, only one of these minority populations (the Italians of Zurich) exceeds 50,000.[10] In Canada, the English-speaking population of greater Montreal alone is well over half a million.

Part of the problem is that the definitions of 'majority' and 'minority' depend upon a series of arbitrary political factors. A population that represents a minority could, in other circumstances, be a majority. For example, the 904,000 English-speakers of Quebec represent a minority within the province.[11] However, they are nearly five times more numerous, in absolute terms, than the 125,000 anglophones who form the majority in P.E.I. In another example, there are nearly three times as many francophones today in Manitoba as there were when it became a province in 1870.[12] But they were a majority then, and today represent a declining minority of less than three percent of the total population.[13]

Canada's problem is that the injustice that would be imposed by cutting off its minorities would be unreasonable, while the positive obligation of offering a full range of minority language services to all individuals in both the French minority outside Quebec and the English minority inside Quebec would be an unsustainable burden upon the country's two majorities.

FOUR VISIONS OF A BILINGUAL CANADA

Four distinct and clearly articulated attempts to develop a comprehensive language policy that would bring justice to the Canadian political system have emerged from the ferment of debate over language policy and linguistic justice:

Pierre Trudeau's 'New Jerusalem': The Personality Principle in Canada
For thirty years, coast-to-coast bilingualism on the basis of the personality principle has been championed by Pierre Trudeau. A strong civil libertarian, Trudeau believes that the key to a just system is for all individuals, wherever

they might be located in the country, to have the right to communicate with and receive services from government in their preferred official language.

Separate But Equal: Canadian Territorialism
The adoption of parallel regimes of French unilingualism in Quebec and English unilingualism in the other nine provinces has been advocated by some academics and some politicians as the only realistic way of dealing with the demands of Canada's two majorities. Although rarely advocated by anybody as a first choice, the Canadian version of territorialism became the working policy of René Lévesque's government, and gained the public support of then-Premier Don Getty of Alberta in early 1992.

Territorial Bilingualism: The Proposal of the Royal Commission on
Bilingualism and Biculturalism
As a sort of practical compromise between the extremes of the personality and territoriality principles, the Royal Commission on Bilingualism and Biculturalism proposed the extension of minority rights to those minorities large enough to survive over the long term. Smaller minorities would not receive full positive rights. This system would have the advantage of imposing only a limited burden on majority populations, while helping most (but not all) of the individuals in the country's minority communities.

Weighting the Scales: Asymmetrical Bilingualism
Another attempt at compromise is the policy known as *asymmetrical bilingualism* under which minority language rights would be extended to only one of the two minorities, while the other would be subject to tight restrictions on its rights. The logic of this policy is that it would use political measures to set right an imbalance in the relative strengths of French and English. This policy is currently favoured by those who feel that French is unable to compete with English on a level playing field and needs a helping hand. A century ago, a mirror image of the pro-French policy currently in vogue was favoured by many English Canadians who felt that their language needed legislative protection because it could not compete with the language of the prodigiously fecund French Canadians.

Of these four, the *Territorial Bilingualism* solution proposed by the Royal Commission on Bilingualism and Biculturalism (the B&B Commission) involves the smallest amount of disruption to individuals and the most limited level of positive obligations. From a utilitarian point of view, it is therefore the most just. In terms of human cost and injustice, the asymmetrical solution is probably the worst. Remarkably, it is the vision towards which Canada is currently moving.

Pierre Trudeau's New Jerusalem

Former Prime Minister Pierre Trudeau stands alone as Canada's most eloquent exponent of a radical and daring experiment in language policy, based on the personality principle. Although he was frequently forced to compromise on questions of language during his long tenure in office, Trudeau has always remained loyal to his belief that both positive and negative language rights should be extended as widely as possible across the country.

So intense was Trudeau's enthusiasm for his vision of a new linguistic regime and his willingness to disregard the fact that he was dividing the state into two unilingual proletariats and a bilingual elite that Keith Spicer, his first Commissioner of Official Languages, took to describing the prime minister's vision as his personal "linguistic New Jerusalem."[14] Less charitably, journalist Peter Brimelow has referred to it as "the Trudeauvian fancy of a co-extensive French nation in Canada."[15] Although Trudeau has never said so directly, it is possible that his ideal vision is of a society in which each individual Canadian would eventually be capable of conversing with equal ease in English and French, as Trudeau himself does.

Fortunately for scholars, Trudeau put most of his ideas about language rights on paper while he was still a university professor. These give a clearer picture of his beliefs than does the much muddier political record, with its inevitable compromises.

The key to understanding Trudeau's adherence to the personality principle lies in grasping his vision of the place of Canada in the world order. Observing the chaos that had been wrought on the world by the nation-state system in the first half of the 20th century, Trudeau concluded in his academic writings that states based upon single nationalities were doomed to eventual extinction. He observed that Canada, by an accident of history, was a multilingual country rather than a nation-state.

From this starting-point, Trudeau developed a Messianic vision of Canada as a prototype multilingual state that could serve as a model of ethnic tolerance to the rest of the world. In an essay published in 1962 in *Cité Libre*, he wrote:

> The die is cast in Canada: there are two main ethnic and linguistic groups; each is too strong and too deeply rooted in the past, too firmly bound to a mother-culture, to be able to engulf the other. But if the two will collaborate at the hub of a truly pluralistic state, Canada could become the envied seat of a form of federalism that belongs to tomorrow's world. Better than the American melting-pot, Canada would offer an example to all those new Asian and African states ... who must discover how to govern their polyethnic populations with proper regard for justice and liberty. What better reason for cold-shouldering the lure of annexation to the United States? Canadian

federalism is an experiment of major proportions; it could become a brilliant prototype for the moulding of tomorrow's civilization.[16]

As a start, this meant that all citizens, wherever located in the country, would be guaranteed full positive rights in either official language. In an essay written in 1965, he stated that the constitution should be amended to include the following words: "It will be the right of every citizen to have an English-French interpreter in his dealings with any level of authority either in the central or the provincial governments."[17]

As a social democrat and a supporter of a generally larger government role in the provision of services, Trudeau recognized, but was not greatly perturbed, by the financial burdens which funding such an extensive system of positive minority rights would impose upon the French majority in Quebec and the English majority elsewhere. He seems to have been aware, long before he became prime minister, that the institutions of government would be turned upside-down. He anticipated that all but the lowest public service jobs would become inaccessible to unilingual people. One might be exempted from bilingual job requirements if one was "an infantry corporal or a minor post office official," but at higher levels, bilingualism would be mandatory. "If a knowledge of English is required in the higher echelons of the civil service," Trudeau wrote, "then the same should be true of French." Personal bilingualism would be an ironclad requirement for admittance into the ranks of the elite. He warned that:

> Of course it will be difficult to test the bilingualism of ministers of the Crown, and no doubt the whole thing will rest upon which men the voters decide to elect. (But it might also be decided by the fact that unilingual ministers would become frustrated when decisions were sometimes taken in French, and sometimes in English within the cabinet.)[18]

Trudeau's bilingual state would guarantee both negative and positive rights to unilingual members of its linguistic minorities, but he seems to have dreamed of creating a country in which each individual would be bilingual, and therefore capable of drawing the best elements from each of Canada's two cultures. In his writings he has nothing but contempt for those who will not strive to learn. Of unilingual francophones, Trudeau wrote:

> No doubt bilingualism is attainable only with some difficulty. But I will not admit that this should be any insurmountable hurdle to men who call themselves intellectuals, particularly when the language they carp over is one of the principle vehicles of Twentieth-century civilization.[19]

His disgust with unilingual anglophones is equally profound:

Generation after generation of Anglo-Saxons have lived in Quebec without getting around to learning three sentences of French. When these people insist, without much gravity, that their jaws and ears aren't made for it and can't adapt themselves to French, what they really want to get across to you is that they will not sully these organs, and their small minds, by submitting them to a barbarous idiom.[20]

The cultural transformation of Canadians would require more than just extensive government services and the sealing-off of the elite to unilingual citizens. Speaking in 1963 at the preliminary hearing of the Royal Commission on Bilingualism and Biculturalism, Trudeau hinted at the need for state-supported migration of French and English-speakers into each others' linguistic milieu on a mass scale:

> [P]ersonally, even with just laws, I do not think that French will become a widely practiced language in parts of Canada where the French Canadians are an infinitesimal minority. It might, therefore, be advisable to contemplate other solutions. For example, we should guarantee labour force mobility, mobility of citizens, so that those who want to live in a bilingual environment can move to another part of Canada.... There comes a moment when it's truly too expensive to speak two languages simultaneously in one country. When that moment arrives, when it's not worth paying the price anymore, it would be better to stop living in such a country.[21]

Linguistically Separate but Equal: Canadian Territorialism

The administrative philosophy of territoriality, pure and unadulterated, has never had its day in the sun as the official ideology of the Canadian government, as the personality principle has, but it has been endorsed from time to time by provincial governments and by editorialists. In Canada, territorialism has never been interpreted as meaning that linguistic minorities in each province should actually be denied either positive or negative rights as a matter of policy. Instead, all jurisdiction over these rights would be turned over to the provincial governments, in the belief that these authorities would probably show more generosity to their minorities if they were no longer bullied into doing so by an overbearing federal government.

To many, this is not a very convincing argument. This explains why the most eloquent descriptions of the ideology come from its detractors rather than its defenders. One passionate condemnation comes from a 1977 federal government publication:

> The federal government rejects the concepts of a Canada divided into two mutually exclusive unilingual separate countries or two mutually exclusive unilingual regions within one country. While these two options have a

superficial appearance of dissimilarity, they amount in practice to the same thing, a province or state of Quebec that is unilingual French speaking and the rest of Canada, or a truncated Canada, that is unilingual English speaking.

The government rejects these concepts above all because they entail a denial of the existence of the official language minority groups of Canada.... It is hardly to be doubted that those who see a Canada divided on linguistic lines, or separated on a similar basis, envisage the gradual absorption of the minorities in the country as the solution to Canada's language problems.[22]

As a rule, the defenders of this vision are not so much enthusiastic about territorialism itself as they are about the potential of this administrative principle to guarantee national unity. The curious parallel between the personality principle put forward by Trudeau and the territorial solution—ostensibly its polar opposite—advanced by his critics is described by Leslie Green and Denise Réaume in a 1991 issue of the newsletter of the Network on the Constitution:

[Official bilingualism's] increasingly vocal critics ... focus on the other alleged purpose of language policy, namely, the promotion of national unity. Yet there is, in this, a strange persistence of Trudeauism. For the critics have still failed to transcend that framework. They remain riveted on the question of how to promote national unity through language policy, offering a revised answer. Now we are told that linguistic 'territorialism' is the cure we need and that Belgium and Switzerland are to be our new role models.[23]

Typical of this sentiment is this statement by George Galt in *Saturday Night*:

There's ... a growing realization that French signs in the post office and unemployment insurance commission in places like Medicine Hat aren't bolstering national unity and may in fact be undermining it by irritating local sensibilities. The solution is obvious: curtail official bilingualism, though I don't advance this view with any pleasure. Bilingualism enlarges rather than diminishes those who attempt it, and we should continue to encourage the acquisition of a second language however we can. But enforce it in federal facilities from sea to sea? No. The least contentious and fairest way out of this tangle is to restrict official bilingualism to the national capital area.[24]

This attitude of weary acceptance that the federal government will be unable to save Canada by trying to save its minorities does not make territoriality a very inspiring rallying point. Although the concept of devolving all language powers to the provincial governments was once endorsed by a royal commission,[25] it has failed to inspire even the provincial premiers who would be its most obvious beneficiaries.[26]

Territorialism also has its share of defenders among Québécois nationalists, although not usually because of any concern for the unity of the country. Quebec separatism is a highly territorial concept, because it is generally accepted by separatists that state-sponsored bilingualism would not survive in the Canadian rump state following secession.

To Québécois nationalists, embracing territorialism means taking a giant step backwards from the dreams of their ancestors, who imagined a French-speaking nation stretching from coast to coast. For years, the Quebec government had acted as a godparent to French-speakers elsewhere in the country. Under the Duplessis administration, for example, Edmonton's French language radio station was supported by payments from the Quebec government, as was the Acadian newspaper *L'Evangeline*. In his biography of Duplessis, Conrad Black asserts that the premier even provided assistance in an "anonymous and totally non-political" way to Franco-Americans in the states of Maine, Massachusetts, and Rhode Island.[27]

These efforts began to be withdrawn during the Quiet Revolution. As early as 1967, historian Ramsay Cook reported:

> In Quebec the current fashion among separatists and quasi-separatists is to advocate writing off the French-speaking minorities everywhere except perhaps in New Brunswick. A corollary, sometimes unstated, is that Quebec should become unilingual (like English Canada) and eventually, no doubt, assimilate the minorities.[28]

The Quebec government's *Secretariat permanent des peuples francophones*, which served as a support agency for francophones outside Quebec, was closed as a cost-saving measure in January 1991. Several years earlier, Robert Bourassa had refused to come to the aid of western francophones when the governments of Saskatchewan and Alberta passed laws revoking the bilingual status that had recently been imposed on their provinces by the *Mercure* decision. In that decision, the Supreme Court of Canada had ruled that both provinces were still governed by the language provisions of the old *Northwest Territories Act*, but that each province had the right to revoke or override these provisions. Premier Bourassa paid a visit to the two provinces in early 1988, when the overriding legislation was being prepared, and stated that he found this legislation to be acceptable and reasonable. Calgary *Herald* columnists Don Braid and Sydney Sharpe made this observation about Bourassa's western trip:

> By [the time of his visit], Bourassa's true mission in the West was clear even to the most naive and trusting observers. He was buying Western silence for his own impending language crisis, the Supreme Court decision on Bill 101 [handed down in autumn 1988]. Bourassa had no interest whatever in protect-

ing French rights anywhere but in Quebec. His goal was to purchase peace and silence at whatever price to minority rights.[29]

The role of protector of the French language beyond its frontiers has now been completely abandoned by Quebec, prompting Pierre Trudeau to note bitterly in a 1992 *Maclean's* article that "the predominant ideology in Quebec doesn't give a fig about bilingualism in Canada."[30] The new belief seems to be that governments can really only control the linguistic destiny of their own territory, because it is only on their territory that they can enact the full range of immigration, education and other measures necessary to stem the English tide. This new harshness echoes in the statements of many nationalists, including Georges Mathews, who wrote in his 1990 separatist manifesto, *L'accord: Comment Robert Bourassa fera l'indépendance*:

> What do francophones outside Quebec do if they really want to live and succeed in French? They move to Quebec. Gabrielle Roy, Jean Ethier-Blais, Daniel Lavoie, Edith Butler, and Antonine Maillet, all have at least one point in common: born in francophone enclaves, they have made their homes and achieved stardom in Quebec.[31]

Territorial Bilingualism: A Just Compromise

Since neither the territorial principle nor the personality principle fits Canada well, the most just arrangement would seem to be a compromise between the two administrative systems. Negative language rights cost the majority nothing, so they could easily be recognized on the full personality principle—in other words, they could easily be extended across the country. Positive rights could be recognized only in those parts of the country where the minority represents a large enough proportion of the local population to ensure that the disutility caused by the positive obligations would be outweighed by the benefits that these rights confer.

This would involve the extension of positive minority language rights only to the relatively limited areas of the country where French or English is the language of the local majority or of a strong local minority, but not of the provincial majority. A closer examination of the language map of Canada suggests that in practice, this would probably mean extending positive rights that Canadians know as *official bilingualism* only to the French-majority regions in eastern and northern Ontario, to francophone northern New Brunswick, and to the west end of Montreal, plus one or two rural districts in Quebec.

This compromise was labelled *territorial bilingualism* when it was first conceived in the 1960s, and most eloquently advocated by the Royal Commission on Bilingualism and Biculturalism.

The B&B Commission was established by Prime Minister Lester Pearson in 1963 and led by André Laurendeau, a prominent journalist and former

Quebec separatist who had since returned to the federalist fold. Endowed with a virtually limitless research budget and drawing on the efforts of a staff of over 200, it published, in addition to six fat volumes of findings, a veritable library of background studies that have become the intellectual foundation of later Canadian scholarship on language.[32]

Although the B&B Commission's voluminous reports contain their share of internal contradictions, and are occasionally unclear, they represent the closest thing that Canada has to an outline language policy based solely on the utilitarian question of producing the greatest good for the largest number of citizens. This principle of focussing solely on utilitarian first principles, which are clearly articulated in the first volume of the commission's report, did not accord particularly well with the views of Lester Pearson, who had established the commission with bountiful goodwill and very little understanding of the nature of the problems he was trying to resolve.[33] The mandate drafted for the B&B Commission by Pearson and Maurice Lamontagne, his Quebec lieutenant, was largely reinterpreted by the commissioners themselves.[34]

The commissioners carefully backed away from any suggestion that Canadians should be burdened with broad new positive obligations. In particular, the Commission rejected the notion, implied in their terms of reference, that Canadians had a duty to become bilingual:

> [Our] terms of reference ... enjoin the Commission to 'recommend what could be done to enable Canadians to become bilingual.' ... But the question of the life and vigour of each language must have priority. The problem of the first language must come first: it is vital; it is more essential for the human being than questions about a second language.[35]

Further in the report, they were even more direct:

> A bilingual country is not one where all the inhabitants necessarily have to speak two languages; rather it is a country where the principal public and private institutions must provide services in two languages to citizens, the vast majority of whom may very well be unilingual.[36]

And finally, they expressed their philosophy in a single phrase: "The objective should be to impose the fewest sacrifices from which nobody benefits ... "[37]

In terms of practical recommendations for the provision of services, this meant that the Royal Commission favoured the extension of language rights for francophone minorities to a variety of specific locations across Canada where they were tightly clumped, but not to the very small number of French-speakers located beyond these regions, or to isolated anglophones living in the most homogeneous French-speaking regions of Quebec.[38]

In its other recommendations, the B&B Commission was similarly moderate. On the question of equitable hiring of francophones and anglophones in the Public Service, for example, it rejected the most obvious methods of boosting the number of French-speakers, who at the time were badly underrepresented. Hiring quotas were rejected, as was enforced bilingualism for individual public servants; instead, the commission proposed that parallel work units be established. In some units, English would be the language of work. In a smaller number of units, proportionate to the francophone share of the national population, French would be the language of work. This would allow more francophones to find job opportunities without imposing undue bilingualism requirements of English Canadian public servants.

Asymmetrical Bilingualism

> Egalitarian situations are not possible, except to the extent that the State creates inequalities favouring the minority.... Equality of status between the majority and the minority produces effects directly opposite to those intended: it minimizes the rights of the minority and maximizes those of the majority. You may find this approach alarming or deplorable, but that's the way things are.
> —*Jacques Leclerc (1986)*[39]

Fear of demographic decline has led much of French Canada to embrace an ideology of language that Bloc Québécois leader Lucien Bouchard, one of its biggest boosters, has usefully labelled "asymmetrical bilingualism."[40] Described simply, asymmetrical bilingualism is the belief that Canadian language policy should use reverse discrimination to "accord compensatory inequalities" to strengthen the French language, in view of the fact (or more correctly, the myth) that French is threatened with extinction. This ideology holds that federal language policy towards the French-speaking minority populations outside Quebec should extend the full range of negative and positive rights, but that many or all of these same rights should be restricted for the English-speaking minority in Quebec. The logic of such a policy, as Bouchard explains it, is that "giving the same weight to French [minorities] as to English [minorities] is unacceptable because it doesn't take into account that French is the only one of the two official languages that is threatened...."[41]

Other supporters of asymmetrical bilingualism offer the same justification. Political scientist Jacques Leclerc puts it this way:

> The cultural imperialism of the Americans, the new czars of culture, is stronger in Quebec than anywhere else because of the proximity of the United States and the attractiveness of the English language.... Small languages, unable to afford to pay the cost of techniques that will raise the value of their language, place themselves in a fragile position....[42]

The asymmetrical view holds that in the nine provinces where French is a minority language, minorities should be shown every generosity, and their institutions liberally subsidized. The active goal of language policy outside Quebec should be to limit or halt assimilation into English. Within Quebec, asymmetrical bilingualism calls for the adoption of whatever measures are necessary to ensure that French continues to grow as the language of an ever-larger proportion of the population. Because demographic trends would not make this happen on its own, asymmetrical bilingualism requires, at best, the bare toleration of Quebec's English-speaking minority. Some of the more extreme supporters of linguistic asymmetry have stated that English should be wiped out entirely within Quebec, but most argue that it should be allowed to survive in a limited and strictly regulated capacity.

Stéphane Dion, a University of Montreal professor, provides a proposal for constitutionalizing asymmetry that is typical of the proposals put forth by its supporters. The "best solution would be a unilateral devolution only to the legislature of Quebec" of all powers over language. The English-speaking provinces, he argues, ought not to receive any additional language powers, because this would result in the loss of protective federal laws and federal subsidies for French-speakers outside Quebec. Anything less than constitutionalized asymmetry, he warns, "asks French-speaking Quebecers to press their interest at the expense of other French speakers. It is doubtful that they would accept it. I would not accept it."[43]

Although most English Canadians would find the concept of asymmetrical bilingualism profoundly disturbing if they were aware of its existence as a well-defined ideology (which most are not), a few have embraced the concept. A tiny minority, like Professor Reginald Whitaker of York University, have come to accept the concept on the same grounds of equality between languages that motivate French-Canadian politicians and academics. In words that could have been penned by a Québécois intellectual or an editorial writer on the pages of *Le Devoir*, Whitaker writes:

> The francophones of Quebec are a majority in that province, but a weak and threatened minority in the larger picture. Extraordinary measures are required to protect the French language within the sole jurisdiction where French is the majority tongue. Francophone minorities outside Quebec are doubly vulnerable and deserve some constitutional protection and an attitude of liberality on the part of the anglophone majority which is in no way threatened in the security of its language.[44]

But collectivist ideals of this sort come more easily to Whitaker, a prominent Marxist, than they do to most English-speaking Canadians. The usual grounds for accepting the gradual encroachment of asymmetry into Canada's language laws has been the hope that the policy will appease Quebec's nationalists.

A typical expression of this sentiment is made in a letter written by NDP

Member of Parliament Svend Robinson in 1989 to Tony Kondaks, one of the founders of Quebec's Equality Party:

> When I spoke of the relatively privileged position of the anglophone minority in Quebec, it was in contrast to the position of the francophone minority outside Quebec, including in my own province of British Columbia. The evidence in support of this argument is compelling. I support the fundamental principles of Bill 101 and believe that they have been responsible in large measure for the relative linguistic peace in Quebec in recent years.[45]

The present-day advocates of asymmetrical bilingualism would probably be surprised to learn that this ideology had an earlier existence among the Orange Lodges of Ontario. In the first few decades following the turn of the century, many English-speakers felt perfectly comfortable arguing, as Toronto mayor Horatio Hockin did, that full rights should be extended to anglo-Quebecers, but denied to francophones unfortunate enough to reside outside the province. After all, Hockin explained in the House of Commons, "it must be plain to anybody who understands English that this is not a bilingual country."[46] At the time it fell to French Canadian nationalists like Henri Bourassa to call for equitable treatment and the extension of francophone language rights beyond Quebec's borders, just as full English-language rights existed within the province.

Strikingly absent from the ideology of asymmetry in either its historical or its modern incarnations is any concern for its impact on the aggregate well-being and happiness of the Canadian population as a whole. Abstract questions of the well-being of languages themselves are treated as far more important than concrete concerns about the well-being of human beings.

Among the Québécois nationalists who form the main body of support for asymmetrical bilingualism, such considerations are probably irrelevant. To many, nationwide asymmetry in the treatment of English-speaking and French-speaking minorities, plus generous federal subsidies to their provincial governments, is simply the price that must be paid if they are to be convinced to temporarily set aside their ultimate ambition of seceding from Canada and establishing an independent Québécois state. From this pragmatic point of view, the only concern of language policy ought to be the impact it has on the strength of the French language. As one commentator notes, "if this results in the English community being diminished, it is not necessarily meant that way, but the result is not an important concern. . . . "[47]

SUMMARY

Of the four visions of linguistic policy laid out in this chapter, only one is entirely focussed on the single short-term goal of achieving the greatest good for the greatest number of citizens. This is the sole objective of territorial bilingualism, as advocated by the B&B Commission. Although the members of the Commission never rejected grander objectives, their vision did not involve making sacrifices of short-term goals in order to achieve them.

The other three visions of linguistic policy presented in this chapter specifically reject short-term justice as their ultimate goal. Instead, they are based on visions of the imagined end results of specific policies. Each of them assumes that applied injustice or inequity in the short run will lead to greater good in the long run. In Trudeau's vision, the greater good is the creation of a model multilingual state. In the territorial vision, it is national unity, or guaranteed provincial autonomy, or both. In the asymmetrical vision, it is the security of the French language. These ends are, in a sense, like the final result of a complicated mathematical equation. The components of each equation are a series of sociological, political and economic factors.

A key problem with these three visions is that each pins its hopes on projections that may prove invalid, on assumptions that may prove to be myths, or on statistics that may not work. The dangers here are particularly evident in the personality-based vision of Pierre Trudeau and in the asymmetrical approach, since both assume that governments can control the language choices of whole communities. But even the territorial approach adopted by federalists like George Galt is a two-step approach which assumes that fully empowered provincial governments would treat their minorities with enough dignity to cause language tensions to be defused. The historical record suggests the opposite.

Justice, by contrast, is not an end but a means, a process rather than a product. Devising a policy intended simply to be fair requires many fewer steps and much less use of fallible analysis than one intended to mould society. One of the beauties of the recommendations of the B&B Commission is that they remain as fresh today as they were a quarter of a century ago, even though their authors believed the same myths and made the same erroneous assumptions common to all students of language at that time.

A further flaw with policies like those advocated by Trudeau, George Galt and Svend Robinson, is that while justice is not a divisible goal nor one given to compromise, longer-term political objectives are. Legislation passed in the name of achieving some more abstruse political goal is subject to lobbying, to political pressures and to compromise. One of the most disastrous results of Canadian adherence to policies based on applied short-term injustice has been that politically advantageous compromises have led to the embodiment in law of policies based on contradictory and incompatible ideologies. To justify each policy to the public, contradictory explanations must be offered. It becomes impossible to justify each conflicting language policy on the basis of a single, comprehensive vision of Canada's linguistic identity.

As Canadians have become confused about the ends of public policy, they have grown alienated from the federal government and even from the country itself. One of the most important reasons why the federal government has failed to rein in separatism in Quebec, despite its emphasis on language policies advantageous to the position of francophones and of the French language, is that it has never been able to develop a consistent vision capable of inspiring Canadians and of serving as an alternative to the Quebec government's clear and inspiring nationalist vision of Quebec as a secure homeland for the French language in North America.

Paradoxically, then, visions that focus mainly on the long term can ultimately prove damaging to national unity.

The chapters that follow will explore some of the myths and erroneous assumptions that invalidate these multi-stage visions. Chapters Two and Three will use Canadian history to show how difficult it is to adopt and consistently adhere to long-term language policies in the face of intense political pressure. Chapter Four will demonstrate that much of the power that governments are commonly assumed to have over language does not actually exist.

CHAPTER TWO

Linguistic Intolerance and Demographic Decline: A Canadian History

> ... both English and French are very much alike. Their respective intolerance tends to assume the same forms.
> —*Dominique Clift and Sheila McLeod-Arnopoulos (1980)*[1]

FROM THE MOMENT they got their first taste of responsible government nearly two centuries ago, English and French Canadians have been using their political institutions to take away each other's rights.

Restrictive language laws in Canada date back nearly to the year 1800.[2] Each one of these restrictions has been rooted in the fears of the linguistic majority of the day—whether that majority be French or English—that its numbers were declining relative to the size of the minority, and that it stood in danger of being overwhelmed.

Using history as a guide, two patterns become apparent. Both are vital to our understanding of why elaborate end-based language policies are likely to fail.

First, when the speakers of either the English or the French language have judged their demographic fortunes to be on the rise, they have taken a relaxed, tolerant *laissez-faire* attitude towards the other. When either language has been on the decline relative to the other, the speakers of the declining language have taken political measures to stop the slide. These measures have included restrictive language laws, riots, rebellion, separatism and even open civil war.

Second, the prevailing ideologies or world views within society change over time, and with this change comes a shift in popular beliefs about the extent to which government is able to manipulate population trends and the processes of assimilation.

In the early and mid-19th century, it was not widely believed that governments were capable of controlling the languages that individuals chose to speak. Government's ability to manipulate the relative strength and size of different language groups was thought to extend mainly to immigration and settlement controls. Since most immigrants in those days came from Britain, the general perception was that the government could influence the demographic picture by restricting the number of English-speaking immigrants to Canada, by redirecting them away from areas of French settlement, or by depriving them of the right to vote, but that it could do little else. As a result, controls in these areas were the main focus of demands for government action.

Around the turn of the century the focus for demands shifted to education, which had become a government monopoly in most provinces, and was becoming mandatory in some of them. The belief was that education could serve as a tool of minority expansion and cultural retention, so the ability to limit minority-language education was perceived as the most effective way to limit the vitality of linguistic minority communities.

More recently, with the rise of the welfare state, governments have come to be seen as virtually omnipotent. As a consequence, appropriate spheres for linguistic manipulation are now seen to include sign laws, restrictions on the language of work in the private sector, government hiring and promotion practices, and subsidies to the arts, to say nothing of the traditional areas of immigration and education.

The general rule has always been this: whenever a language community considers its own long-term survival to be threatened by the prevailing demographic trend, it tries to use the power of the state to do *whatever seems possible* to stop or reverse that trend.[3] The fear of decline establishes the urge. Popular beliefs about government's ability to control trends determine the means that will be promoted by members of the 'imperilled' majority.

Just advocating restrictions on the rights of minorities does not mean, of course, that such measures will come to pass. Large minorities are able to protect themselves by parking their votes with a single political party, and thereby using this party to ward off some of the threats to their language rights. The precise means by which this is done will be discussed in Chapter Three. But certainly, the *extent* to which members of the majority will attempt to enforce restrictive language laws, and the *types* of restrictions that they will try to impose, are determined solely by their perceptions of linguistic decline and their beliefs about the effectiveness of state action.

Language Conflicts Since 1759

Since the Conquest in 1759, there have been three periods of shifting growth and perceived decline in the relations between English and French, and therefore three periods of fearful reaction against the prevailing trends. Sandwiched in between have been two phases of relative calm and good relations, corresponding to times when neither linguistic group felt threatened. The three periods of fear and reaction are defined as follows:

The Rise of English: 1760-1840
In less than a century, English rose from non-existence in Canada to majority status. The tensions this caused helped lead to the rebellion of 1837.

The Revenge of the Cradles: 1850-1920
French Canada's population soared, and its people flooded across the borders of their traditional heartland, causing English-speakers to fear that their language would be overwhelmed. English Canada reacted with restrictive language and education laws, and sometimes with violence.

The Quiet Revolution and the Separatist Threat: 1960-Present
Declining birthrates ended French Canada's ability to keep up with English Canada's immigrant-based population increases. The French language fell into rapid decline outside of Quebec. In Quebec, the provincial government reacted by restricting minority rights to reinforce the dominance of French in the one province where the language was most secure.

THE RISE OF ENGLISH: 1760-1840

In the century between the Conquest and 1850, the French speaking proportion of the Canadian population declined from absolute dominance to less than half. Even in Lower Canada—today's Quebec—one out of four people spoke English by the middle of the 19th century. English, Scottish and Irish immigrants flooded off the ships at the ports of Quebec City and Montreal. The largest share moved on to the wilderness districts of Upper Canada, claiming for the English language an area that for two centuries had been French Canada's hinterland. Many others stayed in Lower Canada. It appeared as though the French language might be wiped out in British North America.

In The Beginning . . .
Prior to the American Revolution there had been little interest among English-speakers in settling in the colony of Quebec; British merchants made up perhaps one percent of Quebec's population at the time of the unsuccessful American invasion of Canada in 1775-76.[4] After the war, United Empire Loyalists were encouraged by the colonial administration—and often forced—to settle in areas outside of French Canada.[5]

As a result of such policies, the total English-speaking population of those parts of the colony of Quebec lying east of the Ottawa River (i.e., within the borders of today's Quebec) was only 1,000 by 1785. Half of these were Irish fishermen who settled on the rocky coast of the Gaspé Peninsula, hundreds of miles from the centres of French-Canadian civilization in the St. Lawrence River valley.[6] Most of the rest were Irish farmers and lumberjacks who settled in the western part of the province, along the Ottawa River.

However, the policy of segregating English and French-speaking settlers was abandoned around 1800. By 1831 over half the inhabitants of Montreal were speakers of English.[7] Anglophones represented nearly forty percent of Quebec City's population by 1861.[8] Many English-speakers chose to become farmers and settled in outlying areas of Lower Canada. A road was built from Quebec City to the wilderness area southeast of Montreal known as the 'Eastern Townships.' Scottish settlers joined the Americans who had moved northwards into the area in the first decade of the 19th century.

The decline of French in the early 19th century was so dramatic that a prominent demographer has suggested if the border between Ontario and Quebec had been drawn in 1850 rather than 1791, it probably would have passed to the east of Montreal, due to that city's domination by British immigrants.[9]

The First Rumblings of Discontent

The rapid decline of the French language in its homeland alarmed many French Canadians. In the first decades following the Conquest, the French-speaking 'Canadiens' were too politically primitive and too disorganized to do much about their fears. The colony lacked so much as a printing press before 1764, and had no widely circulated newspapers before *Le Canadien* was founded in 1806.[10]

After 1806, French Canadians gained political and social awareness from newspapers, as well as the novel phenomenon of elected politicians in the provincial assembly (which had been established by the *Constitutional Act* of 1791). These events, coupled with the rapid rise of English in Lower Canada after 1800, allowed the fears of British assimilation to gain wide circulation in a public forum for the first time.

Legislating Language: Immigration Controls

Language and culture were not perceived in the early 19th century as matters that could be subjected to detailed government control. As a result, French Canadian fears were not manifested in detailed language laws. Instead, the concentration was on anti-immigration measures.

Direct control over immigration was beyond the jurisdiction of the Legislative Assembly. However, it was possible for the Assembly to limit the political rights of English-speaking settlers in the Eastern Townships, which held most of the colony's anglophone population. Until the 1820s, the Townships were denied a judicial district, roads, and even electoral representation in the Assembly.

The French Canadian fear of the English-speaking immigrants who were settling the Eastern Townships during this time is well captured in this description from an 1807 edition of *Le Canadien*: "[They are] half-savage people whose forays are as much to be feared in Canada as those made formerly by the Goths and Vandals into Italy."[11]

This initial burst of fear and intolerance was briefly overcome in the 1820s, thanks, oddly enough, to a piece of legislation designed to deprive French Canadians of their political rights. The *Union Bill* of 1822 was intended to merge Upper and Lower Canada. Had the *Union Bill* passed into law, it would have deprived the French of their majority status in Lower Canada. The democratically-minded Townshippers (who were mostly Yankees at this point) found the Bill's grand-scale gerrymandering offensive, so, as it turned out, the Bill's most important practical result was to unite anglophone Townshippers and French Canadians in a common cause.

Opposition to the Bill forged an alliance between Louis-Joseph Papineau, the leader of the French Canadian nationalist *Parti Canadien*, and John Neilson, an English-speaking reformer and legislative assemblyman. Together they focussed their energies on attaining democratic reforms. Neilson journeyed twice to London to oppose the *Union Bill*, which he saw as a power grab by Montreal and Quebec City's wealthy English-speaking merchants.

On his 1828 trip to London, Neilson carried two petitions condemning the governor's arbitrary actions. One petition, originating in the francophone community, contained 87,000 names. The second, from the Eastern Townships, carried 10,000 signatures. Fully one in six French Canadians and one in eight English-speakers had been willing to sign this petition in support of the reformist policies of the Neilson-Papineau coalition.[12] This represented the high-water mark of French-English co-operation. A commission of enquiry was established by the House of Commons in London, and its report advocated many but not all of the concessions that the reformers had demanded. Neilson pronounced himself satisfied, but Papineau felt the concessions to be insufficient, and the coalition ended.

Rebellion in Lower Canada: 1837-1838

Apprehension over British immigration merged in the minds of French Canadians with a revulsion against government arrogance and corruption. Eventually, these factors led to a failed revolution and open civil war in 1837 and 1838.

In the 1830s, demographic fears once again sparked anger and frustration in French Canadians. Because the governor was reluctant to reform the system of seigneurial tenure, under which much good land remained unused, the soaring French Canadian population had pushed the habitant farmers on the overcrowded seigneurial lands to near-starvation. They resented the flood of English and Scottish immigrants who were taking up the best new lands in the colony.

Worse yet, unskilled Irish labourers began to flood the towns, driving down wages and increasing the misery of the landless, poverty-stricken French-speakers who had been forced off their lands by overcrowding. The rural proletariat turned to the towns for employment but found most jobs already filled. One scholar has estimated that at the time of the 1837 rebellion, half of the day-labourers' jobs in Quebec City and sixty percent of those in Montreal were filled by English-speakers.[13]

Irish immigrants also competed with dispossessed French Canadians for unskilled jobs as navvies on the canal works then in progress at Lachine. When the Irish brought a cholera epidemic to Lower Canada in 1832, one French Canadian wrote:

> [The British] rid themselves of their beggars and cast them by the thousands on our shores; they . . . send us miserable beings, who, after having partaken of the bread of our children, will subject them to the horrors following upon hunger and misery; they must do still more, they must send us their pestilence and death.[14]

In 1832, the legislative assembly passed a bill imposing a head tax on immigrants, to be paid by the captains of emigrant ships. This move was opposed by the English-speaking merchants of Montreal and by Upper Canadians. The Montreal *Gazette* accurately described the new law as an attempt to "obstruct that influx of Europeans which, by increasing the number of English

Figure 2.1
French Canadian fears of losing their majority status helped spur the 1837 Rebellion

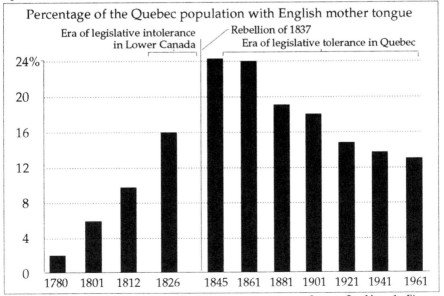

Source: See *Notes for Figures*

inhabitants, threatens soon to [sub]merge the preponderance of the French Canadians in Lower Canada."[15]

In 1834, Papineau's party—which had changed its name to the 'Patriotes'—adopted a series of demands known as the *92 Resolutions*. The resolutions demanded an end to corruption and to government by decree, but also reflected the ethnic tensions at work in the colony. One resolution made reference to British and American settlers occupying the best lands, and another to the disproportionately large share of government jobs being occupied by English-speakers. In all, not less than twelve of the resolutions hint at the deepening ethnic schism in the province.[16]

By now, ethnic conflict had become inseparable from the issue of popular control of the legislative assembly. French Canadians believed that the only way to halt the encroachment of English-speakers would be for the assembly to have total control over the business of the nation. English-speakers, including most reformers, found the Patriote demands (which amounted to a virtual manifesto for independence) to be unreasonable and threatening. Tensions mounted and each side began to arm a civilian militia. French and English militiamen clashed in the streets of Montreal in November 1837, and civil war broke out.

The rebellion in Lower Canada lasted into 1838. British troops were driven back initially, but were soon able to crush the poorly armed Patriotes. Unlike the followers of William Lyon Mackenzie in Upper Canada, the Patriotes were not an unorganized mob. They were numerous enough to require mustering and regimentation. One historian has managed to compile a list of the names of 21,000 open Patriote supporters. There were probably thousands of others. An analysis of these names shows that ethnic polarization was extensive. Only eight percent of the rebels were anglophones—mostly Irish Catholics with no love of the British crown—at a time when English-speakers made up one-quarter of Lower Canada's population.[17]

In light of the above, it is probably fair to characterize the rebellion of 1837-1838 as historian Philip Buckner has done:

> ... the rebellion was precipitated by the economic and social tensions of the 1830s, but the underlying cause was the conflict between the French Canadian majority, which demanded that all power be centralized in the popularly elected assembly, which it controlled, and the British minority, which was no less determined to resist French Canadian domination.[18]

THE REVENGE OF THE CRADLES: 1850-1920

Although the expression itself is quite familiar to most English-speaking Canadians, the full significance that "La Revanche des Berceaux" has had for French-Canadians can only be grasped by reading eulogies such as the follow-

> ing, in which the local French-language newspaper praises the virtues of a man from Beauce County who left some 600 descendants when he finally died at the age of 96: "The grandfather of Mr. Philippon met an honourable death at the Battle of the Plains of Abraham; his grandson has well revenged this death by adding, through his own (sic!) efforts, an entire parish to French Canada."
> —*Richard Joy* [19]

The failure of the 1837 Rebellion put to rest any further attempts to limit the growth and power of the English-speaking community. But the demographic tide was turning anyway. The fertile parts of Lower Canada were almost entirely settled by the middle of the 19th century and virtually all new British immigrants after this date began to move west into Upper Canada. As a result of this influx, by 1851 Upper Canada had passed Lower Canada in total population.

The end of the massive influx of British immigrants to Lower Canada meant that from then on the main source of population growth in the French-Canadian heartland would be natural increase, as opposed to immigration. The higher birth rate of French Canadians caused their percentage of the population of Quebec (now called Canada East) to grow continuously for a full century. The fears of losing their majority status fell away, and for a hundred years Quebec was a model of linguistic tolerance admirable by any standard. The same cannot be said for the English-majority provinces.

The Shoe on the Other Foot: Anglophone Intolerance

> You have every reason to be alarmed at the greater and greater rift between the two groups which make up our country. The first source [of this rift] is found undoubtedly in *nationaliste* pretensions, from the Ottawa River to the Pacific; and these *nationalistes* have succeeded in making the English population believe that the French race wants to impose its language everywhere, as an official language, even in British Columbia, where the French population is not even 2%. These exaggerations are exploited by the extremists of Anglo-Saxonism, and make up the perpetual theme of the Tory press.
> *Sir Wilfrid Laurier (1916)* [20]

The growing French-speaking population spilled over the bounds of the traditional areas of French settlement along the St. Lawrence River Valley. Finding the land immediately to the south and west already occupied by English-speaking farmers, French-speaking migrants began to colonize the unsettled lands scattered between the English-speaking settlements. When empty tracts of land came up for auction or sale, there were several potential French-speaking buyers for every English-speaker.

During the late 19th and early 20th centuries, Quebec experienced mass migration from the countryside to the cities. In Quebec, this phenomenon had a linguistic dimension. Young francophones flooded into the towns and cities, where they provided cheap labour for mills and factories. So many French-speakers moved into the cities that they soon became the majority of the province's urban population. Between 1871 and 1901, Quebec's French-speaking urban population increased by 250 percent.[21] In cities that formerly had English-speaking majorities, like Montreal and Sherbrooke, French gained the upper hand; in Quebec City, the English-speaking community simply vanished. So massive was the flood that thousands of francophones could not find work in the cities of their home province, and emigrated to New England.

By 1891, francophones had grown from seventy-five percent to seventy-nine percent of Quebec's population, and their numbers were beginning to rise in Acadia. Thousands of French Canadians migrated to northern and eastern Ontario, and even New Hampshire and Massachusetts.[22] The growth of French Canada beyond its traditional frontiers led to the ethnic domination of areas that had previously been English, including rural districts in Ontario.

By the 1890s, the near swamping of the French-Canadian heartland by English a half-century earlier had been forgotten. A new self-confident myth began to emerge: that French Canadians would one day, by sheer force of numbers, come to dominate the country, because God had willed for French Canada a sacred mission to be the vanguard of the recapture of North America—and the world—for the Catholic Church. "We believe these emigrants [to New England] are called by God to co-operate in the conversion of America," declared Bishop de Goësbriand in 1868, "as their ancestors were called upon to plant the Faith on the shores of the St. Lawrence."[23]

The enthusiasm of French Canada for this Messianic vision can scarcely be overstated. During the wars of Italian unification in the 1860s, hundreds of volunteers from across Quebec sailed to Europe to help defend the Papal States against the armies of King Victor Emmanuel. This now-forgotten episode was as important to French Canada as Britain's imperial wars were for English Canada; the Church's global mission had come to occupy the same place in the collective imagination of francophones as the British Empire occupied in the minds of contemporary English Canadians.

Some French-Canadians became convinced that their high birthrates would one day permit them to absorb much of English-speaking North America. In 1891, Eduard Hamon, a Catholic priest, even went so far as to publish a book, *Les Canadiens-Français de la Nouvelle-Angleterre*, offering a strategy for the peaceful conquest of New England.

Imperialism was a respectable ideology in the late 19th and early 20th centuries, and French Canadian imperialism was notably pacific, as compared to the British, American, German or Russian variants. But this did not prevent English Canada from reacting with horror to this combination of religious fervour, expansionist enthusiasm and increasing demographic strength. Amid dark mutterings about Papist plots, provincial governments across the country launched waves of retaliation that would last the better part of a century.

THE FIRST ENGLISH REACTION: THE EASTERN TOWNSHIPS: 1849-1880

> In the past 25 years, the French Canadians have largely completed the peaceful conquest of the Eastern Townships. I maintain that what has been done in the Townships without fuss, injustice or civil war, can be repeated in all of north-eastern North America.
>
> —*Jules-Paul Tardivel (1890)*[24]

In the mid-19th century, it was hard for many English-speaking inhabitants of Quebec's Eastern Townships to imagine that their region could ever lose its anglophone majority. In March 1849, one local newspaper ridiculed the notion, comparing its likeliness to the probability of a plague of frogs.[25] But 1849 was also the year when the first stirrings of anglophone demographic discomfort took place in the Townships. Worried about the steady advance of French in their region, 2,500 Scottish and American farmers in Stanstead and Sherbrooke counties signed petitions calling for annexation to the United States, on the grounds that only the Great Republic could protect them from eventual assimilation. In 1850, three English-speaking members of the legislative assembly came out in support of annexation.[26]

The annexation fever of 1849-1850 passed quickly, but by the mid-1860s the French-speaking population of the Townships had more than doubled over 1850 levels. The parliamentary representatives of the English-speaking settlers were now thoroughly alarmed. They demanded special protection in the *British North America Act* before they would give their consent to Confederation.

All that they were able to gain in practice was a compromise arrangement awarding the Townships nine provincial electoral districts with inflexible boundaries so that no future gerrymandering could deprive the region's residents of full representation. The measure had no impact at all on the influx of French-speaking farmers, and by the 1880s, some Townshippers had became desperate and paranoid.

In 1888, A Scottish settler named Donald Morrison gained infamy as the 'Megantic Outlaw.' Morrison, an unsuccessful farmer, killed a lawman sent to arrest him for the harassment of a French family that had bought his family farm at a bankruptcy auction. The local English-speaking Protestant community believed Morrison to be the victim of a Papist conspiracy, and helped him to evade capture for nine months.[27]

Morrison's display of violence was not unique. In the 1870s, a vigilante organization, the Protestant Defence League, founded chapters across the Townships.[28] Armed conflict between English and French-speaking settlers was narrowly avoided in the mid-1870s in Compton County, when a French Canadian land company tried to evict Scottish settlers from land that it claimed.

By the 1890s, however, the spirit of the Townshippers had been broken. Negative measures having failed to stop French-speaking immigration, the English-speaking residents of the Townships seemed to resign themselves to minority status. Scholar J.I. Little explains why they finally gave up:

> The defeatist attitude of the Townships' Anglophone population developed, less because the prize was unattainable than because it was simply not worth struggling for. If the English Canadians had actually wanted the more northerly townships for themselves, if they had felt they were being driven from the region or that there was no escape from it, their attitude would have been very different. But greener pastures lay westward, so their reaction to the French-Canadian colonization movement, though generally hostile, was never sustained enough to present a serious challenge to it.[29]

Unfortunately for French Canadians, the reaction of the Townshippers was only a taste of what the next few decades would bring. English-speakers in other provinces would have their hands on the levers of power in their respective provincial governments, and would be capable of generating a good deal more misery for French Canadians than they had managed in the Townships.

Catholic-Bashing in the Maritimes: 1870-1875

The first acts of government-sponsored discrimination against French Canadians occurred in the 1870s in the Maritimes. Acadian populations rose rapidly in both provinces throughout the late 19th century,[30] leading to Anglo-Protestant fears similar to those that the English inhabitants of the Eastern Townships had already experienced. As a result, public schools policy in New Brunswick and Prince Edward Island during this time was highly intolerant. Restrictions were placed on the constitutional rights of all Catholics, including both the Acadian francophones and Irish immigrants.

Organized intolerance in New Brunswick and P.E.I. took the form of anti-Catholic legislation for several reasons. First, the English-speaking Protestant majorities in these provinces did not regard religion and language as distinct issues. As they watched the number of Acadian and Irish Catholics rise, Protestants in the two provinces concluded that they were under a general cultural assault from the Catholics.

Second, the Catholic schools were perceived to be the most powerful institutions in the hands of the Acadian minority. Education was believed to be the key to assimilation, so it was not thought to be necessary to subject the

Acadians to other, specifically linguistic forms of repression. If access to Catholic schools could be restricted and the curriculum altered, it was believed that minority children would be forced into the cultural mainstream.

A third reason is that the existence of an independently-run Catholic school system was seen as a costly duplication of services. In the late 19th century, provincial governments were turning education into a government-run monopoly. Before this time, primary education had been offered only sporadically and was primarily a church responsibility.

When the provincial governments began to assume the task of offering universally accessible, and eventually compulsory, primary education, provincial authorities attempted to replace local religious schools with a single universal system funded through local property taxes. Because it had always been a church responsibility, school was universally recognized as a place for moral and religious education in addition to the more practical subjects. Because the new provincially-run education systems were intended to be accessible to all, and many communities were considered too small to support more than a single school, considerable effort was devoted to developing a standard system of moral education that would be acceptable to parents of all denominations. This would pave the way for a single school in each community.

The various Protestant denominations were able to agree upon the creation of a school system which would provide a religious education based upon the common foundation of the King James Bible, since this translation was accepted by them all. However, this arrangement was unacceptable to the Catholics, with their vastly different tradition of scriptural interpretation.

In Ontario, where fears of rising French-Catholic numbers were still muted, the extra expense of a second school system was tolerated. A bill creating separate schools was enacted in Ontario in 1863 and entrenched in the *British North America Act* four years later. In Prince Edward Island and New Brunswick, however, the additional factor of demographic paranoia led to a less tolerant solution.

Prince Edward Island's *Public Schools Act* of 1877 provided for a single system of tax-supported non-denominational schools, with no public financial support for Catholic schools. Moreover, in any community where there was an insufficient enrolment in the public school, parents who sent their children to Catholic schools would be fined. The only concession to tolerance was that French-language schools were permitted to continue operating in the heavily francophone western tip of the province and to use textbooks prepared in Quebec for Catholic students, as long as the schools themselves were not overtly Catholic.

New Brunswick's *Common Schools Act* was passed in 1871. School fees were abolished, property taxes were made mandatory and all revenues were directed by law to non-denominational public schools. This amounted to a subsidy of

Protestant schools by Catholic parents, who were required to pay the property tax even if they sent their children to private Catholic schools. For parents who could not afford to pay the tax and private school fees as well, the only option was to send their children to public school.

The *Common Schools Act* was bitterly opposed by the Acadians; in 1875, two men died in the Acadian town of Caraquet in riots sparked by the education law.[31] Nonetheless, it was the Irish Catholics who fought most vigorously against the Act[32]—which was probably quite reasonable, since they were not geographically isolated from the Protestant population, as the Acadians were, and therefore were less able to convince the government to turn a blind eye to its own regulations.

New Brunswick's restrictions would not be fully relaxed for another century. An informal compromise, adopted in 1875, permitted the re-entry of priests and nuns into the classrooms. This measure was as much the work of Irish Catholics as it was the work of the Acadians. However, the compromise was really a divide-and-rule strategy that did little to help the Irish. It meant that in the solidly Catholic communities of Acadia, priests were able to conduct lessons in French and even to give religious instruction to student bodies consisting entirely of Catholic pupils, in schools that were non-denominational only in name.[33] For the Irish, intermingled with the Protestants on the far side of the province from the isolated Acadian population, severe restrictions on access to Catholic education continued.

The experience of New Brunswick's Irish Catholics would be well remembered in Ontario and the West, where the Irish and other non-francophone Catholics would be careful to distinguish themselves from their French-speaking co-religionists when intolerance towards Catholics started to rise in these regions in the 1890s and 1900s.[34] In future battles with the Anglo-Protestant majority, French Canadians would find themselves isolated, friendless and alone.

The Empire Strikes Back: Ontario, 1880-1927

> Ontario will not be safe.... Our eastern gate has already been opened.... Catholic invasion is already streaming through, ... to detach Eastern Ontario from the British and Protestant civilization of which it now forms a part and annex it to the territory of the French race....
>
> —*The Toronto Mail (1889)*[35]

At the time of the British Conquest of Canada, the future province of Ontario contained only a few small settlements of French-speakers. The most important of these was in the Windsor-Detroit region in the province's extreme southwest. Although it contained only a fur-trading fort and a small agricultural settlement, the region was the second most populous part of New France, after the St. Lawrence River valley itself.[36]

The British Conquest ended the flow of new immigrants from France, and the settlement on the Detroit River, now dependent entirely on natural increase and a trickle of migration from Lower Canada to boost its numbers, withered in isolation.[37] For more than a century, Ontario remained, with the exception of the southwestern enclave, entirely British. One result of this was a virtually *laissez-faire* language regime. Possessing no demographic fears, the British majority felt no inclination to pass language legislation of any sort.[38]

By 1880, immigration from Quebec had caused the francophone population in Ontario to grow to just over five percent, and for the first time anglophones were reduced to minority status in one of eastern Ontario's counties.[39] As well, Ontarians were alarmed by news of the rapid expansion of French into the Eastern Townships. In 1885, English became a mandatory language of instruction in all Ontario schools. Five years later, the legislation was extended and English was made the sole language of instruction in Ontario, except where 'impracticable.'

The year 1912 represented the high-water mark of educational intolerance. By this time, a second Ontario county had gained a French majority and two others seemed on the verge of being swamped by the rising tide of French. In response, the provincial government introduced a rabidly anti-French education law under the innocuous name 'Regulation 17.' This law forbade the use of French as a language of instruction beyond the first two grades. By virtue of an amendment passed in 1913, French could still be taught as a subject, but only for one hour a day.

Regulation 17 was the harshest language law ever enacted in Canada. It was designed to force the involuntary assimilation of an entire generation of young Franco-Ontarians, and to frighten away any future migrants from Quebec who might hope to raise their families in the ancestral language.

Regulation 17 enjoyed the support of most Anglo-Ontarians, and united such traditional enemies as the Protestant militants of the Orange Lodge and Michael Francis Fallon, the Irish Catholic bishop of London, Ontario. As one scholar observes:

> ... the Regulation was officially supported by both political parties, and perhaps most vehemently by the Irish Catholic community of that day. Indeed, the only notable exceptions were those, to be found in each party, who wished to go further and to prohibit any recognition at all of the French fact in Ontario's schools.[40]

The reaction within Ontario's French-speaking community was explosive. A new Ottawa-based newspaper, *Le Droit*, was established to lead the battle against the educational law. Non-compliance with Regulation 17 was widespread. Quebecers were also furious, and the issue mounted to the proportions of a national crisis during the First World War, particularly once the conscription

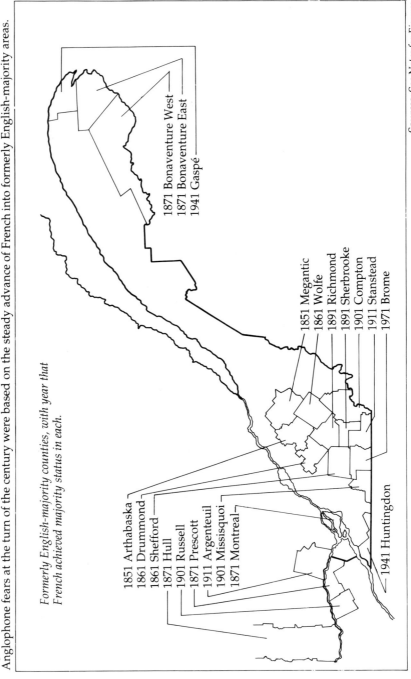

Figure 2.2:
Anglophone fears at the turn of the century were based on the steady advance of French into formerly English-majority areas.

issue had emerged to further divide Canadians along linguistic lines. Agitation by Quebec senators and MPs caused the Senate to pass a motion of 'regret' over Regulation 17, while the House of Commons voted on—but rejected, by a margin of 107-60—a motion of censure against the Ontario government. Pressure from Ontario MPs kept the federal government from exercising its constitutional power to disallow Regulation 17.

Regulation 17 was revoked in stages as Ontarians' demographic fears calmed. In 1927, the government of Premier Howard Ferguson recognized that the regulation was proving unenforceable. On this basis, French was permitted as a language of instruction in areas where recommended by a departmental committee. Continued relaxation of the restrictions continued over a period of several decades, culminating in the active provision by the province of a full range of French-language services, including educational services, in the 1970s and 1980s.

It is significant that these reforms took place at a time when French was no longer perceived to present a threat to the majority status of the English language in Ontario. Between the census of 1931, conducted shortly after the first laws relaxing Regulation 17 were passed, and the census of 1986, the percentage of Ontarians claiming French as their mother tongue dropped by a quarter.[41]

The Reaction in the West: 1890-1920

French and English had been guaranteed equal status in Manitoba under the 1870 *Manitoba Act* and in the Northwest Territories (which included Saskatchewan and Alberta until 1905) under the *Northwest Territories Act*. Schools in Manitoba and the Territories were organized on denominational lines. In practice, most Catholic schools used French. This system remained uncontroversial until 1890, when a wave of anti-Catholic hysteria swept across English Canada.

In that year D'Alton McCarthy, the MP for Ontario's North Simcoe riding, introduced a proposal in the House of Commons for the removal of the provisions of the *Northwest Territories Act* that guaranteed French language rights. If this were not done, McCarthy warned in the House, the use of French would:

> ... grow into what might be called a vested right, so that by-and-by a French Canadian can urge, 'I have left my own home in the Province of Quebec and have gone and settled in the North-West Territories, relying on the faith of an Act of Parliament by which it was said I should be allowed to have my language.'[42]

This measure was defeated in Parliament, and French-speakers in the Northwest Territories retained their rights for a while longer. But in Manitoba, fear of the Church and of a massive immigrant influx from Quebec had reached critical proportions. In 1890, an act of the Manitoba legislature declared English to be the province's only official language.

For the next ninety years, Manitoba would be governed under the provisions of this Act, which bore a remarkable resemblance to Quebec's Bill 101. The *Act to Provide That the English Language Shall Be the Official Language of the Province of Manitoba* provided that English would be the only language of the courts, the journals of the provincial legislature and of acts passed by the legislature. Also in 1890, the Manitoba Government ended all public funding of Catholic schools. The new law effectively ended all French-language education in the province. The Act would eventually (nearly a century later) be struck down by the Supreme Court of Canada as unconstitutional.

The Manitoba Schools Question quickly became a national issue, dominating the federal scene throughout the 1890s. In 1892 and again in 1895, the legality of the schools legislation was judicially confirmed, as was Ottawa's legal right to override the law.[43] Opposition from Ontario MPs, led by McCarthy, was sufficiently strong to prevent the Conservative federal government from passing a bill rescinding the Manitoba schools legislation. In 1896, the new Liberal government of Wilfrid Laurier was elected primarily on the basis of the promise to find 'sunny ways' of solving the schools crisis.

The compromise solution that Laurier and Manitoba's Premier Greenway put in place in 1897 called for instruction to be given in any language other than English wherever there were ten or more students speaking that language. Similarly, Catholic teachers would be hired in any urban school with ten or more Catholics. But the language controversy was not over. In 1916, the provincial government unilaterally rescinded the compromise.

The much-feared flood of French-speaking migrants never materialized. French-speakers have dropped as a proportion of Manitoba's population in every census taken since the turn of the century. As in Ontario, Manitoba's education restrictions were eased gradually over a period of decades as the anglophone majority's demographic fears faded. Full educational rights were finally restored in the late 1960s by the NDP government of Premier Edward Schreyer (which may explain why Pierre Trudeau appointed him Governor General a decade later).

Quebec's Reaction to English Canadian Intolerance: 1870-1920

Remarkably, during the difficult years that followed the passage of anti-French education laws in the other provinces, the Quebec government never considered retaliating in kind. No demographic fears existed in Quebec at the time to warrant such a reaction.

This does not mean, however, that Quebecers were insensitive to the sufferings of French Canadians elsewhere. They were outraged by Manitoba's language laws, and the reaction to Ontario's educational restrictions was so extreme that one deputy in the Quebec legislature accused Ontario's government of being morally inferior to that of Germany—at a time when Canada and Germany were at war.[44] Quebec's school boards were given authorization to send funds directly to Franco-Ontarians to subvert Regulation 17. Nonetheless, the only language law passed by the Quebec government during this period was a measure enacted in 1910 requiring that certain publicly-distributed forms, such as train tickets, be printed in both official languages.

This extraordinary show of tolerance demonstrates more effectively than any other piece of evidence in this chapter that it is *only* feelings of demographic insecurity that can provoke demands for oppressive language laws.

Half a Century of Language Tranquility: 1920-1960

Between the end of the First World War and the late 1960s, Canada enjoyed a period of linguistic tranquility similar to the calm that had prevailed in the two decades preceding Confederation. The main reason for the legislative peace was undoubtedly the country's stable demographic make-up during the period. French Canada still had a high birthrate, but immigration had soared; by the early 1920s it was clear that virtually the entire immigrant population was assimilating into the English Canadian community.[45] Just as the high French Canadian birthrate seemed no longer to pose a threat to English Canada, the flood of immigrants did not seem unduly threatening to the security of French within its heartland. Within Quebec, the proportion of the population speaking French rose modestly from 80.2 percent in 1901 to 81.2 percent in 1961,[46] even though the absolute numbers of immigrants and English Canadians in the province was also posting significant gains.

THE QUIET REVOLUTION AND BEYOND: 1960–PRESENT

> No other linguistic minority combines to such an extent two features: a reason to fear assimilation and the ability to control a modern subnational government. And not any kind of subnational government: the province of Quebec is the most powerful subnational government in all of the OECD countries in terms of its share of resources and its scope of intervention.
> —*Stéphane Dion (1992)*[47]

French Declines Again

The linguistic peace was shattered by two interconnected events that would change the face of French Canada in the 1960s. The first was the precipitous decline in the birthrate among French Canadians. The decline seems to have begun in the 1950s, but it was the census of 1971 that confirmed that the rate had dropped so low that French Canada would no longer be able to renew itself by births alone. The second factor was the explosive growth of secular society and the state apparatus of the Quebec government during the

Quiet Revolution. During the next ten years, Quebec would vocally 'redefine' itself as a much more open, secular, cosmopolitan society than it had ever been before. Immigrants were invited for the first time to assimilate into French Canadian society. French-speaking Quebecers were appalled to discover that most immigrants were not interested in accepting this offer, so they turned to their government to find ways of changing the situation.

The demographic panic in Quebec that continues to this day differs from past panics due to the broad range of measures that the provincial government has attempted to execute in its efforts to ensure the continued dominance of French in the province. Some of the calls for action, such as demands for changes in the province's immigration patterns, or the restrictions on educational rights, echo the actions taken by governments in Canada's two previous demographic crises. However, a whole range of additional measures have been enacted, designed to make French the language of work, of law, of commercial signs, and so on. There have even been measures intended to alter the birth rate.

These innovations reflect the modern Québécois belief that the state can mold society as it pleases—that, as Pierre Trudeau observed in a critique of Quebec nationalism penned during the Quiet Revolution, "the State was nothing in Quebec: now it must be everything."[48]

This new-found Québécois faith in the power of the state to create and manipulate the linguistic destiny of its population has had several consequences. One has been a strong and permanent upswing in the support for independence since the 1960s. Many Quebecers feel independence is the only way of gaining complete control of language. They believe that the provincial government is the only body that can unflinchingly defend the harsh measures necessary to ensure the survival of French, and only through independence can its jurisdiction be extended to every corner of society.

Support for this point of view, and hence for independence, rises whenever Ottawa and Quebec cross swords over language-related issues. Thus, for example, the death of the Meech Lake Accord in 1990 and the protracted constitutional debate which followed sent province-wide support for sovereignty above fifty percent in every poll taken for two consecutive years. Yet prior to January 1990, when the Accord and its all-important 'Distinct Society' clause had seemed safely assured of passage, support for independence had dropped as low as thirty-three percent. Similarly, the passage of Bill 101 in 1977 had the effect of sapping support for independence; some observers believe that it was the sense of security created by Bill 101 that guaranteed the defeat of the Sovereignty-Association option in the independence referendum of 1980.[49]

Language Legislation: 1967-1977

Incidentally, the fact that the sudden emergence of the anglophone demographic threat within Quebec was in large part due to demographic changes within the francophone population—drop in birth-rate and out-migration—rather than amongst anglophones, explains in part why anglophones were caught completely by surprise when the francophone community introduced corrective language legislation.

—*Gary Caldwell (1983)*[50]

Quebec did not progress from a policy of language *laissez-faire* to the restrictions of Bill 101 in a single move; the stages involved in the transformation took place over the course of a full decade.

The first crisis came in late 1967 when the Catholic school board in St-Leonard, a municipality in the northeast part of Montreal Island, attempted to force the children of Italian immigrants to attend French schools rather than the English schools preferred by their parents. The parents resisted, citing their traditional right to linguistic choice. A march to Ottawa was organized, where the parents presented their case to the prime minister. The dispute had soon captured the attention of the entire province. English Quebecers vocally supported the rights of Italians. Francophones were less sure in their response. It seemed discouraging and even insulting that immigrants to Quebec would not want to learn French. However, compulsion was not part of Québécois tradition.

The provincial government of Jean-Jacques Bertrand produced a stop-gap measure in 1968, hoping to satisfy all sides at once. Bill 85, *An Act to Amend the Education Department Act*, attempted to reconcile Quebec's tradition of tolerance with the promotion of French. Parents were to be given the right to choose to educate their children in English or in French, with the proviso that only children capable of understanding English be educated in that language. As well, the provincial minister of education was given the power to take all appropriate actions to ensure that immigrants would learn French. Before it had been passed, the bill was withdrawn and replaced by Bill 63.[51]

Bill 63, *An Act to Promote the French Language in Quebec*, guaranteed freedom of linguistic choice to all, but required that a working knowledge of French be gained by each child, regardless of the main language of the child's education. As well, Section 14 of the Bill declared French to be the language of work in Quebec, although it did nothing to restrict the use of English. A new body, the *Office de la langue française*, was established to promote the use of French in the workplace and act as a kind of language ombudsman for dissatisfied francophones.

Bills 85 and 63 were attempts to seek solutions that would not greatly limit minority rights, showing a continued desire on the part of the government to preserve Quebec's tradition of respect for individual rights.

The results of the 1971 census changed everything. It showed that Quebec's birthrate had dropped to 13.8 per 1,000, down to less than half the rate per 1,000 recorded fifteen years earlier.[52] Another 'leading indicator' of decline was the number of French-speaking children in Canada under the age of four. In 1971, the figure was 485,000, a drop of one-third from ten years earlier. Census figures on home language, which had never been collected before 1971, revealed that far fewer immigrants were assimilating into the francophone community than into the English-speaking community. A demographic study published in 1974 used projections based upon the 1971 census to show that French-speakers might soon find themselves a minority within Montreal or even in the province as a whole. The pressure for more restrictive language legislation became irresistible.

Bill 22, pointedly named the *Official* Language *Act* to emphasize its differences from the federal *Official **Languages** Act*, was introduced in the National Assembly in May 1974. In this law the emphasis on minority rights had been greatly reduced, and intrusions in the name of the majority had expanded. French was declared to be the sole official language of Quebec.

In interpreting provincial laws, the courts were to give precedence to the French version, always disregarding the English text in the event of conflicts. French was to be the sole language of the provincial public service, and of all contracts involving the provincial government. Public servants employed by the province would in the future be legally obliged to use French when communicating with their federal counterparts. Private contractors using English in their dealings with the provincial government were to be given reduced access to public tenders.

As well, in Bill 22 Quebec had for the first time a law that controlled the language shown on signs and which restricted language rights in the workplace and the classroom. The new law embodied the widest range of language restrictions ever imposed by a provincial government in Canada, and elicited a furious response from the minorities. A petition with 600,000 signatures was sent to Ottawa in 1975, demanding the repeal of the Bill. In the provincial election of 1976, thousands of anglophones turned away from the Liberals, voting instead for the nearly-defunct Union Nationale.

But the anger of the English-speaking Quebecers was a less potent force than the heightening demographic fears of French Quebecers. In August 1977, only a few months after its election, the Parti Québécois passed a new, even more restrictive language law.

Bill 101, the *Charter of the French Language*, placed draconian limits on enrolment in English-language schools. Henceforth, education in English would be available only to the children of individuals who themselves had been educated in English in Quebec. In the future, even the unilingual English-speaking children of newly arrived English Canadians migrating from other provinces would be required to attend French schools, as would all overseas immigrants.

All languages other than French were banned from public signs and billboards. Competence in French would become a legal requirement for gaining a licence as a professional. As well, unilingual francophones were promised that they could never be denied any job in any industry due to an inability to speak a language other than French. Provincial legislation would be passed in French only, and records of the debates of the assembly would be published exclusively in French. French would become the sole language of the courts. Municipalities were forbidden to provide services to local populations in English. A 'language police,' the *Commission de surveillance et des enquêtes*, was established to investigate reports of the law being broken, to report infractions to the attorney-general, and to prosecute offenders. One proposal that was discussed but not actually included in the new law would have required film distributors to dub in French all prints but one of any English-language film being shown in Quebec.

Bill 101 is not the only law passed by the Quebec legislature to stop francophone demographic decline. Since the 1980s, the Quebec government has adopted the policy of paying parents to produce more children. The program, nicknamed 'Bucks for Babies,' is based upon a suggestion that dates back to the release of the shocking results of the 1971 census. In 1974, the noted demographer Jacques Henripin called for the provincial government to take action in the form of 'natalist' or pro-fertility policies.[53] This recommendation would eventually be followed by René Lévesque's administration; amounts have crept upwards in successive provincial budgets to the point that today, the Quebec government pays a cash bonus of $7,500 upon the birth of a third child. It certainly cannot be argued that this particular program shows any hint of intolerance, but it does reaffirm the dominance in Quebec of the belief that state measures designed to alter demographics can and should intrude into every aspect of life.

SUMMARY

From whence can such shameful intolerance as Canadians have repeatedly written into their law books conceivably spring, in a nation that prides itself so much on its generosity and openness? And in peaceable times, under what rock does intolerance lurk, waiting to rise up spectre-like to haunt us again? The answer lies in each of us, in how we interact within our language groups, and in how we respond to other language groups.

Everyone with a passing knowledge of Canadian history knows that linguistic intolerance has ebbed and flowed like the tide, but no one really understands why. With careful historical examination, it becomes apparent that when linguistic populations are stable (i.e., neither growing nor shrinking relative to each other), there is peace. When the French language was being swamped by Irish immigrants, however, francophone tempers flared. And when French-speakers poured out of Quebec in large numbers to settle in other parts of Canada and the United States, anglophones reacted with intolerance. They perceived their own language and culture to be in danger, and harsh laws seemed to them to be the only way to preserve the cultural webs that they held dear.

It is a truism that our ancestors saw the world differently than we do. One thing they perceived very differently was the power of government. The early Canadien nationalists of Papineau's day believed that the state was weak, and they attempted only weak oppressive measures. The English-speaking provincial politicians of the late 19th and early 20th centuries believed the state to have greater powers because of its new-found control over education, which became the focus of their attention when they decided to deal harshly with the French 'menace.'

In the second half of the 20th century, the prevailing belief is that governments can control anything they want, including the language people speak and the thoughts that fill their heads. The faith of threatened majority and minority groups alike in the ability of government to control the linguistic and demographic destiny of its people has grown steadily for over a century, in parallel with the rise in the belief of the omnipotent state. It is therefore not surprising that the language laws enacted over the past quarter-century in Quebec are confidently society-wide in nature and scope.

Yet, unbelievably, the true powers of the state in this regard have never been examined critically. It is self-evident that provincial governments can pass language laws that cause their minorities plenty of misery. But the ability to ruin the lives of a few thousand fellow citizens does not necessarily translate into the ability to control the forces of demographics or assimilation, any more than the strength to hold someone's head below the waves until he drowns implies an ability to hold back the tide.

Since federal language policy is to a large extent a reaction to the same real or implied threats that motivate provincial governments, there are important lessons in this for federal legislators as well. Perceived demographic threats are not always real threats. Short-term trends do not always persist in the long term. The influence that we believe government policies to have over the language that individual citizens will choose to speak may be more closely connected to our views of the world than to reality. And finally, the ability of the heavily pressured federal government to maintain a principled stand on any matter relating to language over a long period of time is dubious.

This suggests that any federal attempt to introduce a sophisticated end-based vision of language policy must inevitably suffer from at least two failings. It will be based on premises that are at best are partly faulty, which means that language policies will always be more contentious than expected. As well, Ottawa's practical ability to stick to a single vision consistently over a period of years will be sorely tested, and almost certainly will fail. The first of these two failings will be the subject of Chapters Six through Nine. That the second failing has already happened in practice will be shown in detail in Chapter Three.

CHAPTER THREE

The Victory of Asymmetrical Bilingualism

> ... it comes hard on me to hear honorable gentlemen say that there is no security for [the English minority in Quebec] in the future, but that the French may do anything they choose in the lower branch of the Legislature. But, honorable gentlemen, if the ... Legislature were insensate enough and wicked enough to commit some flagrant act of injustice against the English Protestant portion of the community, *they would be checked by the General Government.*
> —*Sir E.P. Taché,* ***Confederation Debates*** *(1865)*[1]

IN PRACTICE, ALTHOUGH NOT in public pronouncements, the Canadian government actively promotes enforced bilingualism in nine provinces, and tolerates enforced French-only unilingualism in Quebec. This is a complete change of course from the country-wide bilingualism envisioned by Pierre Trudeau when he first came to office. That it has taken place despite his dominance of Canadian politics for more than half of the intervening quarter century reveals just how impossible it is to impose complex, end-based visions of language policy on a country like Canada.

The federal government's language policies touch on every aspect of Canadians' lives. In almost all of these areas, from the hiring practices of the federal public service to the advertising practices that are imposed on federally regulated private businesses, official languages policy has grown increasingly asymmetrical over the past twenty years. Today it clearly favours the French language and French-speakers over the English language and anglophones.

Many critics of official language policies (usually English-speakers, of course) express frustration at the apparent willingness of the federal government to continue spreading the gospel of universal language rights for minorities outside Quebec at a time when the provincial government within that province has repeatedly shown contempt for the rights of its own minorities. One of the most vocal critics is *Forbes'* senior editor Peter Brimelow, who, in his book, *The Patriot Game*, writes:

> The one part of the country where bilingualism is not promoted with the full weight of federal authority is, paradoxically, Quebec. Trudeau's Liberals reacted with extreme caution to the disconcerting spectacle of Quebec, the

jewel in bilingualism's crown, the only part of Canadian society even superficially bicultural, turned to dross.[2]

In fact, this critique is far too mild. On the question of federal government attitudes toward the relative treatment of Canada's two main language groups, it is not the moderate critics who have been closest to the truth, but the bug-eyed radicals on the fringes of the debate. For the past twenty years, federal language policy has been inching closer and closer to openly asserting that Canada should base its treatment of minorities on abstract considerations of equality between languages, rather than on the net well-being of individual Canadian citizens, and that equality of status between languages of unequal strength requires, in practice, the preferential treatment of the speakers of the threatened language (French) over those who speak the dominant tongue (English).

During the last years of the Trudeau era, asymmetrical bilingualism was partly entrenched in the *Canadian Charter of Rights and Freedoms* (although admittedly, Trudeau was reluctant to place it there, and did so only under intense pressure). In the Mulroney years, the ideology has been embraced in Ottawa with enthusiasm, if not exactly with honour, and has, in some departments and agencies, virtually replaced the older concept of equal levels of tolerance for both official-language minorities as de facto federal policy. Today, it is only in programs that are administered indirectly by the elected politicians, such as the Justice Department's Court Challenges Program (directly administered by the University of Ottawa) that Trudeau-style policies based on the Personality Principle linger on unchallenged.[3] Asymmetrical bilingualism has even won the official backing of the Commissioner of Official Languages, Canada's bought-and-paid-for representative of beleaguered linguistic minorities, who now claims he can find little to fault in the way the Quebec government treats its minorities.[4]

Disenfranchising English Canada

[F]rom one ocean to the other, Canada is presenting a bilingual image that is stronger than ever, while in Quebec, for the first time since 1760, the official language is exclusively French. If one sticks to the image, not only is Quebec sovereign, but it has succeeded in partially annexing Canada.
—*Christian Dufour (1990)*[5]

It seems strange, or even politically impossible, that a minority with only a quarter of Canada's population could impose upon the other seventy-five percent a language policy that systematically discriminates in favour of the smaller group and against the larger. To understand how this can happen, it is important to recognize that control of Parliament is essentially a numbers game. As long as Quebec MPs (who hold only one-quarter of the seats in the

House of Commons), are united within the caucus of a single party, they will represent a bloc, or sometimes even a majority, within that party. If the party holds more than half the seats in the Commons, they will have a majority or near-majority share in the party that controls all legislation. This sort of leverage, which finds its basis in the well-known phenomenon of French Canadian bloc voting in federal elections, has ensured that French-speaking Canada's linguistic agenda would dominate federal politics from the moment that Québécois voters began to fear for the survival of their culture in the late 1960s and to move language issues to the top of their political agenda.

Although the phenomenon of leveraged control over the House of Commons has never been analyzed in detail, the principle is understood well enough by Canada's politicians that the battleground in the national *guerre des langues* has largely shifted over the past few years from entrenching asymmetrical bilingualism in law (a victory now largely complete) to setting it permanently in the constitution. Thus far, the strategy has been to do this through constitutionally entrenching structural changes to the Canadian political system that will ensure that French Canada's share of political representation will never fall below twenty-five percent—the magic number that guarantees majority representation in the party holding 100 percent of political power in Ottawa—and to granting Quebec the power to ensure that its own minorities never grow sufficiently large as a share of the provincial population to gain the political means of protecting their own rights. Both 1987's Meech Lake Accord and 1992's Charlottetown Accord contained provisions designed to set this level of representation in stone.

What follows is an explanation of how the ideology of asymmetrical bilingualism has come to dominate Canadian language policy.

The Source of Asymmetry

> A strategy must be developed. The guidelines for this strategy emerge clearly from the present circumstances: 1) The Francophone communities have joined together and will convey a common message. 2) They will demonstrate unflinching discipline and perfect solidarity....
> —*Fédération des francophones hors Québec (1978)*[6]

Canadian politics have always been shaped by a kind of ethnic-based coalition process that ensures that even when governments enact laws that are repugnant to most people in the majority community, the results will still be electorally rewarding to the political parties that advocate the laws. Over the past twenty years, this has led to federal advocacy of asymmetrical bilingualism.

Two factors make this coalition process function. The first, discussed above, is the leveraged control over political parties that minorities are able to gain, as long as they themselves remain united. The second is the higher cohesiveness that minorities tend to have when voting.

Canada's electoral history shows that, except under unusual and temporary conditions, linguistic minorities are far more likely to vote as cohesive units than are the members of the majority. This is probably largely due to the hypersensitivity to ethnic issues that accompanies the uncomfortable sensation—unique to minorities—of being surrounded on all sides by people of another language group. Another factor is that the payoffs that accompany bloc voting are substantially greater for members of a minority than they are for the majority. If the minority splits its votes between two parties, it risks being peripheralized within each of them. If it concentrates its vote on a single party, its influence within that party will be substantially greater than is justified by its demographic presence in the country or province as a whole. Unified support from a sizable linguistic minority means that the party can remain in power with only limited support from the majority community. Accordingly, if party leaders are pragmatic, they will willingly let the linguistic minority set the tone on any issue that is as much or more a political concern for the minority community as it is for the majority, even if most members of the majority community oppose the direction of these policies. This means that whenever language policy becomes an issue of importance to the minority, as it has been to French-Canadians for the past three decades, they will dictate the political unit's language policy.

Their power is not totalitarian, to be sure. If all members of the majority oppose a measure, it will not pass. But if a relatively small percentage of them can be convinced to back it, it will go forward. Observing this phenomenon at work in federal politics, former Commissioner of Official Languages Keith Spicer once described it as "a classically Canadian compromise: upsetting the English enough to convince the French that things are moving, but not enough to provoke the English into throwing a spanner into the works."[7]

The key to the whole process, as Spicer notes, is keeping the compromises just within the bounds of upsetting members of the majority enough to cause them to vote against the governing party. Just how outrageous the legislative agenda can be (in the eyes of the majority) depends mostly upon the relative sizes of the majority and minority communities. The larger the minority, the more it can throw its weight around.

There appears to be a critical mass at which well-organized and highly-motivated ethnic minorities become large enough to dominate those aspects of public policy that concern language and ethnicity. Once this level has been reached, the minority gains enough legislative clout to ensure that it will be granted legislative toleration (if the majority feels threatened by it, due to prevailing demographic trends) or preferential laws and reverse discrimination (if it is the minority that feels threatened by prevailing demographic trends).

It is worth noting that the passage of special legislation does not require that the goodwill of the majority be gained, or that the majority community in any sense endorse the prevailing legislative trend. All that is needed is that the usual pattern be followed, with the minority community more highly motivated to vote along ethnic and linguistic lines than the majority is. As long as members of the minority community continue to vote based more on language issues than on other concerns, and the majority votes based primarily on other considerations, governments will quickly learn that it is good politics to cater to the minority on ethnic issues, and to focus its electoral appeals to the majority on other issues.

Within this framework, enterprising politicians will try to build a tactical alliance between the unified minority population and a portion of the majority community. The combined support of the united minority community and a fraction of the majority community is sufficient to give this party control of the political unit in question. The percentage of the majority community that must be won over to this coalition decreases as the minority's proportionate size within the political unit, be it a municipality, a province, or a country, grows.

This may lead to regular clashes between political elites and the majority ethnic group on language matters, but that is a price that the politicians will usually be able to pay, since they know that it is the minority that has the greater interest on language issues.

This explains why a sizable English-speaking population has been virtually impotent in Quebec politics, while a francophone community that is not (proportionately speaking) very much larger, has been strong enough in federal politics to rewrite Canada's language laws in a way completely unacceptable to the majority of anglophones. In Quebec, where English-speakers and immigrants assimilating into the English-speaking community form 13.3 percent of the total population, a coalition would require the support of forty-one percent of the province's francophone majority in order to represent a majority of the total population of Quebec and therefore gain power.

Contrast this with the situation in federal politics. Francophones form 25.2 percent of Canada's total population, so a coalition party needs to have the support of only thirty-five percent of Canada's anglophone majority to hold power.

The situation is even clearer in New Brunswick, where francophones form thirty-one percent of the total population. In this province, a coalition needs the support of a mere twenty-eight percent of the province's relatively slim anglophone majority to hold power.[8]

A Hundred Years of Beating up on the Little Guys

The twin elements of minority size and of the general lack of internal voting cohesion on the part of Canadian majorities explain why the treatment of the minorities in different Canadian provinces has varied so widely. It also explains why the language policies of Canadian provinces have never been very accurate reflections of the perils of assimilation faced by their majority and minority communities. Language policy has been a far more accurate reflection of the relative political strengths of the linguistic majority and minority communities of the day. When the minority is proportionately smaller—in other words, when it poses less of a genuine demographic 'threat' to the majority—it is far more likely to be the object of restrictive and discriminatory laws than when it is strong. Two examples from Canada's past demonstrate this nicely.

In 1890, francophones represented a mere 7.3 percent of Manitoba's population. Therefore, only fifty-four percent of Manitoba's English-speakers had to be convinced that the French language posed a threat to their way of life for the provincial government to gain the support of an overall majority of the province's population for restricting the educational rights of French-speakers. Likewise, when Ontario enacted Regulation 17 in 1912, Franco-Ontarians represented only eight percent of the Ontario population, which meant that restrictions on their rights needed the support of only fifty-five percent of the English population to gain the support of an overall majority of the province's residents.

The coalition phenomenon also explains the otherwise inexplicable phenomenon of New Brunswick's provincial government restricting francophone educational rights in 1871, when Acadians represented 17.6 percent of the province's population, and then restoring the last of these rights in the 1940s, when the Acadian population had risen to 34.5 percent of the total, and seemed destined to become the majority within a few decades.[9] In 1871, a province-wide majority in favour of restrictions could have been produced with the support of as little as sixty-one percent of the English-speaking population. (In fact, support levels appear to have been somewhat higher.) In 1940, renewed restrictions would have required the support of over three-quarters of the province's anglophones, which would have been virtually impossible to arrange. Later, the province's *Official Languages of New Brunswick Act* would be passed by a provincial government holding every Acadian seat in the legislative assembly, and less than half the seats in the English-speaking parts of the province.

MINORITY POLITICS IN OTTAWA AND QUEBEC

Ethnicity and Party Politics in Quebec

In Quebec, the anglophone minority was strong enough for years to supplement the naturally generous attitude of the French-speaking majority on matters of language. Gradually and quietly, the anglophone electoral strength needed to preserve these rights was eroded. The anglophone percentage of the province's population has dropped steadily—with one statistical blip around 1970—since the

1850s, making it increasingly difficult for English-speakers to build a coalition large enough to block the wishes of the majority francophone community.

The critical point on the scale of proportionate decline, when the anglophone population dropped below a level where it could form a coalition, probably took place around 1930, when the English-speaking population dropped below twenty percent of the provincial total.[10] Starting in 1936, Maurice Duplessis built a long series of provincial governments almost entirely without the support of English-speaking voters. However, anglophone rights remained well-protected by the provincial government, due mostly to the fact that the Québécois fears of the 1930s, '40s and '50s had more to do with Jehovah's Witnesses, who were subjected to police abuse under the notorious 'padlock law,' and Communists than with anglophones. Of course, the substantial financial support that Duplessis' Union Nationale received from English-speaking financiers like J.W. McConnell did nothing to prejudice him against the language rights of anglophones.

Today English-speakers and immigrants who have adopted English as their first official language represent only 13.3 percent of the provincial population. This means that whenever there is even limited majority support of fifty-nine percent or more among French-speakers in favour of a measure that restricts the rights of these groups, the united opposition of anglophones and immigrants can be overridden. Only on issues where francophones are split in virtually equal blocs can the minorities be expected to cast the deciding ballots, as they did in the 1980 referendum on Sovereignty-Association.

This loss of power has happened despite the fact that anglophones have taken a more active interest in Quebec provincial elections since the Quiet Revolution than they ever did previously. Voter turn-out rates among anglo-Quebecers have rocketed since the end of the Duplessis era.[11] As well, since 1970, Quebec's minorities have engaged in bloc voting with a unity and singleness of purpose that makes French Canada's celebrated bloc voting pattern in federal elections seem positively pluralistic by comparison. In 1970, seventy-five percent of English-speakers voted Liberal. In 1973, an amazing ninety-one percent of non-francophones supported the Liberals.[12] In the 1980 referendum, the level of non-francophone unity in support of the No option approached 100 percent. Repeat performances of these bloc voting patterns took place in provincial elections in 1981 and 1985. Even more impressive was a petition signed by Quebec anglophones to protest Bill 22, the restrictive language law passed by the Bourassa government in the mid-1970s. Nearly three-quarters of the province's entire English-speaking population signed the petition; when it was compiled, the list of names was nearly five miles long. Yet none of this activism has had any significant impact on the province's language laws.

A neat illustration of this can be made by contrasting the results of province-wide votes in which different issues have been at the forefront. In the provincial election of 1973, the Parti Québécois campaigned on the issue of independence. Independence was the issue again in the referendum of 1980. Independence is an issue that divides francophones and unites everybody else (against it). In the 1980 referendum, over ninety-five percent of non-francophones voted No.

By contrast, the francophone community was so evenly split that the question of whether or not a razor-thin majority had voted Yes to Sovereignty-Association actually became a hot political issue in the days following the vote.

The answer to the question of francophone preferences in 1980 scarcely matters. The overwhelming and united opposition of Quebec's non-francophones had driven the independence option to defeat by a margin of 702,000 votes.[13]

To some degree, this was a repeat performance of the election of 1973, when the Parti Québécois had campaigned on the promise to make Quebec independent if elected, while the Liberal Party had established itself as the champion of federalism. The appeal of a firm stand on federalism was sufficient to attract only fifty-one percent of the francophone vote, but it also attracted fully ninety-one percent of non-francophones.[14]

These results contrast dramatically with those of the provincial election of 1976 and of the 1992 referendum on the Charlottetown Accord. In both cases, the votes produced a limited but reasonably strong majority vote among francophones in favour of an option resolutely opposed by English-speakers and immigrants. In both cases, the near-unanimous votes of the minorities were swept aside by francophone majorities—even though the francophone majorities were hardly overwhelming.

In 1976, the Parti Québécois swept to power on a wave of euphoria—and a bare majority of the ballots cast by French-speakers. The peculiarities of Quebec's first-past-the-post system allowed the Parti Québécois to win sixty-five percent of the seats in the legislature with only 41.3 percent of the total votes cast in the province.[15]

What is particularly interesting about this election is the way in which it highlights the impotence of Quebec's minorities in influencing the government's handling of the language issue. The Liberals lost a huge proportion of their support among the province's minorities because they had imposed Bill 22, but scholars who have studied the results of the election believe that this did not cause many seats to be thrown to the Parti Québécois.[16]

Under these circumstances, there was nothing that Quebec's minorities could do to stop or slow down the imposition of Bill 101. They had become electorally irrelevant. The process was repeated in the next provincial election, in 1981. The anglophones had returned to the Liberal fold by this time, and voted massively in favour of the party. But their views did not matter. A slim majority of francophones supported the Parti Québécois, which won with 49.3 percent of the total votes cast in the province and a forty-one-seat majority in the National Assembly.[17]

An understanding of this inability of anglophone voters to influence the outcome of provincial elections allowed Georges Mathews to look ahead, while the Parti Québécois was still in power in the mid-1980s, and to predict with impressive accuracy that:

> The Liberal Party will not be much less nationalist, once it returns to power, than the Parti Québécois. There are two main demopolitical reasons for this: the numerical decline of its anglophone base of support and the necessity, if it is to gain power, of electing a significant number of deputies in ridings that have large francophone majorities. The result is that Bill 101 no longer has any significant political opponents.[18]

Final proof of the impotence to which the province's English-speaking population had been reduced in matters of their own language rights came in 1989, when the community once again abandoned the Liberal Party, following the imposition of Bill 178 (a law which the Bourassa government passed in 1988 using the "notwithstanding clause" of the *Canadian Charter of Rights and Freedoms*, prohibiting the use of English on signs).

This time the anglophone community created a party of its own: the Equality Party, dedicated to the universal recognition of individual rights and to full bilingualism. Another minority-rights party, the Unity Party, was also established, and was absorbed into the ranks of the Equality Party after the 1989 election. The intensity and thoroughness with which English-speakers transferred their affiliation to these two parties was startling, as Reed Scowen, a former MNA and parliamentary assistant to Premier Bourassa, recalls:

> On election day, November 18, 1989, the Equality and Unity Parties presented candidates in 35 of the 125 ridings in Quebec (18 in Montreal). When the voting was over, two-thirds of the English community had voted for them and the Equality Party had won the four Montreal ridings with the largest English populations. In the Westmount and Jacques Cartier ridings the Liberals had previously held the seats for over fifty years. In D'Arcy McGee (where the Equality Party leader was elected) and Notre-Dame-de-Grâce, no one but a Liberal had won an election since the ridings had been created. In another seven counties the English parties won over 20 percent of the vote. In a total of 19 Quebec ridings, more than 10 percent of all voters supported the English parties.[19]

In Bourassa's own riding of Saint-Laurent, which is over half non-francophone, the Premier saw his personal margin of victory slip from 82.7 percent of the total votes cast in the January 20, 1986 by-election that won him his seat, to 52.1 percent in the 1988 general election.[20] The largest share of this drop was due to the strong performance of the Equality Party candidate, Ciro Paul Scotti.

Yet despite the virtually complete collapse of the party's support among English-speaking voters, Bourassa's Liberals were returned to power with 49.9 percent of the total votes cast in the province, fifty-nine percent of the francophone vote, and a fifty-nine-seat majority in the assembly. Bill 178, needless to say, was not amended to placate the minorities.

Ethnicity and Party Politics in Ottawa

> Ottawa has never really believed in Canada's bicultural character; and [French Canada's] minor victories in this field have always been obtained as the direct result of manoeuvres that made Ontario tremble because of our electoral strength.
> —*Pierre Trudeau (1968)*[21]

Although the proportion of French-speakers within Canada's population has gradually declined from just under one-third in 1867 TO BARELY OVER ONE-QUARTER TODAY, FEDERAL LANGUAGE POLICY HAS INCREASINGLY CATERED TO FRANCOPHONE CONCERNS RATHER THAN TO THE OFTEN CONTRADICTORY ASPIRATIONS OF ANGLOPHONES. THIS IS DUE TO THE DECLINE OF ANGLOPHONE FEARS OF BEING SWAMPED BY FRENCH CANADIAN BIRTHRATES, AND THE RISE IN FRANCOPHONE FEARS OF MASS ASSIMILATION.

When set against the mass demographic paranoia of English Canadians around the turn of the century, the bloc-voting pattern of French Canada was enough to get the federal government to weakly declare its support of the rights of the persecuted French-speakers of various provinces, but not much more. More recently, the combination of bloc voting in Quebec and of the current widespread Québécois conviction that linguistic perdition is just around the corner have had the effect of turning the federal government into a determined partisan of French language minority rights outside Quebec, and of French-language majority rights inside the province.

The federal government has always been Canada's defender of the rights of linguistic minorities in the various provinces, although admittedly it has been about as ineffectual and wimpish as it is possible for any pretender to white knight status to be. As much as anything else, this is because Ottawa finds itself perpetually at odds with inflamed local majorities who are convinced (all evidence to the contrary notwithstanding) that their language and culture is at risk of being swept aside by the demographic weight of some poor, much-abused linguistic minority.

Ottawa has found itself reluctantly at odds with New Brunswick in the 1870s, with Manitoba in the 1890s, and with Ontario in the 1910s. In each case, the realities of partisan ethnic politics forced it to back down. Sometimes these battles carried serious political costs. Georges-Etienne Cartier lost his seat in Parliament in the 1872 general election largely due to his refusal to condemn New Brunswick's restrictions on Catholic schooling. Charles Tupper's

Conservatives lost the 1896 election because, after years of doing nothing, they suddenly took an overly tough stand on the Manitoba schools question in a calculated attempt to win votes in Quebec. They were replaced by Laurier's Liberals, who introduced a negotiated solution to the Manitoba Schools crisis. In 1916, Sir Robert Borden refused to support a resolution condemning Ontario's Regulation 17. He won the next election, including some seats in the English parts of Quebec, on the basis of English Canadian war hysteria (and a rigged ballot), but his party was completely wiped out in Quebec in the election of 1921, and was reduced to third-party status nationwide.[22]

At moments of intense anglophone unity of purpose, as during the conscription crisis of 1917 or at the time that Riel was hanged, French Canada's point of view could be ignored altogether by federal politicians. But such solidarity among the majority community was rare, and Quebec's collective concerns (which had little to do with language laws, before 1960) were usually treated with considerable respect.

Thus, for example, Mackenzie King was careful to avoid disallowing Premier Duplessis' 'padlock law,' which he personally found despicable, because he could not afford to alienate his Quebec supporters.[23] Later he showed extraordinary skill in avoiding a confrontation over the conscription issue. As well, he gave his Quebec lieutenants (first Ernest Lapointe, then Louis St-Laurent) such high status that his governments were referred to in Quebec as the 'King-Lapointe' and 'King-St-Laurent' ministries, as if they were formal ethnic coalitions along the lines of the Lafontaine-Baldwin or Taché-Macdonald governments of the pre-Confederation era.[24] This care paid off. In all his twenty-nine years as Liberal leader, King never once held less than half the seats in Quebec, and in his two earliest governments, when he had not yet earned the trust of a majority of English Canadians, Quebec MPs actually represented more than half his caucus.

When his long career is considered as a whole, it is clear that King's Quebec support kept him in power despite an English Canadian attitude towards him that was lukewarm at best. Adding together all the federal elections in which King led the Liberals, the party won forty-four percent of the popular vote in the country as a whole, which was usually enough to secure a majority of the seats in the House of Commons. Outside Quebec, the average works out to less than forty percent support for the man who ruled the country for just under a quarter of a century. Within Quebec, however, King's support averaged at more than sixty percent of votes cast, and fully eighty-six percent of seats from the province.[25]

When political contempt was shown to Quebec by English-speaking parliamentarians less wise than King, the reaction from Quebec was sharp and direct. In 1935, for example, R.B. Bennett's Conservatives suffered the loss of all but five of the twenty-four seats they had previously held in the province, when

Bennett refused to add the French language to Canada's unilingual dollar bills.[26] But on the whole, the era before the 1960s can be characterized as having been influenced as much by the moderate and non-intrusive goals of French Canadians as by their collective consciousness and bloc voting patterns. Quebec's influence tended to be used to affect the non-cultural areas of policy that in those days were the province's chief concern. Journalists Sheila McLeod-Arnopoulos and Dominique Clift summarize the pre-1960 era as follows:

> The political alliance between the French and the English business elites of Montreal, as it came to be realized within the Liberal party, gave Quebec a disproportionate weight in the Canadian federal system. Thanks to the disciplined electoral behaviour of the French and to the bloc of votes that they provide in the House of Commons, the business establishment of Central Canada was able to retain control of the whole Canadian economy and to steer the country's development in the direction it saw fit. French support from Quebec was instrumental in beating back successive protest movements which arose in Western Canada and which challenged the supremacy of Montreal. . . . [27]

In addition to economic policy, the loyalty of Quebec voters was won with patronage: "The unshakeable loyalty of Quebec voters to the Liberals was largely due to career opportunities in politics, in the public service, and in the magistrature, which compensated for the closed nature of the business world."[28]

The 1960s changed all this. The emergence of the separatist threat meant that suddenly English Canada had much more to lose from not answering Quebec's concerns. In Parliament, this translated into a weakening of resistance to measures designed to promote the use of French, and to the abandoning of old British symbols such as the Red Enseign and such royalist nomenclature as 'The Queen's Printer.' Suddenly the problem of the unilingual, English-speaking public service, which had been a source of annoyance for French Canadians since at least the end of the Second World War, became a political priority for federal politicians, as did the provision of bilingual counter service at post offices outside Quebec. A royal commission was appointed in 1963 to study the problem of bilingualism, and the Liberal Party turned to Quebec in search of 'wise men' to solve the suddenly urgent question: what does Quebec want?

Quebec, it would become evident later, wanted the ability to impose the French language on its minorities. But it would take Quebecers themselves a few years to realize this. In the meantime, Pierre Trudeau was swept to 24 Sussex Drive on a wave of euphoria impelled, as much as anything else, by the English-Canadian conviction that they had found the man who could give Quebecers whatever it was they were looking for, within Confederation.

Of course, Trudeau had his own idiosyncratic ideas about language policy, and they had nothing at all to do with forcing Quebec's minorities to assimilate into French. The *Official Languages Act*, enacted in 1969, entrenched the notion of coast-to-coast official bilingualism, largely based on copying nationwide the model of Quebec's extensive network of provincially-sponsored English-language services and facilities. There were some notes of protest from English Canada at the thought that someone would have to pay for all the new services and that bilingualism might become an imposition on the individual rather than on the state. But the opposition parties knew the mathematics of winning power, so they were silent, and voted in favour of the bill.

In his first, heady term in office, Pierre Trudeau was free to implement his own grand vision of a bilingual, bicultural Canada. He was rewarded by the loss of nearly half the Liberal seats in English Canada in the election of 1972. Only his iron grip on Quebec and on the francophone ridings of eastern Ontario and northern New Brunswick allowed him to keep a razor-thin two-seat edge over Stanfield's Conservatives in the House of Commons.

But by this time things had started to change in Quebec, too. The 1973 provincial election had confirmed the status of the Parti Québécois as the provincial opposition. Then, newly-released census data showed the French language outside Quebec to be in catastrophic decline and English to be gaining ground even within Quebec. Francophone Quebecers became radically more militant on language matters. Many concluded that the federal effort to save French in the other provinces was doomed, and that all efforts should now focus on strengthening the position of French in Quebec. The first fruit of this policy was Robert Bourassa's Bill 22. Enacted in 1974, it was at the time the most extensive and intrusive piece of language legislation ever imposed in Canada, but it was not enough to placate the popular mood. In 1977 it was repealed and replaced by the Parti Québécois' Bill 101, which raised the bureaucratic control of language to a Kafkaesque art.

Through all of this, Trudeau, the civil libertarian, remained frustratedly silent. He was impotent to stop the swing in Quebec towards restricting individual rights, and he knew it. Had he used the federal government's technical ability to disallow Bill 101, he would have presented the separatists, who were already whispering among themselves over the wording for a referendum question on independence, with a golden opportunity to inflame the anger of Québécois voters. "I don't want to give Mr. Lévesque the choice of timing and issues," said Trudeau,[29] and the issue of disallowance was never raised again.

In any event, even Canadian prime ministers face limits on their ability to make their MPs perform like trained seals, so it is unlikely that Trudeau could have forced his Quebec members to commit political suicide by voting down an enormously popular language law within two years of an upcoming federal election. Evidence of the kind of opposition that Trudeau would have faced within his own ranks, had he tried to push ahead with his vision of a fully bilingual state apparatus on both sides of the Quebec border, can be found in the testimony of eight Quebec Liberal MPs on the subject of the creation of 'bilingual districts' (regions in which services from all levels of government would be guaranteed in both official languages) in Montreal. Although the party whips were successful in keeping all Quebec Liberals silent while the issue was being raised in Parliament, seven of eight MPs who testified before a board studying the issue were opposed to guaranteed government services for Quebec anglophones.[30]

The mood in Quebec had forced the prime minister to remain stonily silent when he was presented with a petition, five miles long, signed by 600,000 English-speaking Quebecers calling for the disallowance of Bill 22. Now he remained equally passive as Bill 101 made a farce of his dream of coast-to-coast minority rights.

Since he was unable to countermand the efforts of the premiers of Quebec, Trudeau could only try to outbid them for the loyalty of French Canada by extending ever further the rights of the *hors-Québec* francophone minorities—in the hope that somebody in Quebec still cared—and by pouring money into the province. Occasionally in moments of extreme boldness, when separatist fortunes were on the wane, he could go further. In 1982, with the referendum on Sovereignty-Association newly won and an exhausting provincial election campaign just freshly out of the way, he was able to slip a few minor guarantees of language rights into the new *Charter of Rights and Freedoms*.

Henceforth Quebec anglophones who had been educated in English in Canada would be guaranteed the right to send their children to school in English (of course, even Bill 101 had not abrogated this right to any great extent, so it was a victory of exceedingly small proportions). But even though René Lévesque had absented himself from the constitutional negotiating table as the Charter was being written, Trudeau did not dare to re-extend educational freedom of choice to immigrants to Quebec, or to include any mention of freedom of choice in language of work or on signs. Fictionally, Canada remained a bilingual country. In practice, Trudeauism reigned only in the nine English-majority provinces, and enforced unilingualism predominated in Quebec.

By his inaction in the face of Quebec's language laws, the prime minister had admitted that he could live with this arrangement. By entrenching a charter of rights in which the language rights of francophones outside Quebec are more extensive than those of anglophones in the province (the former are guaranteed the right to an education in their mother tongue, while the latter are not, unless their parents were educated in English in Canada), he had taken the first step towards making this asymmetrical arrangement permanent.

Of course, the prime minister could still dream that one day Quebec would see the light. His Messianic vision of Canada as a bilingual society was still ploughing ahead in nine of the country's ten provinces, despite the muffled complaints of the locals, and Section 59 of the *Charter of Rights and Freedoms* did contain a clause permitting the legislature in Quebec City to opt into full protection of minority education rights, apparently on the theory that at some moment in the future, the option of being just like the rest of the country would become too tempting for Quebec politicians to resist. To date, the option of exercising this provision of Section 59 has not attracted a following in the Assemblée Nationale.

This reluctance is not difficult to explain, given the fact that another unity policy had badly misfired. The Prime Minister had attempted to buy the loyalty of Quebec with cash on the barrelhead. By pouring intergovernmental transfer payments into Quebec, he had hoped to show that federalism was more financially worthwhile than independence. ('Profitable federalism'— *fédéralisme rentable*—would become a standard Bourassa phrase, in time.) Instead, federal transfers made the province's economically disastrous policy of French-only unilingualism economically feasible. Intergovernmental transfer payments are structured to pay more to each province as its per-capita income declines. Quebec's per-capita GNP took a hosing as the province haemorrhaged anglophones between 1977 and 1987, but during this period the province absorbed $23.6 billion in federal equalization payments (more than all Canada's other provinces combined).[31]

The Parti Québécois was now able to benefit three times over from its policies of linguistic intolerance: first, it could establish itself in the minds of voters as saviour of the French language. Second, the PQ's policies were a simple and direct method of confiscating wealth and power from groups that would never cast votes for it (like anglophones) or make campaign contributions in its favour (like Protestant school boards), and redistributing the surplus to groups that did support it, most notably civil servants and francophone teachers who benefited from the flood of immigrant children forced into their schools. Another benefit of Bill 101 for members of the so-called 'new class' of government employees, school and hospital administrators, and employees of provincial crown corporations was that they were able to buy west-end Montreal homes and Laurentian cottages at a discount as the real-estate market plunged in the wake of the anglo exodus.

Third, and best of all, the federal billions flowed directly into the hands of the *péquiste* finance minister, Jacques Parizeau, and he was able to make sure they found their way to constituent groups likely to support the Parti Québécois. The same man who had become a separatist in the 1960s because he had concluded that the country's economy couldn't survive the illogic of the transfer payment system and the provincial opting-out provision of fiscal federalism,[32] was now placed in charge of spending the largesse that he had earlier predicted would eventually destroy the nation.

Meanwhile, none of the oppressors of English rights in Quebec needed to feel concerned that Quebec's unilateral actions might produce a backlash against francophones outside the province. Every new imposition against Quebec's minorities seemed to incite instead an equal and opposite act of generosity towards French-speakers in the other nine provinces, no matter how small, how demographically unstable or how thoroughly assimilated they might already be. It began to seem even to some separatists that Quebec's future might not be best served by becoming a small independent state, making its way in the world by its own finances. After all, the rest of the country seemed prepared to become Quebec's cash cow. It was in the light of these factors that René Lévesque would renounce separatism in 1983, pronouncing Confederation *un beau risque*.

Pierre Trudeau's vision of Canada as a 'New Jerusalem' of linguistic tolerance, to use Keith Spicer's memorable phrase, was in ruins, but national unity had survived a major test. As well, Trudeau had been carried to a series of election victories remarkable for the contrast between his plunging support in English Canada and ever-rising numbers of Liberal MPs elected in Quebec. In 1968, he had carried a bare majority of English Canada and fifty-six of the seventy-four seats in French Canada. In his final election in 1980, Trudeau won every seat but one in Quebec, and only seventy-three of 207 in the rest of the country, or just better than one-third. By this time his party held only two seats west of Ontario.

It was under Brian Mulroney that asymmetrical bilingualism, and the electoral mathematics on which it is based, would come into its fullest flower. Mulroney swept to victory in 1984 with a strong absolute majority of seats in both English and French Canada. Until the moment of his election, the only indication of his stand on linguistic matters had been a showdown with a hostile audience of Winnipeg Conservatives in 1983, when the then-leader of the opposition had publicly supported the provincial government's unpopular effort to extend French-language services in the province. To many observers from outside Manitoba, this willingness to stand up for minority rights seemed to indicate that, like Trudeau, he would be a strong supporter of minority rights everywhere.

This was a misplaced hope. Mulroney had learned much from Trudeau's years in power, but it seems that he absorbed more information about Trudeau's electoral success than about his political philosophy. In practice, the new prime minister turned out to be a strong supporter of any measure likely to cement his support in Quebec, regardless of the implications for national language policy. The results were Meech Lake, Bill C-72 (the new *Official Languages Act*, which was bitterly opposed by much of the Tory backbench), and several spectacular examples of federal fiscal generosity to Quebec.

Like Trudeau before him, Brian Mulroney paid heavily in English Canada for these policies, especially in the west. By the federal election of 1988, his party had been outflanked on the right by the Reform Party. Reform opposition was enough to throw the majority of seats in British Columbia to the NDP,[33] and even in the Tory heartland of Alberta, the average margin of victory for Conservative MPs was cut by a quarter.³⁴ The Conservatives won only thirty-eight percent of the seats in English Canada as a whole, but they were returned to power nonetheless, having captured sixty-three of seventy-five seats in Quebec.

Mulroney embraced asymmetrical bilingualism throughout his nine years in power with far more enthusiasm than Trudeau had ever shown. This was most evident in the public clashes of the two men over the Meech and Charlottetown Accords, but it was also evident in Mulroney's rhetoric. It is impossible to imagine Pierre Trudeau declaring, as Mulroney did when he was asked about the Bourassa government's decision to invoke the notwithstanding clause in order to ban English signs, that "It is important to emphasize that Quebec has no lessons to learn from anyone regarding its way of treating its language minorities.... I think Quebec is a leader in this field."³⁵

Whether this attitude was the result of genuine belief or merely of political expediency is anyone's guess. In any case, the result was the same. A majority of English Canadians became alienated from Mulroney's government, while Quebec remained reasonably happy with his performance.

CASTING ASYMMETRY IN CONCRETE

With official bilingualism established overtly on the federal level and in New Brunswick and in practice in Ontario since the passage of the province's *French Language Services Act* in 1986, and with enforced unilingualism in place in Quebec, the attention of Canada's political elite has turned to permanently entrenching this arrangement. Much of the federal political agenda of the past decade can be seen as an attempt to freeze Canada's political clock in the present, since the present asymmetrical regime rests on the precarious foundation of a population distribution that cannot be expected to last more than a few years. The proportion of French-speaking MPs drops with every census; some population projections warn that Quebec's proportion of the total Canadian population could drop as low as twenty percent by the year 2031.³⁶

The logic of this new movement seems to be that if the French-speaking proportion of Canada's population drops much below twenty-five percent, it will no longer have sufficient weight in Parliament and at the polls to ensure that the federal government continues to support linguistic asymmetry. Even an impressive level of political cohesiveness will not be enough to permit francophone MPs to maintain control over federal language policy. Similarly, if the proportion of English-speakers climbs above twenty percent of Quebec's population, future Quebec governments will find it politically advantageous to abandon the province's systematic discrimination against English-speakers, regardless of the fact that the francophone majority might remain opposed to this sort of generosity. Should it become large enough, the anglophone minority would become sufficiently powerful at the provincial legislature to start exercising the same sort of influence upon provincial language policy that francophones currently have over federal language policy. Should this happen, Quebec governments would lose their ability to maintain the anti-English laws which serve to dampen the assimilative power of the language, and, one assumes, English would begin to spread at a cancerous rate, until it consumes the whole province.

In the chapters ahead, it will be demonstrated that governments cannot change the fundamentals of the social and economic environment which are the final determinants of whether a language will grow and prosper or wither and die. Nonetheless, it is certainly true that governments can pass an infinite variety of laws *intended* to influence the dynamics of population growth and language interaction. At this level, the assumptions about the political precariousness of language laws within Canada and Quebec are absolutely correct. The historical evidence shows that there really does seem to be a critical mass, around twenty percent of the total population within a given political unit, at which point linguistic minorities become large enough to dictate public policy on language-related matters.

As long ago as 1984, University of Montreal political economist Georges Mathews warned of the consequences that population decline would have for French Canada's ability to control events in Ottawa:

> Each census brings a new electoral map that reduces Quebec's representation in Ottawa. The next enters into effect in 1985 and will mark the end of the period in which the Quebec delegation represented more than half of the absolute majority of seats; it will drop from 75 seats out of 282 to 75 out of 304. After the election of 1988 or 1989, Quebec MPs will no longer be more than a minority within the party in power.[37]

To those who support the asymmetrical system, the only way to guarantee its survival beyond the turn of the century will be to entrench their current gains in the Constitution, where they will be protected from the control of future majorities. If this is done, no future backlash will be able to undo asymmetrical bilingualism, no matter how unpopular it becomes.

The recently-ended Mulroney/Bourassa round of constitutional negotiations revolved around this attempt to freeze language relations into a permanent reflection of a status quo that had served both of these politicians well. This agenda was most obvious in the provision of the Meech Lake Accord guaranteeing that twenty-five percent of all future immigrants to Canada would be shoehorned into Quebec:

> The Government of Canada will ... guarantee that Quebec will receive a

number of immigrants, including refugees, within the annual total established by the federal government for all of Canada proportionate to its share of the population of Canada, with the right to exceed that figure by five percent for demographic reasons. ...[38]

This clause can only be interpreted as an attempt to ensure that Canada's population not be permitted to grow more rapidly than Quebec's, in order to ensure that Quebec would not lose its proportionate share of the seats in the House of Commons. A counter-argument could be presented that this measure was really just a way of ensuring that Quebec would not be deprived of the immigrants it needs to replenish its francophone population, in the event of future federal decisions to limit the number of immigrants arriving in Canada, but this argument would be self-evidently false. Any concern with absolute numbers of immigrants to Quebec could only have been addressed by including a provision guaranteeing a minimum numerical quota for Quebec, regardless of the number of immigrants to the rest of Canada. The Meech Lake accord specifically ruled out the possibility of Quebec being guaranteed a minimum absolute number of immigrants. The reference to percentage figures can only mean that Prime Minister Mulroney and Premier Bourassa were searching for a way to permit Quebec to retain its proportionate size within Canada without having to reform its language laws or make itself attractive to immigrants in any other way.

The Meech Lake Accord's immigration provision is worded with a vagueness that makes it impossible to know exactly how it would have been enforced. As one federal official wondered out loud at the time, "How do you guarantee that Quebec will receive a certain proportion of immigrants, when you've got free movement of persons in Canada?"[39] Canadians may yet learn the answer to this mystery, since a bilateral federal-Quebec agreement closely resembling this aspect of the Meech Lake Accord was signed shortly after the Accord itself had died in 1990.

With the immigration argument thus secured, 1992's Charlottetown Accord upped the stakes and called for Quebec to be guaranteed, in perpetuity, a minimum of twenty-five percent of the seats in the House of Commons. This percentage would remain in force regardless how small Quebec's proportion of the total Canadian population might shrink, thus fixing in stone the political base of asymmetrical federalism for decades or even centuries to come, no matter how small a share of the total Canadian population continues to speak French.

One alarming aspect of this arrangement was overlooked even by its critics during the course of the 1992 referendum on the Charlottetown Accord. Under its provisions, once the number of Quebec seats had dropped to the statutory minimum, the Quebec government would have had a powerful incentive to completely destroy its English-speaking minority, so as to ensure that none of

Quebec's share of seats would be wasted on MPs likely to vote against the concept of asymmetrical bilingualism. Under the Charlottetown Accord, even the slightest English-speaking residue within Quebec would have represented a threat to the continuance of the ruling order.

SUMMARY

When, and why, did the national dialogue on linguistic equality that began in earnest in the 1960s evolve into the system of asymmetrical bilingualism that currently dominates Canada?

The answer is that the change did not occur at any one specific point. Canada's journey from one form of linguistic injustice to another has been a slow historical and political process that has very little to do with the search for justice and very much to do with the exercise of raw political power.

At the root of this political progression (or, equally, regression) is the golden rule of parliamentary power in a deeply divided society: any political bloc with the cohesive support of between twenty percent and a quarter of the population can usually guide the political agenda on the isues that concern it most, as long as the rest of the population is not paying too much attention.

Knowingly or not, Canada's most successful political leaders, from Mackenzie King to Brian Mulroney, have let this golden rule guide their legislative hand. All of these prime ministers appreciated what support from Quebec meant to their ability to remain in power. The golden rule has made each of them pliable on issues relating to Quebec, which has increasingly come to mean pliability on issues relating to the French language.

In the last three decades, the pressure on these politicians to adopt asymmetrical language policies has grown ever more intense. There is now more than mere partisan advantage at stake. There is the fate of the nation itself, since the cohesive francophone bloc not only holds the twenty percent of Commons seats needed to influence the legislative agenda, it also now wields the sword of separatism. It was this extraordinary combination of positive and negative incentives that was necessary to beat asymmetry's stiffest opponent, Pierre Trudeau, into submission. Since his resignation a decade ago, the ideology has reigned in Ottawa, supreme and unopposed in any meaningful sense.

CHAPTER FOUR

The Limits of Language Policy

There's every reason to fear that [language] legislation will have results exactly opposite to those it is intended to produce. If there is one single painful lesson to learn from the American experience of the 1960s, it's that there are limits to "social engineering" and that social measures, no matter how well-intentioned, have unexpected and counter-intuitive side-effects.
—*Yvan Allaire (1974)*[1]

Assimilation.

The word rings out like an alarm in the ears of Canadians, conjuring up images of repression and intolerance. Because guilt by association has burdened the concept with the weight of hundreds of individual acts of cruelty, a meaningful understanding of assimilation is lost on most Canadians. At best, the process of assimilation is seen by our political leaders as a dangerous element, like electricity or nuclear fission, that can ultimately serve to strengthen society but may kill its handlers. At worst, it is seen as an evil to be halted at all costs. Neither view is remotely accurate.

Assimilation is an impartial process, neither good nor evil. How languages rise, intermingle, and ultimately vanish has very little to do with king and country, although tyrants and political leaders throughout history have dreamt that it were otherwise.

This chapter examines the forces that both cause and inhibit assimilation, and stresses government's inability to change or control the course of demographic language trends. Like oil and water, language and political muscle do not mix.

Castles Built on Sand

Both the federal government and the Quebec provincial government have built their language policies on the naïve belief that the processes of cultural assimilation can be controlled by fiat. This flies in the face of mountains of evidence that governments cannot substantially affect the cultural choices of large groups of individuals. Even under political regimes more repressive than anything dreamed of in Canada, oppressed and abused minorities have shown a remarkable resistance to forced assimilation. This fact bodes poorly for the success of Quebec's policy of requiring all immigrants to assimilate into the French language.

On the other hand, Ottawa's policy of halting the assimilation of French-speakers from Gravelbourg to downtown Toronto also flies in the face of the evidence. Members of linguistic minority groups are often willing and even anxious to adopt the language and customs of the surrounding societies. They do so because they seek acceptance, and also because of the potential opportunities that assimilation will open to them. This suggests that the federal government will fail in its attempt to freeze Canada's demographic map by providing the country's scattered minorities with lavish exhortations and vague incentives not to assimilate into the surrounding majority.

as-sim-i-late \vb -lated; -lating 1: *to absorb into the cultural tradition of a population*

Assimilation is a complex concept, which applies to all the cultural and ethnic characteristics that an individual possesses, including religion, diet, etiquette, attitudes towards a thousand questions, and even personal grooming habits. Somewhere in the midst of all this is language assimilation. Simply learning a second language does not mean that a person has assimilated into the ranks of that language's native speakers and abandoned his own ancestral tongue, although it certainly opens the door to the possibility.

For practical purposes, linguistic assimilation could be said to be the stage at which an individual feels more comfortable speaking an acquired tongue than his or her native language. This transposition of new languages for old sometimes happens in adults, but it is a matter of statistical record that it occurs most often in children. Assimilation is particularly likely to happen if the language a child learns at its mother's knee is different from the language of the child's playmates and schoolmates. Within a short period of venturing into the playground the child becomes as comfortable in the language of his or her friends as in his or her mother tongue, then more comfortable. For adults, the process of growing more comfortable in an acquired language is slower and more difficult, and in some individuals it is impossible.

The key to understanding language assimilation is to recognize that language is a tool that allows individuals to communicate with each other. Because most people naïvely think of language in its more glorious roles, as the medium of poetry and literature, we forget that even in its most exalted uses it is no more than a tool of verbal or written communication. Like any other tool, language is judged by its usefulness, and its users will quickly (although often reluctantly) drop it in favour of another language if that one shows itself to be a better tool for most or all of the communications functions that a language must fulfill: for business, shopping, entertainment, friendship and love.

If learning a second language were costless and painless, assimilation would be even more widespread than it is already. However, the costs of learning a second language are substantial, and they increase with age. Children pick up second languages with the same annoying ease with which they learn to use computers. Some children have such a high level of natural ability that they even manage to attain workable skills from Canada's abysmally ineffective system of grade school second-language education. For the average adult, however, it takes 1,600 hours of full-time intensive training to become fluent, according to language training estimates prepared by the federal government.[2] This is the equivalent of studying forty hours per week, for ten months on end. The same federal estimates indicate that getting enough second-language ability to limp along semi-comprehensibly requires about half as many hours.

It is not surprising, therefore, that each individual's decision to learn or not to learn a second language is made on the basis of a rational cost/benefit analysis of the usefulness that a second language will have as a tool for securing jobs, promotions, or even lovers, weighed against the substantial cost and inconvenience of the learning process. Once an individual is bilingual, the same kinds of decisions will repeatedly be made about whether to maintain or upgrade his or her second-language skills—or about maintaining skills in that individual's mother tongue, which can also get rusty if the language is no longer regularly used.

LINGUISTIC SURVIVAL IN A SMALL WORLD

> Within a radius of a few hundred kilometres from my study, even as I write these lines, a dozen or so Indian languages are breaking down, their vocabulary and structure in total disarray; only a few dozen elders can speak them fluently, and there is at least one case known of a language spoken by one single person.
> —*Jean Laponce, Vancouver (1987)*[3]

In all economically advanced, trade-dependent societies, the long-term trend is for linguistic and cultural differences to diminish over time. Improvements in communication and transportation technology throughout the 19th and 20th centuries have permitted the exchange of ideas and of cultural information on an ever-intensifying level. The cultural products that boost the quality of life are now easily transferred from culture to culture and across international boundaries. For example, American movies, music and television are seen all around the globe, and in almost every country in the world there is frequent and often worried discussion in the media about the 'Americanization' of culture.

Yet American culture is enticing to the rest of the world largely because it is itself an amalgam of useful or enticing cultural products of foreign origin that have met and spread from the immigrant centres of New York, Chicago and Los Angeles. As economist Thomas Sowell writes in his book *Ethnic America*:

> American culture is built on the food, the language, the attitudes, and the skills from numerous groups. The old Anglo-Saxon Puritan resistance to social recreation was long ago overwhelmed by the German easygoing attitude of good clean fun, which is now considered the hallmark of Americans in general. American popular music has its roots in the black musical tradition that produced jazz and blues. . . . Nothing is more American than hamburgers or frankfurters, although both names derive from German cities. Pizza and tacos are not far behind. None of these features of American culture is descended from the British settlers. They are a common heritage, despite ethnic diversities that still exist. Budweiser is drunk in Harlem, Jews eat pizza, and Chinese restaurants are patronized by customers who are obviously not Chinese.[4]

These 'American' cultural goods have all had a strong influence on French Canadian culture, which is far less distinct from the culture of English-speaking North America than it was a century ago. French Canadians, who seemed wonderfully exotic and quaint to travellers of the 18th and 19th centuries, and even to French writer Louis Hemon when he arrived from Brest in 1911, today eat the same food and wear the same clothes as Americans, English Canadians, Italians, Germans and Japanese. Increasingly, the same trends move us all, regardless of ancestral culture.

The ease with which cultural goods are now transmitted across borders can upset the stability of nation-states. The oppressed populations of Communist Eastern Europe gained access to the ideals of capitalism and consumerism and brought their countries' regimes toppling down because of the insistent, unstoppable flow of information from America and Western Europe. Even in Nicolae Cauceseau's hermetically sealed and totalitarian Romania, the socialist empire could not shield its population from the knowledge that the rest of the world was a freer and materially wealthier place.

Assimilation Pressures

> Since the end of the Nineteenth Century the rate at which languages have been disappearing has been particularly high—the inevitable result of the supremacy of the strong languages. Dozens more will have disappeared by the end of the century; one hardly need mention that the disappearance of a language is never a spectacular event.
>
> —*Jacques Leclerc (1986)*[5]

The ease with which information is nowadays transmitted between cultures, and the natural attractiveness of many new cultural forms, has put pressure on individual languages. It is more expensive for smaller language groups to produce cultural goods in their own tongue, so it makes economic sense to import these goods.

Using cultural goods produced by other cultures—from textbooks to movies to instruction manuals for stereo equipment—often involves learning the language of that culture, and this need for full or partial proficiency in a foreign tongue in turn limits the usefulness of the ancestral language. This is one of the factors explaining why many of the world's smallest language groups have vanished with the progress of the 20th century. Even as the world's population has grown, the number of languages that have a realistic chance of long-term survival has been steadily decreasing.[6]

In Canada, the world-wide homogenizing trend can be seen in the gradual disappearance of most of the aboriginal languages that dominated the country before the arrival of the Europeans. Of Canada's dozens of indigenous languages, only four still have more than 5,000 speakers.[7] Most aboriginal Canadian tongues have already disappeared and are preserved today only in the books of academic linguists, if at all.

The Elements of Linguistic Survival

> Our language [Occitan, spoken in southern France] is dying because reality no longer takes place in Occitan. And what purpose do our words serve, when there is no longer any meaning with which to fill them?
> —*Péire Pessamessa, Occitan writer*[8]

To survive and expand in the modern world, linguistic communities must contain certain institutions in which the communal language can be used. The communities themselves must conform to a certain minimum size, or else young people will be forced to conduct social and courtship activities with members of other groups, with the result that future generations will probably be raised in another language. These conditions apply equally to small self-contained linguistic communities, like those that continue to speak Canada's aboriginal languages, and to outlying language enclaves of some larger, far-removed cultural centre. Examples of communities in the latter category include the immigrant communities found in many Canadian cities, the francophone villages of the Canadian West, or the few English-speaking towns that still survive in mostly-French regions of Quebec like Argenteuil County or the Gaspé Peninsula.

A McGill University study conducted in 1964 among immigrants in Montreal showed that members of minority ethnic communities prefer to conduct their affairs among other members of their own language group over the additional effort needed to contact members of other groups. The greater the degree of institutional completeness in an ethnic community, the greater its ability to retain the loyalty of its members.

The most important factor of institutional completeness was found by the researchers to be the existence of internally-managed religious institutions, because "Churches are very frequently the centre of a number of activities; associations are formed and collective activities are organized under their influence and support."[9] Second in rank of importance among institutions were local publications, such as newspapers, produced by the ethnic group for the consumption of its members. Third in importance was the existence of welfare, support and health institutions.

Together, these linguistic institutions permit the linguistic community to be culturally self-contained. In other words, a complete set of these institutions permit members to carry out the majority of their social interactions (especially marriages) without leaving their own cultural community.[10]

On their own, however, this small list of institutions will only provide short-term defence from assimilation, which is bad news for most smaller languages. Only 140 of the over 2,000 languages in existence in the world today have sufficient numbers of speakers to support at least one university, which is probably an essential feature of long-term linguistic survival in the modern world. Without the availability of university training in their own tongue, it is impossible for the speakers of a language to conduct the higher-strata activities of a commerce-based society, like medicine, law or engineering, without learning another language.[11] This is not, strictly speaking, a problem for isolated linguistic enclaves that belong to larger language groups, like the francophones of P.E.I. or the anglophones of the Gaspé, but it does presuppose that individuals seeking a higher education will have to move far away. Often, they do not return.

Population density is also an important factor in the survival of linguistic communities. As long as it is relatively easy for speakers of a minority language to find other speakers of the same language with whom to carry out their daily activities, they will not feel the need to learn a second language. The more they require knowledge of a second language, the better they will normally learn to speak it (they will have more opportunities to practice) and the less they will feel the need or desire to return to the use of their mother tongue.

The ease with which life may be lived in one's native language is mostly a result of the number of fellow speakers who live in the limited geographical area in which day-to-day activities take place. As University of British Columbia language scholar Jean Laponce puts it, "The density of the minority population must be such that one does not need to use another language with the grocer, restauranteur, lawyer, or politician."[12]

Isolation: the Ultimate Guarantee of Language Preservation

It is possible to imagine a language and a culture being transmitted in spite of

the surrounding environment, but an unusually fierce determination and
uncommon readiness for sacrifice would be required.
—*Report of the Royal Commission on
Bilingualism and Biculturalism*[13]

At one time, before the development of automobiles, radio, television, movies and recorded sound, it was possible for small linguistic communities to exist in perfect security for generations, due to their relative isolation from the rest of the world. In the context of such isolation, members of these communities had no need to learn any language other than that which they shared with their ancestors and their most immediate neighbours. The outside world, and the languages it spoke, were irrelevant.

An extreme example of this primitive context can be found in the multiplicity of languages spoken in the Stone Age societies that existed in perfect isolation until very recently on the island of New Guinea and its surrounding archipelago of smaller islands. Many of these societies did not make contact with the outside world until the second half of the 20th century, making the region a sort of living laboratory for the study of primitive cultures.

In 1961, sociologist J.C. Anceaux recorded the existence of fourteen different indigenous language groups and an even greater number of dialects on the island of Yapen (population 20,000), off the coast of New Guinea.[14] With each village existing in virtual isolation from all the others for centuries, the inhabitants of Yapen had been able to maintain distinct languages with only a few hundred speakers each. One healthy dialect, called 'Aibodeni,' had only 150 speakers at the time of the Anceaux study, yet seemingly had survived for many years.

Although this level of fragmentation is extraordinary, the same general rule holds true in any society in which the great mass of communications take place at the family and village level. Travellers in mediaeval Europe, for example, frequently complained that every village or county seemed to have its own dialect. In India, before the arrival of the British, the saying arose, 'Language changes every nineteen or twenty miles.' A similarly extraordinary heterogeneity of tongues was one of the main reasons why the Catholic church found it useful to employ a single *lingua franca*, Latin, as its language of internal communication, and why the Russian Orthodox Church conducted its affairs in Old Slavonic.

The natural isolation of the primitive world is now a thing of the past. In order to be absolutely certain of ensuring their survival in the long term, small linguistic communities would have to cut off most contacts with the outside world. While this is technically feasible, it involves sacrifices that most people would find unpalatable. To see why, consider the case of the minority language group that, more than any other in Canada, has successfully maintained its linguistic identity.

Hutterites and Francophones in the Canadian West

The Hutterites of western Canada have successfully adopted isolation as a way of maintaining their cultural identity. Members of this small religious splinter group have embraced a form of agrarian communism as a central feature of what they believe to be the ideal Christian life. Hutterites live in large communal farms with average populations of between sixty and 120 individuals. All property is owned in common, and each communal farm is self-sufficient, providing its own religious, educational and other cultural services.

The Hutterites are scattered in communities across the prairie provinces and show much better cultural resiliency than do prairie francophones. Seventy years after they arrived in Canada en masse in 1918, and four centuries after they were driven out of Germany for their extreme anabaptist beliefs, almost all the 20,000 Hutterites in Western Canada continue to speak their ancestral dialect of renaissance German. This contrasts dramatically with western Canada's francophone population. Only nineteen percent of the 432,000 persons in the four western provinces who report themselves to be of French ancestry still speak French at home.[15]

Before the Second World War, Canada's economy was sufficiently localized and fragmented for isolated linguistic pockets to exist across the country, and for some pockets, like the British Columbia town of Maillardville and the rural French communities of northern Alberta, to continually expand in size. As long as small agrarian communities could survive in relative isolation from the rest of the world, French-speaking minority populations were able to prosper across Canada, and English speakers could survive without assimilating in remote regions of Quebec. Although greatly outnumbered in the prairie provinces, Western francophones built thriving rural parishes. Isolated in their prairie communities for the better part of a century, they managed to maintain their culture and speak an entirely different language than that which was used in the surrounding towns and on nearby farms. This era came to an end with the advent of widespread radio and television and of the automobile in the mid-20th century. The linguistic enclaves have been disappearing in stages ever since.

As long as the cultural isolation of a low-technology society was guaranteed, French-speaking communities could spring up in the most unlikely regions of Canada. However, the removal of the veil of isolation has always resulted in the assimilation of these ethnic enclaves. For example, in 1917 a colony of French speakers was established at Welland, a few miles from Niagara Falls, when workers were imported to fill posts at a local factory during a wartime labour shortage. Although the French community in Welland continued to thrive for decades, the assimilation caused by daily contact with English has since virtually wiped out the community. By 1986, only 3,445 persons, or 7.7 percent of Welland's population, still spoke French at home.[16]

Equally remarkable is the story of British Columbia's French-Canadian town. In 1909 the Fraser Mills Lumber Company established the town of Maillardville on British Columbia's lower mainland, and peopled it with lumberjacks from the Hull and Sherbrooke regions of Quebec, who were attracted by high wages. This French-Canadian town continued to grow until the 1930s, when its population peaked at around 150 families.[17]

This sort of activity was economically justifiable seventy or eighty years ago, given the very low wage demands of French Canadians at that time. The workers of that day were much more self-sufficient than they are today. In the case of Maillardville, the lumbermen from Hull built their own houses. No municipal services like sewerage were needed to meet the living standards of the day. The only cost imposed upon the Fraser Mills Lumber Company was the contribution of materials used in the construction of the parish church and a new school. As demographer Richard Joy explains, such self-sufficiency is no longer imaginable:

> Today, a company wishing to bring in a French-Canadian workforce would be faced with a staggering bill for all the amenities which would be necessary to fully satisfy the requirements of the new workers and of their families; it is unlikely that this initial cost could ever be recouped from savings and labour costs. Thus it is unlikely that we shall ever again see massive recruiting of the type common during the last century.[18]

The French-Canadian mill workers at Maillardville needed only their church and their schools to maintain and preserve their culture, so for a few decades linguistic purity was easily maintained. Today, many more institutions, including television and radio stations, shopping facilities, hospitals, and other public institutions would also be required. Also needed would be many direct government services, from tax and regulatory documents in French to French-language service at the local vehicle licensing office. Very little of this, of course, is currently available in British Columbia.

Isolation would also mean an end to friendships and romances with English-speaking Vancouverites, and would require the avoidance of work in jobs that require English. This is the way that Hutterites avoid assimilation. They socialize only with other Hutterites, they marry only Hutterites, and they restrict themselves to agricultural activities, selling their produce *en masse* and thereby avoiding significant individual commercial contact with the rest of the world. Individual Hutterites do not own televisions or cars. Although these practices have helped preserve their language, they do not represent a lifestyle that most people would be willing to accept.

THE MYTH OF EFFECTIVE LANGUAGE LEGISLATION

Neither the federal government's attempts to rescue tiny minority communities on the verge of collective annihilation nor Quebec's attempts to quash the half million Anglo-Montrealers whenever they show signs of life have had the desired effect. Federally-sponsored incentives meant to encourage language retention have tended to be too puny to be taken seriously by, for example, Manitoba or Nova Scotia francophones slowly merging into the surrounding English-speaking milieu. Meanwhile, Quebec's efforts to make life difficult for anybody not proficient in French have been more effective at making people leave the province than at winning over the new recruits that the language needs if it is to prosper within the province's bounds.

These policies are based on a myth, accepted without question by most Canadians, that patterns of language use can be effectively controlled by government. In its least sophisticated manifestation, this belief takes the form of the assertion that somehow the simple fact of group control over a government will ensure language security, while the lack of such control will probably guarantee assimilation. Thus, for example, Jacques Leclerc declares in his book *Langue et Société*:

> The languages of Scandinavia bear witness to the protection that political control brings to small languages. Whether it is Swedish (8 million), Danish (5 million), Finnish (5 million), Norwegian (4 million), or even Icelandic with its 238,000 speakers, these languages ought to hold their own as long as they continue to maintain a hold on the political power in their respective states.[19]

He warns:

> Languages without countries are disarmed languages, without demographic force and without economic or military power. At best, they can hope to have a modest and strictly local cultural force, and to retain the good will of those who hold power.[20]

The myth of a mystical link between state power and linguistic security is virtually unchallenged in Canadian intellectual circles. As a result, it often takes the form of assertions that are, frankly, silly. The normally astute Jean Laponce warns that without state control, languages will not be used much for scientific research and publication:

> Languages without states, defenceless languages . . . are also languages without cultural power other than locally. The foremost among them in scientific culture is Ukrainian; but it accounts for no more than 0.1 per cent of the articles listed by *Chemical Abstracts* for 1980. . . .[21]

Although the accuracy of the statistic that Laponce cites is unquestionable (his book, *Languages and Their Territories*, includes a table listing the number of scientific papers published world-wide in each language), it is absolutely without meaning. Over sixty-four percent of the scientific papers published in the year cited were in English.[22] But it is obvious that English-speaking countries do not produce sixty-four percent of the world's scientists, nor publish sixty-four percent of the world's scientific journals. English is simply the accepted *lingua franca* of the world's scientific community. Scientists who hope to have their work examined beyond the borders of their own country are forced to recognize that English is the only effective medium for securing an international audience, just as Renaissance scholars realized that in their day Latin was the only mutually comprehensible language of scientific and philosophical discourse, and 19th century diplomats recognized the need to speak French.

Language and the Pursuit of Happiness

There is a more sophisticated argument in favour of the effectiveness of state control over the assimilation process. This argument concentrates on the fact that each individual's choice to learn and use one language instead of another is made on the basis of rational choices designed to make the individual happy—to increase his or her 'utility function,' as the economists like to say. One factor in an individual's happiness is the value of his or her language as a tool of economic advancement. This suggests that state interventions that boost or reduce the usefulness of each language can strongly influence individual choices to learn and use one language or another.

Government manipulation of the economic value of each language is, therefore, expected to cause individuals—and particularly immigrants who have to learn a new language anyway—to change their choice of which of Canada's two languages to adopt.

However, happiness is not exclusively the result of externally tradable economic factors. Factors such as the extent to which a language is a useful vehicle for relations with other members of the family and the immediate community play a role. These elements are beyond the control of government.

This can be illustrated by reference to the language choices made by members of Quebec's largest immigrant community. In 1970, just as the federal and Quebec governments were starting to build their language edifices, Jeremy Boissevian published a detailed background study on the Italian community in Montreal for the Royal Commission on Bilingualism and Biculturalism. In it, he warned that attempts to manipulate patterns of language use would run into a tangle of complex personal choices:

> The Italian Canadian may have ambivalent attitudes towards the French and

British, but he wishes above all else to be left alone. He does not wish to be forced into a public statement of why he chooses a French bride, or why he sends his children to an English school, or why he regards the British as gentlemen and the French as extravagant. Because he studies English and sends his children to study English, it does not mean that this language governs his complete social life. If language to the French Canadian is the symbol of his culture, its quintessence and the embodiment of this social and political status, for the Italian it is merely a socioeconomic tool. He uses English to his boss, French to his workmates, Italian to his friends from other regions of Italy, and a local dialect to his closest kin and *paesani*.[23]

This means that when governments attempt to manipulate the linguistic allegiances of groups within society, they will find them much less tractable than the simplistic economic model would suggest.

Why Ottawa Can't Stop Assimilation

On maps showing Canada's language distribution by colour, the red used to symbolize English stretches unbroken from Ottawa's west-end suburbs to the Pacific Ocean. French forms a smaller patch of blue stretching from Ottawa's eastern outskirts to about the middle of New Brunswick, where the map turns red again. For any francophone cast into the midst of the vast sea of red extending from Nepean to Nanaimo, or for any anglophone dropped into the smaller sea of blue, the gentle but insistent pressures exerted by living in an environment in which hardly anybody speaks his or her language would be an everyday reminder of the advantages of assimilation. Federal government services in his or her native tongue might be an enjoyable luxury, but they would play only an insignificant role in questions of overall language choice and daily use.

The federal government seeks to slow the assimilation of official-language minorities and to make it possible for unilingual speakers of either official language to travel in comfort to any corner of the country, but it is hampered by its inability to impose overtly repressive measures. Individuals cannot be punished for using the dominant language of the region, as they are legally forbidden under the provisions of Bill 101 to use English for many purposes in Quebec.

The best the federal government can do is to subsidize some minority services, provide a few others itself, and to force some private federally regulated companies, like airport concessionaires, airlines, and communication companies, to provide money-losing services in the second language. These efforts are a considerable burden on the Canadian taxpayer, but they are far too small to make a meaningful difference to the way people live their lives.

There is strong historical evidence from Europe that attempts on the part of governments to prevent minority-language assimilation are doomed to fail.

One of the most diligent efforts to save a dying language was attempted by the Irish Free State, starting in the 1920s. As the traditional national language, Gaelic was given a place of honour on Irish postage stamps and bank notes, taught everywhere in the schools, and given various other forms of state support. Entire departments within the Irish civil service were instructed to employ Gaelic as their internal language of work. Even the country's official name was changed to the Gaelic name 'Eire.' Nonetheless, Gaelic has become increasingly rare, and is today confined to remote areas in the country's west.

Officially-sponsored and generously subsidized efforts to save the Swiss language of Romansch, spoken in the Swiss canton of Grisons, have been equally unsuccessful. In the case of Romansch, the language is so far in decline that it is unlikely that there remain any unilingual speakers of the language, other than small children who have not yet spent any time outside the home and who are not yet old enough to go to kindergarten, since only a few thousand families still use the language at home, and even the simplest forms of social interaction outside the home now require the use of another language.

Further evidence that generous minority-languages services cannot prevent assimilation from taking place may be found right here in Canada. In some districts of rural Quebec, isolated farming communities and fishing villages have been populated by English-speakers for generations. Until the Parti Québécois came to power in the 1970s, these communities were able to enjoy all government services in English. Nonetheless, each one of these regions has been suffering a decline in the percentage of unilingual English-speakers for decades. In some cases, the descendants of the original English-speaking settlers are now mostly unilingual francophones, with only their Irish or English family names to remind them of their ethnic origins.

The lack of impact of government services on the assimilation of anglophones in these communities is most strikingly illustrated by the decline of English on the Gaspé Peninsula, which was originally settled by Loyalists in the 1780s. Initially, the assimilative pull in the region was towards English rather than French. Protestant French-speakers from the island of Jersey in the Channel Islands migrated to the Gaspé, where they adopted the language of the local majority.[24]

Throughout the 19th century the region remained sufficiently isolated and self-sufficient that it had an assimilation dynamic of its own. One result was that it retained its English-speaking majority in every census up to and including the 1931 enumeration.

The decline of English commenced with the introduction of a French-Canadian economic innovation in the 1920s. Formerly, the fishermen had lacked an adequate distribution network for their fish, which they had sold to a monopoly customer, Charles Robin and Company. The Robin Company had also been able to gain a control over the local credit supply and through a combination of ruinous rates of interest and low prices for fish, had reduced the fishermen to the nautical equivalent of sharecropper status.

French Canadian fishermen's co-operatives gave the English-speaking Gaspesians a way to escape the cycle of poverty. The new arrangement also exposed the English-speakers to an assimilation dynamic that is close to a mirror image of the situation faced by francophones in western Canada. English-speakers joined enterprises started by entrepreneurial francophones, and moved out of their tiny isolated fishing villages into the larger regional centres, where French was the language of work and life. The diversification of the local economy led the anglophones to jobs in mining and forestry where French again predominated, through sheer force of numbers.[25]

Throughout this period, English services and English schools continued to be available, sometimes at considerable expense to the local school boards. One study shows, for example, that in the 1955-56 school year, the anglophones enjoyed both a Protestant school board and complete English facilities within each of the local Catholic boards. "The number of [English-speaking] students under a local school board ranged from 186 at Chandler to six at Cap d'Espoir. In every case the English-speaking Roman Catholic students were taught in their mother tongue in a separate class."[26]

The generous service had no noticeable impact, and the English language in the region has entered into terminal decline. By 1991, English, the former majority language, was the home language of only 10.9 percent of the local population in the two census districts that most closely correspond with the boundaries of the old English-majority county.[27]

Why Quebec Can't Force Assimilation into French

> It is the social milieu, more than any other single factor, which determines whether the French language could survive in any part of the country... school laws and other legislation had only a secondary influence.
>
> —*Richard Joy (1967)*[28]

Examples abound of minority cultural groups that have refused to assimilate into the majority despite intense government pressure to do so.

Examples from Europe show that state intervention does not guarantee the assimilation of minorities. The progressive, state-sponsored domination of the French language within France in the post-revolutionary period has been enormously influential in Canada, but the story of the rise of French in the formerly multilingual kingdom of France is misleading. Peter Mentzel, a historian at the University of Seattle, gives the standard interpretation of the phenomenon of official-language domination in France, Britain and elsewhere:

> [A] common vernacular language of administration, state education and

military commands was an important tool in the extension of the modern state's bureaucratic control. Thus, "national" languages are largely the creation of modern nation states, not the other way around.[29]

About half the population of pre-revolutionary France spoke French. Since that date, the language has virtually wiped out the country's smaller regional languages.

In truth, none of the smaller languages really ever stood a chance, and most of them probably would not have survived direct competition from French even in the absence of legal restrictions on their use. Each language was confined to one or another of the peripheral regions of the country, and even before the revolution of 1789 none was more than a fraction the size of French. French was the language not only of regulated activities like education, but also of unregulated commercial transactions.

The Russian, German, Ottoman and Austrian Empires controlled Eastern Europe before the First World War. By way of comparison to the French, it is worth observing that none of these four great empires was successful in imposing its own language or culture on its minorities. Equally unsuccessful were their successor states, the mini-empires of Yugoslavia, interwar Poland, and the post-1868 Hapsburg Kingdom of Hungary.

Russian history is a virtual litany of failed attempts at forced assimilation. Forced Russification was completely unsuccessful in causing the assimilation of the Poles in the 19th century, or even of the much smaller Volga German and Crimean Tatar populations in the 20th century.[30]

It is interesting to note that Jacques Leclerc and Jean Laponce, the same academics who warn, in passages quoted earlier, that languages unprotected by state power are "defenceless," "disarmed," and "without demographic force," are both sufficiently careful scholars to report that the decline of peripheral languages in Britain and France was due mostly to factors beyond the control of government. Leclerc writes:

> As long as Brittany and Wales remained agricultural societies protected by relatively high levels of geographical isolation, Breton and Welsh held their own despite the linguistic pressure (francizing or anglicizing) of school, administration, and government. But the economic prosperity of French in France and of English in Britain has attracted the Breton and Welsh populations to zones where the dominant language reigns, to the towns in particular. In less than a generation, industrialization and urbanization have cost Breton and Welsh half their speakers.[31]

Laponce describes the decline of Breton in terms that make it hard to believe that government intervention was the main factor in its decline, or that government intervention could have saved it from decline.

Until the Second World War, Breton was holding its own despite the strong Francizing pressure of school and government and Breton acquiescence in learning French. The local language survived through the family and the church, thanks to the relative isolation of the region. The autonomist Breton movements of 1960-1980 were ineffective and tardy countermeasures against the increasingly close integration of Brittany and the rest of France as the result of urbanization, industrialization, mass tourism, easy communication, and large-scale interminglings of population.[32]

Linguistic Survival in the Face of Legal Adversity: Two Canadian Examples

In Canada, the best examples of minorities that have refused to assimilate despite government pressures are the francophone minorities in Northern New Brunswick and in Ontario's Eastern tip.

In New Brunswick's Madawaska and Gloucester counties, French remains strong and English is less widely spoken than it is in most of Quebec. Madawaska's population is over ninety-five percent French-speaking, and Gloucester county is 81.5 percent French. English has always been a mandatory subject in New Brunswick schools and the use of French in schools was largely restricted by provincial law between 1871 and 1940.[33] Yet in this overwhelmingly French social environment, the education laws have had no demographic effect. The proportion of the francophone population capable of conducting a conversation in English in the less homogenous of these two counties is only forty-one percent.[34]

This demonstration of the extent to which bilingualism is determined primarily by economic factors is repeated in Eastern Ontario. In 1911, one year before the provincial government's infamous Regulation 17 made French-language education effectively illegal, 42,600 residents of Ontario's two easternmost counties declared themselves to be of French origin. Sixty years later, when the last of the educational rights taken away by Regulation 17 were finally being restored, the number of county residents using French as their home language had grown to 45,000. Their percentage of the local population had remained constant at between sixty-seven and sixty-eight percent.[35]

SUMMARY

When governments treat their citizens like commodities, the chief product they manufacture is misery. This is true whether citizens are treated as economic machines to produce wealth that the politicians can then tax and redistribute, or as language machines, to carry out the state's cultural aims. But confiscating wealth is easier than emptying the minds of entire populations of all their thoughts and re-encoding them in a different set of language symbols. In short, government lacks the godlike powers it would need if it were really to master the forces of assimilation.

Languages change when it is necessary, and die out when they are no longer useful. Governments can try to halt or speed this process by trying to manipulate the relative usefulness of different tongues, but there is no well-documented example of a government successfully rescuing a dying language or destroying a strong one.

Meddling with the natural flow of linguistic trends can have painful economic implications. Witness the mass exodus of people, money and jobs out of Quebec after the passage of Bill 101. As long as states are unable to completely restrict individual freedom of movement, governments will have to face up to the fact that they cannot go too far with restrictive legislation. The target groups of harsh policies can simply divorce the state and move elsewhere. This doesn't mean that the target group has suffered less than the perpetrators, or that such policies will not produce an agreeably homogeneous language environment in the political unit in question. But this will be matched by a most disagreeable poverty, for the systematic oppression of a strong and vibrant minority is an expensive business.

The same impotence applies in reverse to policies designed to stop the assimilation of small, dying language communities. The assimilation process is taking place due to the economic and social attractiveness of the dominant language. Governments can fork out massive sums of money in an attempt to sustain these small communities, but not nearly enough to compete against the sheer size, power and attraction of the large and vibrant culture and society that beckons from just the other side of the language divide.

History and an understanding of the mechanics of assimilation make it clear that governments should not involve themselves in costly attempts to assimilate unwilling minorities, as the government in Quebec has attempted. Equally, they should refrain from pouring taxpayers' dollars into the pockets of minuscule minority-language communities, as is the practice of the Canadian federal government.

CHAPTER FIVE

Assimilation and the Failure of Federal Action

> For fifteen years, the spectre of "polarization" has haunted the reports of each successive Commissioner of Official Languages: English gradually pushing French towards the east, French pushing English to the west. This tendency has been growing more and more pronounced over the past three decades: English Canada is becoming more exclusively English, and Quebec is becoming unilingual French.
>
> —*Jacques Leclerc (1986)*[1]

TWO YEARS BEFORE the *Official Languages Act* was introduced in Parliament, and one year before Pierre Trudeau swept to power promising to make Canada bilingual from coast to coast, the death-knell of Canada's official-language minorities was quietly sounded. Richard Joy, an Ottawa engineer with no background in demographics or linguistics, wrote and self-published a book, *Languages in Conflict*, in which he foretold the inevitable downfall of the English language in Quebec and of French in the other provinces.

Joy had been prompted to write about demographics by his private curiosity as to whether the children born to him and his francophone wife should be considered French Canadian or English Canadian. Careful research based on an exhaustive study of the the 1961 census led him to unexpected conclusions. By the time he finished writing, his book had become a haunting prophecy of the unstoppable decline and inevitable disappearance of the very same minorities that Official Bilingualism would soon be attempting to save.

Joy believed that no amount of political effort would stop the decline of the minorities; the social and economic difficulties faced by individuals trying to survive as minorities in isolation from the main population centres of their own culture would far outweigh even the most generous efforts of the federal government. In consequence, neither subsidies nor minority-language services would make a noticeable dent in the prevailing assimilation trends.

This analysis turned out to be flawlessly accurate. Both Canada's official languages have declined dramatically over the past quarter century in their respective minority regions. Even more striking has been the complete inability of the federal government to stop this decline, even though it has spent billions of dollars trying. This is a confirmation of the thesis that governments cannot stop or slow assimilation by legislative fiat.

Twenty-five years after the introduction of the *Official Languages Act*, the continued decline of French outside Quebec and of English inside the province serves as proof that efforts to build a bilingual nation have been an exercise in futility. In retrospect, it seems it would have been easier for the Canadian government to legislatively move the Rocky Mountains to Quebec than to save the isolated French-language communities scattered in their shadow, or to stop the erosion of English communities in Quebec's Gaspé Peninsula and the Eastern Townships.

Federal Language Policy: A Legacy of Failure and Deception

Even today, the message of *Languages in Conflict* still seems unexpectedly brutal and frank:

> Although Montreal may well retain its bilingual character, the English-speaking population of other parts of Quebec will probably decline in absolute numbers, not merely relative strength. Outside Quebec, French will continue to be spoken in the border counties of Ontario and New Brunswick but will virtually disappear from Southern Ontario, the Atlantic Region and the Western provinces. . . . If this forecast is accurate, then our politicians and editors should commence now to prepare the public for the inevitable by showing that the disappearance of linguistic minorities is a natural phenomenon, rather than the consequence of some "genocidal" plot. If the public is not so prepared, then the psychological shock when the minorities do disappear could be far more harmful to Canadian unity than will be the actual disappearance.[2]

This gloomy message was lost in the sea of enthusiasm surrounding Canada's centennial celebrations; in 1967, it seemed that Canadians could overcome any challenge. Copies of Joy's book were returned to him unsold by the few bookstores that had agreed to stock it.[3] Cassandra-like, its dire and accurate warnings were forgotten as billions of dollars and millions of man-hours were devoted to the task of shoring up the declining official-language minorities. By the end of the decade, the country had embarked on the language policy experiment that is still in place today.

In the quarter-century since Joy wrote his book, the assimilation of the French minorities outside Quebec and a few border regions of Ontario and New Brunswick has virtually been completed. Beyond the limited regions on the geographical peripheries of Ontario, New Brunswick and Quebec that Joy earmarked thirty years ago, the minorities are, for practical purposes, extinct. This runs contrary to numbers cited by the federal government, but Ottawa's favoured 'mother tongue' statistics can be shown to be meaningless. They are used to create the illusion of large minorities—particularly francophone minorities outside Quebec. This is supposed to strengthen national unity by fooling the Québécois into believing that separation will lead to the loss or destruction of a large proportion of the French Canadian nation.

If these francophone minorities are nothing more than statistical illusions, it follows that federal language policies designed to halt the progress of polarization are merely expensive exercises in futility. The geographic polarization of language, or "linguistic segregation" as Joy called it, is a force beyond the control of the Canadian government. In the isolated minority communities of different parts of Canada, the language of the local post office is not nearly as important as the language of friends, neighbours and co-workers. The interactions that have the strongest impact on assimilation are precisely those that are furthest beyond the grasp of government. This impotence will be clearly revealed by statistics showing that minority decline has not slowed since the *Official Languages Act* went into effect.

LIES, DAMNED LIES, AND LANGUAGE STATISTICS

> [They use] statistics as a drunken man uses lamp-posts—for support rather than illumination.
>
> —*Andrew Lang, Scottish humorist*

In complete disregard for overwhelming evidence to the contrary, the federal government continues to maintain that, rather than polarizing, the French and English languages are increasingly intermingling. This view is as contrary to the facts as it is possible to be, but it can be made to sound convincing if the statistics are manipulated the right way.

Consider the comments made in 1992 by Dr. Victor Goldbloom, the Commissioner of Official Languages:

> A million French-speaking Canadians, a number equivalent to the total population of Manitoba or Saskatchewan, live outside Quebec. About a million people in Quebec are English-speaking, two-thirds of them by mother tongue.[4]

In the same vein, a recent article in the Montreal *Gazette* observed that between the 1976 and 1986 censuses, the number of people living outside Quebec with French as their mother tongue had increased from 908,000 to 946,000. "That," records the *Gazette*, "is hardly taking the fast road to extinction."[5]

In one sense, the *Gazette* is correct. Mother tongue figures were up. (They rose again in the 1991 census to 947,000.)[6] The official language minority communities would now be virtually extinct if the census numbers that the newspaper and Dr. Goldbloom cited were meaningful. But these statistics have no value at all.

There are two reasons why these numbers are meaningless. First, 'mother tongue' is a poor measure of the size of language minorities. However, it is the yardstick used by most departments and agencies of the Government of Canada most of the time, and by the Commissioner of Official Languages all the time, when they are speaking of the size of Canada's minorities. Second, the boundaries of the French Canadian and English Canadian heartlands do not precisely match the borders between Quebec and its neighbouring provinces, thus giving an illusion of minority strength.

"Mother Tongue" versus "Home Language"

The data collected from the census of Canada produces several different measures of minority populations. The favoured measure of the Commissioner of Official Languages and the one most often cited in the media is 'mother tongue,' which is defined on census forms as the first language learned by the respondent in childhood and still understood.

The problem with mother tongue is that it fails to take into account individuals who have integrated into another culture or who have a partner from another linguistic background, choosing to speak their partner's language in their daily life. This means that for thousands of Canadians, mother tongue figures are a generation out of date. This phenomenon may sound uncommon or improbable to those who have not experienced it, but it is not. Nearly ten percent of all Canadians speak a language other than their mother tongue at home.[7]

It was in recognition of this phenomenon that the Royal Commission on Bilingualism and Biculturalism recommended in 1967 that the census of Canada take a new measure of language, based on the language most often spoken in the home.[8] This measure, adopted for the first time in the 1971 census and nowadays generally referred to as 'home language,' gives an up-to-date picture of language use.

The results of using this new measure are dramatic. Measured by home language rather than mother tongue, the French-speaking minority living outside Quebec at the time of the 1991 census drops by more than one-third, from 947,000 to 607,000.[9] Moreover, comparisons to previous censuses show the number of persons speaking French at home outside Quebec to be in rapid decline. In 1981, there were 672,000 persons living outside Quebec who told the census that French was their home language. This represents a drop of ten percent in the past decade alone.

Another significant indicator of the well-being and usefulness of a language is the number of unilingual speakers it can claim. If this number is a high proportion of the total number who use the language at home, then the language is shown to be useful for a full range of social and commercial activities. If the number is low, this is a signal that the language is no longer a truly useful medium of communication, and is dying out.

Hubert Guindon explains the interaction between widespread bilingualism and assimilation:

> The fact of the matter is that when everyone is fluent in English, maintaining a level of fluency in French . . . becomes an artifice not grounded in the needs of social interaction; and those who try to maintain the [social frontier between French and English] are more apt than not to be viewed as narrow-minded if they are young, old-fashioned if they are not. As a consequence, fluency in French steadily decreases. . . . [10]

By this token, the French language is in serious trouble outside its Quebec-centered heartland. Only 151,000 French-speakers residing outside the province are unable to speak English in addition to their mother tongue, according to the 1991 census. Five out of six francophones outside Quebec, in other words, have taken the first step towards assimilation. Some of these bilingual francophones may go no further along this path, but many others will.

Actually, things are even worse than this. Many of the 151,000 who are unilingual never set foot outside their own homes. They do not speak the language of the local majority because they are never in contact with it. This group includes senior citizens who are in the care of their children or of an institution. Many people in this situation forget their second language, and can no longer be considered bilingual. An even larger proportion of this class of 'transitional unilinguals' are very young children who have not yet grown old enough to make friends outside their own household, or to attend kindergarten.

If these two age groups are dropped and the focus is narrowed just to persons aged five to sixty-five, the number of unilingual francophones outside Quebec is cut by another one-third. Outside Quebec, there are only 101,000 unilingual French-speakers who belong to age groups likely to have contact with the outside world. This is less than one-ninth the number of mother tongue francophones cited by the Commissioner of Official Languages. And this is only half the story.

The Heartland Measure

An impediment to accurately measuring the extent of French in its heartland is the fact that the most commonly cited aggregate language data do not accurately reflect the realities of language distribution in Canada. All census data, including language data, is compiled on a province-by-province basis.

This means that any trends that do not take place exclusively within a territory conforming precisely with provincial borders will be distorted in the published data.[11] Because the real boundaries between North America's

English and French-speaking regions conform loosely but not perfectly to Quebec's borders, accurate measures of the health of the French language will only be possible if the bounds of these regions are accurately mapped and the relevant statistics are then applied to these adjusted areas.

A simple test is needed to determine which geographical areas qualify as parts of which linguistic region. The most important criterion for whether an area should be considered part of the Quebec-centred French-language region (which I shall henceforth refer to as the 'French-language heartland') is whether or not it is possible to conduct all or most of life's activities in French. A similiar test can be applied to see whether any town, neighbourhood or rural area is part of the English-language heartland. Therefore, the linguistic adherence of any individual community can be measured using a variety of language measures, such as mother tongue, home language and unilingualism versus bilingualism on local populations.

For a community to be part of the heartland region, it must not only consist mostly of French-speakers, but also be located close to the main body of French-language speakers. Some rural districts still exist in western Canada and in the Atlantic, in which French is the language most often used by the local populace. But these linguistic enclaves, or "language islands," as one scholar has labelled them,[12] are mostly in catastrophic decline and simply cannot be compared to, or lumped in with, the main body of French-speaking culture in and around Quebec.

Of course, such comparisons do get made. But they are no more useful as guides to the overall health of the French language in its heartland than the declining English-speaking enclave in Argenteuil County is as a measure of the overall health of English in the vast English-speaking heartland that covers most of North America.

The search for a precise linguistic frontier is made yet more complex by the existence of some localities that are dominated by French and surrounded by English-speaking areas, yet which are geographically close enough to the heartland to draw sustenance from it. It is difficult to tell whether these should be thought of as language islands, or as language peninsulas, apart from the heartland yet closely enough linked to it by ease of transport and communication to be a part of it.

In a small number of Canadian communities, including some neighbourhoods in central Montreal and in the Ottawa-Hull suburbs of Aylmer and Orleans, it is possible to live one's life unilingually in either language. In such situations, every man is an island. Or a peninsula, at any rate. Invariably, these situations exist because of the fortuitous location of the community at the very edge of the English-speaking and French-speaking heartlands, where all of life's necessities may be drawn in English from one side of the dividing line, or in French from the other.

Such regions have been described as "bilingual regions," since rates of bilingualism tend to be quite high in these areas, or as "contact regions" or "transition zones."[13] The last name is probably the best, since it reflects the fact that these areas are usually in flux, as one language gradually rises to predominance and the other fades.

Probably the simplest way of differentiating between language islands and peninsulas is to impose an arbitrary test as to whether the trip to the main body of the heartland can be made with ease. If you can get in your car and drive without refilling the gas tank to the 'mainland' of your language bloc, then your community can reasonably be considered also to be a part of this mainland or heartland, even if it appears on the map to be isolated. If you have to stop and fill your tank or ask for the restroom key in what is (to you) a foreign tongue, then you live in a linguistic island. Even if all your neighbours, or the entire town, converses in the same language as you, your neighbourhood or town is an island if a foreign-language rest stop is still required to land you in your own heartland.

The need to resort to such complex descriptions goes a long way towards explaining why most statistical measures of language are based on the provincial boundaries of Quebec, rather than the more meaningful heartland measure.

At any rate, once the rest-stop test has been applied, the bounds of this heartland can be traced. The overlap of the French-Canadian heartland into Ontario, New Brunswick and a corner of the state of Maine takes place in four areas:

- Northern New Brunswick is home to 216,000 francophones. One county (Madawaska) is over ninety-five percent French-speaking;
- Ontario's north-east contains 73,000 francophones;
- The eastern tip of Ontario is inhabited by 148,000 French-speakers;
- The Madawaska Valley in northern Maine, which hugs the border with Quebec and New Brunswick, is home to approximately 30,000 Franco-Americans.[14] This small French-speaking colony is not separated geographically from the French Canadian heartland (there is even one house that lies partly inside Quebec and partly in Maine), and so far the presence of an international border has not posed enough barriers to integrated social activities, marriages and so on to produce effective isolation from the Canadian side of the border. Should the border ever become a more substantial obstacle, the colony will cease to be part of the heartland, and will face eventual assimilation.

The extension of parts of Canada's English-speaking heartland into Quebec takes place in three areas:

- Pontiac County in west Quebec, which has a small English-speaking majority of 11,000;

- The North Shore of the Gulf of St. Lawrence, which is dotted with communities culturally identical to those in Newfoundland. Newfoundland is accessible only by water, but so is the rest of Quebec. This region contains 4,000 anglophones;
- West-end Montreal, which is the largest English-speaking metropolitan centre in Canada's five eastern provinces, with 462,000 inhabitants for whom English is the language of choice.[15]

Once the population figures have been adjusted to reflect the real geographical boundaries between French and English rather than Quebec's political boundaries, it is possible to sketch a more accurate picture of the nature of the minorities.

The big surprise is the extent to which English- and French-speakers are segregated. Of francophones as measured by home language, 6.1 million—nearly ninety-seven percent of all French-speaking Canadians—live within their linguistic heartland. Only 198,000 francophones, as measured by home language, live elsewhere in Canada.[16]

Over ninety-eight percent of English Canadians live beyond the borders of the French-language heartland. Using the home language measure, only 267,000 English-speakers live within its bounds.[17]

Three Kinds of Minority

The French-speaking population outside Quebec really has three faces. First, there are border regions of Ontario and New Brunswick that form the eastern and western parts of the French-language heartland. Here, francophones form an absolute majority and have easy access to the rest of the heartland. French continues to survive, even prosper. French communities are highly concentrated and institutions such as French schools are well-established and actively used.

Of 607,000 Canadians residing outside Quebec who reported in the 1991 census that French was the language spoken most often in their homes, over two-thirds lived in a few counties of north-eastern Ontario and northern New Brunswick, in regions so close to the Quebec border that they could reasonably be described as part of the Québécois heartland. Only 198,000 French-speaking persons, or slightly over three percent of all Canadian francophones, lived outside this restricted area. Thus, beyond the eastern suburbs of Ottawa and the rural counties hugging Quebec's boundaries, francophones, as measured by home language, represent a minuscule 1.04 percent of the population of the nine English speaking provinces, where they form an ethnic presence a good deal less demographically significant than the speakers of Chinese and not much larger than those who speak Italian in their daily lives.[18]

It makes no sense to compare the situation of one French-Canadian living in Hawkesbury, which is a completely French town half a mile from the bridge

Figure 5.1
The further one travels from Quebec, the higher the percentage of francophones capable of speaking English

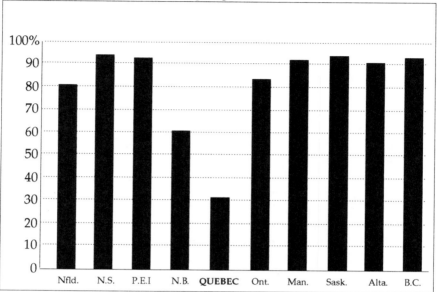

Source: See *Notes for Figures*

across the Ottawa River to Quebec, and another living in the English-speaking environment of downtown Calgary or Vancouver. But this is precisely what aggregate figures do when they are calculated on the basis of provincial boundaries, because they ignore the slight overlap of French Canada's borders with those of Quebec. This is not a fact which serves the cause of national unity. The existence of French-majority counties contiguous with Quebec's eastern and western borders will not make French-speaking Quebecers feel a sense of loyalty and 'belonging' to Canada, the way that a chain of vibrant francophone communities extending from Cape Breton Island to the Peace River district is supposed to do. On the other hand, the existence of these minorities on the outside edges of Quebec has caused some indépendenistes to suggest that a sovereign Quebec should annex the relevant parts of New Brunswick and Ontario.[19]

The impact of the heartland phenomenon on the size and strength of the minority populations cannot be overstated. It is clearly illustrated by bilingualism rates across the country. The further away from Quebec one travels, the higher the ratio of bilingual francophones to bilingual anglophones becomes, indicating that the relative social and economic value of French is dropping. Outside Quebec, fully three out of four francophones are bilingual, a number that continues to rise the further one travels from Quebec: eighty-three percent

Figure 5.2
The further one travels from Quebec, the lower the percentage of anglophones capable of speaking French.

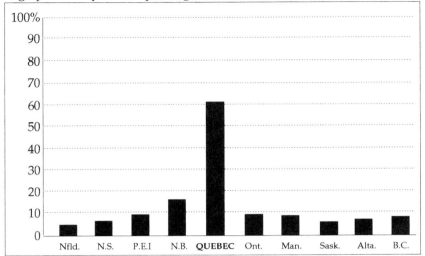

Sources: See *Notes for Figures*

in Ontario, ninety-two percent in Manitoba, ninety-three percent in Saskatchewan, and so on. By contrast the number of anglophones capable of speaking French falls: sixty percent in Quebec, ten percent in Ontario, eight percent in Manitoba, and five percent in Saskatchewan.[20]

The second face of the three faces presented by the French-speaking minority is found in English Canada's big cities, where many Quebecers have moved, almost as immigrants from foreign countries would move, without any real hope of passing on their ancestral languages to their children. So great is the assimilation rate in these cities that Ottawa's French-language newspaper, *Le Droit*, refers to the cities of southern Ontario as "les fours crématoires des franco-ontariens"(The crematoriums of the Franco-Ontarians).[21] This is only a mild exaggeration.

With each census, a larger and larger proportion of the francophones living outside the Quebec-based heartland are moving into English Canada's cities. Once in Toronto or Winnipeg or Edmonton, it is virtually impossible for a francophone to remain unilingual or even to avoid complete assimilation. Winnipeg has the French Canadian ethnic neighbourhood of St. Boniface and Edmonton has several small partly-French neighbourhoods, which provide an environment in which one's ancestral tongue retains some limited usefulness, because some private services and social interactions can take place in French. But in Toronto, Calgary, Vancouver and the rest of English Canada's cities, there is not even this limited cultural protection.[22] The 75,000 French Canadians who have moved to English Canada's largest cities[23] have no environment, beyond their own households and a few social clubs, in which they can even practice their language.

The third face of the French-speaking minorities can be found in the rural townships and parishes that lie scattered in a sparse patchwork across the English-speaking provinces. These old-fashioned farming communities are what most people imagine when they think of English Canada's francophone minorities. In truth, they represent only around one-fifth of the francophone minority in the English-majority provinces—about 127,000 souls in all, as measured by home language.[24]

At different points of time in the past, the French-speakers in these communities represented majorities or near-majorities in the regions that have since become eight of Canada's nine English-speaking provinces. In the mid-18th century, the future provinces of New Brunswick, Nova Scotia and Prince Edward Island were overwhelmingly French-speaking. In the years preceding the American Revolution, the majority of the white inhabitants of what would become Ontario were French. At various points in the mid-19th century, the territories that would later become Manitoba, Saskatchewan, Alberta and even British Columbia contained more French-speakers than English-speakers.[25] Seventy years ago, a quarter of Canada's French-speaking population lived outside of Quebec, and francophone settlers from Quebec were opening up the last of the virgin farmland in northern Alberta. As late as 1951, Ontario and New Brunswick were recording progressively larger proportions of francophones in their population with each successive census.

Today, the small and mostly isolated communities that once made up this *hors Québec* vanguard of the French Canadian culture are suffering a catastrophic decline that has not been halted or even slowed by the *Official Languages Act* and the host of other federal measures intended to make it possible to live in French outside Quebec.

In many of these areas there is little cultural residue left to save. The Windsor region, for example, had a French-speaking agricultural and military populace as early as the mid-eighteenth century, and one-third of the population spoke French at the time of Confederation. By 1991, only 1.6 percent of the local population still claimed to use the language at home.[26]

It is the agrarian economic status of French communities in these provinces that has traditionally protected them from overwhelming contact with English. In Manitoba, most French-speaking parishes are located in the southeast corner of the province, where until recently they were able to enjoy partial isolation from the English-speakers who dominate the rest of the province. In Saskatchewan, the tiny French-speaking minority is clustered in the south, near Gravelbourg. Most of Alberta's French-speaking communities are grouped in the rural districts north of Edmonton. In Nova Scotia and Prince Edward Island, the francophone population lies in remote farming and fishing communities far removed from the main population centres. Newfoundland's minute French Canadian minority lives in what was once the most isolated spot imaginable—a rugged peninsula on the island's west coast separated from St. John's by a narrow isthmus, a range of mountains and 300 miles of wilderness.

Each of these communities existed in a rural environment where an older order was able to survive for decades. Maintaining a lifestyle characteristic of Quebec francophones of an earlier era, they maintained a high birth rate, large extended families and a strong loyalty to the Catholic Church.[27]

Such continued isolation protected these communities not only against influences from English Canada, but also against the changes sweeping mainstream French Canadian culture in faraway Quebec. Just as isolated immigrant communities around the world have been left behind by evolving cultures in the home country, these isolated communities were left behind by Quebec. Their situation parallelled that described by Japanese writer Yasuo Wakatsuki, who has made this observation about the cultural results of the isolation of Japanese emigrant communities abroad, "If you want to see Japan of the Taisho Era (1912-1926), go to Brazil; if you want to see Japan of the Meiji Era (1868-1912), go to America."[28] Those who wished, in the 1950s and 1960s, to observe a living relic of the agrarian, church-based French Canadian society of the 19th century would have done just as well to go to the French areas of southeastern Manitoba as to visit Quebec itself.

Today this can no longer be said. The extinction of the rural francophone way of life is virtually complete. One indication of the extent to which the francophones of the west have come to live their lives in English is indicated by the results of a survey conducted by Gérard Jolicoeur. In the mid-1960s, Jolicoeur visited the rural townships of south-eastern Manitoba to determine which activities were being conducted in French, and which in English. This corner of Manitoba has always been the part of western Canada in which French has had its strongest hold. Among Jolicoeur's findings: although most local residents used French at home, half the hours they spent listening to the radio were devoted to English programming, and almost three-quarters of television viewing was done in English.[29] This was in the 1960s, before the advent of cable television, satellite dishes and other technological improvements that have made cultural isolation even more difficult. The number of unilingual French-speakers in Manitoba has dropped from 7,954 in 1961 (the last census before Jolicoeur began his study) to a negligible 1,905 today.[30] Of these, less than 400 are between the ages of five and sixty-five.

The almost complete annihilation of French as a language of everyday use is brutally confirmed by reviewing the data on the ages of unilingual francophones in the Maritimes and the other western provinces. The figures reveal

Figure 5.3
A portrait of two dying francophone communities...

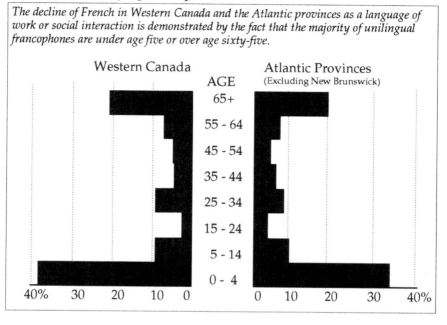

The decline of French in Western Canada and the Atlantic provinces as a language of work or social interaction is demonstrated by the fact that the majority of unilingual francophones are under age five or over age sixty-five.

...and two vigorous francophone communities.

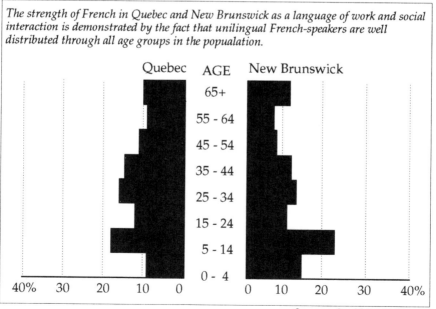

The strength of French in Quebec and New Brunswick as a language of work and social interaction is demonstrated by the fact that unilingual French-speakers are well distributed through all age groups in the popualation.

Sources: See *Notes for Figures*

that there is virtually no one left west of Ontario or east of New Brunswick capable of living fully in French. Only 5,430 francophones living west of the Ontario-Manitoba border are incapable of conducting a conversation in English, and of these, sixty percent are either children under the age of five, who have not yet had to learn any other language than that spoken at home with their parents, or elderly persons over the age of sixty-five. Among those of school age and working age, only 2,195 individuals in all of western Canada were capable of speaking French but not English. The figures for Atlantic Canada are equally devastating. There are only 945 unilingual francophones in the Atlantic provinces, excluding New Brunswick, who are not small children or senior citizens.[31]

Therefore, the depressing truth is that in exact opposition to the claims of the *Gazette* and Dr. Goldbloom cited above, the French outside Quebec are indeed taking what the *Gazette* referred to as the "fast road to extinction." The real news is not that the scattered communities outside Quebec are on this road; it is that they have already arrived at its terminus, and that their journey was neither reversed nor slowed by the federal billions spent on their behalf.

THE DISINTEGRATION OF THE ANGLOPHONE COMMUNITIES OF RURAL QUEBEC

Outside Montreal, Quebec's English community in Quebec has suffered a precipitous decline which resembles, in every particular, the decline of the French outside of their Quebec-based heartland. At the height of their powers and proportionate strength in the 1830s and 1840s, English-speakers represented over a quarter of Quebec's population. Not only were they a majority of the population in Montreal, they also represented nearly forty percent of the inhabitants of Quebec City. In 1841, nineteen Quebec counties had English majorities,[32] and the English-speaking population of the Eastern Townships was numerically more significant than that of Montreal. Newspaperman Robert Sellar was able to write, "When I came to Huntingdon [in southwestern Quebec] in 1862, the county was as solidly Protestant as any in Ontario."[33]

Today, English-speakers in Quebec are virtually confined to a single city. Eighty-five percent of the province's anglophone population lives within twenty-five miles of downtown Montreal. Only a single county in rural Quebec (Pontiac County, due west of Ottawa on the north shore of the Ottawa River) still has an English-speaking majority—and that by a bare fifty-five to forty-five percent margin over French.[34] Moreover, Quebec's English-speaking enclaves are all pressed against Quebec's borders with Ontario and the United States. English- speaking west-end Montreal is a twenty-minute drive from the Ontario border. The Anglo-Saxon farming communities of the Eastern Townships are within minutes of Vermont and New York State but are dying out nonetheless.³⁵ The English-speaking towns just north of the Ottawa River in west Quebec survive mainly because they are largely bedroom communities for Ottawa.

Elsewhere in the province, English is virtually extinct. Beyond the Montreal urban community and the two tiny rural districts mentioned above, English is the preferred language of only three percent of households.³⁶

As with the French-speakers of the other provinces, the English-speakers of Quebec have more than one 'face,' or settlement pattern. The small English-speaking farming and fishing communities that lie scattered across the rural regions of the province are perfect mirror-images of the traditional francophone communities of Nova Scotia or Saskatchewan. They are small, isolated, vulnerable to encroachment from the local majority, and either doomed to extinction or already extinct.

The second and much more visible face of English Quebec is the urban community of west-end Montreal. This face is vital, much more vigorous even than the Acadian community of northern New Brunswick, and is every bit as much an integrated part of the English-speaking heartland as Madawaska County is an integrated part of the French-speaking heartland.

Unlike the francophones outside Quebec, the English-speaking minority in Quebec has no third face, in the form of an 'immigrant' population in the major urban centres. The anglophones who migrate to Quebec from other parts of Canada in search of job opportunities almost always locate themselves in west-end Montreal, which simply is not the same cultural experience as being a francophone in west-end Toronto. There are a tiny number of English-speaking migrants who relocate to Quebec City, but most of them are federal civil servants temporarily in town on French-language training.

The inability of federal measures to stop the decline of minorities is demonstrated tidily by a comparison between the two faces of English Quebec. In the rural regions, as well as Quebec City, English has been in continuous decline for at least a century. This decline has been neither stopped nor slowed by the extension of federal services in English to minority communities as small as the one in Barkmere, where there are only thirty anglophones, or Ristigouche-partie-sud-est, where there are forty-five.³⁷

In these rural areas, even the provincial government has been relatively generous in its treatment of the anglophones. Bill 101's school law has had no impact at all on the English-speakers of rural Quebec, since they are nearly all covered by the provision of the law exempting persons educated in English in Quebec from the requirement to send their children to French schools. A similar exemption makes it possible for the anglophones of rural Quebec to become doctors, lawyers or engineers without speaking French. In addition, the language-of-work laws imposed under Bill 101 have little impact on English-run

Figure 5.4
Federal language policies have not slowed the decline of French outside its heartland.

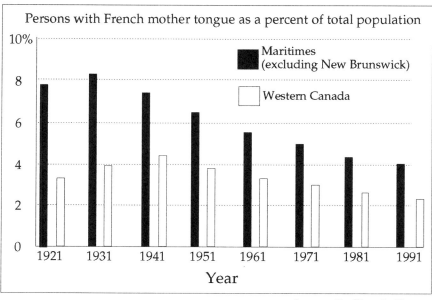

Sources: See *Notes for Figures*

Figure 5.5
English has been in decline outside its heartland for decades. This trend has not been influenced by federal language laws.

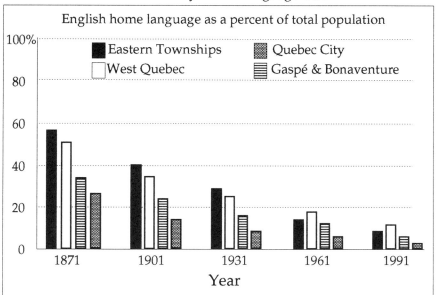

Sources: See *Notes for Figures*

businesses in the rural enclaves, since almost all such establishments fall below the fifty-employee minimum size for mandatory 'francization.'

Add to this the construction of English-language CBC retransmission stations across Quebec, and the anglophones of rural Quebec can honestly be said, in dramatic contrast to their fellow anglophones in Montreal, to be better served in their own language by government than ever before.

Yet the areas continue to decline at least as rapidly as the English-speaking population of Montreal, which has suffered the full brunt of each of the province's language laws. In Montreal the decline is clearly the result of the exodus that followed the imposition of Bill 101. As late as 1971, increasing absolute numbers of English-speakers had been recorded in Quebec in every single census for two centuries, thanks virtually exclusively to the growth of English-speaking Montreal. In the countryside, it is simply the continuation of a long-term trend. If federal measures were effective in turning back the tide of assimilation, it would have been logical to expect that the anglophone populations of the rural areas would have started to stabilize after 1970. Nothing of the sort has happened.

HOW MINORITIES CHOOSE TO ASSIMILATE

Just like disappearing minorities everywhere else in the world, the francophones outside the French-language homeland and the anglophones of rural Quebec are not dying out because they are being forced to assimilate. They are dying out because they choose to do so. This sounds improbable, and in a sense it is. No minority ever chooses to decline and fade. But at some point it becomes easier for the individuals who are its members to integrate into the society that surrounds them than to fight to retain the ancestral language. As the language becomes less and less satisfactory—compared to the language of the local majority—as a means of communication with the people one meets in daily life, the opportunities to perpetuate the ancestral lifestyle and language start to fade.

As members of the linguistic minority become increasingly fluent in the majority tongue, their interest in retaining the ancestral language starts to wane. And as these two factors destroy the language from within, the ease with which individuals can transport themselves to a different part of the country or province permits those who still do cleave strongly to the ancestral culture to move to more congenial surroundings. Together, the loss of linguistic opportunity, the loss of enthusiasm for keeping up the language, and the ease of movement back to the heartland account for the disintegration that each of Canada's official languages has experienced in its minority regions.

Loss of Opportunity

One can trace the patterns of assimilation in the west by observing the very high rates at which francophones marry outside their linguistic community. In Saskatchewan, fifty percent of francophones marry anglophones. In Alberta the rate is nearly fifty-five percent. In British Columbia, the rate is over sixty percent. Intermarriage between francophones and anglophones in western Canada means assured assimilation: ninety-six percent of mixed anglophone and francophone married couples speak English at home. Together, these figures mean that almost half of the children born to western francophones will be brought up in English.[38]

The same phenomenon is at work in rural Quebec. English/French intermarriages outside of west end Montreal almost always lead to the assimilation of the English-speaking partner and the raising of children in French. This is nicely illustrated by the fate of three of the more illustrious sons born to interlinguistic marriages outside west-end Montreal. Prime Minister Louis St-Laurent was born in Compton County in 1882 to a francophone father and an anglophone mother named Ann Broderick. He grew up fluently bilingual, but with a preference for French. The same happened three-quarters of a century later with former Deputy Prime Minister Jean Charest, whose mother was also an anglophone. Pierre Trudeau, who was raised in a French-speaking suburb of Montreal, also chose to adopt the language of his father over that of his anglophone mother, Grace Elliott.

Loss of Interest

In the cities of southern Ontario, demand for French education is surprisingly weak, given the relatively large numbers of French-speakers who have moved there; it remains underutilized even when actively offered. Toronto is the best example of this surprising lack of interest: with 100,000 citizens of French origin in a city of three million, metropolitan Toronto offers six French-language primary schools. Together, these schools have been able to attract less than 1,800 students.[39]

Evidence of declining group identity among individuals who have married into the majority community or who are the children of linguistically-mixed marriages are hard for researchers to track, but one fairly reliable indicator is the circulation figures of minority language newspapers, which Richard Joy refers to as "barometers" of group identity.[40] As loyalty to and identification with the ancestral minority group declines, readership of these newspapers will also decline. By this token, group loyalties are rapidly vanishing among western Canada's francophones. Today, the Winnipeg-based newspaper *La Liberté et le Patriote* has only half of the circulation it had in 1970, even though the French-speaking population on the Prairies has only fallen by one-third over this period.[41]

Figure 5.6
Federal legislation has been unable to stem the decline in minority-language education.

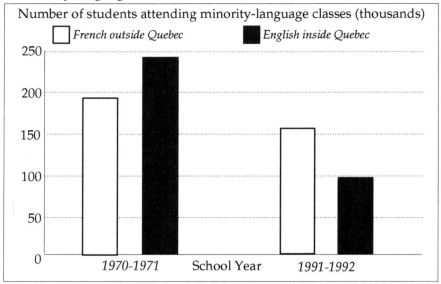

Sources: See *Notes for Figures*

Likewise, an indication of the slow demise of English in the French-language heartland can be found in the declining health of the English-language newspapers outside of Montreal. In Argenteuil County, north of the Ottawa River and west of Montreal, English-speakers formed a majority of the population until 1911. Today, their numbers have declined so substantially, and their ability to maintain local institutions has collapsed so much that the local English-language newspaper, the Lachute *Watchman*, has been reduced to six pages. Since early 1993 it has been forced to publish in the form of an insert placed between the sports pages and the classified ads in its former rival, the French-language *Le Progrès*.[42]

In Quebec City, the last English-language daily newspaper, the 200-year-old *Chronicle-Telegraph*, reduced its frequency of issue from daily to weekly in 1972. It survives as little more than a community news-sheet, kept alive not by reader interest but by a technicality in federal language legislation that requires federally regulated companies in bilingual regions (which Quebec City is, under federal law) to publish advertisements in the English media as well as in French. As a result, the *Chronicle-Telegraph* is able to generate advertising revenues in a market where there is no longer any demand for newspapers in English.

Ease of Departure

Another phenomenon is of interest because it closely resembles the well-known exodus of the English-speaking community of Quebec: the youth are leaving. Francophones who leave to study in Quebec are not returning to the other provinces, just as younger English-speakers of child-rearing years are leaving Quebec.[43] This is not a new phenomenon; well-known western francophones who departed permanently for the broader horizons of Montreal and Quebec City include novelist Gabrielle Roy, who left Manitoba in the 1930s, and former governor-general Jeanne Sauvé, who abandoned Saskatchewan to continue her studies in the east. Famous Franco-Ontarians who moved to Quebec include the Dionne quintuplets. The Maritimes has also produced its share of famous Quebecers.

THE DISAPPEARANCE OF THE FRANCO-AMERICANS

> The French Canadians are flowing over our borders. The victory won by men of the English race, on the Plains of Abraham, is being avenged by women of the race of Montcalm. New England is lost. The swarms descending from the French hive are taking possession of the land.
> —*New York Commercial Advertiser (October 1890)*[44]

One hundred years ago, French Canadians were flooding into New England at such a rate that many observers, both English-speaking and French, were convinced they would soon dominate the region. Today, the French language has nearly vanished in New England. At first glance, the virtually complete assimilation of the francophones of New England suggests that the processes of assimilation really can be manipulated by governments. French survives in pluralist Canada; in America, the francophones were swallowed up by the melting pot.

This impression is false, even though there is no doubt that the American authorities were anxious to assimilate their French-speaking minority, as is shown by this extraordinarily insensitive passage from a letter sent by President Franklin Roosevelt to Mackenzie King in 1942:

> All of this leads me to wonder whether by some sort of planning Canada and the United States, working towards the same end, cannot do some planning—perhaps unwritten planning which need not even be a public policy—by which we can hasten the objective of assimilating the New England French Canadians and Canada's French Canadians into the whole of our respective bodies politic.[45]

In fact, the rise and decline of the French Canadian minority in New

England had very little to do with deliberate assimilationist policies. The francophones of New England were assimilated because they did not inhabit a geographically remote region well-isolated from the attractions of American culture. Instead, they were integrated into dozens of towns and villages with English-speaking majorities, scattered across the American north-east from Maine to Rhode Island.[46] This geographical dispersion left them open to integration with the majority when a change in American immigration law in 1930 cut them off from their linguistic heartland.

From about 1850 to 1930, hundreds of thousands of French Canadians fled south from rural poverty in Quebec and Acadia to find employment in the textile mills of New England. It has been calculated that in this period, fully one-third of the entire French Canadian population was living in the United States.[47] So great was this migration that it can reasonably be argued that French Canada's modernization into an urban and middle-class society took place primarily in the United States rather than in Canada.[48] In New Hampshire, fully thirty percent of the state's population is descended from Quebec francophones. This is a level as high as that in New Brunswick. Yet today there are virtually no French-speakers left in this state or elsewhere in New England.

Before 1930, migrants crossed easily back and forth across the border. There was no requirement for immigrants to obtain work permits or visas; borders in the 19th and early 20th centuries served to stop the free movement of goods, not the free movement of people. In the glory days of the French Canadian expansion into New England, the labour markets and social networks of Quebec and the states immediately to the south were closely linked. Francophones flowed into New England when the Canadian economy was weak. When it strengthened, many flowed back.[49] This had important implications for the cultural viability of their New England settlements, as Father Edouard Hamon noted in 1890:

> To me, their chances of survival appear much more favourable [than those of any other immigrant group in the United States]. The colonies, in effect, are in constant physical contact with the motherland. The eastern states where they are established touch on the borders of Quebec. In a few hours on the train, the Canadiens find themselves again on their native soil, in the bosom of the ancient parishes, among their parents and friends.... And in any case, where is the Canadien who passes more than a few years without returning to see his country?[50]

New cohorts of job-seeking French-speakers were constantly travelling south; at no point between 1900 and 1930 did the number of first-generation immigrants from the heartland drop below one-third of the total French population of the United States. Earlier, it had been even higher.[51] As well, there was substantial reverse migration. French Canadians who had made their fortunes in the U.S. sometimes returned to Quebec to retire, while others who had left their families behind in Quebec returned after briefer sojourns. This meant that to a very large degree, the 'petits-Canadas' of the region were really just extensions of the French Canadian heartland.

Immigration restrictions imposed at the beginning of the Great Depression changed everything. Starting in 1930, permanent entry into the United States was forbidden to any person not holding a work visa. Visas were only issued to those who could demonstrate that they would be guaranteed a job, or that they would be supported by relatives already residing in the U.S. At once, the supply of new French Canadian workers came to a halt. Net immigration dropped from 130,000 in the decade preceding the new law to zero in the decade following.[52] Return emigration to Canada also dropped sharply. Separate figures for Quebec do not exist, but the total annual figures for native-born Canadians returning from the United States tell the story. In the average year between 1925 and 1929, 36,000 Canadians returned to the country of their birth after sojourning in the United States. In the average year between 1935 and 1939, the number dropped to 4,300.[53]

The end of the easy mobility that had previously existed had the effect of isolating the New England francophones from the cradle of their ancestral culture, leaving them vulnerable to the intrusions of English-speaking culture. The post-war period saw the advent of television and American cultural media penetrating into the community. Isolated from the heartland in Quebec and Acadia by the now-closed international border, the French language didn't have a chance. Without warning, they had been caught in the trap that eventually finishes off all immigrant groups. Raymond Breton describes, in clinical terms, the phenomenon that destroyed them:

> Ethnic communities are formed, grow, and disappear; they go through a life-cycle.... If the rate of [im]migration is low or nil, the ethnic public will progressively decrease, because even a high degree of institutional completeness will not prevent some integration into the native community. With time—and it may be quite long—the ethnic organizations will themselves disappear or lose their ethnic identity, completing the life-cycle of the community.[54]

Today, only a handful of French-speakers exist in New England to lament the loss of their language and culture. Language assimilation has been so complete that even the leaders of Franco-American organizations are often unilingual English-speakers, whose only connection to the French language is ancestral.[55]

It seems hard, at first, to accept that even in the heart of the American 'melting pot,' it was natural demographic forces rather than deliberate policies of assimilation that led to the vanishing of the Franco-Americans. Proof that this is the case lies in the story of the single area of New England where the

French-speakers were never assimilated. In Maine's Madawaska Valley, on the state's northern border with New Brunswick and Quebec, a vigorous Acadian society exists to this day. The keys to its survival have been precisely the factors that were absent in the larger Franco-American communities further south. In the Madawaska region, French-speakers have always been able to stay in close physical contact with their Canadian cousins across the border. Thus, all the really important activities of life have continued to take place back and forth across the border, regardless of the immigration laws:

> Life at this border has its idiosyncrasies. A baby born to an American family living in the town of Madawaska, Maine, will most likely enter the world in Edmundston, New Brunswick—since Madawaska has no hospital—and therefore can claim dual citizenship according to both United States and Canadian law. Intermarriage between the valley's Canadians and Americans is so common you need a scorecard to keep track.[56]

Nearly as important as their easy access to their culture's heartland for the French-speakers of the Madawaska has been their relative isolation from New England's English-speaking majority. The only systematic survey of New England's French Canadian population in its glory years was conducted in 1890, which showed that out of over 170 cities and towns in the six New England states with substantial francophone populations, French Canadians formed a majority in only twenty. Of these, twelve were parishes in the Madawaska Valley.[57]

It is only in the vaguest sense that the U.S. government can be said to be responsible for the assimilation of its French-speaking population. Their demise was largely due to the shutting of the border, but the immigration law of 1930 was certainly not enacted with the assimilation of the French Canadians in mind. One point, however, is certainly clear: the Franco-Americans of New England did not lose their language because of the absence of an American parallel to the *Official Languages Act*, and they would not have been saved had one existed. In the United States as much as in Canada, legislation plays, and has always played, a minor role in the assimilation process.

SUMMARY

Canada's French and English communities have virtually completed the process of polarization or linguistic segregation. French has been confined almost entirely to Quebec and a few neighbouring counties in Ontario and New Brunswick. English has been eliminated from almost all of Quebec except west-end Montreal. The disappearance of Canada's official-language minorities, first predicted in 1967, is nearly complete.

The process of polarization has continued at full speed for the past twenty years despite the introduction of the *Official Languages Act* in 1969, and a host of other federal language initiatives since that date. This reveals embarrassingly the inability of the federal government to stem the decline of the minorities. The federal government is impotent because factors beyond the control of any government have limited the economic and social viability of English in Quebec and of French elsewhere. Despite Ottawa's best efforts, the members of the minority populations still must choose assimilation if they wish to remain where they are, or migration if they wish to retain their language.

In spite of this trend, the bulk of Canadians still believe there are thriving minority communities right across the country. The federal government, ever mindful of Quebec separatism, does what it can to encourage this misperception among its citizens.

Deception is the only aspect of federal language policy that has actually achieved its goal; none of Ottawa's policies, grants or subsidies to tiny scattered minorities have done anything to slow or stop their assimilation. Public policy is no obstacle in the way of the juggernaut of demography.

The federal government should recognize that it is beyond the power of any state to prevent minorities from assimilating when they choose to do so. The present federal practice of hiding behind misleading statistics and declaring Official Bilingualism a successful antidote to the predominant assimilation trends is dishonest and should be discontinued. Once this is done, the government will be able to turn its attention far more effectively to helping Canada's *real* official-language minorities—the smaller but far more vibrant French communities of eastern Ontario and northern New Brunswick, and the anglophone population living on the western half of Montreal Island.

CHAPTER SIX

Speaking in Tongues: The Delivery of Official Language Services

> The turn of phrase attracts the reader's attention and obstructs understanding: "The Government of Canada *is committed to ensuring that* ... " (Article 39). "The Government of Canada *is committed to enhancing* ... " (Article 41). This text is destined to become the law of the land. ... But what is the effect in law of an article in which "The government commits itself"? The incursion of political vocabulary into the law introduces an unwelcome element of uncertainty into the understanding of its mandates and obligations.
> —*Government of Quebec, internal report on the new Official Languages Act (1988)*[1]

IN ALL OF CANADA's language battles, no other issue highlights more clearly the rift between minorities and majorities than the subject of minority official-language services. This is because minority-language services are very much a zero-sum political game. It costs money to provide every new service, and for the most part, that money comes from tax revenues collected from members of the majority. As well, minority-language services can only be provided by bilingual public servants, and in every region of the country a disproportionately large share of the qualified applicants for such positions are themselves members of the local linguistic minority. When services are extended to new regions, federal employees in these regions who have the misfortune to be unilingual can be forced out of jobs they have held for years. But when services are retrenched, members of the minority feel stripped of traditional rights, or even that they are being turned into strangers in their home communities.[2]

Polarized interests of this sort are more conducive to dialogues of the deaf than to reasonable compromises. So it is hardly surprising that when it comes to the question of services, legitimate concessions to the minorities are frequently taken as an affront by the majorities, while suggestions to place even moderate restrictions on services are regarded by the minorities as evidence of bigotry.

One might have hoped that the fact Canada has two majorities (the French in Quebec and the English elsewhere) and two corresponding minority populations would have produced a little moderation on each side. A constant emphasis on the equal size of these two minorities is certainly the key feature of the federal government's public justification of its present policy of widespread French-language services outside Quebec and widespread English-language services inside the province.

The fact that moderation has not been much in evidence is mostly due to the claim of equality itself, which the federal government believes will have the effect of enhancing national unity by showing that Ottawa's minority services policies do not unduly favour either the French-speaking or the English-speaking minority.

In a pattern that gets repeated in many other areas of federal language policy, the emphasis is placed on trying to create a policy which will reconcile the incompatible goals of equality of outcome for each language community as a whole and equality of treatment for individual members of either of the two language groups.

In this case, the equal outcome that is sought is that equal numbers of francophones outside Quebec and anglophones inside Quebec are to be offered services in their mother tongue. Because of the very different geographical dispersion of Quebec's compact anglophone community and the widely dispersed francophones in the rest of the country, it is much easier to reach a large number of Anglo-Quebecers with English-language services than to reach an equivalent number of francophones elsewhere with French-language services. This means that equality of outcome could most easily be achieved through the formal adoption of asymmetrical rights to federal services for anglophones in Quebec and francophones outside. Francophones living outside Quebec would be eligible for services in French when anglophones living inside Quebec in identical circumstances would not.

This solution has been proposed by some Québécois academics, but clearly it is not saleable to English Canada, where equality of treatment is held sacred. English-speaking Canadians expect that, for example, an anglophone living in the municipality of West Montreal (which is three-quarters English) should have the right to services in English, just as a francophone in New Brunswick's Madawaska County (which is over ninety percent French) would have the right to services in French. Likewise, it seems reasonable to most English-speakers that neither an isolated anglophone in Quebec's ninety-eight percent French Beauce region, nor an isolated francophone living in similar circumstances in British Columbia, ought to expect to receive services in his or her native language.

But equality of outcome for the two language communities and equality of treatment for the individuals who make up these communities do not easily mesh. The attempt to find a solution that makes everybody happy at the same time traps the federal government into extending the positive right to services far more widely than would be justified under any logical system. Ottawa comes dangerously close to attempting to provide services to every last speaker of minority official languages no matter how remotely located they are in the heartland of the other official language. In extending these services so widely, Ottawa violates the basic principle discussed in Chapter One, that the provision of services to any minority should not place a burden on the majority that outweighs the benefits being bestowed on the recipients of the services.

DEMOGRAPHICS AND THE PROPAGANDA OF UNITY

Language *equality* is the mortar that binds Canada together.
—*Brian Mulroney (1989)*[3]

For the federal government's network of minority-language services to serve effectively in its role as a guarantor of national unity, it is important that the number of francophones who benefit from it be larger than the number of anglophones, and that the intrusions of English-language government services in Quebec be no more onerous or highly visible from the perspective of the francophone majority than are French-language services outside Quebec. As long as these conditions are being met, minority language services can be held up as an example of the benefits that Confederation bestows on the French language.

So according to the official story, the federal government provides bilingual services to ensure the well-being of nearly one million francophones outside Quebec and of a somewhat smaller English-speaking population inside the province. This is a good argument for national unity, so it is unfortunate that it bears no resemblance to the truth. By any objective measure, there is a vast disproportion in size between the French-speaking population outside Quebec and the much larger English-speaking population within.

This is an inconvenient fact for a policy designed to appear not to favour either group, so the federal government is always careful to couch its defence of existing rules on service-provision on the basis of 'mother tongue' figures (based on the first language that an individual learns in infancy). These figures show a healthy and growing francophone population outside Quebec, and a declining but still substantial population of anglophones inside the province. The mother tongue figures at the time of the 1991 census were 947,000 francophones outside Quebec and 599,000 anglophones inside.

Mother tongue figures reassuringly show both groups to be large enough to justify the enormous costs of servicing them. This satisfies anglophones. The substantial size advantage of the francophone community outside Quebec shows that federal policy favours neither group unduly, but that in practice, the federal language regime somewhat favours the French language over the English. This satisfies francophones.

These are signal advantages, so it is unfortunate that mother tongue figures mean absolutely nothing, in terms of providing information about who actually speaks which official language, and therefore who benefits from minority language services. Mother tongue statistics are always a full generation out-of-date, ignoring the intermarriage and assimilation that affects literally hundreds of thousands of Canadians.

The idea that Canada's two minorities are large, vibrant communities, or that the francophone community has a substantial size advantage over the anglophone minority, bear little resemblance to reality. Measured by home language, the size of the francophone population outside Quebec drops by more than one-third, to 607,000. The contrast with the situation in Quebec is even more astonishing. The English-speaking population of Quebec as measured by home language is 716,000 (plus another 100,000 immigrants who speak a non-official language at home but use English as their main language of communication with the outside world). This is much larger than the mother tongue figure cited by the federal government, and it is nearly twenty percent larger than the population of francophones living outside Quebec.

How the Myth of Equality Leads to Bilingual Services on Baffin Island

In truth, the situation is even more unequal than this, and even more problematic for a federal government trying to maintain national unity by maintaining services to Canada's two minorities. They are geographically distributed on completely different patterns.

Eighty percent of all home-language English speakers in Quebec live within a twenty-five-mile radius of downtown Montreal. By contrast, the 607,000 francophones of the other nine provinces, as measured by home language, are thinly scattered from the Atlantic to the Pacific.

Because migrants from Quebec have travelled to the other provinces mostly as job-seeking immigrants, large numbers are concentrated in the big cities, where they almost always represent only a minute fraction of the local population. In these situations it is not really possible for francophones to conduct their lives, or at least that part of their lives that involves interactions outside the immediate family, in French. The same rule applies to the much smaller proportion of Quebec's anglophones living beyond west-end Montreal, but because this small area holds the vast majority of Anglo-Quebecers, the problem of geographical dispersion is really a French Canadian one. The few communities outside Quebec where French-speakers form a homogeneous majority are for the most part tightly pressed against the province's eastern and western flanks.

As a result of these dramatically different settlement patterns, a policy of protecting and serving only the communities outside Quebec in which a substantial portion (say, ten percent) of the total local population is made up of unilingual or semi-bilingual francophones, and only the communities inside Quebec in which unilingual anglophones are similarly numerous, would lead to a three-to-one asymmetry in favour of the Anglo-Quebecers.

Figure 6.1
Three Measures of Minority Population Size

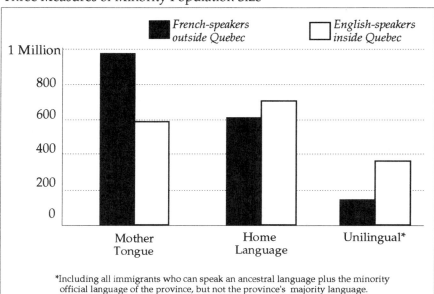

Sources: See *Notes for Figures*

Ottawa fears that such a solution would be politically unpalatable to francophones, and would be a particularly poor way of achieving the public-relations and national unity goals that are such a vital aspect of all federal language policies. Since the goal of equal coverage is all-important to federal politicians, the only alternative has been to extend bilingual services to every corner of English Canada, in order to reach as large a proportion as possible of the scattered francophone population outside Quebec. Under the latest set of rules, which were introduced in January 1992, bilingual services reach ninety-two percent of francophones outside Quebec[4]—and the bilingual regions of Canada have been extended to include Toronto, Calgary, and Frobisher Bay, on Baffin Island.

Frobisher Bay, included by virtue of its 220 French-speakers, thereby qualifies for mandatory French-language services from Canada Post, the CBC, the RCMP, the Department of Fisheries and Oceans, and six other federal agencies.

But a policy of offering bilingual services only to francophones outside Quebec would be unsaleable even to a population as docile as Canada's anglophones. To placate them, the same extremely broad criteria for designating bilingual regions are applied within Quebec as in the other provinces. This has had the result of extending English-language services to Quebec City, where the unilingual

English-speaking population of 1,700 (including unilingual babies and toddlers) represents three-tenths of one percent of the municipal population.

Ottawa's attempt to please everybody has produced a situation that leaves nobody happy, and that mostly cancels out its own national unity goal. It is rather doubtful that Quebec's appetite for Canadian unity has been increased by the imposition of English-language service on corners of the province where, save for federal policy, the language would never be spoken.

Propaganda Made Secret

It would probably be possible to back away from this extreme situation in order to adopt more common sense rules on service to the public if the decisions about where to direct minority-language services were being made on the basis of an impartial standard commanding widespread respect. But in Canada, these decisions are made by politicians on the basis of arbitrary criteria, so they garner no more respect than they deserve.

This problem can be traced to a simple and seemingly innocuous feature of Canada's original bilingualism law, the 1969 *Official Languages Act*. The Act proclaimed that English-language services should be provided in Quebec, and French-language services should be provided elsewhere, wherever "there is a significant demand" for such services, but it failed to include a definition of significant demand. This meant that specific numbers were never discussed in parliamentary debate before the Act was passed. The public was never given a chance to express its views on the extent to which it was willing to see minority services expanded, or on what balance between services and costs which it viewed as most fair.

The phrase "significant demand," and a similar definition, "where numbers warrant," have since been repeated in the 1988 *Official Languages Act* and in the *Canadian Charter of Rights and Freedoms*. But the concepts remain undefined in law and untested by national debate and discussion. The benefits that isolated francophones enjoy when French-language government services are made available in British Columbia, or that handfuls of anglophones can enjoy in the Saguenay, have never been weighed against the costs that these impose on the surrounding majority population, or on Canadian taxpayers. Decisions about where to provide services, and to whom, have been made instead in the semi-private surroundings of Parliamentary committee-rooms.

To avoid criticism of specific actions taken under this policy, over the past two decades the federal government has progressively shrouded its detailed actions on service to the public behind increasingly thick layers of bureaucratic obscurity. By now its actions have become so well-hidden that simply learning which regions of the country receive bilingual services requires recourse to the *Access to Information Act*.[5]

This practice of information-deprivation puts an end to many specific instances of public criticism, but it arouses the suspicion of both of Canada's two majority populations and does little to comfort the minorities. Besides, secrecy sits poorly on a policy that is more a propaganda exercise designed to give a boost to national unity than a genuine effort to improve the general welfare. Bashful propaganda is a contradiction in terms, or at least a sign of a very confused administration, but it is the essence of federal policy on minority language services.

A BRIEF HISTORY OF BILINGUAL SERVICES

> ... the Trudeau government firmly intended to create a maximal number of bilingual districts based on the generation-behind-the-facts mother tongue data. Like pieces in a jigsaw puzzle, the bilingual districts inside and outside Quebec were to lock together English and French Canada, at least from the Atlantic to the Rockies, in an overall language map expressing the geopolitical quintessence of Canadian unity in duality.
> —*Charles Castonguay (1979)*[6]

In the Bad Old Days . . .

For many decades following Confederation, the federal government made little effort to provide services to the public in French. The struggle of early French-rights activists for basic services in their language seems alternately noble, for their persistence and dignity, and pathetic for the extreme modesty of the goals they hoped to achieve.

Train schedules in Quebec itself were often printed only in English before 1910. Postage stamps were unilingually English until 1927. In 1935, Prime Minister R.B. Bennett rejected a private members' bill that would have created bilingual money, although he grudgingly granted that he would permit the French language to be added to certain banknotes, as long as these bills were circulated only in Quebec.[7] His proposal for dual economies was judged a national insult by French Canadians (it also defied the laws of economics), and his party lost most of its Quebec seats in the next election.

Nonetheless, it was not until 1945 that bilingual baby bonus cheques were issued, and not until 1962 that the French language was added to all other government cheques. One of the primary reasons for the creation of the Royal Commission on Bilingualism and Biculturalism in 1963 was that, nearly a century after Confederation, the federal government was finally prepared to acknowledge that the level of federal services being provided to French-speakers outside Quebec was inadequate.

The Bilingual Districts Proposal: 1967

The first volume of the B&B Commission's multi-volume report, issued in 1967, provided a solution to the problem of minority-language government services that would have formed a strong and permanent basis for a reasonable and moderate regime of service-provision, had it been adopted in the form recommended by the Commission. Unfortunately, nothing of the sort happened.

Having examined the government service models of several other bilingual countries, the Commissioners chose to closely emulate the system used in Finland. Finland's population is slightly less than five million. Most of the population speaks Finnish, but a small proportion, located mostly in peripheral areas of the country, is Swedish-speaking. This makes Finland similar to either Ontario, with its small percentage of francophones largely clustered in the province's eastern tip, or to Quebec, with its anglophone population clustered at one end of Montreal Island. This made Finland's successful method of providing services to its minority a perfect model for the French-speaking minority outside Quebec, or for the English-speaking minority within Quebec.[8]

Under Finnish law, the country is divided linguistically according to the linguistic composition of each *commune*, or municipality. Most communes contain a Finnish-speaking majority of over ninety percent, so they are designated unilingual Finnish and government services are available in no other language. However, if the Swedish-speaking proportion of any commune's population is ten percent or more, the commune is declared bilingual and services are mandated in both languages. In the very small number of communes where Swedes form more than ninety percent of the population, government services are offered in Swedish only.

The Finnish system offers two important advantages. The first is flexibility. Inevitably, population patterns shift over time, and the designated communes are able to shift as well. To prevent very small population fluctuations from affecting the language designation of any individual commune, unilingual communes are not redesignated as bilingual until the minority share of the commune's population reaches twelve percent, and bilingual communes are not made unilingual until the minority has dropped to eight percent.

The second advantage is that services are offered everywhere in the country where it can realistically be said that "numbers warrant" or where there is "sufficient demand," but in no regions where these conditions do not apply. There is no confusion in the mind of any Finn as to what "sufficient demand" means.

Based on these factors, the B&B Commission recommended the adoption of a system of bilingual districts virtually identical to the one in Finland.

The Commission identified fifty-four census divisions in eight provinces which met the ten percent rule, as indicated by the admittedly out-of-date mother tongue figures in the 1961 census.[9] Implemented as shown in a map supplement accompanying the Commission's report, the bilingual districts would have contained a total population of 4.6 million, of which 1.2 million would have been members of the respective official-language minorities. This system would have been imposed upon only a relatively small number of majority-community members (3.4 million), but these districts would still have been sufficient to provide services to sixty-seven percent of francophones living outside Quebec and to eighty-nine percent of anglophones within the province.[10]

Botching the Bilingual Districts: 1969-1975

Federal Bilingual Districts
4.(1). Under and in accordance with this Act, the Governor in Council or any member of his family (i.e. his wife, children, cousins, grandchildren, nieces . . . well you get the point), may, whenever they get the urge, establish one or more bilingual districts if they so choose.
4.(2). A bilingual district will be designated by the boundaries so imposed by the Governor in Council or any member of his family (as listed in major part in 4.(1) above) . . .
4.(3). Alterations of established districts shall be permitted for various and sundry reasons which we have yet to decide upon, so long as they are approved by the Governor in Council (his family has no say in this one).
"The Unofficial Official Languages Act,"
by Marisa Akow, an eighteen-year-old student (1986)[11]

The 1969 *Official Languages Act* entrenched the idea of bilingual districts in law, but it also sowed the seeds of their destruction. The *Act* adopted the system recommended by the B&B Commission, but incorporated a significant modification designed to gradually introduce Trudeau's visionary ideal of a bilingual country filled with bilingual citizens, coast to coast. This secondary purpose of the bilingual districts system was never stated in the text of the *Official Languages Act*, but it is clearly indicated by the details.

Section 9.1 of the Act stated that all federal agencies were required to provide bilingual services "at each of its principal offices in federal bilingual district[s]." The B&B Commission had stressed the importance of basing the location and size of each district on impartial criteria, as in Finland. Instead, the Act stated that an appointed board, christened the 'Bilingual Districts Advisory Board' (BDAB), would be given wide latitude to base the boundaries of bilingual districts on a variety of criteria. Boundaries could be based upon municipal boundaries, school districts, census districts, or federal or provincial electoral districts. Bilingual districts would be created wherever recommended by the board.

Districts could be created or expanded at will, following each decennial census, but the Act provided no means for districts to be shut down or reduced in size if the numbers within their boundaries declined to a level that no longer justified the provision of minority-language services. Clearly, the districts were intended to be ratcheted upwards both in size and number, serving as tools by which the state could gradually turn the Canadian people into the bicultural supermen envisioned by Trudeau.[12]

Two reports were produced by the Bilingual Districts Advisory Board; their contents took much of the shift in power in Canada away from Trudeau's philosophy to the ideology of asymmetrical bilingualism.

The report of the first Bilingual Districts Advisory Board was published in 1971. It recommended that minority-language services in French be provided in thirty-six districts of various sizes across Canada's nine English-speaking provinces. Many of the districts were tiny; one, located on Newfoundland's Port-au-Port Peninsula, contained a francophone population of only 749. Other districts in Manitoba and Saskatchewan were even smaller.[13] All of this was in keeping with the Trudeau vision. The vision was even more pronounced in Quebec; the entire province would be a single enormous bilingual district, in which both federal services and (provisional upon the hoped-for consent of the provincial government) provincial services would be made available in English. The logic of this move seems to have been that the bilingual districts system would serve as a lever to convert all of Canada to the bilingual paradise envisioned by Trudeau, and that the process could proceed more rapidly in Quebec, because English had already made far greater inroads there than French had made in the rest of Canada.[14] New Brunswick was also proposed as a single large district. Over time, the rest of the country had the potential to become a single vast bilingual district as well.

This agenda was not stated explicitly, so it is possible that the arrangement proposed by the advisory board would have been saleable to the Quebec government had it been presented a few years earlier, when fears of francophone demographic decline were less pronounced. The 1971 census, conducted just a few months after the board's report was released, put an end to any notion that Quebec politicians would be willing to expand the privileges enjoyed by English-speakers. The census showed Quebec's birthrate to be in free fall, and that even within the province's borders, most immigrants and indeed many francophones were adopting English. Soon the Bourassa government began planning restrictive language legislation, and the Parti Québécois started to build the framework that would eventually become Bill 101. In the event, the report of the Bilingual Districts Advisory Board was rejected out-of-hand by the Quebec government, and a second Board was established in Ottawa.

A second report was not completed until 1975. Its findings were significantly influenced by the Board's attempt to use bilingual districts as a vehicle for the promotion of national unity. One of its purposes appears to have been to help stem the rise of the Parti Québécois by altering the ideological underpinnings of bilingualism. This time, "... the rights of linguistic minorities themselves [were to be] subordinated to more abstract sociological considerations of language equality."[15]

As a result, the 1975 Report was a complete victory for the Québécois nationalist, asymmetrical vision of Canadian bilingualism. The new report recommended bilingual districts in English Canada that were both more extensive and more populous than those recommended in 1971.[16] But it was in Quebec that the differences between the 1971 and 1976 reports were most remarkable. Not only had the idea of a single all-inclusive district been abandoned, but the vast bulk of the English-speaking population was to be excluded from any legislative protection at all. Montreal, the home of three-quarters of Quebec's English-speaking population, was to be exempted from inclusion in a bilingual district on the basis that traditional protections for their language rights would be sufficient, and also on the basis of the peculiar argument that English Canada had a unilingual metropolis in the form of Toronto, so French Canada needed a unilingual metropolis too.[17] In total, Quebec would contain only five bilingual districts with a total minority population of only 78,000, while the rest of the country would contain twenty-five bilingual districts with a total francophone population of 594,000.[18]

These recommendations created an uproar among the Advisory Board's own membership. Four of the ten commissioners wrote dissenting reports. One commissioner stated:

> ... if it is impossible to recommend a bilingual district in the census metropolitan area of Toronto, because its French minority is only 1.7 per cent of the population, I fail to see how this can be any kind of a justification ... in denying a bilingual district in the census metropolitan area of Montreal, where the Anglophone minority is 21.7 per cent of the population. If such a line of reasoning had been taken to its logical conclusion, the Board would have abstained from recommending one single bilingual district anywhere in Canada for the simple reason that it was impossible to recommend one in British Columbia.[19]

Another commissioner had this acid comment on the designation of all of New Brunswick as a single large district:

> If all of New Brunswick is declared a federal bilingual district, there is no way to distinguish [the Public Service's] obligations in Moncton or Edmundston from their obligations in St. Stephen or Sussex. The job of the Bilingual Districts Advisory Board is to locate the populations of the two official languages in order to recommend the areas which should be able to function in both languages. To fail to do this in New Brunswick, it seems to me, is to cast doubt upon the whole notion of formally defined bilingual districts. One might as well go on to say that, since the overall figures for Canada meet the

requirements of the law, the whole of Canada should be declared a [single vast] bilingual district.[20]

Introducing Bilingual Districts Through the Service Entrance: 1975-1988

The high level of dissent within the Board itself discredited the Board's report and with it, the entire concept of openly designated bilingual districts. Upon receiving the completed report, the Trudeau government announced in the House of Commons that it was rejecting them, and promised instead to introduce its own set of proposals for bilingual districts. These proposals were never made public.[21] Instead, the government turned to the "sufficient demand" clause of the *Official Languages Act*, and began to quietly extend bilingual services to those areas of the country where, in the eyes of the cabinet, such demand existed.[22]

When those areas of Canada in which bilingual services would be offered was codified and published (for internal use only) in 1982, it showed a list of bilingual service regions far more extensive than had been proposed by the B&B Commission, and more symmetrical than had been proposed by the second Bilingual Districts Advisory Board.[23] The total minority population served had increased to 1.1 million, of whom 63.2 percent were Anglo-Quebecers and 26.8 percent were francophones living outside Quebec. The most egregious inequities of the 1975 BDAB report, such as the exclusion of Montreal, had been eliminated.[24] At last, by acting secretly, the government had been able to enact a policy roughly approximating Trudeau's vision of widespread bilingual services.

The *Canadian Charter of Rights and Freedoms*, also adopted in 1982, gave constitutional protection to the concept of significant demand. However, a numerical definition of significant demand is studiously avoided in the *Charter*. The same vagueness is also present in the 1988 *Official Languages Act*. The Act simply states that every federal institution has the obligation to offer services in both English and French wherever there is sufficient demand. Instead of defining this concept, the Act states that "sufficient demand" will be whatever the federal cabinet decides it ought to be.[25] It recommends that the size of any local minority population should be taken into account, but so may be "any other factors that the Governor in Council (i.e., the Cabinet) considers appropriate."[26]

With secrecy and arbitrary cabinet discretion over the extent of bilingual services now entrenched in law, it was only a matter of time before partisan and electoral consideration would cause the party in power either to overextend minority-language services, or to retrench them unjustly. As events would have it, it was the former that came to pass.

Bilingual Districts *A Mari Usque ad Mare*—The 1992 Regulations

Following the passage of the 1988 *Official Languages Act*, the earlier regulations defining areas of bilingual service became obsolete, since they had derived their authority from the now-repealed 1969 Act. The Canadian legislative system is not always known for its speediness, and new regulations on service regions were not issued until 1992.

The new regulations extend bilingual services to every major city in Canada and to most smaller centres as well. This is due to the government's rejection of Trudeau's 1982 bilingual service areas.

A policy so clearly favourable to greater numbers of English-speakers than French-speakers (it extended federal services to more than twice as many Anglo-Quebecers as francophone residents of other provinces) would have been wildly unpopular with francophone leaders and the French-language media, had its existence not been kept secret. This meant that the district boundaries created in 1982 could not have survived a public debate on the size and location of districts such as the one that followed the passage of the new *Official Languages Act*. It was therefore politically necessary to wipe the slate clean, and thus open the way for new ideas.

One of the first new ideas was an odd proposal known as *potential demand*, which originated in a confidential document produced in 1987 by the Treasury Board (while the new *Official Languages Act* was still working its way through parliamentary committee). The document proposed that minority-language services be extended to certain areas of the country where there was no meaningful demand for such services, on the theory that the insistent "active offer" of services in the language of the local official-language minority would create its own demand. The proposal called for bilingual services to be offered in regions "where significant demand does *not* exist, but where there is a *potential* for it to develop. . . . . These provisions are intended to stimulate demand. . . ."[27] Bilingual services, it suggested, could be offered by federal institutions in these parts of Canada for a three-year period to see if the repeated "active offer" of minority-language services would generate the demand that could exist if every person with the minority mother tongue chose to reactivate their native language when using government services.

As a definition of areas of potential demand, the Treasury Board proposed extending federal services in its reach to areas with minority populations far smaller than had ever previously been considered: any census metropolitan area (i.e., a city with over 100,000 persons) in which 5,000 persons or more spoke the minority language, or any smaller city or rural district in which the minority represented 500 or more individuals.[28]

Over the next few years, the Treasury Board expanded and developed the concept of potential demand. In 1991, it circulated a document to all members of parliament showing which areas of the country would be offered bilingual services.[29] In addition to the other categories, services were now to be extended to any municipality in Canada with an official-language minority of five percent or more, with no numerical minimum on the number of individuals being served. This means that in some small townships with populations around 100, bilingual services would automatically have been mandated in order to serve the needs of minorities of less than half a dozen individuals.

When regulations on services to the public were finally issued on January 1, 1992, the *potential demand* idea had been dropped.[30] Nonetheless, since 1992 Canada's *de facto* bilingual districts have covered most of the country's populated areas and contain over sixty percent of the national population. Every one of the country's major metropolitan areas is designated as a bilingual area, even though the percentage of the local population speaking the minority language is frequently as low as one or two percent. Metropolitan Toronto is designated to receive French-language services because of a francophone population that represents only half of one percent. So is Quebec City, where anglophones represent only 1.6 percent of the population.[31] In total, all twenty-five of Canada's urban centres are affected, as are 441 other municipalities.[32] In these regions, 2,155 government offices and service outlets have been designated bilingual.[33]

SYMPTOMS OF A SYSTEM IN CHAOS

In carrying out its impossible mandate of coast-to-coast services, the present regime imposes two types of burden upon majority populations. The first is the closure of many federal civil service jobs to members of the majority community, because only bilingual individuals can be expected to work in an English environment and serve French customers, or vice versa. The second is a high dollar cost, which translates into higher taxes. An estimate of the total annual cost of second-language federal government services (which is explored in more detail in Chapter Twelve), places this figure at over $150 million each year.

These are the fundamental problems, but there are spin-off difficulties as well. There is, for example, the impossible nature of the federal goal of providing a meaningful level of French-language services in every major urban centre in English Canada. Thus far, the promise to provide high-quality services throughout the country has been completely hollow.

There is also the question of whether or not there is any genuine level of interest among minorities in these services. In at least in some of the more remote regions, such as metropolitan Toronto, a high level of interest in such services simply does not exist.

Finally, there is the impact of the imperative to provide services in both official languages on the quality of service that the affected institutions are able to offer to the public as a whole. A brief look at the federal court system shows that the effect can, in some cases at least, be seriously negative.

Brother, Can You Spare a Job?

> People do not have a God-given right to work in the Public Service. They have the possibility of doing so, but the purpose of the Public Service is to provide services to a *clientèle*. And if according to this country's Charter of Rights and Freedoms, that *clientèle* is entitled to receive services in the language of its choice, in English or French, our two official languages, will that right be paramount or will it be outweighed by the promotion of an employee who, all things considered, does not have to work in the Public Service and could find a job elsewhere?
>
> —*Raymond Garneau, MP (1988)*[34]

Whenever minority-language services are extended to a new region of the country, that region experiences a decrease in the number of local public service jobs open to unilingual members of the majority. If you speak only French in Quebec, or only English outside Quebec, you will not be eligible for a wide variety of government posts in areas that are designated bilingual.

There is a significant difference between the cost in jobs and the cost in dollars caused by minority services. The burden of the dollar cost falls on all taxpayers, whether they are part of the minority or the majority. While it is true that members of the country's two majority communities pay the lion's share and that the minorities reap all the benefit, there is at least some small measure of common ground between all Canadians.

The same cannot be said for the conflict over jobs. The level of bilingualism among francophones outside Quebec is high (around 84.7 percent), whereas among anglophones in these provinces it is very low (around 6.3 percent).[35] Naturally, when jobs open up that require fluency in both official languages, members of the minority language group become ideally suited for the positions.[36] The federally-funded advocacy groups that lobby for the maximum extension of government bilingual services are keenly aware of this. Thus, for example, the *Fédération des francophones hors Québec* reported in 1991:

> The federal government is there, ready to up the ante, to establish the official languages coast to coast. The federal public service [has] opened its creaky doors to *le fait français*. Who, outside of Quebec, can fill bilingual positions? Why, the Francophones, of course![37]

To some degree, this conflict of interest between members of majorities and minorities is unavoidable. As former Liberal MP Raymond Garneau observes, the purpose of the public service is to serve the public, and services cannot be provided by individuals who are incapable of communicating with their clients. But there must be a balance between the cost to the community that is shut out from employment and the community that gains not only from the services themselves but from the opening of new public service job opportunities to which they are uniquely well-suited.

A Boy and His Dog

> The backbenchers ... fear that "significant demand could be downsized to mean one constituent and [his] dog."
> —*Alberta Report (1988)*[38]

The complete loss of the balance between costs and benefits can be demonstrated by looking at what happens in each of the dozens of small communities with minority populations of less than 500, where bilingual services have been extended as a result of the 1992 regulations. Many of these towns, such as Vawn in Saskatchewan (with a population of sixty-five), are too small to receive more than minimal federal services, but each of them at least has a post office, or is served by a post office in a neighbouring town.

In each case, the local post office must have three bilingual staffers. Representatives of Canada Post Corporation have testified before a committee of Parliament that providing full-time bilingual counter service at a single post office requires the presence of three bilingual clerks—one to fill the post on a regular basis, a second to fill in during lunch hours and coffee breaks, and a third to fill in when either of the first two clerks is on vacation.

The management of Canada Post is prohibited by its collective agreement with the Canadian Union of Postal Workers from choosing which unionized worker will serve the public at each office. Therefore, every time a post office is declared bilingual, it must send three employees on a six-month language training course. This costs tens of thousands of dollars in wages, plus teaching costs, for every single post office wicket so designated.[39] And the practical benefits of this expense remain dubious, since nobody can become genuinely bilingual in six months, as Canada Post chairman Sylvain Cloutier ruefully observed before Parliament's Standing Committee on Official Languages.[40]

In the most extreme cases, it is possible to have more people serving the minority than there are customers for this service. Vawn, Saskatchewan is guaranteed bilingual post office service because mother tongue tables in the 1986 census report that it has a francophone population of twenty. The total population of this tiny municipality is only sixty-five, which means that the twenty francophones represent more than thirty percent of the local population, qualifying Vawn for automatic bilingual designation.[41]

This means that Vawn, like any other 'bilingual' area, must be assigned three bilingual post office employees. A twenty-to-three ratio among service recipients and service providers is silly enough, but it is possible the situation is even worse than this. The francophone population of Vawn is quite possibly lower than twenty, and is recorded as twenty because mother tongue statistics have been used rather than the more meaningful home language measure. Unfortunately, accurate home-language data is not available for small towns like Vawn, because only one census form in five contains a question on the language spoken most often in the home (the question on mother tongue is included in every census form). However, in Saskatchewan as a whole, only three out of ten persons of French mother tongue continue to speak French at home.[42] If this pattern holds true for Vawn, then there could conceivably be only a single francophone family in the town who almost certainly use English in all their interactions with the outside world.

The Law of Language in the Language of Law

It is difficult at first grasp to understand the extent to which regulations such as the ones created by the 1988 *Official Languages Act* can create new and unnecessary expenses for the government, and odious (or career-ending) new obligations for the employees of the affected institutions. The extent to which the benefits newly bestowed on the minorities are facile and unimportant is also hard to see. To illustrate both the expense and the utility of these new regulations, it is worth reviewing in detail one of the many dozens of federal institutions affected by these regulatory changes.

Revisions to the regulations governing Canada's federal courts have taken the right of the accused to address Canadian courts in the language of his or her choice and transformed it into the right to dictate the language of all court proceedings. This in turn has evolved into the preposterous requirement that each one of Canada's courts must be fully equipped and staffed to provide bilingual trials at any time. This rule applies uniformly in all parts of the country, including regions as solidly and unilingually English as Newfoundland and as solidly French as Quebec's Lac St-Jean region.

Sometimes it happens that the defendant or the plaintiff in a given court case will be a member of the linguistic minority in the region where a court proceeding is being held. In recognition of the fact that this circumstance might make it difficult to obtain a fair trial, the *Canadian Bill of Rights*, enacted in 1960 by the Diefenbaker government, instructed that no Act of Parliament should be interpreted so as to:

> ...deprive a person of the right to the assistance of an interpreter in any proceedings in which he is involved or in which he is a party or witness, before a court, commission, board or other tribunal, if he does not understand or speak the language in which such proceedings are conducted.[43]

This right was confirmed in the 1969 *Official Languages Act*.[44] An amendment to the *Criminal Code* in 1978 strengthened the right, and in 1982 the right to use either French or English before the courts was entrenched in the constitution. Section 19(1) of 1982's *Charter of Rights and Freedoms* guarantees that "Either English or French may be used by any person in, or in any pleading in or process issuing from, any court established by Parliament."

Section 19(1) was interpreted narrowly in a 1986 case titled *Société des Acadiens du Nouveau-Brunswick v. Association of Parents for Fairness in Education*. The Supreme Court ruled that court officers did not have to be bilingual in order for federal courts to be bilingual, as long as a translator was present whenever requested by a party to the court proceedings.[45]

This ruling deprived the minorities of no meaningful rights. Under the Criminal Code, all defendants in all criminal proceedings were already guaranteed the right to a trial in their own language (including a bilingual judge, jury, counsel and court reporter), anywhere in Canada.[46] Rights concerning all other legal proceedings in Canadian courts remained solidly protected by the strong existing guarantees of simultaneous translation. As well, in Ontario, Quebec and New Brunswick, the only three provinces with sizable minority populations, almost all civil proceedings were already available in either language.[47]

Nonetheless, a perception had developed among some members of minority communities that they had lost an important aspect of the guaranteed right to trial proceedings in fully bilingual courts. The argument was made, with much sound and fury, that the 1986 ruling represented a step backwards. There was a minor uproar among the leadership of several minority-rights advocacy groups. New Brunswick legal scholar and royal commissioner Michel Bastarache, for example, demanded rhetorically, "Are the language rights of a taxpayer when purchasing a stamp to be regarded as greater than that of a litigant to defend himself in Court?"[48]

In truth, all that had been lost was a measure of convenience. Both French-language and English-language criminal proceedings continued to be available everywhere, but the extra effort involved in assembling a complete set of fully bilingual court officers in some regions of the country could add months to a trial. In one second-degree murder case tried in French in British Columbia, for example, the trial took four months longer than it would have otherwise, because the deputy sheriff "had to pore over subscription lists of French-language newspapers and magazines to find prospective jurors," and because a court reporter had to be flown in from Quebec City.[49]

Nonetheless, with an election approaching, the Mulroney government must have felt that it could not afford to risk the ire of minority-rights activists. It agreed to include the right to a fully bilingual trial in the new *Official Languages Act* then being debated in the House of Commons. The resulting text of Section 16 (1) of the 1988 *Official Languages Act* reads, in part:

Every federal court, other than the Supreme Court of Canada, has the duty to ensure that ... if both English and French are the languages chosen by the parties for proceedings conducted before it in any particular case, every judge or other officer who hears these proceedings is able to understand both languages without the assistance of an interpreter.

In the future, therefore, every federal court will be obliged to have at least one judge, one reporter, etc. on its staff who is fluently bilingual.[50]

Since most judges currently on the bench are not bilingual, and there is a shortage of other court officials who can speak and write in both languages, Canada's entire court system has been left in a sustained state of technical violation of the law, which has resulted in some mistrials being declared as a result of the lengthy delays involved in piecing together trials that can be considered bilingual under the tough new definition. In one Manitoba case, *Regina v. Allain*, the accused was granted a stay of proceedings which effectively freed him when a one-year trial delay was found to violate his constitutional right to a speedy trial. In an Ontario case, *Regina v. Belleau*, the accused was summarily acquitted because the indictment had been written in English only. Defences of minority-language individuals on technical grounds such as these are now becoming commonplace.[51]

To correct the problem, it will be necessary to place lawyers with a comprehension of both official languages at a comparative advantage in appointments to the bench. For the sake of extending a right that is of microscopic importance west of Ontario and east of New Brunswick (where it had already existed prior to 1988), the *Official Languages Act* has placed a permanent impediment in the way of the majority of Canadian lawyers (including, one has to assume, the majority of good candidates) who might otherwise serve as federal judges. Aside from the obvious discrimination inherent in this new rule, it is unlikely that the legislated need to make many future appointments to the bench from an artificially small pool of bilingual lawyers will improve the quality of Canadian judicial decisions.

Unrequited Love, Coast to Coast

Despite the extraordinary sensitivity that federal policy has shown to all the needs, real and perceived, of Canada's official-language minorities, it is doubtful that they do all that much good for many of their intended beneficiaries in those parts of the country where the minority populations are marginal. It is simply not possible for government measures alone to make it possible to adequately conduct one's life in English in Quebec, once one wanders from the anglophone enclave of west end Montreal, or French in the Yukon. As Charles Castonguay, the University of Ottawa mathematician who has become a mordant commentator on Official Bilingualism, has observed:

The average Canadian spends only a few hours each year with federal service providers, so the possibility of using his preferred official language [in transaction with the government] doesn't weigh too heavily in the ensemble of his linguistic activities.[52]

Once a local minority population has acclimatized itself to its unilingual surroundings, it takes a lot of federal prodding to get even a glimmer of interest in using the ancestral language. In British Columbia, only thirty-four percent of francophones bother to make the effort to use French when using federal government services.[53] This is simply a reflection of the fact that most members of Canada's official-language minorities are, by necessity, already bilingual. Only in the border regions of Ontario and New Brunswick and in west end Montreal are there meaningful numbers of unilingual adults. In the rest of the country, unilingual members of the minority-language community are so rare that there would not be enough of them to populate a good-sized town or fill a stadium.

Broken English

> Important: Under no circumstances should you directly or indirectly suggest to clients that they speak your language or oblige them to do so, even if it is quite obvious that they are bilingual.
>
> —*"Good Morning . . . Bonjour"*
> *(a behaviour manual for public servants)*[54]

The federal government goes to extraordinary lengths to service all minority-community members of this microscopic unilingual population. A manual circulated to receptionists and other public servants in bilingual posts warns them that in some regions of the country, members of minority communities have lost the habit of conversing with government officials in their mother tongue. Therefore, it advises, public servants must greet each member of the public in both languages (thus the title of the manual—"Good Morning . . . Bonjour") and continue the conversation in whatever language they think is the citizen's mother tongue, even if the person has switched to the language of the local majority.

"Often," the manual explains, "clients will act this way [switching to the majority language] because they think it is easier for you to communicate in your first official language. . . ." It is therefore the public servant's responsibility to prove his or her ability. However, in a concession to the reality that some minority members prefer to speak accented English than to be served in incomprehensible French, the manual adds that if all else fails and "it becomes obvious that they prefer to use the [majority] language, do not insist. *You* are at *their* service."[55]

The epidemic of broken Public Service French causes francophones in

English Canada, understandably, to throw up their hands in despair. In an effort to improve the quality of second-language service, the federal government has initiated programs to boost the fluency of employees assigned to bilingual posts. The most obvious way to do this is to have them converse in the minority language, but this is no easy task in places like Vancouver, where it is the francophone minority, not anglophone public servants, who get ample opportunity to hone their second-language skills. As such, some of the government's language proficiency exercises have the scent of desperate measures. In one bizarre effort, twenty-six English-speaking but ostensibly bilingual Revenue Canada employees in Vancouver were given one-hour of paid time each week to speak to each other in ungrammatical French, in the hopes that this would somehow improve their skills.[56]

Lost in Toronto: Linguistic Experiments in the Real World

The federal government has promised to deliver far more than it is genuinely capable of providing. Examples of this failure are everywhere, raising the question why the promise was made in the first place. One amusing example of how easily the system can break down took place when a francophone from Montreal decided to make an informal test of the federal promise to provide bilingual services to the public at airports, railways stations and ferry terminals across Canada. Afterwards, he gave a report of his adventure to Mordecai Richler, who immediately recounted the story in an article published in the *The Atlantic*:

> A Montreal friend of mine, though thoroughly bilingual, testily attempted to book a flight in French at the Toronto airport. But absolutely nobody at the Air Canada desk could speak the language. Finally, the help of a Dutch immigrant porter was enlisted and my friend was led onto the airplane grasping a form that declared the following disability: SPEAKS FRENCH ONLY.[57]

The federal government is certainly capable of dictating that services will be provided in both official languages, but actually making these services available on a practical basis is much more difficult. Regulations issued in 1992 to define the areas where sufficient demand exists to offer minority-language services specify that in large urban areas like Quebec City, Calgary or Toronto, federal services will be offered "at a proportion of offices or facilities that is at least equal to the proportion of [the minority] population in the [metropolitan area] to the total population. . . ."[58] This means that since French is the mother tongue of 1.7 percent of Torontonians, 1.7 percent of all federal offices of each federal department and agency in the city must provide services in French as well as English. (The number of offices must always be rounded upwards, so if any federal agency has only a single outlet serving Toronto, that outlet must provide service in both official languages even though this means that the service is being offered at 100 percent of federal offices in the city.) In short, the services will be brought directly to the minorities. On paper, at least, Toronto is equipped with sufficient federal services to support a thriving francophone enclave.

Like Richler's friend, I conducted an experiment for this book to determine whether the federal government's elaborate efforts to provide French-language services in English Canada's cities would make it possible for a francophone moving to Toronto to interact with federal agencies exclusively in French. I decided to use the postal service as my guinea pig, since the post office is the federal agency most frequently contacted by the public and the one with the largest number of service outlets in any city or town. There are about 600 postal outlets in metropolitan Toronto, meaning that bilingual counter service is legally mandated at ten of these locations.[59]

To carry out this experiment, my research assistant, who is bilingual, contacted Canada Post claiming that her unilingual French-speaking father would be moving to Toronto, where he would want to use his own language to buy postage stamps. The obstacles she faced in trying to determine which of the city's postal outlets offer services in French give some idea of the obstacles that would face a genuinely unilingual French-speaking Torontonian attempting to exercise his or her rights.

On November 23, 1992, an initial request for information on the locations of postal outlets offering French services was placed by telephone to the public services branch of Canada Post's national headquarters. My assistant was promised that she would be contacted shortly with information on the locations of all bilingual outlets.

After waiting a week and receiving no response, she telephoned again. This time she was given a toll-free Toronto number to call. During the next week, she called the Toronto number at least two times each day and sometimes more, but found that it was always busy. Finally, she called Ottawa again and was given a local number for the same office in Toronto. Unlike the toll-free number, this one was not busy, but the person on the other end did not have the necessary information, and could only give her a second Toronto telephone number to call.

At the second number she was informed that while information on the bilingual post offices was not available, it would be possible to obtain service at any postal outlet in Canada by approaching the service desk and requesting, in French, that the outlet call Canada Post's head office for translation services by telephone.

Unconvinced, she called Head Office once again and asked for an address to which a written request for the locations could be directed. She mailed her request to this address on December 23—fully a month after beginning her search—and received a written reply on February 1, 1993.

The whole process had taken nearly seventy days and consumed considerably more time than the average person would be willing to devote to the effort. Because I have to pay my assistant for the time she spends on these efforts, cost considerations have precluded any similar experiments for the fifty-one other federal departments and agencies that claim to offer the French-language services in Toronto.[60]

THE SOLUTION: TERRITORIAL BILINGUALISM ON THE FINLAND MODEL

Every multilingual country that does not offer services in all its official languages over the entire extent of its territory has rejected, in practice, the administrative principle of personality. On the other hand, the administrative principle of territoriality has been rejected, in practice, by every country that does not systematically deny all minority language rights to its citizens, whenever they stray from the province, state or canton in which they form the majority. Once an in-between position has been decided upon, the only question becomes which point on the spectrum of intermediate choices should be chosen. This means that, for practical purposes, the question becomes one of defining the size and shape of bilingual service areas. This may be done openly or, as in Canada, in secret.

Canada's current position clearly leans far too much to the 'personality' end of the spectrum. But how far should Canada swing the other way? And how can such a move be made politically feasible?

Returning to First Principles

In making all future decisions on where to provide or not provide bilingual services, the federal government should attempt to build principled solutions that focus entirely upon the problem of counterbalancing the justifiable expectations of the majorities with those of the linguistic minorities. This would entail abandoning the traditional post-1969 practice of using bilingual districts to achieve additional goals. These goals have ranged from Trudeau's dream of building a new culture to the ongoing federal government obsession with building national unity on the back of every aspect of language policy, to the asymmetrists' view that language districts should be designed to boost the fortunes of one official language at the expense of the other. None of them should have a place in federal policy on service to the public.

The temptation to start fiddling with the borders of districts for the sake of ulterior motives has in the past been too much for our politicians to resist, but there is reason to hope that circumstances have changed. For one thing, there is now twenty years' worth of evidence that simply providing minority-language services is not enough to halt the forces of assimilation in their tracks, or to redirect them in some new way.

Since minority-language services cannot alter the dynamics of assimilation and population movement, their only logical purpose must be to provide aid and comfort to minority-language individuals in the carrying-out of their daily lives. This is a modest goal, and one far less likely to cause contention than the grandiose visions with which Canada's politicians have thus far been armed.

Bilingual Districts on the Finnish Model: What's Involved

The Finnish model, advocated by the B&B Commission a quarter of a century ago, provides a perfect mechanism for achieving this modest and inoffensive goal. If it were applied to Canada using some practical modifications outlined in the following paragraphs, the Finnish system would have the impact of limiting federal French-language services outside Quebec to *four* regions: northern New Brunswick; eastern Ontario; northern Ontario; and some rural townships in Nova Scotia. Similarly, English-language services within Quebec would be restricted to west-end Montreal Pontiac County, and a portion of the Eastern Townships.

The first aspect of making the Finnish system work in Canada would be to do away with the secrecy that is involved in the present process of defining bilingual districts. In Canada, as in Finland, there must be no room for politicians or bureaucrats to manipulate the borders of bilingual districts, or to control them in any other way. The formula by which regions are designated bilingual would have to be open and simple, unlike the current formula, which is thirteen pages long in each official language.[61]

Since the process of deciding which area is to become a district is essentially a numbers game, the percentage of the population that must belong to the minority community in order for a district to qualify as bilingual would have to be set, openly, in the text of the law, as opposed to being decided by the cabinet after the law is passed.

A strong case can be made for the Finnish precedent to be followed precisely, with ten percent serving as the base figure. A simple amendment to the existing *Official Languages Act* would be sufficient to replace the present meaningless phase "where numbers warrant" with a simple formula based on the ten-percent principle. If the Finnish model were followed exactly, districts would be established in all municipalities with linguistic minorities of over ten percent, as recorded in the previous decennial census. New districts would be created following future censuses in additional municipalities if a minority population previously below ten percent rises to above that level. As well, municipalities previously accorded bilingual district status would have this status revoked whenever the minority population falls below ten percent.

As in Finland, it would probably be an advantage if the model were to allow for a minimum of leeway in either direction. Finnish communes not designated as bilingual in the previous census are not accorded bilingual status until their minority-language population reaches twelve percent of the local population. By contrast, existing districts do not have their status removed until their minority-language population drops to eight percent. Nonetheless, ten percent remains the benchmark.

Adapted to the Canadian situation, this model presents some minor problems. Most notably, our municipalities vary wildly in size and population. All three prairie provinces have many tiny municipalities of only one or two hundred people, in which a minority of perhaps a dozen have French as their home language. Under the legislation in place in Finland, this would require the establishment of many tiny bilingual enclaves, often in townships where no federal services are offered. The choice in this situation would then be between providing federal services in both English and French to all the surrounding townships as well as the one that is bilingual, or else ignoring the fact that a bilingual district exists.

A more practical solution to this situation would be to have a minimum size limit on districts. A reasonable argument could be made that if the minority-language population in the municipality in question is less than some arbitrary number, and if the municipality does not form a single continuous area with other municipalities with a total minority-language population that surpasses this arbitrary number, then the township should not be eligible for bilingual status, even if the ten-percent criterion is met. It is hard to believe that a small, isolated minority in such a situation would survive assimilation for very long anyway, regardless of the federal services provided for its benefit.

Making Reform Politically Feasible

To be politically feasible, the adoption of openly-defined bilingual districts based on the Finnish model would have to be acceptable both to the majority French-language population inside Quebec and to the English-speaking majority outside Quebec. In practice, it would be necessary to prove to Québécois nationalists that English would take a step backward in their province, and demonstrate to anglophones outside the province that French would no longer be 'shoved down their throats.' Given the starting-point of today's overextended bilingual service area boundaries, this should be relatively easy.

A few additional alterations, which are improvements in their own right, could be made which would also have the effect of further solidifying the political support for a Finland-based system.

First, the peculiar practice of designating entire metropolitan areas bilingual could be ended under the new rules. As things currently stand, the entire territory of the metropolitan areas of Winnipeg, Ottawa-Hull and Montreal are designated bilingual in order to service linguistic minorities that are highly concentrated in individual parts of these cities. Yet very large sections of each of these cities are completely unilingual in the language of the provincial majority. In the case of Ottawa-Hull, the bilingual district encompasses the entire National Capital Region, which covers 1,050 square miles on the Ontario side of the Ottawa River and 750 square miles in Quebec—a total area nearly as large as Prince Edward Island. In the case of Montreal, the bilingual district is 1,350 square miles, and recently grew by twenty-five percent for no other reason than that Statistics Canada had arbitrarily adjusted its definition of the boundaries of the Montreal Census Metropolitan Area.[62]

Logically, only the parts of each city in which the minority is concentrated should be guaranteed services in the minority's language. The effect of this refinement would be particularly striking in Montreal, where it would no longer be necessary to provide post office service in the homogeneous francophone neighbourhoods in the eastern half of the city. This would help reduce the fears of English encroachment in these key centres of nationalist militancy, so it would have a beneficial effect from the point of view of national unity. Services in English in Montreal could, and should, be limited to government offices serving census tracts in which ten percent or more of the local population had indicated on the latest census that it would prefer to receive services in English.

As an additional guarantee of the security of the majority languages, and in particular of the French language in Quebec, bilingual service regions could be permanently restricted to the geographical areas they occupied at the time of the first census taken under the Finland system. In other words, a downward ratchet would be set permanently in place. Towns or census tracts could be stricken from the list of bilingual areas and made unilingual should the minority-language population drop below eight percent of the total, but no new territory would be added, even if in some future census the minority-language population rose to above twelve percent. This, of course, is the precise opposite of the ratchet set in place in 1969, which was intended to spread out and eventually envelop the nation. It would provide a sense of security to Quebec francophones who fear the gradual geographic spread of English across their province, and would do much to ease the way for the adoption of openly-designated bilingual areas.

The other side of this equation, of course, is that whenever a numerically large minority-language population (say, over 5,000 individuals), living together in a closely-defined community, forms a minority of less than ten percent of the population of a large urban centre, then bilingual services should be provided within that part of the city, regardless of the failure of the minority to meet the usual municipality-by-municipality ten-percent test.

The 5,000-individual criterion is borrowed from the Federation of Canadian Municipalities, which advocates its use for the purposes of municipally-provided services.[63] It would apply to a very small number of cities—Winnipeg, and some of the individual municipalities within the metropolitan Montreal

Figure 6.2
Bilingual Service Areas in Canada, 1992.

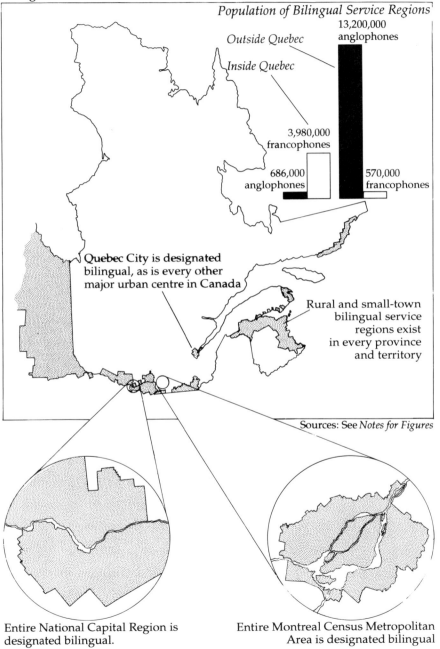

Entire National Capital Region is designated bilingual.

Entire Montreal Census Metropolitan Area is designated bilingual

Figure 6.3
Bilingual Service Areas in Canada (Proposal)

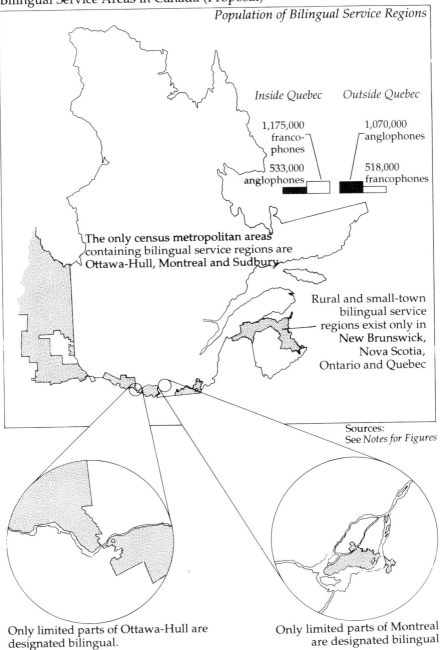

area. It would not apply to Toronto or Vancouver, despite the large numbers of French-speaking immigrants to these cities, because the francophone populations in these metropolitan areas are not sufficiently concentrated. There is no census tract in Toronto, for example, in which the percentage of the population speaking French at home exceeds five percent. Nor would it apply to the dispersed English-speaking minority of Quebec City, which is similarly lacking in a strong neighbourhood base. Even in the cities where it did apply, it would not create a large number of bilingual civil service positions, and therefore would not substantially limit the job opportunities for members of the unilingual majority.

A final, very important innovation would be to base all measures on home language figures rather than on the mother tongue figures that are currently used in delineating minority-language service areas. Mother tongue figures are a reflection of history, not of current reality. It makes no sense to provide minority-language services to individuals who are no longer committed to using that language in their personal lives. Richard Joy has gone further and suggested that the census should actually include a question asking each individual to list his or her preferred language,[64] but since such a question does not yet exist, home language is the most logical existing basis for the delineation of service areas.

The formula I have proposed is, by necessity, entirely arbitrary. A perfectly good case could probably be presented in favour of setting the threshold percentage for the creation of bilingual districts at fifteen or twenty percent rather than at ten, or for adjusting the minimum population requirements. It must be observed, however, that as long as Sections 16-23 of the *Charter of Rights* remain in effect, the terms under which bilingual districts are legislated will have to remain relatively generous, or the legislation will be rejected by the courts as unconstitutional.

This proposal would probably meet with at least the tacit approval of the Quebec government. Despite the frosty reception given by the Bourassa government to the bilingual districts proposals of the first Bilingual Districts Advisory Board, which sought to create a single vast bilingual district in the province, Quebec politicians have always been willing to listen to reasonable proposals for bilingual service regions. In 1972, a provincial royal commission proposed that Quebec should emulate Finland by forcing all municipalities in which anglophones represented more than ten percent of the population to publish all official documents in English.[65] A 1984 amendment to Bill 101, enacted by René Lévesque's government, created bilingual districts for the purposes of municipal government services in all cities and towns where anglophones represent half or more of the municipal population. While fifty percent is far from generous, a precedent had been set: even separatist governments were willing to recognize the validity of the bilingual districts concept. In 1986, Bourassa once again investigated the possibility of creating bilingual districts for the purposes of extending broader rights to erect English-language signs.[66] He was rebuffed by the minority-rights group, Alliance Quebec, but another precedent had been set. On this evidence it is clear that there is no longer any need to hide the fact that Canada has bilingual districts within Quebec, for fear of rocking the political boat.

SUMMARY

In spite of a determined effort to offer bilingual services to everyone in Canada, the federal government never set out to determine if such a policy was at all wise, or practical, or even possible.

It is none of these. The current regime of universal bilingual services is impossible to deliver and pay for; it outrages local majorities, lends imaginary and mostly fictitious support to minorities too small to make any practical use of the extra government attention or often even to want it, and is implemented secretly, making everyone suspicious of the motives behind it all.

The whole notion of making government services a pillar of national unity is misguided. The link between national unity and the quality of French-language service at government offices in Halifax is probably not as intimate as some of our politicians and bureaucrats are inclined to imagine. Meanwhile, the problems that near-universal bilingual services have created are difficult to ignore.

One reason for the confusion is that the public lacks the information to make an intelligent analysis of the costs of services and of the number of people who are benefitting from them. The federal government could compile and release this information, but it has a vested interest in not doing so, since costs are high and benefits extend to a very limited clientele. As long as the public lacks hard evidence to back any estimated cost of minority-language services, those who speak out against the extension of services can be dismissed with a wave of the hand as malcontents or bigots.

The solution to the mess lies in a version of the never-implemented recommendation of the Royal Commission on Bilingualism and Biculturalism to institute bilingual service areas. The solution to non-intrusively offering bilingual services in Canada is to create a few bilingual districts in those parts of the country where the official language minorities live in sufficient concentrations to significantly benefit from services in their own tongue. If bilingual districts were implemented in Canada, bilingual services would be delivered in a cost-effective and honest manner, where they are actually needed. Equally importantly, this system would silence disgruntled local majorities. This matters not only because majorities have rights too, but also because it is the majorities, in the end, who will decide whether or not Canada remains united. It is in our interests to treat them well.

CHAPTER SEVEN

Passing the Buck: Legislating Language Use in the Private Sector

The state has no place in the bedrooms of the nation.
—*Pierre Trudeau (1967)*[1]

SINCE 1967, the State has recognized that it has a duty to keep out of the bedrooms of the nation, but today federal language laws extend to the content label on every pillow-case and mattress in Canada, to say nothing of prophylactic wrappers.

The federal government has shifted much of the burden of creating a bilingual society in Canada onto the shoulders of private citizens, through a series of regulations mandating privately-owned manufacturers and service-providers to offer services to the public in each official language.

In passing regulations on language use in the private economy, government is trying to force the private sector to do what it cannot itself hope to do in a free society: to make its language policy omnipresent, even in the most personal, informal parts of society, which our traditions and our ideals have always taught us should be off-limits to the state.

For the politicians, one advantage of enforcing language policy through regulations on the private sector rather than through direct government action is that it transfers the costs of the policy to private society, often in the form of hidden boosts in consumer costs and downward nudges in purchasing power. The political advantage of this course of action is seen most dramatically in the difference between the annual language-policy budgets of Ottawa and Quebec. Ottawa's policies largely take the form of direct payments for government-provided services, language training, subsidies to minority-language advocacy groups, and transfers to provincial departments of education for minority-language education programs. The official annual budget for all of this is $653 million, and the real cost to the federal government is substantially higher. The Quebec government, by contrast, has built its entire language policy around the mandatory private use of French, whether on signs, in the workplace, or at school. Very few additional government-provided services are created under the terms of Bill 101. In consequence, the annual direct cost of the legislation to the provincial treasury is a mere $28 million, most of which consists of the operating budgets of enforcement agencies like the *Commission de protection de la langue française* and the *Office de la langue française*.[2]

The Commerce of Languages

For sheer volume and detail, no other area of language legislation beats the minutely detailed laws and regulations governing the language(s) in which Canadians carry out their private lives. Everything from country-of-origin labels, to store signs, to warehouse order forms and rubber stamps are subject to language laws. Private companies and individuals in Canada can find themselves legally obliged to advertise in French when they would prefer to do so in English (or in English when they would prefer to do so in French). One Quebec government regulation even instructs professionals to order French-language professional journals whether they want them or not.[3]

Nobody knows for certain how many laws in Canada regulate the language of private activities, and no individual can possibly come close to ploughing through all the regulations, orders-in-council, court decisions and regulatory-board rulings enacted under these laws. One gallant effort, published by Emmanuel Didier in 1987, listed thirty-nine federal laws and numerous other provincial laws, as well as several hundred legal precedents set by court rulings.[4] But even this list is far from complete.

The reason for this spectacular array of laws is the fundamental contradiction between the wrong-headed belief among Canadian bureaucrats and politicians that government can and must exercise total control over language, and the fact that Canada is not a totalitarian state in which these rules can be imposed by brute force. Since government does not directly control every aspect of private life as it does every breath and twitch issuing from the Public Service, and since it does not directly subsidize every aspect of private life in the way it funds the school system, it cannot control language use in private society the way it does in these institutions. Instead, it seeks to impose its vision through regulations that mandate certain individual actions and forbid others. These regulations are intrusive. In the language of political philosophy, they impose 'positive obligations,' since they force individuals to engage in activities they may find distasteful, humiliating, or expensive.

Ottawa has mandated strict bilingualism from sea to sea, with one eye on the pie-in-the-sky dream of a country of bilingual citizens and the other on defusing separatist ardour with another layer of indirect subsidies to the French language. The *Assembée nationale* in Quebec City, equally true to form, has mandated strict unilingualism both in areas within its jurisdiction and in a few that are *ultra vires*. In the world of private services as in the world of public services, the result in practice of Ottawa's enforced bilingualism and Quebec's enforced unilingualism has been the imposition of mutually contradictory language laws with asymmetrical costs and benefits for French- and English-speaking Canadians.

Bilingualism Before Balance Sheets

For the federal government, the challenge is to force private companies to provide bilingual services where it is unprofitable to do so. Ottawa requires that private firms falling under the jurisdiction of its regulatory agencies provide bilingual services everywhere in the country, as a condition of being permitted to continue operating.

One example of how this is done: all private contractors at federal installations must provide bilingual services whether they are needed or not. This applies mainly to airports, but also to railway stations and ferry terminals. Bilingual services must be provided at restaurants, cafeterias, car rental outlets, foreign exchange wickets, duty free shops and hotel registration counters. One regulation requires airport video games to provide bilingual instructions, lest unsuspecting francophones lose their quarters playing Pac-man at the Calgary airport.[5] Regulations this detailed seem amusingly silly, but sometimes they can really hurt.

At Fredericton's airport, the tightening of federal language regulations required the replacement of all seven unilingual waitresses at the airport restaurant and all eight staffers at the airport's car-rental booths. Fredericton is in a region of New Brunswick that is well over ninety percent English-speaking. Airport car rental agents reported at the time that there had never been any customer problems due to language.[6]

Another incident, reported by former provincial legislator Morton Shulman in the Toronto *Sun*, involved an attempt by the general manager of Toronto International Airport to force all private companies operating stores and services at the airport to provide fully bilingual services. Under pressure from a federal cabinet minister who had asked an airport vendor a question in French and received a reply in English, the general manager instructed all airport leaseholders that:

> We will seek evidence to show that the employers have made reasonable efforts to employ bilingual staff by advertising in areas with substantial Francophone populations, by offering to pay moving expenses or premium wages for bilingual capability, or offering various other economic or social benefits that would achieve the desired results.[7]

Shulman writes that he followed up on this story by calling the transportation ministry in Ottawa. This is a description of what followed:

> I could not believe that the federal government could be quite this stupid and called the department of transportation where I spoke to one Margaret Martin

who described herself as a parliamentary liaison officer. When I asked her whether she really wanted the unilingual English speaking clerks at Toronto Airport fired, she replied, 'Well, it is the law in this country that they have to be bilingual.'[8]

Ostensibly, the purpose of such regulations, insofar as they apply to airports, airlines, gas stations and so on, is to ensure that the 'travelling public' will be able to enjoy bilingual service anywhere in the country. But left in the hands of overzealous bureaucrats anxious to curry favour with their political masters, the language regulations have had a tendency to spin out of control. In 1989, the department of transportation ordered investors in a new golf course located on land leased from the Victoria, B.C. airport to provide signs, scoreboards, sales slips and promotional brochures in both French and English, and to have a translator on call whenever golfers were using the course. Transport Canada agreed to drop these demands only after the investors had approached the media with the story. Afterwards, an embarrassed official admitted to a Canadian Press reporter that the only travelling likely to take place at the golf course would occur in golf carts.[9]

Referring to the Fredericton firings, journalist Peter Brimelow notes:

> The essentially symbolic nature of Transport Canada's reform is . . . important to note. Since most Francophone New Brunswickers live in the north and east of the province, Francophones arriving in the south-central city of Fredericton must brace themselves anyway to face a largely Anglophone population, unless they propose to spend their entire visit in the airport.[10]

In other words, mandated bilingual private-sector services, just like bilingual public-sector services, are intended not so much to improve the quality of life of individual Canadians as they are to be yet another argument in favour of national unity and against Quebec separation.

Privatization vs. Institutional Bilingualism

> Bilingualism presents a serious obstacle to the privatization of the major Crown corporations, as these corporations are important vehicles for the national language policy across the country. The contributions to the national language policy of Crown corporations such as the Canadian Broadcasting Corporation, Air Canada, Petro-Canada and the Canada Post Corporation explains, at least in part, the lack of progress that has been made thus far in privatizing them.
> —*Library of Parliament Research Report (1990)*[11]

In the minds of many Canadians, imposed bilingualism at post offices and airports across the nation is a virtual metaphor for Official Bilingualism. Once privatized, federal agencies would be free to cast aside the rules that require them to offer services in both official languages. This has led to a successful effort on the part of the Commissioner of Official Languages to have the federal government pass legislation requiring privatized agencies to offer bilingual services.

In practice, this imposes substantial permanent costs of the operation on privatized crown corporations, making it difficult for them to compete effectively with their private-sector rivals.

The most obvious example of this kind of regulatory handicapping took place when Air Canada was privatized. In the mid-1980s, the Commissioner of Official Languages lobbied successfully for a special law to guarantee that the airline be required to continue complying fully with the *Official Languages Act*, despite the fact that it was no longer a government agency (the Act was designed to impose obligations only on the federal government). The result is that even as a private company, Air Canada is still obliged to offer bilingual services everywhere it flies.[12] Currently, the Commissioner is advocating that the mandate of the *Official Languages Act* be expanded to cover privatized airports.[13]

Similar pressures were placed on Petro-Canada as it was prepared for privatization. The Standing Joint Committee of the Senate and House of Commons on Official Languages expressed concern that French-language service in stations along the Trans-Canada Highway west of Winnipeg would not be provided by a privatized Petrocan, which might start putting other priorities, such as return on investment, before minority-language service.

The Joint Committee also worried that Calgary might lose its special status (for gas station purposes) as a bilingual city. Reporting on the committee's hearings, Ottawa *Citizen* columnist Marjorie Nichols wrote:

> The Petro-Canada chief raised . . . hackles [on the Joint Committee] when he said that he doubted the Crown-owned oil company would ever have a Francophone component equivalent to the country as a whole. MPs and Senators also had difficulty with Hopper's arguments against bilingual stations in Calgary, which is, after all, the head office of a Crown corporation.[14]

The requirement to continue providing services in both languages is only one aspect of the bureaucratic intrusions into Canada's privatizations. There are insistent pressures from Ottawa to engage in language-based discrimination in their hiring and firing practices. William Hopper, the Chairman of Petro-Canada, was raked over the coals by the Standing Joint Committee on Official Languages for suggesting that a privatized Petro-Canada would make "no effort in the Calgary oil patch to recruit French-speaking professionals into the industry."[15] Similarly, Air Canada was pressured by the Commissioner of Official Languages to continue to "promote the equitable participation of members of both linguistic communities in the company's administration" following privatization.[16]

Although the evidence is only circumstantial, it appears that in the process of privatization crown agencies have knuckled under to the pressure to use preferential hiring and firing techniques. Between 1979 and 1991, fully 97.8 percent of all federal government layoffs due to privatization took place among anglophone employees, despite the fact that English- and French-speakers are represented almost perfectly equitably (i.e., in about a three-to-one ratio) in Canada's crown corporations.[17]

Permanent Press

In a move designed to boost the fortunes of declining English-language local newspapers in Quebec and French-language newspapers elsewhere, it is now federal policy to require that private companies subsidize the minority press by placing unneeded and unread advertisements.

Federally-regulated private-sector companies are required to provide public information in both official languages on services they are offering or bids they are making for government contracts, whenever they conduct business in any "region of significant demand" (in other words, in any of the bilingual districts, created in 1992, that stretch from Vancouver to Halifax, including most of what lies in between). In theory, the placing of these ads helps the local official-language minority to have a fair shake at winning tenders or to learn of services available in their region without having to use the majority language.

Given the very small circulation of the minority papers, which reach only about twelve percent of readers in their own client communities,[18] it is doubtful whether these mandated ads have much practical value to their nominal beneficiaries. However, they do have a practical cost: private advertisers are forced to pay a total of $2 million each year to these newspapers.[19]

Sometimes the pressure to advertise in the minority media is made by means of subtle pressures, and sometimes by more direct means. In 1990, the Commissioner of Official Languages took Air Canada to court in an attempt to force the recently privatized airline to advertise in small French-language weekly newspapers outside Quebec. Air Canada had incurred the Commissioner's wrath by spending over a million dollars on English-language advertising in the Montreal *Gazette* and other English-language media in Quebec, but only $247,000 on French-language media outside Quebec.[20]

The attempt to force Air Canada to spend more on advertising seems to have had only a little to do with actually servicing francophones outside Quebec. The Commissioner's chief objective seems to have been to force private industry to inject advertising revenues into the minority-language weeklies, which are mostly either money-losers or only marginally profitable—a subject that had been discussed at length in his presence at a meeting of parliament's Standing Joint Committee on Official Languages not long before the case against Air Canada was launched.

That federal efforts to keep marginal local newspapers alive have been successful is best illustrated by the story of the *Chronicle-Telegraph*, Quebec City's only English-language newspaper, which is the subject of an admiring article in a 1991 issue of the Commissioner's in-house publication, *Language and Society*.

The *Chronicle-Telegraph* was once a prosperous, widely circulated newspaper which served a substantial English-speaking community. The anglophones of Quebec City have, however, long since assimilated or moved away, and the *Chronicle-Telegraph* lives on only because federal regulations classify the city as bilingual, as the *Language and Society* article explains:

> The secret to survival for Quebec City's only English newspaper is simple: hard work, and a daily flip through local newspapers to find out who is breaking the federal government's *Official Languages Act*. Calls for tender, notices of land expropriation and CRTC hearings, as well as services offered by federal departments, by law must be published in both official languages in independent media where it exists. The law applies to federal services in areas categorized as regions of significant demand. Quebec City falls into this category.[21]

A glance through a typical edition of the *Chronicle-Telegraph* reveals this to be true. Each issue of the newspaper is only eight pages long, printed on two folded sheets of newsprint. It contains no hard news; the lead story in one recent issue was about community recycling programs. The classified ads section in this issue contained only nine items, including a single personal ad and a single notice of an apartment for rent. The *Chronicle-Telegraph* is nothing more than a moribund community newspaper. Oddly out of place are the three main advertising features: two-thirds of one page is filled by an ad from Canadian National Railways for its double-stack freight containers ("the wave of the future in freight transportation"), while two calls for public tenders, including one to dredge the ship channel of the St. Lawrence, also take up considerable space.[22]

What the article in *Language and Society* neglects to mention is that Quebec City's demographics make the cost of advertising in the newspaper a complete waste of money. Despite the fact that greater Quebec City is designated as a bilingual region, only 1.4 percent of its 638,000 residents speak English at home. Only 1,700 members of Quebec City's tiny English-speaking minority—less than three-tenths of one percent of the city's total population—are incapable of conducting a conversation in French.[23]

CANADA'S CORNFLAKES CONUNDRUM: THE COST OF LABELLING LAWS

> Twenty years ago it was cornflakes boxes. Now it's sailors' manuals. Just another symbol in the endless debate.
> —*The Ottawa Citizen (1991)*[24]

The symbol of legislated bilingualism most intimately etched into the Canadian psyche is the bilingual cornflake box. It says something about the Canadian character that the impassioned rhetoric and heated debate over the issue that defines the nation has taken as its central metaphor these humble cardboard containers. Cornflake boxes and all other packaged products have been required under federal law since 1974 to be printed in both official languages.[25]

When Pierre Jeanniot, the former president of Air Canada, suggested to a parliamentary committee that some aspects of Official Bilingualism should be eased, the headline in the next day's Montreal *Gazette* screamed, "SCRAP BILINGUAL CEREALS: JEANNIOT."[26] When Ottawa *Citizen* columnist Roy MacGregor wanted to sum up what he felt was an unjust characterization of Albertans as bigots, he wrote they were being compared to Klansmen burning cereal boxes on their front lawns.

To many opponents of Official Bilingualism, the bilingual labelling requirements of 1974's *Consumer Packaging and Labelling Act* are the paradigm of enforced wastefulness. To its supporters, this opposition is a clear demonstration of a refusal to compromise. In fact, in financial terms, Canada's labelling laws are by far the most burdensome aspect of Official Bilingualism.

It is impossible to calculate with any precision the scope of that burden, since it is spread over thousands of manufacturers and importers, and ultimately over millions of consumers who must pay higher prices for products that could have been placed on store shelves at a lower cost if there were no laws regulating the language of packaging. However, it is possible to determine a conservative 'floor' cost as the minimum dollar figure which these labelling laws impose on the economy. The total cost imposed on Canadian consumers by the *Consumer Packaging and Labelling Act* is not less than $2 billion per annum.

The reason why only vague outlines of the law's cost can be drawn is that the dollar costs of bilingual labelling are inextricably tied with the costs of Canada's other labelling and packaging requirements. In Canada, all clothing items are required to bear bilingual content labels and all packaged products must be sold in bilingual jars, tins or wrappers. This is a major imposition, since it makes it difficult or impossible for overseas or American manufacturers to 'piggyback' items destined for the Canadian import market onto longer and therefore cheaper production runs destined for the much larger American market. Even Canadian exporters must separate their Canadian production runs from those intended for the American market, which reduces these manufacturers' competitiveness in the international marketplace by making it impossible for them to piggyback small initial production runs for foreign clients with their larger production runs intended for domestic consumption.

Although it is easy to see how this adds to costs, the problem is that it is difficult to separate out the cost of bilingual packaging requirements from other labelling requirements imposed by the Canadian government. Clothing labels, for example, must include a special code number, usually called a 'CA' number, identifying the producer or importer. Some other products fall into the same category. Most prepackaged foods cannot be imported because of elaborate Canadian regulations limiting the size of packaged goods permitted on Canadian shelves to a series of specifically-enumerated metric sizes (known as 'hard metric' sizes). Regulations state that peanut butter is limited to eighteen specific jar sizes, while tissues must be sold only in quantities of 50, 60, 100, 120, 150 or 200. One intrepid inspector from the Department of Consumer and Corporate Affairs reports having caught a store selling cheese slices in illegal 227-gram packages instead of the 225-gram sizes required by law. In a fit of generosity, he let the incident pass unpunished.[27]

As well, all packaged food products sold in Canada must contain ingredient lists enumerating the contents in a certain manner which is neither better nor worse, but certainly different, from the system used in the United States. Certain claims about the health benefits of products may not be made on labels intended for the Canadian market. Most important of all, in terms of effect on restricting access to the Canadian market, every food product, bar of soap, bag of charcoal briquettes, etc., must show its volume or weight exclusively in metric, to the exclusion of all other measures. Pounds, ounces, gallons and pints are strictly forbidden on Canadian labels, even if this is in addition to a metric size.

With so many factors at play, it seems unimaginable that any specific cost could be attached to the bilingual aspect of Canada's labelling requirements.

In fact, such a calculation can be made (although admittedly not with much precision). The first step in making this calculation is recognizing that some of the restrictions mentioned above can be circumvented, while others exist only because the bilingual labelling requirement already has shut off the Canadian market to all products packaged for the American market. (Once products labelled for the U.S. market have been shut out, additional labelling restrictions can be added without imposing meaningful additional costs.) The requirement for hard metric package sizes falls into the first category, while the requirements for metric labelling and for the listing of ingredients in a specific manner fall into the second category.

According to sources in the Canadian retail industry, the hard-metric size requirement may be circumvented with relative ease. If a product is produced outside Canada in a package that does not match the Canadian size requirements, it can be relabelled as containing a somewhat smaller quantity than it really does hold. This is legal because the size listing on packages is merely a statement of the *minimum* quantity contained therein. In the case of the cheese slices mentioned earlier, the producer could have complied with the law by listing his cheese as containing 225 grams, even though the true weight was 227 grams.[28] According to these same retail industry sources, because of the ease with which fictitious sizes can be listed on products sold in Canada, the hard metric size requirements add up to no more than five percent of all costs imposed on consumers by Canadian packaging and labelling laws.

Metric labelling replaced imperial measures in the 1970s at the same time as bilingual labels were being introduced. Ideologically, the metric sizing had much the same justification as the adoption of the maple leaf flag ten years earlier. It distanced Canada from its colonial past, and removed another symbol that might be considered objectionable by French Canadians. The move was bitterly opposed by the same sectors of society that had opposed the adoption of the new flag.

Given that the maple leaf flag had imposed no new costs on society, while the new labelling laws amounted to a non-tarriff trade barrier driving up the cost of many products for Canadian consumers, it is unlikely that metric labelling could have been imposed on its own without unleashing a politically deadly storm of protest had it not been coupled with bilingual labelling laws. Where only a weak national unity argument could have been made for metric labels, a strong one could be made for bilingual labels. So the cost of relabelling was imposed on the Canadian public because no politician dared to speak against a policy calculated to strengthen national unity.

In short, then, virtually the entire dollar cost of Canadian packaging and labelling laws can be traced back to the bilingualism requirement.

Debbie Doesn't Do Canada

Although it is now clear that the lion's share of the economic burden imposed by the *Consumer Packaging and Labelling Act* is the consequence of the law's bilingual labelling requirement, establishing the total cost of the law is still difficult. The problem is that there is no sure way to tell which products would drop in price, and by how much, if the bilingual labelling requirement was removed.

A few broad rules can, however, be sketched out. Clothing and textile prices would be affected only minimally, because labelling is almost an afterthought in these businesses. Automobile prices would also probably not be greatly affected, although there have been cases of cars that have not been imported into Canada due to the labelling laws.[29] The biggest costs are borne by packaged goods, which includes all tinned and boxed products and anything packaged in plastic. The costs are least significant on high-priced products where the price of packaging is a small component of the total unit value, and most oppressive on low-priced products like chocolate bars where packaging is a substantial percentage of the total cost.

One buyer of food products for a grocery chain gave me the example of individually-wrapped chocolate-covered angel food cakes. In Canada, these are sold under the brand names 'Jos Louis' and 'Wagon Wheels.' He could have purchased an American-made equivalent called 'Little Debbies' at half the price of the Canadian cakes, but only if he joined a long production run. Doing a special short run for the Canadian market in bilingual packaging would have effectively doubled the price. This price leap ended the business deal, and Little Debbies never did make it to the Canadian market. But this experience demonstrates that at least in this one product category, the impact of the *Consumer Packaging and Labelling Act* is a doubling of prices.

Asked for a conservative estimate of the number of products that are raised in price due to the bilingual labelling requirement, the same buyer estimated that at least twenty-five percent of the products he carries would drop in price if the requirements were repealed. He stressed that the percentage might be much higher, because "some American suppliers are scared to do business with Canada thanks to all the crazy rules, and they won't even talk to me at trade shows down in the States."

Assuming that the average cost savings on this twenty-five percent of packaged foods was a modest twenty percent (or less than half the cost savings that would be attained on Little Debbies), this would amount to a savings of five percent on all packaged foods sold in Canada. Total sales of packaged foods nationwide in 1992 were $30 billion. This means that in food products alone, bilingual labelling laws cost Canadian consumers a minimum of $1.5 billion each year.

Similar costs are added to cleaning products, toiletries, motor oil, and every other product category that is purchased by Canadians in packaged form. In these broad categories, total retail sales in 1992 were $20 billion. Assuming an average added cost factor of only ten percent (in recognition of the fact that per unit prices are generally higher than they are for packaged foods), and again assuming conservatively that only one-quarter of all products would see a price decline, the average savings to Canadian consumers for products in these categories would be $500 million.

The total of these two amounts is $2 billion. It should be stressed that this is a bare-bones minimum. It may well be that bilingual labelling costs Canadians far more than this amount. It certainly does not cost them less.

Mr. Pearson Doesn't Go to Washington

Of course many Canadians disregard the packaging laws and drive across the border to buy their unilingually-labelled groceries in the United States. This would seem to include a sizable number of the francophones who are the intended beneficiaries of bilingual labels. Large malls in Plattsburgh, New York and Burlington, Vermont were constructed specifically to cater to the Montreal-based cross-border trade.

The *Consumer Packaging and Labelling Act* receives little public criticism because its costs are so obscure and its burden so widely spread among the whole population. Nonetheless, it does occasionally cough up a victim visible enough to attract media attention.

A *Globe and Mail* story from 1991 records the fate of Richard Pearson, a shopkeeper in the town of Salmo, B.C., who was cut off from his main source of supply in Spokane, Washington because his wholesaler's packaging did not measure up to the requirements of the Act.

As Pearson explains it, high transportation costs made it impossible to bring goods from Vancouver into his shop at a reasonable cost. Spokane was the only reasonably-priced source of supply for his store. However, Pearson was informed by the Kelowna branch of the Department of Consumer and Corporate Affairs that he would be unable to continue importing merchandise into Canada unless he could relabel it to conform with the Act. According to the *Globe and Mail* report, Pearson's merchandise violated a number of the provisions of the *Act*, including the requirement that all food packaging contain lists of ingredients and that all sizes be listed in metric.

However, these problems arose only with selected merchandise. Pearson expressed the opinion to the *Globe* that it was the bilingual labelling that had proved to be the insurmountable hurdle. For a while, he struggled pathetically to conform with the law, tearing English labels off some items and erecting in-store signs in French. These efforts were inadequate. Informed by Consumer and Corporate Affairs in March 1991 that he was selling improperly labelled merchandise, and that he could be fined up to $5,000 for each item, he was forced to auction off most of his inventory. By the end of May he was out of business.

When the local representative of Consumer and Corporate Affairs was contacted by the *Globe and Mail* he gave a response that goes a long way towards explaining why Official Bilingualism has generated so much anger: "If he is going out of business, that's his problem, not ours. . . . All we did was send him our guidelines."[30]

Bill 101: The Mother of All Clauses

Bill 101, Quebec's *Charte de la langue française*, is best known in the rest of the country for its total ban on English signs. The more outlandish examples of sign-smiting oppression have been the stuff of back-page newspaper stories across Canada for nearly two decades: a town is forced by the provincial government to add a hyphen to every sign in the city, because the municipality's name (Pointe-Claire) is French with the hyphen in, English with the hyphen out. Another town is forced to replace hundreds of street signs with offending words like 'street' and 'road.' One shopkeeper is charged for having a sticker on his front door with a picture of a Welsh dragon and a word written in Welsh, while another is charged for inviting in his clientele with the word 'Welcome' painted onto his store window in thirty languages. Department stores erect scaffolds to remove the possessive apostrophe in their names, while a CBC radio host and a Montreal *Gazette* columnist worry on-air whether a two-letter store sign indicating that service is available inside in either official language might be unlawful because it has dared to use the letter 'E,' which implies the word 'English,' instead of the letter 'A,' which would imply the more acceptable 'Anglais.'

Despite all the attention, sign laws are probably the least important aspect of Bill 101 (and anyway, this aspect of the *Charter* has since been superseded by other provincial laws). Of far greater significance are the law's language-of-work provisions, which have caused thousands of anglophones to flee the province, and with them, thousands of jobs. Effectively, the language-of-work laws have had the effect of making it impossible to gain a professional licence in Quebec unless one is capable of speaking French, and have institutionalized the French language as the official language of work in all enterprises employing over fifty people. Some firms (notably head offices of Canada-wide corporations) have been exempted, to prevent them from moving to Toronto, but the atmosphere of uncertainty as to whether the restrictions on English in the workplace might be extended to include formerly exempted categories of business has prevented most new firms from moving in.

As a consequence of the large-scale abandonment of Montreal by English-speaking businesses and professionals, and the unwillingness of other English-speakers to move in to replace them, the province has suffered enormous drops in income and sales tax revenues. One francophone investor has recently estimated the cost to the provincial treasury between 1976 and 1986 at $20 billion in lost income tax revenues alone.[31]

This burden would have been unsustainable had it not been for federal complicity in the implementation of Bill 101. To be sure, Ottawa did not respond when demands were made for outright direct federal subsidies for the law. It ignored this request for aid, for example, from Montreal professor Roger Miller:

> The most dysfunctional effect of the *Charter of the French Language* has been to impose extra costs on head offices in Montreal. Other provinces do not impose such costs. . . . [More] bilingualism in Canadian business firms . . . would reduce extra costs on head offices located in Montreal and obviate the need to transfer head offices. To stimulate bilingualism within Canadian business firms, the Canadian government could persuade publicly regulated

industries such as transportation, telecommunication and banking to become more bilingual.

The advantages of leaving Quebec, Miller explained, would be greatly reduced if the federal government would agree to use "constant persuasion to encourage Canadian firms to promote linguistic duality in their head offices regardless of location...."[32]

Instead of this direct form of support, the federal government became the paymaster of Bill 101. While Quebec engaged in the economically self-destructive action of driving out a large percentage of its wealthiest and best-educated ethnic group, Ottawa funded the process, through its formula of government-to-government 'Equalization' payments. Before the ink had dried on the language law, University of Western Ontario economist Thomas Courchene had already explained how Canada's existing equalization payment system would subsidize it:

> As far as equalization payments for personal income are concerned ... for each additional percentage point that Quebec's share of Canada's population exceeds its share of the income base, federal equalization payments will increase by approximately $75 million. This reduces substantially the cost to the Quebec economy of a wholesale outflow of non-French speaking Quebeckers, assuming that they are in the top half of Quebec's income distribution. Put more bluntly, the structure of the federal transfers is such as to lend incentives to the Parti Québécois to come down harder on the English-Quebecker, under Bill 101, than would be the case if Quebec were an independent nation.[33]

Although his comments on the subject were never publicly recorded, it is highly unlikely that Pierre Trudeau, the first prime minister trapped into paying this subsidy, approved of it in any way. But with a referendum on Sovereignty-Association approaching, the fragile state of the nation's unity demanded that provocative federal initiatives in the area of federal-provincial relations be avoided. One of the most important issues in the 1980 referendum turned out to be the 'Battle of the Balance Sheet,' in which federalist and separatist politicians debated whether or not Quebec was receiving more money from Ottawa than it was contributing in the form of federal income and sales taxes. Therefore it is not surprising that the formula for equalization payments remained untouched, and the federal coffers opened ever wider to the provincial government, as the province's average personal income figures stagnated relative to the rest of Canada.

SUMMARY

In much of this book, I try to offer compromise solutions, obtainable through amendments to the policies I critique. This chapter is an exception.

There is nothing positive about the language restrictions placed by government on the private sector. These regulations place the burden of costs upon private businesses, who in turn pass it on to all of us. The benefits even to Canada's official language minorities are minuscule, but every Canadian must suffer a substantially lower standard of living.

If a shirt manufacturer knows his market is made up of both English-speakers and French-speakers, then it is in his best interest to see that the labels on his shirts are in both languages. This is natural private sector bilingualism. It occurs when and where market forces deem it necessary. If francophone consumers choose to not tolerate unilingual English labels, they will send a message which manufacturers will not fail to hear. On the other hand, if their message is that they'll settle for English-only packaging on some of the products they buy in return for a lower price, then producers will respond to that too. But it is certainly illegitimate to impose bilingual labelling and packaging from Cape Spear to the Klondike, with seventy-five percent of the attendant cost falling on English-speakers, in order to attain a benefit that francophones themselves might not choose to accept, if given the choice on an item-by-item basis.

Much the same can be said for every other form of mandated private sector bilingualism. If customers at gas stations in Calgary or car-rental booths in Fredericton want their service in any language at all, they can make their wishes known and entrepreneurs will respond. That's why banks in parts of Toronto now offer counter service in Cantonese. It's why Vietnamese-language newspapers thrive in several cities, despite a total absence of force-fed advertising revenues from Air Canada and CN Rail.

The state has no place in the bedrooms, the boardrooms or the store shelves of the nation, so long as citizens conduct business in an honest manner and continue to pay their taxes. Free individuals, freely associating, can take care of all the rest.

CHAPTER EIGHT

The Lord of the Files: The Bureaucracy of Language in the Federal Public Service

> We are not saying Canadians need to be bilingual for every job in the federal civil service—only for the top job.
> —*Edmonton Journal (1993)*[1]

THE PUBLIC SERVICE of Canada hires, promotes and systematically discriminates on the basis of language. For more than twenty years, Canada's largest employer, which provides jobs for over half a million Canadians,[2] has made use of hiring and promotion policies designed to appear to discriminate against anglophones and in favour of francophones, on the theory that affirmative action for French-speakers is an effective weapon in the war against Quebec separatism.

To be effective in boosting national unity, the system cannot discriminate openly, but it must also avoid complete secrecy. It must permit the federal government to sing out of both sides of its mouth, providing concrete, irrefutable statistics of francophone success in the Public Service for the benefit of its francophone clientele, while carefully hiding the mechanisms by which these results are achieved, so as not to give anglophone critics a solid target for their suspicion that they are the victims of what amounts to linguistic racism. The discrimination is hidden in the form of redefining the job requirements of Public Service posts on a mass basis to make these jobs more easily accessible to francophones than to anglophones.

Tens of thousands of Public Service jobs have been redesignated as 'bilingual-essential' (i.e., open only to persons who can speak both official languages) even though there is no job-related need to give them this designation. Because two-thirds of Canada's bilingual population is made up of native French speakers, it is twice as easy to fill a typical bilingual-essential post with a francophone as with an anglophone. Hence, every time a position is unnecessarily redesignated, it becomes an additional affirmative-action post, twice as likely to be filled by a francophone as by an anglophone.

Nonetheless, the 'bilingual-essential' system hurts rather than helps the job prospects of the average French-speaking Canadian. This seems counter-intuitive, but it is true, due to the fact that most francophones are themselves unilingual.

Until the late 1960s, English was the language of work in all but a small proportion of Public Service jobs. This had the practical effect of discriminating against any French-speaker who did not speak English as fluently as his own mother tongue. Despite much propaganda to the contrary, the system imposed since the end of the 1960s has not corrected that injustice. In fact, of the few jobs that were open to unilingual francophones twenty years ago, over one-third have since been reclassified as bilingual, meaning that they are no longer open to francophones incapable of speaking English.[3] In addition, the system of bilingual post designations discriminates against the ninety percent of English-speakers who cannot perform the same feat of multi-linguistic virtuosity in reverse.

BILINGUAL QUOTAS AND THE PROPAGANDA OF UNITY

> A mutually reinforcing circle of influences has been developed: the designation of bilingual and French positions has resulted in the appointment of more francophones; the working environment has thus become more attractive to francophones; more francophones have presented themselves for appointment to the Public Service; more francophones can be appointed because of the bilingual and French positions; and so on. The most tangible indicator of progress is the fact that francophones are now represented in the Public Service in almost exact proportion to their numbers in the total population. ...
> —*Kenneth Kernaghan (1978)*[4]

Because the existing policy discriminates against a larger number of anglophones than francophones, the superficial impression is left that French-speakers as a whole are its beneficiaries, thus inflaming the anger and even the hatred of many English Canadians. Yet it is this impression itself that is the real reason for enacting the system of bilingual quotas. As long as total numbers of francophones in the Public Service are high, the illusion is created that Canadian unity bestows tens of thousands of job opportunities on the average Québécois. No readily available statistic reveals that most of these posts are actually closed to most French-speakers, so the illusion is maintained and national unity is given a little boost. The truth is that the system functions extremely poorly at performing the straightforward affirmative-action role of promoting francophones at the expense of anglophones, because it has been enacted and administered in a roundabout, secretive and indirect way, rather than through the more direct mechanism of outright quotas for francophones.

To be sure, the statistics appear impressive, as long as they are not properly understood. By 1991, francophones made up twenty-eight percent of all Public Service employees,[5] three percent higher than their share of the Canadian population. As well, full statistical equality has been achieved in crown corporations,[6] and in the few areas of Public Service employment where the proportion of francophones does not exceed their representation in Canada's population as a whole, the proportion nonetheless exceeds the percentage of French-speakers in similar jobs in the private sector.[7] Moreover, French-speakers are statistically over-represented in every region of the country except New Brunswick, and even there they hold exactly the proportion of posts that their numbers warrant.[8] The numbers in which francophones hold government posts have been steadily increasing since the mid-1960s, and the rate of increase shows no signs of slowing.

The Tall and the Short of the Matter—An Analogy

> ... the use of quotas in hiring and promotion should be viewed as a last resort to eradicate deep existing social inequities, if it is used at all. We must be sure that in removing inequities we do not merely compound them, *even for the group we are trying to help.*
> —V. Seymour Wilson and Willard Mullins,
> *Canadian Public Administration*[9]

It seems impossible that a new, artificially created bilingual elite that is two-thirds francophone has had, as one of its primary results, an increased level of discrimination against the average French-speaking Canadian. Still, this is the case. The easiest way to illustrate how this could happen is by way of analogy.

Imagine that in order to make up for a century of discrimination and under-representation, a political decision has been made to boost the number of women employed by the Public Service. As well, imagine that in order to hasten the process of hiring women, Public Service personnel managers are put under tremendous and unrelenting pressure from their elected masters in Parliament to hire women on a preferential basis. They are not permitted to do so openly, however, because the politicians fear a negative reaction from male voters. Under these circumstances, the traditional principle of merit hiring could not be openly violated in favour of quotas. Affirmative action would have to be introduced on the sly.

Inevitably, the bureaucrats would search for a way of incorporating some quality that women possess more frequently than men into the definition of 'merit.' If this sounds improbable, consider that a ministerial commission in British Columbia has recently recommended doing precisely this. As described in an article in *British Columbia Report*, the commission proposes to:

> [open] the door for a full-fledged employment equity program by paying lip service to the long-held merit principle on one hand, while trying to redefine the term "merit" on the other. [The report states:] "What requires examination

FIGURE 8.1
The practice of designating posts "Bilingual Essential" hurts anglophones disproportionately...

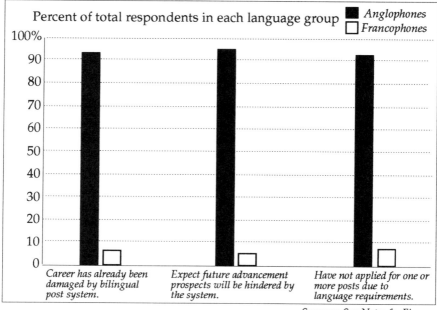

...And gives the false impression of helping francophones as a group...

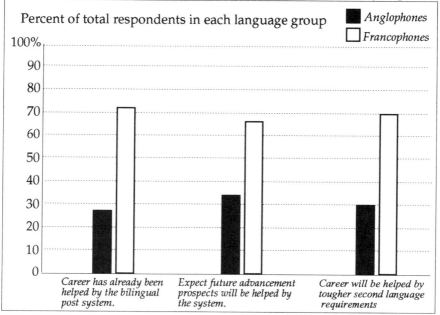

...But in reality it hurts the unilingual majority in both language groups

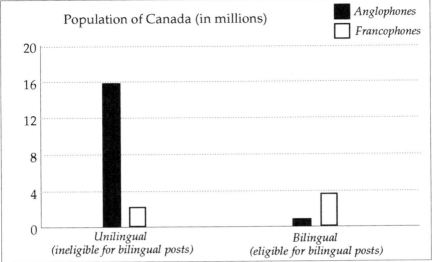

Sources: See *Notes for Figures*

are the specific factors of merit and the application of the merit principle" to hiring. In other words, the principle of merit would be redefined to include factors such as gender and ethnicity.[10]

The precise manner in which merit might be redefined is not specified by the commission. One possibility, which admittedly is unlikely in practice, but which serves the purpose of our analogy well, is that the public servants attempting to covertly introduce affirmative action might take note of the fact that on average, women are shorter than men. 'Shortness' could then be incorporated into the definition of merit. More short people would be hired, and hence a disproportionate share of women.

The parallel of this analogy should now be clear. 'Men' represent anglophones and 'women' represent francophones. Shortness is equivalent to second-language ability. Of course, it is silly to suggest that height could ever have any logical connection to most civil service jobs. But it is just as ridiculous to claim, as the federal government does, that both English and French are essential skills for the majority of jobs currently designated bilingual, since most could be equally well performed exclusively in one language or the other. The only real difference between height quotas and bilingual quotas is that the lunacy of the first is evident to the uninitiated, because height is a *physical* characteristic unrelated to job performance while the lunacy of the second becomes obvious only upon reflection, because bilingualism is an *intellectual* characteristic unrelated to job performance for most posts other than translators, receptionists in bilingual regions of the country and a limited number of supervisory posts.

The analogy doesn't end happily. Male public servants would notice a disproportionate number of women filling *short-essential* posts, and would incorrectly conclude that women as a class were benefiting from the program. They would be resentful, hurt, and in some cases, they might become bigoted women-haters.

In fact, women as a class would not benefit from this kind of hidden quota, because unlike simple affirmative action quotas, it excludes many women. Only those women below a certain specified height would benefit; the cut-off height designed to exclude most men would exclude a large number of taller women as well.

Something like this has happened in the Public Service. Bilingual-essential post designations have made it more difficult for most French Canadians to get jobs in the Public Service than it was a quarter of a century ago, and have simultaneously turned francophones into the undeserving object of anger and resentment on the part of English-speaking public servants who have seen their own careers damaged in the name of a spurious, statistical illusion of language equality.

How Badly Has the Bilingual Post System Hurt Anglophones?

> The careers of civil servants who are not bilingual and who have devoted many years of their lives to the service of their country must not be prejudiced in any way by measures to develop bilingualism.
> —*Lester Pearson (April 6, 1966)*[11]

In the mid-1960s, when his government first began to implement measures to boost the numbers of francophones in the Public Service, Prime Minister Lester Pearson rose in the House of Commons to give his personal guarantee that the policy of making more space for francophones would not be permitted to hurt the careers of English-speaking public servants. Pearson's Commons speech of April 6, 1966 has been repeated mantra-like ever since as proof that the policy of bilingualism in the Public Service is designed to be fair and equitable to anglophones as well as francophones.

Unfortunately, well-intentioned policy pronouncements do not always translate into reality. In 1971, when an anglophone public servant appealed a denied promotion on the basis of Pearson's statement, the Public Service Commission Appeals Board ruled that the parliamentary ruminations of politicians have no legal weight—and therefore, presumably, that they do not prevent the simultaneous public advocacy of policies precisely opposite to those actually being adopted.[12]

The extent to which twenty years' worth of redesignating posts bilingual has hurt the careers of anglophone public servants is revealed by the results of a survey undertaken by the Professional Institute of the Public Service of Canada (PIPSC), the trade union representing those federal employees who have professional credentials. In 1990, PIPSC polled its membership on how their own careers had been affected by the language regime in the Public Service. The union received 7,687 responses.[13]

The results, released in 1991, clearly indicate that the majority of anglophone public servants find their personal interests have been harmed by the bilingual quota system, while only a small group of bilingual public servants count themselves as its beneficiaries. Over one-third of English-speaking respondents answered that the federal government's language-based hiring and promotion practices had negatively affected their advancement opportunities in the past, while over half believed that their future promotion prospects would be hurt by these policies. Nearly forty-two percent indicated that on at least one occasion in the past they had not bothered to apply for a position because of its bilingual language requirements.[14]

By contrast, only three percent of anglophone respondents felt that their careers had been helped by the practice of designating posts bilingual. Only six percent expected their future careers to be enhanced by the tightening of bilingualism requirements for managers.[15]

Another interesting result, which goes a long way towards explaining why English Canadian civil servants are often so angry at their francophone colleagues, comes when anglophone and francophone responses are compared. Almost all the respondents (93.4 percent) who felt their advancement opportunities had been hurt by the federal government's official languages policy were anglophones. Of those who felt that managerial positions had been closed to them by recent increases in the second-language requirements of the posts, almost all (95.4 percent) were anglophones. Finally, of those who reported that they had not even bothered filling out applications to compete for new posts because they felt they would get stopped by a language requirement, 92.1 percent were English-speakers.[16]

In a sense, the anglophone public servants are just the tip of a much greater iceberg, which consists of those 17.8 million Canadians who can speak English but are unable to conduct a conversation in French. This vast group represents eighty-six percent of all non-francophones in Canada and just under two-thirds of the total Canadian population, yet its members can no longer look forward to the prospect of building decent careers with their country's largest employer.

How Badly Has the Bilingual Post System Hurt Francophones?

Unilingual francophones lose out even more severely than do unilingual English-speakers. This, of course, is because unilingual French-speakers are no better qualified to hold a 'bilingual-essential' post than they are to hold a post where English is the only language of work. But francophones have been saddled with an additional handicap. The proportion of Public Service positions open to anglophones has shrunk, but francophones have witnessed the *absolute number* of posts open to them shrink as well. Today, unilingual anglophones can still apply for sixty-four percent of Public Service jobs. By contrast, only twelve percent of Public Service positions are open to unilingual francophones.[17]

As more and more posts have been reclassified bilingual, fewer and fewer have remained open to the unilingual speakers of either official language. But the decline has been particularly sharp on the French side. In 1974, the first year for which records exist of the number of posts designated unilingual and bilingual, 18.8 percent of all Public Service positions—over 34,000 jobs in all—were open to unilingual French-speakers. By 1992, only 25,000 positions were still fillable by persons not capable of speaking English. Even in Quebec itself, 53.2 percent of federal jobs had been classified bilingual.[18]

This massive reclassification is mostly the work of the bilingual francophones already entrenched in the Public Service. Since 1977, the government has paid an annual bonus of $800 to all qualified occupants of bilingually-designated posts. This has given bilingual public servants a tremendous incentive to have their posts classified 'bilingual-essential.'[19] But once a post has been so classified, it is virtually impossible to reclassify it as unilingual, even when its former occupant retires or is transferred.

The result is a multitude of unnecessary bilingual posts in Quebec. The Commissioner of Official Languages estimates that instead of 53.4 percent, only fourteen to sixteen percent of Public Service positions in Quebec should be designated bilingual, and the rest should be open to unilingual francophones.[20] Likewise, it is hard to justify the rule, adopted in 1977, that only bilingual persons would be able to supervise 'either/or' positions (positions open either to English-speakers or to French-speakers), without regard for the possibility that many of these posts, particularly in Quebec, will always be filled by francophones.[21] This rule has had the effect of removing a large number of supervisory posts from the reach of the average Quebecer.

Sometimes the bilingual designation of Public Service posts in Quebec seems comical, as in this example unearthed by the Ottawa *Citizen* in 1991:

> There's a federal government office in Quebec where the positions of eight employees have been designated bilingual.... The Industry, Science and Technology Canada officers ... have been asked just once in the past two years to use their bilingual capabilities for which they are paid an extra $800 a year. An English caller telephoned their offices. He had the wrong number but they were able to direct him to the right one.[22]

As amusing as stories like this may seem, their consequences are severe:

Figure 8.2
The number of posts open to unlingual francophones has decreased, thanks to the system of designating posts bilingual

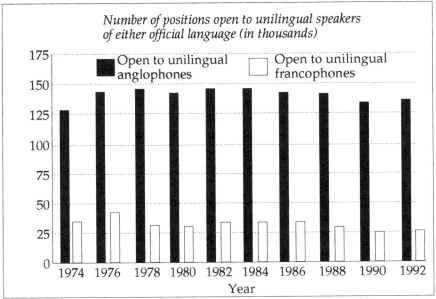

Sources: See *Notes for Figures*

the permanent sealing-off of a vast employer to the majority of Quebecers. The uncomfortable knowledge that most federal government positions within their own province require them to be capable of speaking English can hardly be considered likely to cause Quebecers to embrace Canadian unity.

Conspiracy Theory #63
In a system this confused and duplicitous, it is tempting to hunt for conspiracies. Indeed, in the higher levels of the Public Service there does exist a sort of half-cooked conspiracy of silence which is rendered largely ineffective by the simultaneous and completely contradictory desire to shout from the rooftops—at least to francophone audiences—that Ottawa has adopted preferential hiring policies designed to enrich and empower francophone bureaucrats. To the extent that it functions at all (and very little functions as intended, when it comes to official languages in the Public Service of Canada), the 'conspiracy' works like this:

1. *Public Service managers are put under intense and relentless pressure to hire and promote more francophones, by hook or by crook.* The following passage from

the minutes of the February 10, 1987 meeting of Parliament's Standing Joint Committee on Official Languages is an example of these pressures:

> *Jean-Robert Gauthier* [MP from Ottawa-Vanier]: The Canada Post Corporation hires people every year because others leave; some retire, some die, and others get tired of working for you. What is your annual personnel turnover rate? With a turnover of 15% or 20% a year, for example, can you replace people under affirmative action programs for women, the handicapped and francophones?
>
> *Mr. Cloutier* [President of Canada Post]: That is exactly the direction in which we are heading. In addition, every three to six months, we plan to monitor how many positions have been vacated as a result of turnover.[23]

2. *Senior civil servants must respond cautiously to the incessant demands of their political masters for additional tampering with the merit system.* Increasingly elaborate means have been sought by the bureaucracy to avoid the sort of career-ending jolt that would come to a senior public servant caught by the media or Public Service unions trying to promote one language group over the other by means of overt quotas. This is particularly true since affirmative action-style quotas are expressly forbidden under the *Public Service Employment Act*.[24] Thus, for example, follow-up research shows that Mr. Cloutier of Canada Post was not foolish enough to actually introduce outright quota hiring for French-speakers as he had promised to the Standing Joint Committee.

3. *One way to avoid being caught in the crossfire is to hide the paper trail of documents that might expose the discriminatory nature of Public Service hiring practices through the use of arcane bureaucratic language on all documents.* This masks bureaucratic decisions, including hiring decisions. It is presumably for this reason that the Treasury Board publishes an instruction booklet for the use of deputy ministers and other senior administrators, which provides guidelines on how to phrase any written references to quota hiring in nearly unintelligible prose, thus gaining a margin of safety from media scrutiny. The following instructions are offered on how to write documents, known as 'Letters of Understanding,' that outline each department's linguistic staffing practices:

> Does the department give equal employment opportunities to Anglophones and to Francophones?
>
> *Non-Acceptable answer:*
> "The department uses imperative staffing in order to recruit bilingual Anglophones in Quebec. Regarding participation in Northern and Eastern Ontario, Francophones represent 3 employees out of a staff of 20; the department intends to recruit at least 3 others during the coming year."

More-acceptable answer:
"The department is making every effort to ensure that its effectiveness reflects the presence of the two languages communities. It aims for an eventual francophone participation rate at 21% in the Scientific category, based on labour market data. The actual participation rate in this category being at 15%, the department estimates that a rigorous application of Treasury Board policies will permit it to attain a rate of about 18% in the next few years."[25]

"Rigorous application of Treasury Board policies" is, of course, code language for designating posts bilingual-imperative in order to ensure that two-thirds of new recruits are francophones. In both the acceptable and the non-acceptable responses, quota hiring is regarded as good and necessary. Observe that, with the exception of the slightly different numerical goal in the second wording, the two are precisely the same—but the second is less quotable!

THE BIG PICTURE: THE HISTORY OF PUBLIC SERVICE BILINGUALISM

When Dinosaurs Ruled the Earth

For a full century following Confederation, francophones were the victims of systemic under-representation in the federal Public Service.

In 1964, for example, French-speakers were under-represented in all but five of the twenty-five largest departments and agencies in the Civil Service of Canada.[26] Even at the lowest salary level, French-speakers were under-represented, holding only 23.7 percent of posts at a time when they represented twenty-eight percent of the national population. Their numbers decreased with each level of seniority. Only 10.4 percent of public servants in the top salary bracket were French-speakers.[27]

Worse yet, statistics collected at the time indicated that French-speakers advanced more slowly though the Public Service ranks than did English-speakers who had entered government employment at the same time and in the same departments. This slow rate of advancement could not be attributed to external factors such as the lower general level of education among French Canadians; measurable and significant differences in rates of advancement existed between French and English Canadians with identical levels of education.[28]

These problems were the result of the fact that the Public Service conducted its affairs almost entirely in English; the investigations of the B&B Commission confirmed that there was no evidence of deliberate bigotry in hiring and promotion.[29] Because English was the only language of the Public Service, all francophones who did not speak English fluently were at a perpetual disadvantage in the workplace. The need to work in a second language discouraged many French-speakers from applying for Public Service jobs. Among those who did apply, only the ones with extraordinary language skills could ever hope to compete as equals with English Canadians. In short, Canada's largest employer had inadvertently adopted a policy of systematic discrimination against a quarter of the country's population. As the B&B Commission explained in 1969:

> Where one language is dominant, those of another mother tongue are systematically excluded from posts of command unless they become perfectly fluent in the dominant language.... [Francophones are] genuinely unable to do the work as well as the English candidate whenever that work consists in large part of the manipulation of symbols in English.[30]

It was this simple phenomenon, more than anything else, that explained the perpetual disadvantage faced by francophones.[31]

For decades, the federal government simply ignored the problem of francophone under-representation. By the time Lester Pearson became prime minister in 1963, the question had become a serious political issue, cited by Québécois nationalists as one of their greatest historical grievances with Confederation. With separatism becoming increasingly popular in Quebec, the new prime minister was anxious to eliminate all hints of discrimination or language inequality in all federal institutions.

Within a year of taking office, Pearson established the B&B Commission to search for long-term solutions to the language problems that seemed to be threatening Canada's unity. However, the Commission did not submit recommendations on Public Service staffing until 1969. In the intervening six years, a system of ad hoc staffing reforms was adopted which has formed the basis of Public Service staffing ever since. The basic tool of this stopgap system was the redesignation of individual Public Service positions as bilingual, so that only a bilingual person (which usually meant a francophone) could fill the position. To facilitate this process, the *Public Service Employment Act* was rewritten in 1967 to include a clause stating that second-language ability henceforth would be considered a component of merit. This change made it possible to use bilingual post designations as a form of low-visibility affirmative action, without violating the legally enshrined principle that Public Service hiring and promotion must be done strictly on the basis of merit.

Twenty years later, a Public Service Commission brief, drawn up for presentation to a parliamentary committee, explained the reworked definition of merit this way:

> The Public Service Commission has noted that various media reports ... have suggested that to consider a person's linguistic qualifications in a selection process is an infringement upon the *Public Service Employment Act*, which

requires selection according to merit and nothing else. As there appears to be some confusion or misconceptions about this issue, the Commission wishes to offer your Committee some explanation as to how merit is applied in the selection of candidates for positions in the Public Service.

The *Public Service Employment Act* ("1967") states that for the purposes of assessing merit, the Commission may:

"... prescribe selection standards as to education, knowledge, experience, *language*, residence or any other matters that, in the Commission's opinion, are necessary or desirable, having regard to the *nature of the duties to be performed*." (Emphasis added.)

This provision as well as the selection standards which the Commission has adopted make it clear that the only qualification which can be demanded of candidates for a position are those which are called for by the duties of the position. ... In this context, when the knowledge of both official languages is a requirement of the position either because the incumbent serves the public, or, in bilingual regions, because he or she supervises both francophone and anglophone employees, such knowledge becomes an element of merit and in order to apply the principles of the *Public Service Employment Act*, the selected candidate must meet this and all other requirements at the time of appointment. ...[32]

The full implications of this statement become clearer when another Public Service Commission document is cited:

"Since the time of Prime Minister Pearson's statement in 1966 on bilingualism in the Public Service, an implicit assumption of official languages policies has been that the establishment of a bilingual institution requires a maximization of individual bilingualism among employees *through the creation of as many bilingual positions as possible*." (Emphasis added.)[33]

Enacted in haste without a clear set of objectives, these hiring and promotion practices have twice collapsed in chaos and been totally rewritten (in 1973 and again in 1977), and have required numerous minor reforms on other occasions. Even with these adjustments, they have succeeded in creating only the statistical illusion of equality, as we have already seen.

As envisaged by Pearson, the reforms had wildly optimistic objectives: to provide full statistical equality between anglophones and francophones in all branches and at all levels of the Public Service, to allow every department of the Public Service to operate easily and fluidly in both languages at once, to provide each public servant with a fluent understanding of the other official language, and to build national unity by turning the federal Public Service into a vast centre for francophone employment on a scale rivalling the giant new French-only provincial bureaucracy being established in Quebec by Premier Jean Lesage. Also, national unity demanded a headlong rush to achieve equality in the shortest possible space of time. Quotas were adopted in order to cause full statistical equality to be reached as soon as possible, since equality would have taken years to attain under a process of strictly equitable hiring and promotion, if the normal practice of replacing retiring public servants on a merit basis had been followed.[34]

Although it was Lester Pearson who began this process of frantic, panic-driven reform, Pierre Trudeau would institutionalize it. In May 1968, Trudeau succeeded Pearson as prime minister. One of the first items on his list of legislative priorities was to make his predecessor's tentative and ad hoc language reforms permanent. Strangely, given Trudeau's personal taste for precise, rationalistic legislation, the new and comprehensive *Official Languages Act* did not incorporate systematic, detailed reforms to Public Service staffing.[35] Instead, Pearson's hastily contrived measures were allowed to remain in place and additional informal pressure was applied to individual departments to speed the process of achieving full statistical equality. The exact means of promoting equality within each individual department was left in the hands of regulatory agencies and bureaucrats, who would carry on the battle for equality by means of administrative memoranda.

In choosing not to adopt open, systematic reforms, Trudeau removed the hiring-and-promotion issue from its proper home in the high profile, publicly debated world of parliamentary legislation and placed it in a shadowy netherworld where reforms would be subject to arbitrary change, unnecessary delays, bureaucratic secrecy, and politically motivated hidden agendas.[36]

Trudeau and the Rejection of the B&B Solution (1969-1972)

Trudeau's decision seems even stranger in light of a creative alternative to Pearson's stopgap system that had been made public, to great fanfare, in 1969. The third volume of the B&B Commission's report was released that September. This document, which contained the most thorough study ever attempted of language in the Public Service, was harsh in its condemnation of Pearson's quota-based reforms.

It noted that the disruption of the merit system had a negative effect on Public Service morale,[37] and stressed that "only those positions where use of the two official languages is part of the daily routine should qualify as positions with special language requirements."[38] As well, the Report maintained that the bilingual status of any individual post should be reviewed regularly, since the functions of each post would inevitably change over time.[39] In other words, no post would ever be designated *permanently* bilingual—as was happening regularly by 1969, and has been happening ever since. Instead, every post would be capable of reversion to unilingual status, should circumstances make this appropriate.

The B&B Commission envisaged the existence of only a tiny number of designated posts which would be open only to bilingual candidates. These would be limited to areas like translation, "where bilingualism defines the function,"[40] and to a small number of very senior posts such as Section Head, Assistant Deputy Minister, and Deputy Minister, where the duties of the post would include communicating regularly with unilingual politicians from both official language groups, or with unilingual subordinates from both groups.

As an alternative means of boosting opportunities for francophones without resorting to quotas or preferential hiring, the B&B Commission recommended dividing the Public Service into 'French-language units' in which all work would be performed in French, and 'English-language units' in which all work would be performed in English. Under this system, almost all jobs would be open to unilingual speakers. At first there might be a preponderance of unilingual English jobs, but as anglophone employees retired and francophones joined the Public Service, French-language units would expand at every level of seniority, to include a proportion of jobs equivalent to the French-speaking share of the Canadian population. There would be equitable representation without resorting to affirmative action, or expensive language training, or cultural engineering.

Trudeau seems to have had two reasons for not adopting this eminently fair and practical solution. First, he apparently felt the 'French language unit' system would take too long to implement, while the separatist threat was an immediate problem demanding immediate solutions. As he had once observed in another context, "we can't tell Quebec, 'Cool it fellows, in forty years we'll be able to talk to you.' . . . We might save some money . . . but we wouldn't save the country."[41]

Second, it should not be forgotten that Trudeau had, several years earlier, expressed his belief that unilingual speakers of either official languages should be excluded from all but the most junior bureaucratic posts. (See his comments on this subject, which are quoted in Chapter One.) Briefly stated, his agenda involved using an ever-expanding network of bilingually-designated jobs as a tool to gradually force all Canadian public servants to become bilingual, as part of a grand scheme to create a new culture out of the amalgamation of English Canada and French Canada.[42] Language-based work units for unilingual public servants would have thrown a wrench in this plan.

Things Fall Apart: 1972-1973

Instead of language-based work units, a decision was made that the Public Service would promote francophones through the use of bilingual posts.[43] In 1971, the Treasury Board issued a directive instructing that by 1975, sixty percent of all executive positions in Ottawa and half of all administrative posts were to be staffed by bilingual personnel.[44]

Although the national-unity function of these bilingual quotas was not advertised in English Canada, it was no secret. As Sandra Gwyn put it in a 1976 article published in *Saturday Night*, in the early Trudeau years, "bilingualism was often—everyone knew this but no one would say it—a synonym for francophone."[45]

René Lévesque, who was fully aware that his party's separatist option was the real target of federal hiring quotas, referred to Ottawa's scramble to hire more francophones as "Operation Panic."[46] Meanwhile, another *Saturday Night* article noted a curious fact about the time frame of the quotas: "Politically, the 1975 deadline [for quota hiring] just happens to correspond with René Lévesque's 'deadline for Confederation.' "[47]

The 1972 federal election nearly brought an end to the experiment in unity-via-quota. Trudeau's Liberals came within two seats of being forced out of office. The Liberals did badly in English Canada, where they placed a poor second to Stanfield's Conservatives. Nowhere was the decline more precipitous than in Ottawa, where an anti-Liberal wave of frustrated anglophone public servants swept away incumbents in several traditional Liberal 'safe' seats.

Gérard Pelletier, who was Trudeau's minister of communications at the time, recalls that in late 1972 there was an unseemly rush among deputy ministers to dispose of the system of bilingual post designations.[48] A compromise with English-speaking public servants was necessary if the system was to be saved.

This compromise would set the pattern for all future reforms to the Public Service. Changes would be made to accommodate unilingual anglophones already in the system, but de facto francophone quotas would be more firmly entrenched than ever.

From the point of view of anglophone public servants, the most important compromises included a new rule granting language training at government expense to unilingual public servants occupying any positions that were designated bilingual during their tenure at the post.[49] As well, all employees aged fifty-five or older occupying positions designated bilingual would be exempted from the language requirements of their positions. All applicants, including unilingual ones, would be considered for bilingual posts, as long as they expressed a willingness to learn the other official language. Public Service unions would receive prior notice whenever a position was redesignated bilingual. Finally, the quotas set for 1975 would be pushed ahead to 1978.

In return for letting select unilingual anglophones gain access to the bilingual category, the quota system would be substantially tightened. Control over the language designation of every position in the Public Service was centralized and placed in the hands of the Treasury Board, while the role of individual administrators was reduced to methodically applying the instructions they received from on high.

The National Capital Region was designated a "bilingual region of work," along with several other regions of the country, meaning that any francophone public servant in a non-bilingual post could demand to work exclusively in French, regardless of previous contracts or arrangements. (In theory, any anglophone working in Ottawa in French could now demand to work exclusively in English, although it is unlikely that anybody was actually able to take advantage of this right, in a civil service that still operated almost entirely in English.) This new right meant that superiors would have to be universally bilingual, as this passage from a government publication of the period explains:

> In dealing with the concept of "free choice" of language of work ... it must be emphasized that for the concept to be operative in the broadest sense, certain employees must have language obligations imposed upon them. The "language right" of an employee to be supervised in his preferred official language becomes the "language obligation" of his supervisor.[50]

Therefore, in the future, all supervisory posts would be designated bilingual, not just the sixty percent previously targeted.

Finally, the quota system would be further entrenched by means of an all-party parliamentary resolution endorsing the system.

Things Fall Apart ... Again: 1973-1977

The new system began to unravel as soon as it was implemented. Unilingual public servants realized that the formal creation of a ceiling, above which unilingual staff would never be able to be promoted, would have the effect of ending their chances for advancement. One civil servant explained to Sandra Gwyn a few years later what happened next: "We knew damn well you had to be bilingual to have any hopes of promotion, so we made damn sure that our own positions were designated bilingual, and for their own sake, the jobs of everyone else in sight. That way, we'd all have the right to learn French."[51]

The 1973 regulations had been designed as a one-way ratchet; it was easy to designate posts bilingual, difficult to undesignate them. Suddenly, the number of posts classified bilingual soared out of control. In 1973, as the plan was being implemented, Treasury Board president Bud Drury estimated that 20,000 posts would eventually be designated bilingual. A year later, his successor, Jean Chrétien, reported that 53,000 posts had been so designated. By 1976, the number was up to 60,000, and the Commissioner of Official Languages was reporting that these classifications "bear distressingly little relation to on-the-job needs, except by distant and often disputable projections."[52]

Language training was a particularly glaring failure. Only eleven percent of graduates from French-language training were actually fluent in the language.[53]

As a result, tens of thousands of ostensibly bilingual positions were filled by ostensibly bilingual anglophones who could barely construct a sentence in French. "You have to keep forcing yourself," one nominally bilingual anglophone explained, "to inflict yourself on your French Canadian colleagues."[54]

In the confusion, it was no longer possible to keep unilingual anglophones out of posts which were genuinely in need of bilingual incumbents, so French-language service to the public stood in danger of deteriorating. This was a public relations disaster which Ottawa could scarcely afford, with the separatists on the verge of sweeping into office in Quebec. Worse yet, the profusion of anglophones occupying bilingual posts had effectively ended the usefulness of the system of designating positions bilingual as a form of affirmative action.[55] Two commissions of inquiry were hastily established, and detailed reforms were undertaken in 1977.

The Turn of the Screw: 1977-Present

The 1977 reforms sorted out some of the chaos created four years earlier —particularly the excessive centralization—but they ratcheted the standard of bilingualism yet another notch higher. By now the government had caught itself in a trap. Unless each set of reforms was stricter than the last, Ottawa would be accused by the watchful Parti Québécois of abandoning francophone interests. The bilingual francophone public servants already in federal employ, who served as highly visible symbols of the material advantages of national unity, could be promoted to new and more unifying heights only if the door were shut more firmly on their unilingual compatriots. It would be bad public relations to redesignate thousands of bilingual posts unilingual, even if this might allow more unilingual French speakers into the Public Service. The action would be interpreted as proof that the Public Service had reverted to its traditional status as an English-only old boys' club.

On this basis, the government extended the bilingual quota system to all crown corporations. As well, it chose not to remove the bilingual status of the thousands of wrongly designated positions, creating instead a new 'bilingual-imperative' category.

A bilingual-imperative post was to be one in which the need for the job to be conducted in both official languages was so immediate that occupants could not learn their language skills on the job. All applicants for imperative posts would have to be bilingual before occupying their job. Positions clearly suited for the bilingual-imperative designation included those posts where public safety was involved, or where the post served a market with a customer base that was partly French-speaking and partly English-speaking.

The logic of creating a distinction between ordinary bilingual posts and bilingual-imperative ones is strange in the extreme. Logically speaking, all bilingual positions in the Public Service should be staffed on an imperative basis. It is difficult to maintain, as the Public Service Commission does, that there is a need for thousands of posts to be filled by bilingual personnel, but that many such posts can be staffed for years at a time by individuals who are incapable of speaking both languages. If bilingualism is an inherent part of the job description for any post, then it makes as little sense to appoint a unilingual person to the post as it would to hire persons without pilot's licenses as government pilots, or non-swimmers as lifeguards. In fact, one prominent legal scholar has suggested that the unilingual staffing of posts that genuinely require bilingual skills would probably be a violation of the federal government's constitutional obligation to provide service to the public in both official languages.[56] As initially created, therefore, the designation 'bilingual-imperative' meant genuinely bilingual, while 'bilingual-essential' meant *make-believe bilingual*.

The imperative category was only partly designed to restore bilingual services where they were genuinely required. A second purpose was to re-establish a category of employment that would once again create de facto affirmative action hiring for francophones, now that the 'bilingual-essential' category had been gutted. Technical revisions adopted in 1981 (and still in effect today) alter the mechanism by which posts are designated bilingual-imperative, to assure that an ever-larger proportion of federal jobs are being designated imperative.[57] This is important, since the percentage of non-imperative jobs held by francophones is dropping gradually, as anglophones continue to take advantage of the 1973 regulations granting them the right to on-the-job training.[58]

From 1980 onwards, regulations on the language regime within the Public Service have been an unending series of regulatory band-aids, trying to patch up an essentially unworkable system. One particularly glaring symptom of the general disorder is the federal government's inability to abolish the $800-per annum 'bilingual bonus' that was introduced in 1977 as a temporary six-year measure. Pressure from bilingual public servants has turned this expensive program into what Ottawa watchers call a 'sacred cow,' immune from government tampering despite its destructive nature.

The most significant band-aids have been the Public Service clauses of the new *Official Languages Act*, Bill C-72, which was passed in 1988. Unlike the original 1969 Act, this one deals extensively with bilingualism in the Public Service. The Act follows the pattern of the 1973 and 1977 regulatory packages, in that it ratchets up the intensity of bilingual quotas by formalizing in law quotas that had previously only been enshrined in Treasury Board directives and a resolution of Parliament.[59]

SYMPTOMS OF CHAOS AND COLLAPSE

The system of preferential hiring through bilingual quotas is in the final stages of a terminal illness. The inherent self-destructiveness of the system can be seen by examining it from a variety of angles: language training, language of work, and even from the point of view of Canadian demolinguistic trends.

Language Training

> There are still some [public servants] who are not making an effort [to become bilingual]. They require interpretation. And yet, there are people out there who speak a minimum of three languages—thousands of them! If someone cannot learn the language after trying fifteen years, the only solution is to throw him out.
>
> —*Vincent Della Noce, MP (1985)*[60]

In 1962, the Glasscoe Report on Government Organization had recommended that public servants be made bilingual upon entry into federal employ, and that language training be made available to all.[61] Language training facilities would allow all public servants to learn the other official language at no personal cost—in terms of either financial or opportunity costs—in order to compete with other public servants who are already bilingual.

The federal government has since attempted to set up just such a network of facilities, and has completely failed. There is a good reason for this. The task is impossible.

Second-language training for public servants was introduced in 1964.[62] At the time, ambitious policy-makers believed that it would be relatively easy to retrain most unilingual government employees in English or French. Listeners at the annual convention of the National Civil Service Federation in 1965 were informed that:

> The ultimate objective of the comprehensive language training programme for the federal Public Service is the achievement over a period of time of sufficient fluency and facility in both languages by members of the Public Service to permit the day-to-day business to be conducted interchangeably in either or both languages without the necessity of translation services in routine matters.[63]

Nearly three decades later, the vision of a Public Service populated by hundreds of thousands of workers equally comfortable in both English and French seems fantastical. Experience has proved the task of creating bilingual skills on a mass basis to be significantly more difficult than originally anticipated. Internal estimates calculated by the Public Service Commission in 1990 indicate that the average unilingual public servant requires 1,600 hours of linguistic training to learn a second language.[64] To train an individual full-time for 1,600 hours requires that he or she take a ten-month leave of absence from work while on language training.[65]

Even if a temporary replacement could be found for every unilingual worker who wanted language training, the costs of paying ten months' full salary to a worker who is producing no work at all during his or her period in language training is so high that no more than a tiny percentage of civil servants can ever be sent to learn a second language.

The statistics on federal language training tell this story eloquently. In 1990, public servants spent 1,212,418 hours (over 600 person-years) at government expense learning to speak French. A further 183,278 hours, or ninety-one person-years, were spent training francophones to speak English.[66] Assuming that the average public servant participating in the language training program was being paid $20 an hour, this represented an expenditure of nearly $30 million in salary costs alone. The cost of teachers and of instructional materials boosts this total much higher, as does the high failure rate. As long ago as 1978, one estimate put the cost of producing a single genuinely bilingual public servant at $206,000—over a half million dollars in today's money.[67]

Because of the enormous cost, language training is strictly rationed. Public servants who hope to enrol in second-language courses must pass a test showing that they have the natural ability to learn quickly. Failing this test means permanent exclusion from second-language courses, and hence from most promotions.[68] In 1991, only 2,280 unilingual English-speaking public servants and 395 unilingual French-speaking public servants were able to participate in government-sponsored language training.[69] This represents less than two percent of all unilingual persons employed in the federal Public Service. Moreover, many of these participants were involved in part-time study only, and others were on 'refresher' courses to update rusty second-language skills. Given that 163,000 of the 234,000 persons employed by the Public Service of Canada are unilingual, the production of a completely bilingual Public Service would require 130,000 person-years of training, at a total cost of $4.3 billion in lost work hours alone.[70] Yet even this would be only a temporary solution, since all new unilingual public servants entering the workforce in the future would require second language training.

The Language of Work

> The state can play the blind man but not the deaf mute. To arrange for 30 percent of Canadian public servants to be francophone is one thing; to arrange for this francophone 30 percent to work in French is another.
> —*Jean Laponce, Languages and their Territories (1987)*[71]

Ironically, the bilingual quota system has completely destroyed Trudeau's vision of a fully bilingual civil service in which French would be spoken as widely as English. English is still, after twenty years, the dominant language of the Public Service. Despite two decades of constant emphasis on the right of francophones to speak their own language at work, the language is only slightly more widely used today as a work language than it was in the 1960s.

Fifteen years after Trudeau came to office, Gordon Robertson, former Clerk of the Privy Council, was still able to report that "in interdepartmental meetings, English is spoken virtually 100 percent of the time."[72] More recent figures indicate that most francophone public servants still have to speak English on the job, while anglophone public servants—including anglophones holding bilingual positions—almost never find occasion to use French.[73]

This situation still exists because most recruitment of French-speaking public servants is done through the bilingual quota system. The result is that most francophone public servants are bilingual, while most anglophone public servants are not. The numbers here are not much different than they were thirty years ago. In 1965, eighty-three percent of francophones in the Public Service were bilingual; today, seventy-five percent are. Eight percent of anglophone public servants were bilingual in 1965;[74] by 1991, the figure had climbed only to seventeen percent. What happens when unilingual anglophones and bilingual francophones work together is explained by a Department of National Defence report:

> There are two principle reasons why BUs [bilingual work units] still produce much of their written work in English only: too many anglophone incumbents, who make up approximately 78% of the total BU strength, are not bilingual. Francophones are invariably fully bilingual and in fact frequently find it easier to do their work in English than in French.[75]

One result is that the employment deck is still stacked as heavily as ever against those French-speakers who are not fluently bilingual, since they must continue to struggle in jobs where their communication skills are *by definition* inferior. These individuals are not at all helped by increases in bilingual hiring quotas, but the federal government is unable to respond to their needs, having long ago rejected the idea of French-language work units. Caught in a trap of its own making, all that the federal government is able to do is give the illusion of overcoming this inherent discrimination by increasing yet further the number of posts designated bilingual. This worsens the problem by closing the door on an ever-increasing proportion of Public Service jobs (including all senior posts) to non-bilingual francophones, but at least the statistical illusion of French Canadian participation lingers on for a little while longer.

Just Who Occupies Those Bilingual Positions Anyway?

Even the best illusionist cannot perform the same tricks forever and assume that his secrets will not eventually be discovered. The statistical illusion that is the whole *raison d'être* of the current system has been uncovered by a number of writers, but the information does not seem to have filtered its way to the public. Should the Quebec media or the *Péquistes* ever successfully bring this information to the Quebec public's attention, a powerful argument for national unity will have been destroyed.

As long ago as 1975, political scientist Léon Dion reported that Québécois francophones were under-represented and francophones from outside Quebec were over-represented among French-speaking bureaucrats.[76] A book published later that year put a more precise number on this assertion:

> Nine out of ten of the Francophones are from either Ontario or Quebec. To be exact, 51 per cent of the Francophone middle-level is from Quebec and 40 per cent from Ontario. This represents a decided over-representation of Franco-Ontarians since less than 10 percent of the total French Canadian population resides there. . . . Among Francophones what is noteworthy is the high proportion (43 percent) from Ottawa and Hull. The narrow base of Francophone recruitment is even more striking when the numbers from the proximate French-speaking areas of Ontario are added to it, bringing the total to 51 per cent. In contrast, only 37 per cent originated from Montreal or other points in Quebec.[77]

Time has not improved this situation. The proportion of Ontario francophones who speak English has been rising steadily since the 1970s, making them more qualified than ever to fill bilingual positions, while the number of bilingual francophones in Quebec has remained stagnant.

Another problem exists, which almost certainly guarantees the eventual destruction of the bilingual quota system: the rising number of English Canadians who have taken the message of Official Bilingualism seriously and learned French. Because English Canada's population is so much larger than French Canada's, even a slight increase in the percentage of English-speakers who master the French language will have the effect of ending the usefulness of the quota system as a means of preferential hiring for francophones.[78] In 1986, 64.9 percent of Canada's bilinguals were francophones. By 1991, the figure had dropped to fifty-seven percent.

Even the illusion of francophone over-representation will soon be under attack, bringing an end to the usefulness of the bilingual quota system as a means of bribing Quebecers to support a united Canada. Therefore, even if fairness and equity were not at issue, it would be time to re-examine alternative methods of securing a reasonable linguistic balance in the Public Service.

A PRACTICAL SOLUTION: UNILINGUAL WORK UNITS

> Since research has shown that bilinguals strongly prefer to use their mother tongue when talking to bilinguals of the same mother tongue, we can conclude that if a feature of an organization is a need for teamwork and there is a preponderance of bilinguals of one mother tongue (rather than a balance of both), the organization will tend over time to become unilingual, even though all its members are bilingual.... On the other hand, the sort of organization that could maintain a true bilingualism is one that is segmentable, in the sense that individuals do a great deal of their work alone or in small units where many conversations involve small groups working face-to-face, in which it is possible for people to feel relatively comfortable using their first language. Such a structure could even tolerate the presence of a substantial proportion of unilinguals, as long as unilinguals of different languages need not converse directly with one another, or can find a bilingual as a translator.
> —Sanford Borins, *The Language of the Skies* (1983)[79]

The Solution of the Bilingualism and Biculturalism Commission

Twenty years ago, the members of the Royal Commission on Bilingualism and Biculturalism determined that the fundamental flaw with hiring and promotion in the Public Service was the lack of French-speaking work environments. Solve this problem, they asserted, and equitable hiring and promotion would take care of itself, without any need for quotas, preferential hiring, or any deviation from the traditionally-defined merit principle.

Their solution is as valid today as it was then. After all, the fundamental problem is still that people are forced to learn a second language in order to get ahead in Ottawa.

The most important aspect of the Commission's proposals was its recommendation that the federal government create a network of 'French-language units':

> The essential idea of the French-language unit is that its personnel—both Francophone and Anglophone—will use French as the language of work. This requirement will not entirely exclude the use of English, but it will sharply circumscribe it. Generally, only French will be used within designated French-language units and between these units and the senior officers of their departments. In communication between the French-language units and other units, a policy of receptive bilingualism will apply.[80]

French language units would be created in each department of the Public Service and would be vertically integrated, allowing individuals to rise to high levels of seniority without learning English.[81] In Ottawa, the number of jobs located in units designated as French-speaking would be proportionate with Canada's French population, to ensure equality of opportunity for both official

Figure 8.3: The French-language unit (FLU) system (theoretical model)

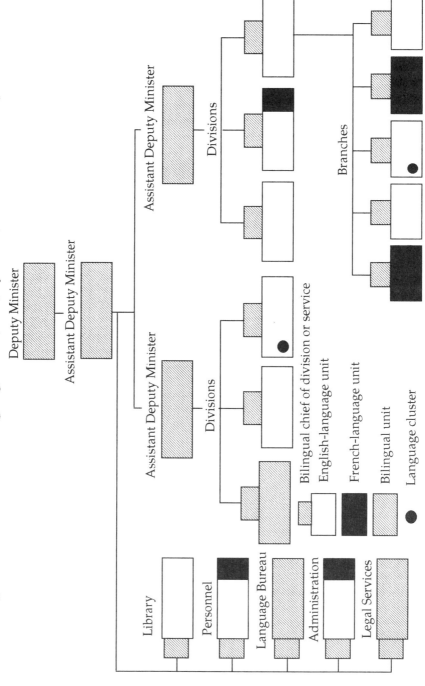

language groups. In the field, French language units would be heavily concentrated in Quebec, with a smaller number located in French-speaking areas of Ontario and New Brunswick to allow equitable job opportunities for the members of the local populations.[82]

By implication, any work unit not designated as a French-language unit would operate as an English-language unit. The B&B Commission's report carefully notes that French-language units would be open to anglophones with sufficient French language skills, and that the creation of French-language units would not limit francophones with a sufficient command of English from pursuing job opportunities in English-speaking parts of the Public Service.[83] This would preclude the danger of linguistic 'ghettoization' within the Public Service.

As the schematic chart on page 193 shows, the B&B Commission envisaged the existence of posts which would be open only to bilingual individuals, but these were to be limited to areas like translation, "where bilingualism defines the function,"[84] and to a small number of senior posts such as Section Head, Assistant Deputy Minister and Deputy Minister.

The key to fairness was the entrenchment of a proportionate share of jobs, in which French would be the language of work, rather than requiring that the jobs be filled by persons whose mother tongue is French. As long as this was done, the federal government would not be creating a grandiose quota system, in which linguistic background counts for more than merit. Instead, the government would be creating the closest thing possible, in a country of two linguistic communities, to a genuinely level playing field in federal hiring and promotion. Members of each language group would have access, on a per-capita basis, to an equal number of posts at each level of seniority. As Commissioner of Official Languages Keith Spicer wrote in 1975, when the federal government was toying with the idea of tossing aside bilingual designations for individual posts in favour of the language based work unit-system:

> [This policy] is sound ... from every point of view: Anglophone bilinguals may apply to work in [French language units] on the same terms as Francophones. This avoids the danger of an "ethnic" ghettoization repugnant to Canadian society, and allows strongly motivated Anglophones to develop further the language skills many have acquired at public expense.[85]

Under such a system, bilingual persons would continue to benefit from access to all jobs in the civil service (both in French-language and English-language units), plus a continued monopoly on the relatively small number of jobs that would remain bilingual (translators, receptionists and individuals serving the public in bilingual regions of the country). But their elite status would be gone.

Although it was never taken seriously in Ottawa, the system of unilingual work units has been implemented elsewhere, and has proven to be a great success. These successes bear closer examination, since they form such a striking contrast to the disaster of Ottawa's quota system. As well, the past two decades have produced a few refinements on the B&B Commission proposals that would prove to be beneficial additions, should Ottawa at long last adopt this system.

Language-Based Work Units in the Private Sector

Although the members of the B&B Commission do not seem to have been aware of it, the system of unilingual work units they proposed is remarkably similar to the standard practice among successful bilingual companies in the Canadian private sector. A study by Robert N. Morrisson, published a year after the Commission had published its proposals for the federal bureaucracy, described the staffing practices of forty-one Canadian companies providing 21.5 percent of the jobs in Quebec's industrial sector. Morrisson found that the companies had for the most part divided their operations into unilingual work units linked by what he called "linguistic bridges" (in other words, supervisors or unit members who were capable of speaking both French and English).[86]

One consequence of this system was that francophones were well represented among certain types of management functions where French was particularly useful, such as industrial relations and sales. This compensated considerably for their under-representation in categories of management that involved out-of-province work (and, in consequence, the frequent use of English).

Language-Based Work Units in the Canadian Military

The Canadian Armed Forces have been subjected to bilingual post designations at least as severe as those in the rest of the Public Service—so much so in fact, that one minister of defence was prompted to blurt out at a Parliamentary hearing: "The Canadian Forces [seems to have] believed the intent of the *Official Languages Act* was to establish as many bilingual positions as possible, regardless of whether there was a necessity or a possibility of filling them."[87]

Nonetheless, there are parts of the military where the language regime has not been applied in the usual manner. In fighting units, it is necessary to have the ability to communicate rapidly and effectively in times of extreme stress—in other words, to operate at peak efficiency at exactly those moments when one's ability to use a second language is most likely to fail. For this reason, some military units are divided on the basis of language. The famed Royal 22nd Regiment—the 'Van Doos' of Val Cartier—operate entirely in French, as do the destroyers HMCS Skeena and HMCS Algonquin. Other units operate entirely in English.

Unfortunately, the French Language Unit/English Language Unit model has been tampered with repeatedly in an effort to institute a language regime on the model of the Public Service,[88] so the military is full of strange hybrids like 'Bilingual Language Units' (of which there were 738 in 1991), and French language units with minimum percent quotas of anglophones who are on immersion training. Being neither fish nor fowl, it is not surprising that these units do not function well, while genuinely unilingual units provide satisfactory work environments for unilingual personnel.

The New Brunswick Model

An interesting variant on the B&B Commission's language-based units proposal is the "target team" model presently being instituted in the provincial civil service of New Brunswick.[89] Under this model, individual *positions* in the provincial Public Service are not designated 'English-essential,' 'French essential,' or 'bilingual-essential,' as are posts in the federal Public Service. Instead, as in the B&B Commission's system, each of the *functions* and *services* provided by the provincial government is defined as requiring the use of one, the other, or both languages.

Employee groups, or 'target teams,' are then identified within the Public Service to fulfil these functions. Employees are grouped within these teams. Individual positions within the teams have no language designation. The team as a whole, however, is required to meet established language requirements in terms of service to the public.[90] The primary innovation of the target team approach is that some teams will offer services in both languages, even though most people on the team are unilingual. As originally conceived, even the B&B model did not permit this level of flexibility.

The target team system assures that high-quality services provision in both official languages remains the Public Service's top priority, while providing the widest possible job flexibility for unilingual public servants. This approach could easily be married to the English/French Language Unit concept, with which it already bears much in common. Under such a hybrid system, each target team would be designated as either English or French, and the designated language would become the normal internal language of the team. Most posts could be filled by unilingual anglophones or francophones (as appropriate to that team's language designation), but a relatively small number of bilingual posts would remain in some teams for jobs that fulfil such innately bilingual team functions as translation, reception and secretarial functions in bilingual regions, and other aspects of service-provision.

If properly designed, a staffing system based on the New Brunswick model would have the effect of dividing the Public Service into teams in which either English or French (but rarely both) would be used as the language of work. This would cause many job opportunities to be opened up both to unilingual anglophones and to unilingual francophones.

Under the 'target team' approach, unilingual work units would probably evolve naturally elsewhere in the Public Service, with a number of positive results for the majority of Canada's French speakers. For one thing, unilingual francophones would no longer face a substantial hiring and advancement disadvantage as compared to their bilingual counterparts. As well, for the first time ever, it would be possible for a majority of French-speaking public servants to carry out their jobs entirely in the French language.

A Further Refinement . . .

One important flaw with the otherwise excellent proposals of the B&B Commission is that they assumed that above a certain level of seniority, bilingualism would be necessary for all public servants. The Commissioners seem to have believed that up to a relatively senior level, unilingualism would be possible, but at a higher level, bilingualism would have been as much a requirement under the B&B proposal as under the existing system.

The reason for this insurmountable barrier above a certain level is that, sooner or later, as one proceeds up the bureaucratic ladder, it would be necessary to place somebody in charge of supervising or co-ordinating both French-language units and English-language units. This individual would have to be able to communicate in both official languages. This need for bilingual people to coordinate unilingual people would have the effect of creating a 'glass ceiling' for unilinguals, similar to the one that exists under the present system, where no supervisor is permitted to have a lesser level of second-language ability than the most highly skilled of his or her subordinates. The primary difference under the B&B Commission's proposal is that the glass ceiling would be set at a higher level of seniority.

A recent report by the Professional Institute of the Public Service (PIPSC) suggests a common sense way of permitting unilinguals to rise above either of these glass ceilings. PIPSC recommends that:

> . . . in areas where services must be provided in both official languages according to government regulations, the personnel at the service level should be bilingual as well as the immediate supervisor in order to be able to evaluate the quality of bilingual services provided. All other upper supervisory levels can be unilingual since they evaluate management skills only.[91]

With this refinement made, it should be possible for unilingual francophones or anglophones to advance as far as the rank of assistant deputy minister or even (as long as the minister they serve speaks their language) to the ultimate level of Public Service seniority—deputy minister itself. Equitable hiring and completely merit-based promotion would have been married at last.

SUMMARY

There is no denying that francophones were under-represented in the Canadian Public Service in years past. But this injustice has long since been overcome, and past inequities are no justification for deliberate present-day injustices. Insensitivity on the part of our parents' generation is no excuse for us to make a positive virtue out of today's systematic discrimination. Besides, a policy of systematic discrimination should at least have the virtue of actually helping its designated beneficiary group. Most Québécois are as firmly and permanently excluded from the Public Service by the bilingualism barrier as the anglophones who are its intended victims, and they know it.

So it is doubtful, to say the least, whether the bilingual quota system is helping, rather than hurting, the cause of national unity. Since the system's sole reason for existing is to foster unity, it is time to admit that it has failed to perform its intended function, and kill it.

No one would suggest that official language abilities ought to cease entirely to be considerations in Public Service staffing and promotions. But consideration need not mean wholesale application of inflexible 'language requirements' that categorically exclude all whose second language proficiency falls short of the specified level. There are positions for which such intractable language requirements are appropriate. Quality control in a translation bureau, for example. In such positions, there is an actual 'language requirement' in that incumbents cannot do the job without the specified high level of second language proficiency. But in most Public Service positions that are today designated bilingual, functions can be done—were done, in many cases—by unilingual public servants.

Many jobs, performed once-upon-a-time in English only, could be done unilingually in English once again, or unilingually in French. Does anyone really care what language their tax forms are processed in or the language in which tens of thousands of other jobs are performed in hermetically-sealed government offices far from the public eye (and ear)?

In short, there are practical alternatives to the current approach. All that is required is to set aside the current policy of awarding each post a linguistic designation, to create language-based work units, and thereby to open the Public Service to all members of the public who are willing and competent to serve.

The whole system should be reformed by introducing genuine merit hiring, for both anglophones and francophones, for the first time ever. This can be done only if the Public Service is divided into parallel hierarchies of English-language and French-language work units in which unilingual speakers of either language can rise to the top (or close, anyway) without having to speak the other language.

CHAPTER NINE

Language and Education

The right of citizens of Canada under subsections (1) and (2) to have their children receive primary and secondary school instruction in the language of the English or French linguistic minority population of a province:
(a) applies wherever in the province the number of children of citizens who have such a right is sufficient to warrant the provision to them out of public funds of minority language instruction; and
(b) includes, where the number of those children so warrants, the right to have them receive that instruction in minority language educational facilities provided out of public funds.
—*Section 23,* **Canadian Charter of Rights and Freedoms** *(partial text)*

[Section] 23 (1) (a) shall come into force in respect of Quebec . . . only where authorized by the legislative assembly or government of Quebec.
—*Section 59 (partial text)*

EDUCATION HAS ALWAYS been central to Canadian language conflicts, from the murderous Caraquet riots caused by New Brunswick's *Common Schools Act* of 1871 to the burning of the Quebec flag in schoolyards by immigrant children protesting Bill 101.[1]

Perhaps this is why Canadian education policy, more than any other aspect of federal language policy, has been redesigned primarily as a propaganda tool, to show Québécois voters the depth of Canada's commitment to subsidizing and supporting the French language.

Asymmetrical bilingualism dominates the Canadian education system to an extent unrivalled in any other area of language policy. In Quebec, the right to receive primary and high-school education in English is legally available only to a privileged and shrinking minority of anglophone children whose parents were themselves educated in English in Canada. This right is passed from generation to generation as an hereditary privilege. Ottawa did not create this rule, but it did entrench it in the constitution.

By contrast, outside Quebec, the right to receive an education in French has been extended, in principle, to a degree of generosity unsurpassed in the rest of the world. Although practice has not quite caught up with the cutting edge of jurisprudence on this matter, it is only a question of time before it will be the right of every francophone parent, Canadian-born or immigrant, wherever located, to have his or her children educated in French in schools supported by the local taxpayers, regardless of cost.

The dichotomy between the rights extended to Canada's francophone and anglophone minorities is entrenched in the Constitution, as a feature of the 1982 *Charter of Rights and Freedoms*. Section 23 of the Charter, which deals with language in education, does nothing to protect the right of immigrants to Quebec to choose the language in which their children will be educated. On the other hand, it does guarantee the right of francophones (including francophone immigrants) to educate their children in French, as long as the "number of those children so warrants." There exists no exact definition of this phrase. However, almost from the moment that Section 23 became law in 1982, Ottawa has been subsidizing court challenges designed to cause the legal definition of the phrase to be interpreted as generously as possible.[2]

Asymmetry is also evident elsewhere in the education system. French-immersion classes have spread from coast to coast, and now contain 295,000 students nationwide.[3] This is partly the result of generous federal transfers to provincial departments of education in support of French immersion, but mostly it is due to fierce pressure from unilingual anglophone parents who are aware that children who cannot speak French will never be able to build careers in the Public Service, the diplomatic corps, the military, any crown corporation, or an increasing variety of federally-regulated private businesses. The parental pressure from anglophones is even more intense in Quebec, with the result that immersion in that province begins as early as kindergarten and that a majority of Anglo-Quebecers feel that immersion should be made mandatory for all English-speaking children.[4]

English Canadians are so used to hearing of the benefits of French immersion that they forget how odd it is that there is no such thing as English immersion. The very concept is unlawful in Quebec, below the CEGEP (senior high school) level, and it simply is not offered anywhere else in Canada.[5] All of the hundreds of millions of dollars devoted to immersion education every year by various levels of government is channelled exclusively into French-language teaching.[6]

There are two central conflicts in the unending battle over language in education. The first is the widespread belief that if an individual receives his education in English, he will be assimilated into Canada's English-speaking community, and that assimilation into the French community will be the natural and inevitable result of schooling in French. This perception, which has nearly universal acceptance by government, the media, academia, and the public, has been the source of such oppressive schooling laws as Ontario's Regulation 17 and Quebec's Bill 101, among others. Despite the tears that have been shed over policies founded on this belief and the billions that have been spent on them, it is completely, demonstrably false.

The second source of conflict is the fact that minority language education is expensive. There is a high cost associated with setting up separate school boards, teaching facilities, and sometimes expensive extras such as busing children to minority-language schools. Minorities plead that the extra expense is necessary, while majorities insist that the financial burden is unreasonable and draws scarce resources out of the regular school system.

The conflict of financial interest has led to disputes over language of education even in regions of the country where there exist no demographic fears based on the belief that education is a source of assimilation. Financial considerations have been the cause of restrictive language-in-education laws from British Columbia to Newfoundland. Yet here, too, the conflict is based on a fundamental misunderstanding—in this case, the peculiar belief that all schooling must be tightly controlled and regulated by the government, with all financing of education taking the form of direct payments to the provider of the services, without any intervention or control on the part of the minority-language parents.

This chapter will argue that the solution to the conflicts caused by minority language education lies in the adoption of a system of education vouchers issued by provincial governments to minority-language parents. This solution would produce lower-cost, higher-quality minority education and in addition would allow parents to develop the curriculum to their own taste.

Conflict #1: Education as the Guarantor of Assimilation

In each of Canada's major French-English battles over education during the past century, the same argument has held pride of place in the arsenal of those seeking to diminish minority rights. Education, it is explained, is the key to assimilation. If minority-language schools are allowed to operate unrestricted, the demographic weight of the minority will continue to grow until it threatens the security of the majority. This argument is completely incorrect, even though it has been repeated from Manitoba in the 1890s to Quebec in the 1990s.

To be sure, there are elements of individual colouration to this monotone argument. In Manitoba, the perceived danger was that migrants from Quebec would flood into the province if the schools and other institutions were not made uninviting. In Ontario in 1912, it was believed that only high rates of assimilation in the schools could lessen the impact of high birthrates among Franco-Ontarians. In Quebec since the 1970s, the argument has been that the English do not themselves pose the demographic threat, but that 'allophone' immigrants from overseas will fail to assimilate into the French-language majority if they are permitted to attend English-language schools.

Although this belief is incorrect in Quebec's case as much as in the others, it does rest on an important bit of truth: that only the assimilation of new immigrants into the French language will be able to compensate for sagging birthrates among francophones. But it is incorrect to conclude that every time the child of an immigrant is enrolled in an English-language school instead of a French one, a future francophone is lost, as completely and permanently as if the child had been stolen by gypsies. And it is certainly incorrect to continue this line of thought by assuming that each lost child will become a member of Quebec's own English-speaking minority, thereby adding to that community's demographic weight and assimilative pull on the rest of the province. This fundamentally erroneous point of view is summed up tidily in this passage from a recent book by University of Montreal professor Georges Mathews:

> The concentration of young allophones, the children of Bill 101, in certain French schools [draws] attention to the enormous challenge of integrating new arrivals in Quebec society. Since 1986, there has been a surge in immigration, but two-thirds of all immigrants do not understand French when they land. As there are two communities in Montreal ready to receive them, and since there is, even today, no obvious reason why a non-francophone would choose the French rather than the English community, integration in the French milieu requires a supplementary effort on the part of the community. We know that if nothing changes in the linguistic choices of the immigrant population, current demographic trends suggest that the relative importance of francophones in Montreal will decline.... [7]

This psychological distinction between immigrants who are expected to become the source of renewed French Canadian population growth and anglophones already residing in Quebec is one of the main reasons why both the Parti Québécois and Robert Bourassa's Liberals have never attempted to limit the education rights of Quebec's native anglophone population. The two-century-old English-speaking population of Montreal and the Eastern Townships is seen as more or less indigestible, and therefore not a promising source of conscripts for assimilation.

Conflict #2: The Question of Cost

Even in the periods of relative toleration that have punctuated Canada's bursts of demographic angst, minority-language education has remained a contentious issue because of the high costs that minority-language education has normally involved. The dispute over these costs, and the burden which they impose upon the majority population, can be traced back to the beginnings of state-supported education in the mid-19th century. In 1846, when an attempt by Upper Canada's superintendent of education to centralize school administration led to Canada's first-ever dispute over language in education, the focus of concern was the division of scarce local property-tax revenues between French and English-language educational facilities.[8]

This theme was repeated in the New Brunswick and Prince Edward Island *School Act* disputes of the 1870s, where anti-Catholic intolerance was mixed with a desire to gain control of all tax revenues for the Protestant school systems. In 1905, the *Alberta Act*, creating Canada's ninth province, was delayed in Parliament for five months by a bitter dispute over entrenching an expensive system of parallel sectarian school boards in the new province's constitution. The dispute led to the resignation of Laurier's Minister of the Interior, Clifford Sifton; the parliamentary debate became the longest that Canada had yet experienced.

The same issue was central to Quebec's debates over education policy in the 1960s, before anyone had seriously contemplated using education as a mechanism for the forced assimilation of immigrants. It simply seemed wasteful to run four parallel school systems: French Catholic, English Catholic, English Protestant and French Protestant. The plethora of overlapping school boards led to the creation of a provincial commission of inquiry in the mid-1960s. In the 1970s and 1980s, attempts by the provincial authorities to implement various recommendations on school board consolidation would be fought bitterly by anglophone parents and teachers who feared the weakening or loss of any traditional English-controlled institution. The consolidation debates would add to the atmosphere of hostility over the schools in Quebec, which was already substantial for other (obvious) reasons.

BILL 101: AN IN-DEPTH LOOK AT EDUCATION AS THE GUARANTOR OF ASSIMILATION

Whenever and wherever in Canadian history provincial laws have over-ridden individual freedom of choice in education in order to forcibly join minority children to the majority linguistic community, the results have been fundamentally inhumane. In effect, these governments have regarded the children as raw meat to be fed into an educational system conceived of as a giant sausage-making machine; put through the grinder, students were expected to emerge as neatly packaged assimilation statistics. This was the attitude of the Manitoba government in 1890 and of the Ontario government in 1912. Today it is the attitude of the Quebec government towards its immigrant population. It is this attitude that permits Stéphane Dion of the University of Montreal to gush with academic delight over a new batch of figures: "among the allophones [the percentage attending French schools] increased from 38.7 to 72.7 between 1980 and 1989. The effects of Bill 101 are spectacular here."[9] In Dion's view, and that of the government as well, the actual impact of the whole process upon the student is of distinctly secondary importance.

The casual attitude towards the well-being of individual immigrant students is reflected over and over again in the comments of Bill 101's enthusiasts. Dion, for example, concludes his statistical observation by noting casually that even though many immigrants are angry and frustrated because they are unable to send their children to English-language schools, the important thing is that "the results are encouraging for the French language."[10]

Even half-hearted attempts to humanize the system are greeted with derision. For several years following the imposition of Bill 101 in 1977, some school boards illegally accepted immigrants into English-language classes. The practice ended fairly quickly, once the provincial government began to tie school funding to compliance with Bill 101. As an additional measure, the illegal students were denied the right to obtain provincial certificates of graduation. Shortly after the Liberal party was returned to power in 1985, it introduced a law granting amnesty to these students.[11] This measure was perceived by the nationalists to abandon the French language in its hour of need. The well-being of the ex-students, who had effectively been cut off from further education by the withholding of their credentials, was simply not an issue.

A similar mini-crisis arose in 1991 when Michel Pagé, the provincial minister of education, observed to a reporter from the Montreal *Gazette* that in light of the fact that enrollments in English-language schools in the province had fallen by over fifty percent since 1976, it might be time to consider lifting Quebec's ban on English-language schooling for the children of immigrants from English-speaking countries. Pagé quickly backed down in the face of criticism in the French-language media, and told the *Gazette* the next day that he had been misquoted and that he would never support such a modification.[12]

A somewhat different crisis, which reveals the same inflexible attitude, had arisen fourteen years earlier, when Inuit parents in northern Quebec had refused to allow their children to be forced into French-language classes. The province, which was taking charge of Inuit schools (formerly run by the federal government) as a consequence of one of the provisions of the James Bay Agreement, was unwilling to extend the right to be educated in English, Cree and Initut—the traditional language of northern schools—to children who had moved from other provinces or the Northwest Territories since 1973. According to one author writing on the subject of the Quebec Inuit dispute:

> It is hardly possible to imagine anything more disruptive to school children than to have the language of instruction arbitrarily shifted in such a manner against the wishes of parents and students alike, all done to serve some remote political end.[13]

In the end, the province chose to deal with the crisis by sending armed police north to protect the local French-speaking authorities and to ensure that it could bargain with the Inuit from a position of strength.[14]

Most striking of all, however, is the text of Bill 101 itself. Here it is stated, in the precise logical wording of the law, that members of immigrant minorities will be expected to sacrifice their personal well-being for the sake of the well-being of the French language. Section 81 of the law graciously exempts all non-francophone children with serious learning disabilities from the additional burden of having to get their education in French. Any child who is at least three years behind in his studies qualifies as having such a disability. However, a 1984 order-in-council amending Bill 101 warns, "disabilities caused by a change of cultural or linguistic surroundings are not considered to be serious learning disabilities...."[15] In other words, a ruined education caused by enforced enrollment in a French-language school is a reasonable price to pay to gain one more foot soldier in the war against assimilation.

The foregoing paragraphs may leave the false impression that Quebec's education policies are bigoted, in that they force non-francophones to bear the entire cost of maintaining the French language. This is not the case, for while allophones are obliged to be educated exclusively in French, most anglophone children are not affected by the law. As well, it bears mentioning that the burden of the anti-assimilation struggle extends to young francophones as well. One of the most contentious aspects of Quebec education policy is the Department of Education's policy of not permitting French students to receive any English lessons before the fourth grade. While serving as Minister of Education, Claude Ryan announced that provincial transfer payments would be cut off to schools teaching English before the fourth grade or for more than three hours a week at more senior grades. He explained the policy by stating the "we've long understood that premature exposure to English might not be compatible with the best development of the child."[16]

To some degree, Ryan's concerns can be traced back to the findings of Quebec's 1965 Royal Commission on Education, which had recommended delaying English lessons for francophone students until their grasp of French grammar and vocabulary was strong enough to guard against the intrusion of grammatically incorrect borrowings from the English language, known as "anglicisms."[17] But it has to be assumed that a substantial part of the logic behind the limit on English classes is the desire to delay the learning of English to a later age to ensure that linguistic loyalties, not just grammatical skills, will be cemented. This is certainly the attitude adopted by language scholar Jacques Leclerc in the following:

> Studies ... demonstrate beyond any doubt that bilingualism is very positive for children from dominant groups who acquire a functional level in a second

language ... because they don't risk acculturation (assimilation into another culture). On the other hand, bilingualism and a bilingual education aren't nearly so good *for the children* of minority groups ... even if the bilingual minorities find socioeconomic advantages in being bilingual, they risk assimilation if the second language dominates in too many social roles, penetrating eventually even into their homes.[18]

It would be difficult not to be sympathetic to the desire to preserve and perpetuate *any* language and culture, but there is something sinister in the suggestion that a population should as a matter of policy be denied a specific class of knowledge that confers "socioeconomic advantage." Some anglophone commentators would take this criticism further, suggesting that the true goal of Quebec's ruling elite is to create a unilingual French-speaking clientele, dependent upon its bilingual leaders for guidance in a mostly English-speaking world. Mordecai Richler, who is never bashful about taking note of inconsistencies between what the nationalists say and what they do, notes that Jacques Parizeau hired an English nanny to look after his children.[19] Reed Scowen, a former aide to Robert Bourassa, remarks that it is "astonishing" to talk of the best interests of a child in terms of his or her right to be isolated from knowledge of English, while ignoring the fact that bilingual francophones in Quebec have higher average incomes than unilingual French-speakers.[20]

If this really is the intention of the ban, it may be turning out to be successful. Richler writes that an Anglo-Quebecer businessman he knows told him, "Years ago, if we placed an ad in the papers looking for a bilingual employee, a good many of the applicants were Francophones. Now they are for the most part Anglophones, Italians or Greeks. The young Francophones are being forced to revert to unilingualism, which will deny them the most jobs whether this province separates, drifts out to sea, or whatever."[21]

Unlike Bill 101, which has strong support from the francophone majority, the policy of limiting the access of francophone children to English second language instruction has not favourably impressed the majority of French-speaking parents. As long ago as the 1960s when the first surveys on the issue were conducted, francophone parents favoured giving their children adequate instruction in English. A poll conducted in the mid-1960s on behalf of the B&B Commission found that ninety-five percent of French Canadians agreed that "French-speaking children should learn English in primary school."[22] This consensus exists to the present day. Following Ryan's announcement, newspapers in Quebec were filled with stories of local boards of education that had been violating the ban at the request of French-speaking parents.[23]

The Feudalization of Education Rights in Quebec

> Bill 101 makes access to English schools a hereditary privilege, a concept foreign to ordinary democracy.
> —Editorial, Montreal **Gazette** (October 19, 1988)

In the space of half a dozen years in the 1970s, Quebec moved from a regime of free choice in education to one of complete state control. The province moved first to a system under which education in English would be available only to those who could speak English (under Bill 22), and then to a system under which it would be restricted to those who *are* English (under Bill 101). For its first five years in force, Bill 101 was even more restrictive than this. Only children of parents who had been educated in English *in Quebec* would be eligible to attend English-language schools. Parents from other parts of Canada would be treated like any other 'foreigner,' and would be forced to send their children to French school.

This particular provision of Bill 101, known as the 'Quebec Clause,' was rolled back in 1982 when Parliament adopted the *Charter of Rights and Freedoms*. Under the Charter, the right to receive an education in English would henceforth be extended to any child of parents educated in English in any province of Canada. Although a liberalization could hardly be faulted, the practical effect of the two laws combined is to turn the right to attend school in English into a hereditary right, passed down from generation to generation among a single ethnic group, while all others are excluded because of their ethnicity.

The hereditary, ethnically discriminatory nature of education rights in Quebec will be heightened by the province's 1993 package of language law amendments, Bill 86. One provision of the Bill is designed to compensate for an unexpected phenomenon. In the wake of Bill 101, so many anglophone Quebecers chose to enroll their children in French schools that within five years, one anglophone student in seven was enrolled in French schools (as opposed to French immersion classes in English schools).[24]

Now that a first generation has passed through the school system in the post-Bill 101 period and some of the first anglophones to attend French schools are parents themselves, they have made a horrible discovery: under the terms of Bill 101, their own children are ineligible to attend English schools for all or part of their own educations.

Bill 86 remedies the problem by permitting the right to attend English schools to skip generations. Once again, a selective liberalization has had the effect of entrenching a right with limited bloodlines. Inevitably, this will become an explosive issue as the ethnic British proportion of the English-speaking population (who are by far the largest group holding this hereditary right) continues to decline, and the immigrant, non-white portion of the English-speaking population continues to grow. Eventually it will be seen as a right reserved, on the basis of ethnicity, for Anglo-Saxons only—but not for the visible minorities who will form the majority of Quebec's English-speakers.

What Would Happen in Quebec Under a System of Free Choice?

In fact, there is no evidence to suggest that the absence of restrictive laws would cause allophone students to flood massively into the English-speaking school system. Historically, free choice led to most immigrants choosing to school their children in English, but this decision seems mainly to have been due to flaws in the French system rather than to the intrinsic desirability of assimilating into the English rather than the French community. The 1966 report of the provincial government's Parent Commission on Education found that the relatively poor quality of the education provided in French-language schools was a prime factor.[25] This in turn was the result of problems that have since been corrected. For example, the French Catholic school system did not provide many of the prerequisites needed to enter university, while the English Protestant system did.[26]

The adoption of the *College d'enseignement général et professionel* (CEGEP) system of professionally-oriented high schools in the wake of the Parent Report has solved this second problem; new school funding procedures solved the first. Until the 1970s, school boards had been funded entirely by local property taxes. Higher tax assessments on supporters of the Protestant school boards had meant that the funds "available for the education of the average English-speaking pupil was many times that which could be raised per French-speaking child."[27] Direct payments from the provincial government to local school boards have since eliminated this inequity.

Another problem mentioned by the Parent Commission was the inadequacy of instruction in English as a second language in French schools. This was partly the result of a bizarre rule that forbade the hiring of Catholic teachers in the Protestant system, or of Protestant teachers in the Catholic system. In practice, this meant that French was taught to English students by anglophone teachers, and English to French students by francophone teachers. Neither program of second-language instruction was particularly good, but in the economy of the 1960s and 1970s, when English was still a much more economically valuable language to know than French, immigrants concluded English unilingualism seemed preferable to French unilingualism.

The provincially appointed Commission of Inquiry on the Position of the French Language added to these comments in 1972 by observing that immigrants had been made to feel unwelcome in the Catholic school system. Jews, for example, had been legally classified as Protestants and required to attend Protestant, English-language schools.[28] By the 1960s and early 1970s, the English-speaking schools had developed into an open, heterogeneous system, while French-speaking schools still maintained a closed and unwelcoming curriculum and structure. Whatever its other failings, the practice of force-feeding tens of thousands of allophone students into the French system for the past twenty years has by now overcome this problem. Nowadays, over one-third of the students in Montreal's French-language schools are immigrants.[29] A sophisticated network of *classes d'acceuil* (welcoming classes) have been developed to ease the cultural and linguistic transition for students, and supplementary French courses created to boost skills.

All of this does not mean that there would not be a substantial shift to English-language schools if the ban were lifted; some students would unquestionably make the change. But there would be no stampede. Even in a completely *laissez faire* school environment, the power of attraction of English-language schooling over French would never come close to 1970 levels. It is even less likely that francophone students would flood into the English-language school system, since even when the English system was at the height of its powers of attraction, only three percent of Montreal's francophone school children were attending English-language schools.[30]

A system of partial *laissez faire*, in which freedom of choice is enlarged only to include the children of immigrants from English-speaking countries, would have the effect of decreasing enrollment in French schools by only one percent, even if every single newly-eligible student were to switch to the English system.[31]

One indication of the kind of impact that complete free choice would have for children of all linguistic backgrounds may be gathered by observing the linguistic choices of allophone students at the senior high school (CEGEP) level, where free choice is still permitted in Quebec. In 1976, only sixteen percent of all allophone first-year CEGEP students elected to attend school in French. By 1992, the percentage had risen to forty-four percent.[32]

The reintroduction of free choice into the school system would probably even prove to be beneficial for the health of the French language. Children do not assimilate into the French language simply because they attend French-language school, or into English because they attend an English school. The schoolyard and hallway environment, rather than the classroom itself, is the determinant of language preference, and this is an element completely beyond the control of the educational authorities. The factor deciding whether English will predominate over French, or vice versa, is simple demographic weight. If more than half the children in the school have a predisposition towards one language or the other, their weight will pull along the rest of the student body.[33]

Logically, then, it is an advantage to lower the number of 'anglophile' students (allophone students who already lean towards English because of preschool exposure to the language) in the French-language system to a digestible level—i.e., to a level where they do not predominate in any schools, and are therefore more likely to be assimilated than to be assimilators.[34]

Figure 9.1
In the only part of the Quebec school system where free choice exists, French is growing steadily more popular

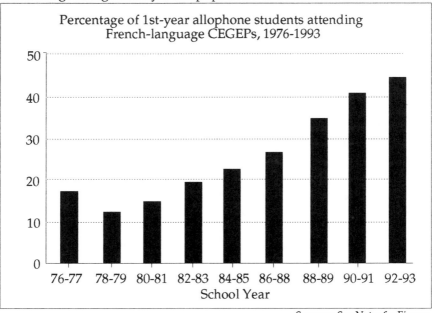

Sources: See *Notes for Figures*

This process could be accomplished by reintroducing free choice for immigrant parents. Better yet, vouchers could be issued, allowing them to choose freely among existing systems of education or to establish new alternatives of their own. If, as is likely, many parents were to opt to reject all the existing alternatives in favour of their own, they would almost certainly insist upon fully bilingual educations for their own children (as even the anglophones do nowadays). A certain degree of emphasis might be placed upon ancestral languages, but this hardly represents a threat to the predominance of French.

Meanwhile, a regime of voucher-driven free choice would make Quebec a much more desirable destination for overseas immigrants, and would significantly drive down the numbers of immigrants choosing to leave for the other provinces where immigrants in the main urban centres must send their children to increasingly decrepit public schools with decreasing educational standards.

The French-language teachers' union and school boards can be reliably counted on to oppose any such move towards freedom of choice, and presumably even English-language public school teachers in Montreal would speak out against a regime of free choice that does not grant them priority access to students being schooled in English. But one has to wonder whether it is not time for politicians in Quebec to decide whether they place a higher priority on placating the unions or on preserving and building the future of the language they profess so dearly to love.

SECTION 23: THE QUESTION OF COST

> In so defining the rights contained in section 23, Chief Justice Dickson refused to formulate a single rule of general application to govern the implementation of section 23 rights. In his view, section 23 "simply mandates that governments do whatever is practical in the situation to preserve and promote minority language education." Under his interpretation of section 23, however, no government can know with certainty what section 23 demands of it until a court "breathes life" into this provision.
> —*Christopher Manfredi (1993)*[35]

For more than a century following Confederation, francophone minority populations across Canada struggled, with very limited success, to secure the legal right to educate their children in French, at public expense. (This right had always been secure for English-speakers in Quebec—even Bill 101 did not cut off access to English schools to the majority of the province's English-speaking population.) Section 23 of the *Canadian Charter of Rights and Freedoms*, which guaranteed this right for the first time, was in some ways the ultimate victory of the 'personality principle' of language rights in Canadian law, and the crowning achievement of Pierre Trudeau's career-long struggle to entrench these principles in law.

Although Section 23 extended the rights of English-speakers in Quebec by extending the right to attend English-language schools to the children of parents educated in English in other provinces, the main beneficiaries of the new law were francophones living in the other nine provinces. (As a side note, it should be observed that only Section 23(b) is constitutionally binding upon Quebec. Both Section 23(a) and 23(b) are constitutionally binding on the other provinces.)

At first, some provinces attempted to give an ungenerous interpretation to the words "where numbers warrant," but court appeals in the mid-1980s established that this could mean as few as a dozen students.[36] The courts also ruled that it would be impossible to guarantee full francophone control of French-language education unless new French-language school boards were established. This guaranteed that French schools would be funded, but it also added expensive new layers of administrators and parallel networks of services. This, in turn, was made more complex by an additional court ruling that the established sectarian dichotomy in some provinces between 'Public' (Protestant) school boards and 'Separate' (Catholic) school boards would not serve as an acceptable framework for establishing universal French-language schooling, since this would force French-speaking non-Catholics to attend Catholic schools. Nor could the old system of denominational schools, entrenched in the constitution since 1867, be abolished.[37] This ruling led to the proliferation of even more school boards.

In some parts of the country, the result has been a mass of duplication and confusion. The Regional Municipality of Ottawa-Carleton, for example, now has eight school boards. Education is bisected into Ottawa and Carleton sectors, bisected again along religious lines, and divided again along linguistic lines. A total of eighty-eight school trustees are needed to administer all these boards; the high cost of paying them all means that there is a major public outcry every time one or another of these groups of trustees suggests voting itself a salary hike.

The new set of rules precipitated by Section 23 has led to battles in dozens of tiny communities over the establishment of new boards of education. These tiny wars have become so commonplace, they are no longer reported in the major media. A typical story, recounted in the Sarnia *Observer* in 1991, describes how a local English-language elementary school was closed due to low enrollment (about 100 students), then reopened as a French-language school with only thirty-seven students. The extremely high teacher-student ratios and per-student fixed costs for heat, light and rental costs for school facilities ensure that the extra cost per pupil to Sarnia rate payers will be in excess of $4,000.[38]

Traditionally, each province's majority could treat the educational aspirations of its linguistic minority with as much or as little generosity as it saw fit. Insensitivity to these aspirations was the general rule, punctuated by periodic bursts of outright bloody-mindedness. Since the adoption of the *Charter*, things have been dramatically different. Armed with their new legal powers, it is now the minorities that are becoming insensitive to the needs of the majority.

This new arrogance is expressed in the comments of some of the key players in the minority-language education game. Asked by the *Globe and Mail* for his comments on the high cost of creating overlapping new boards of education, Laurent Joncas, the president of the Franco-Ontarian Teachers' Federation, stated, "It's a question of rights, not money. If it were a question of money, none of us would have rights."[39] Likewise, D'Iberville Fortier, the former Commissioner of Official Languages, was unperturbed that the newfound legal rights of the francophone community might upset some people in provinces where the French are dwarfed by other minority languages, as is the case in each of the western provinces:

> If you are in a province where 14% of the population is of Ukrainian origin,

obviously this creates a little malaise in giving schools to one group simply
because it is one of the two official languages. We appreciate this, but there is
a price to pay for belonging to a country. This price is not very high.[40]

This situation has always been difficult to accept on the basis of group
equality or of individual justice. In more recent years, it has taken an enormous
leap of faith in the ability of French-language education as an instrument of
national unity to justify the extraordinary status of French over other non-indigenous languages. Today, there are more Chinese-speakers in Greater
Vancouver alone than there are francophones in all four Western provinces
combined.[41] In Toronto, where French-language education must by law be
available, French is only the tenth-most frequently spoken language, behind
Vietnamese, Tagalog and Punjabi, among others.[42] If the French-majority
regions of eastern and northern Ontario and northern New Brunswick are
excluded, French is only the second-largest minority language in English
Canada (slightly ahead of Italian and far behind Chinese).[43] It is rarely concentrated in pockets large enough to financially justify the creation of the normal
sort of school board—a situation that is not true for any number of highly
concentrated minority language groups in Toronto, Vancouver or Calgary.
Costs per student will be extravagantly high when, as in Sault Ste. Marie,
francophone parents demand not just a new school, but an entire new school
board to satisfy the needs of fifty-seven students.[44]

As well, the demands are no longer simply for the right to be educated in
French. For several years, there has been an effort to extend the interpretation
of Section 23 to mean that children have the right to a fully segregated, publicly
funded education, free from any interactions with anglophone students. Francophone educators point to the findings of an Ontario ministerial report from
1972, which found that "much more often than not, the mixed or so-called
'bilingual' school is a one-way street to assimilation for the French-speaking
student."[45] This, of course, is a repeat, outside of Quebec, of the same
phenomenon that has been making a mess of Bill 101's attempt to assimilate
immigrant schoolchildren through the schools. It is the language of the
playground, not the classroom, that determines linguistic loyalties.

Activism among francophones since 1982 has revolved around ending the
existence of the bilingual schools and the creation of unilingual French schools.
The influential 1990 *Mahé* decision of the Supreme Court involved a dispute
over this issue starting at a school in Edmonton, where educators felt that the
Department of Education was preventing them from creating a totally "French
environment."[46]

Similarly, in 1990 a French-language school in Midland, Ontario chose to
segregate its students on the basis of ethnic background. To decide the group
in which each individual student would be placed, parents were distributed

questionnaires asking whether or not their children are "pure French."[47] Francophone educators in Esquimalt, British Columbia, took a more direct route to solving the problem of playground assimilation. They elected to construct a fence to separate the anglophone French immersion pupils of Macaulay Elementary School and the francophone pupils at Ecole Victor Brodeur, which shares the same building and the same playground.[48]

Needed: Low-Cost Minority Education

Remarkably, a century and a half of unending dispute over the question of minority-language education has produced no insights and no solutions. The debate still boils down to a struggle between minorities trying to divert as many dollars as possible in their own direction, and majorities trying to keep down or eliminate this cost. In practice, the debate is still, as it has always been, little more than a raw power struggle.

The most important change, therefore, has come not with a growing sophistication in the solutions being debated, but with a shift in the relative strength of the majority and minority participants in each province. This change was brought about by Canada's adoption, in 1982, of the *Charter of Rights and Freedoms*. Section 23 of the Charter guarantees the right of official-language minorities in every province to establish their own publicly funded boards of education "where the numbers of . . . children warrant." Before 1982, many provinces had been ungenerous with their minorities.[49] Even in provinces where generosity was shown, it was always contingent upon the goodwill of the provincial majority. This led the Fédération des francophones hors Québec, in a 1978 publication, to complain that:

> [Even] in Manitoba, Ontario and New Brunswick, instruction in the French language is not available as a fundamental right but as a conditional right which is more in the nature of a privilege than of official and statutory recognition.[50]

After 1982, goodwill no longer needed to be a factor in the equation. Provincial departments of education had no choice but to loosen the purse-strings.

Arguably, it would be appropriate to solve the problem by repealing Section 23 of the *Charter of Rights and Freedoms*, or better yet, to rewrite it to provide a more detailed and practical definition of "where numbers warrant." However, the harsh practical reality is that there is no possibility of redesigning Section 23. The language-related section of the Charter can be amended only by the unanimous consent of all provincial legislatures, and the history of the Meech Lake and Charlottetown Accords shows that unanimity is virtually impossible to obtain.

A more realistic alternative would be to search out a lower-cost method of providing minority official language education. Fortunately, this should not be difficult. Canada's primary and secondary education systems are antiquated, inefficient enterprises modelled after the centralized, highly regimented 19th-century factories that seemed to be the height of modern practicality when our school system was being established a century ago. This rigid, top-heavy structure, with its layers of bureaucrats and administrators, has a desperate need for economies of scale. Whenever a parallel system is established under the Section 23 rules, a whole new set of parallel bureaucracies must be established, without any of the population base to support it. Fixed costs remain high, the number of students low, and the per-student cost soars.

If the minority-language schools established under Section 23 were to be more cost-sensitive, they could probably produce high-quality education for relatively small enrollments at a cost no higher (and possibly lower) than the price of educating a student in the mainstream system. The trick would be to keep costs down by giving those who are demanding the educations, francophone parents, an incentive to keep costs down. This could be done by adopting an innovation known as the voucher system, currently being introduced with great success in parts of the United States.

Vouching for the Future

As implemented in several American jurisdictions, school 'vouchers' are certificates issued by state or municipal governments directly to parents.[51] Each voucher normally has a value equivalent to the average cost of educating one student in that state for one year. The government will redeem the vouchers for cash when they are presented to the department of education by a school that meets pre-established departmental standards. However, each school can only present as many vouchers as it has been provided by parents. This means that parents are able to band together and demand certain standards of performance from a school before they will consent to allow their children to attend. If the school is unable or unwilling to comply, the parents can turn to another school and make the same demands.

The use of vouchers induces competition between schools; each school is forced to work to improve its standard of education in order to attract more parents and more vouchers. Vouchers have been used with considerable success, most notably in Vermont, in parts of New York City and in Milwaukee, where the schools involved have undergone significant improvements in the standard of education delivered to students. Improvements in quality have taken place because students and parents are empowered to walk away from poor schools, but must compete with each other to gain entry to the best schools. This inter-student competition improves work attitudes.

The voucher system also allows parents to school their children at home, if they so choose. Such parents would simply redeem the voucher themselves, and collect the money. Of course, parents would be required to meet the same provincially-mandated educational standards as any regular school, as is presently the case for parents who have chosen to practice home schooling without benefit of vouchers.

Where to Use Vouchers

Vouchers could serve as a one-step solution to the problem of minority-language education. There are 108,000 school-age francophone children living outside Quebec. Of these, more than half reside in the parts of Ontario and New Brunswick where French is the language of the local majority.[52] These youngsters benefit from long-established French-language school boards. In these regions, French-language education is not an issue, since it costs no more to educate a francophone student than a local anglophone. The same is true in reverse, in the English majority parts of west Quebec, Montreal and the Eastern Townships. The voucher solution would produce substantial cost savings in the rest of the country, where minority populations are too small to justify the cost of full-size school boards. The total extra cost of French-language education in these mostly anglophone regions is approximately $250 million. The voucher system might have usefulness for the very small anglophone minorities in the Eastern Townships, the Gaspé and in Quebec City. The extra costs imposed on the Quebec government by the need to educate children in these regions in English is over $70 million.[53]

Used in these regions, vouchers would have a number of advantages. They could be used as a constitutionally-viable way of fixing the cost of educating official-language minority children at a level no higher than that of educating children in the majority language. If, for example, it costs $5,000 to educate the average child in a given province for one year, vouchers for $5,000 could be issued to the francophone parents upon request. The parents would then be able to establish schools, school boards, or classes within the existing schools, depending on the solution that seemed most suitable to their individual circumstances.

The American experience has confirmed, many times over, that whenever parents are given control of the finances of their childrens' education, costs tumble dramatically. This is due mainly to the absence of bureaucracy, empire-building and non-classroom expenses in parentally-controlled systems. In California for example, the annual cost of educating a child in the public system is $4,260, but private schooling costs, on average, only $2,600.[54] This suggests that, once freed from the impractical constraints of the school board system, parents will be able to assure their children of the education to which Section 23 entitles them, without imposing any additional costs at all on taxpayers.

With minority language education costs under control, the primary cause of alarm to local majorities would disappear. So too, presumably, would the intolerance that majorities have displayed toward minority-language education.

At the same time, minorities would be freed from their role of petty, grasping supplicants demanding more and more privileges from the public purse through an endless series of court challenges designed to extract ever more funds from the unwilling majority. Demands for segregated schoolyards and distinct school boards seem the height of greed and privilege when they are paid for by additional monies extracted from a majority that regards them at best as luxuries and at worst as a form of educational apartheid. Paid for by the minority itself, they would be completely acceptable. Of course, with public funding limited to the amounts paid out in vouchers, minority-language educators might be less inclined to demand some of the more esoteric things they have taken to requesting since Section 23 became law.

Additional expenses could be undertaken by minority language schools funded by vouchers only if the voucher money was spent sparingly enough to leave a surplus for these purposes. Failing this, additional funds would have to be raised by approaching the parents of students and asking them to contribute—from their own pockets. This would not be a unique prospect, since private schools have fundraising drives all the time. But it would certainly be an accurate test of whether or not the parents really feel the additional expenditure to be worthwhile.

A further advantage of the voucher option is that it would effectively remove the "where numbers warrant" floor on educating children in a minority official language. Home schooling—the direct education of children by their parents—is permitted in most provinces, but it is prohibitively expensive since it requires, in practice, that one parent stay home full-time with the children. This parent cannot enter the job market and earn an income. Parents who are too isolated to band together with neighbours in support of a local minority-language school could stay home to teach their children, using the funds from the voucher to purchase materials and texts and also to cover the costs of filing reports to show that provincial standards are being met, and even to pay themselves a small 'teacher's salary' out of the residual value of the voucher.

A variation on this would be made possible if provincial departments of education were to issue 'micro-vouchers.' These would be divisible vouchers, allowing the parent to redeem part of their voucher's value in return for individual teaching services. With the use of micro-vouchers, parents would be able to remove their children from classes for part-days or for part of the school week in order to have a portion of their education provided in French. Thus, children could take certain courses such as language, literature and history in their mother tongue, and the rest of their education in English at a regular public school. Even where the local francophone population is too small to support a full French language school, the most important aspects of culture could be covered by the micro-vouchers.

Vouchers and Interest-Group Politics

A final benefit of the voucher system is that it would free minority language parents from the tyranny of local minority language school boards. One unfortunate aspect of directly tax-funded school boards that are not financially answerable to individual parents is that the administrators of school boards— majority language and minority alike—tend to become bureaucratic empire-builders, as much concerned with expanding their control over ever-larger sums of money and numbers of students as they are with providing for the needs of the children under their care. It is due to pressures from these educational bureaucrats, rather than from parents, that the language battles of the 1970s in Montreal took place.

As Marc Levine shows in his incisive study, *The Reconquest of Montreal*, Protestant and Catholic boards fought bitterly over who would have access to the immigrant children necessary to prop up declining enrollments; the needs of young Greeks and Italians were secondary in importance to the bureaucratic imperative to protect turf and the jobs of teachers and administrators. Levine writes:

> Although the main concern over Montreal school enrolments involve Francophone cultural security, there were also some vital economic issues at stake. Simply put, the declining enrolments in French-language schools threatened the jobs of Francophone teachers and school administrators. The rivalry for Montreal's new ethnic minorities was not only an issue of linguistic demography; it was also a battle over which linguistic community, in an era of shrinking school enrolments, would attract sufficient numbers of immigrant children to keep schools open and protect educators' jobs. It was no accident that Francophone teachers and their students formed the core of an expanding coalition calling for language policies restricting access to Montreal's English-language schools: their material well-being was at stake.[55]

Thus, it is difficult to believe that nationalist zeal was all that was at work when the *Corporation des enseignants du Québec* warned, in opposing a piece of proposed schools legislation, that "school structures in Montreal must serve the francophone majority."[56] Striking much more closely to the heart of the matter was the comment of Stanley Frost, the vice-principal of McGill University, who rejected an earlier piece of legislation because it "spells the end of the English language teaching profession in Quebec."[57]

In the end, it was the francophone teachers and boards who won, and the English-language teachers and boards that lost jobs and closed schools. In the first ten years following the introduction of mandatory French language schooling for immigrants, enrollment in English schools fell by forty-eight percent, while French-language schools experienced a drop of only fourteen percent.[58]

Similar, although smaller-scale, battles between English and French school boards and teachers' unions take place in every other province each time there is a dispute over minority language schools. It is no accident, for example, that when the Ontario Court of Appeals heard testimony in 1984 on whether the province was constitutionally obliged to extend more generous schooling provisions to its francophone minority, representatives from six English-dominated school boards and teachers' associations intervened before the bench to argue that it did not, while representatives from three French-language school boards and teachers' associations took the opposite stand.[59]

Not surprisingly, the imperative to protect their own economic interests applies as well to the teachers and administrators of the dozens of tiny French-language school boards springing up from Newfoundland to British Columbia. Just as the demands of professional educators in Montreal eventually poisoned the atmosphere in that city and made rational discourse impossible, the most extreme demands for French-language schooling come not from francophone parents but from professionals seeking a monopoly over their children's educations. It is the educators rather than the parents who are most active in demanding segregated schoolyards and the barring of anglophone children from attending French-language schools. It is the educators who have declared that it is the purpose of French-language education not only to teach children their ancestral culture, but to inoculate them against the impurities of English culture and the English language. This division between francophone parents and francophone educators was most dramatically shown in 1985, when more than 300 Acadian students in Cheticamp, Nova Scotia, were kept out of school by their parents to protest the redesignation of their school as French-only. The parents objected that the redesignation, which had taken place despite their efforts, would impair their children's ability to learn English.[60]

Vouchers would free francophone parents from being drawn into the political battles that some of these administrators have chosen to initiate. No longer would francophone parents be forced to send their children to a single local French-language school run by teachers and administrators with a monopoly choke-hold over French-language education in the region. Should a school's curriculum be undesirable to the parents, they could simply band together and establish a new school. Likewise, if they find the local educators to be more interested in political lobbying than in apolitical educating, parents could cut them off.

If, as is sometimes the case, the parents concluded that their children would be better off receiving additional French instruction within a mostly English school, it would be each set of parents, as an individual family unit, that would make the decision. Some parents might choose one option, some might choose another. In attempting to satisfy this clientele, educators would have to serve parents' agendas rather than their own.

Given the many merits of the voucher system, a reasonable argument can be made that education vouchers should be extended to parents in the country's two majority communities rather than to minority parents alone. While this is true, it is worth noting that there are powerful interests opposed to the introduction of free choice in schooling, including the administrators and educational bureaucrats who would lose their jobs and their political power under a system based on parental initiative.

Although most teachers presently employed by the provincially-run school monopolies would probably find employment (and greater freedom to do their work) under a voucher system, the teachers' unions would no longer hold the keys to power as the sole suppliers of education. Unions are therefore militantly opposed to any change to the present system. The experience in the United States, where administrators and teachers' unions have successfully thwarted nearly all attempts to introduce vouchers, despite an education system far worse than Canada's, suggests that the widespread introduction of vouchers is not politically feasible.

However, the introduction of the voucher system for official-language minorities in regions where they do not always have established school boards should face no interest-group opposition. The administrators and unions have no cause to oppose vouchers for minorities, since their battle to retain monopoly control over minority-language education was lost with the passage of Section 23. The minorities have been placed permanently beyond their grasp for over a decade.

SUMMARY

In the past as much as the present, conflicts regarding education revolved around the belief among majority-community members that the only way to deal effectively with annoying or worrisome minorities is to deprive them of education rights in their own language. This idea is misguided to say the least. Using coercion in an attempt to forcibly manipulate the culture of whole populations, or to wrench cultural decisions out of the hands of parents so that they may be placed in the palms of unfeeling bureaucrats, is utterly repugnant to a liberal society. The fact that such efforts are ineffectual merely renders them pathetic, as well as shameful. This combination of misguided beliefs and misbegotten ends once shaped education policy in several English-majority provinces; today it shapes education policy in Quebec. In the English-speaking provinces, the main source of conflict is the cost involved in creating new and mostly unnecessary segregated school boards on the outdated 19th-century model for the francophone linguistic minority.

In Quebec as well as elsewhere, the introduction of greater parental choice would help resolve these disputes. Outside Quebec, the introduction of an educational voucher system would place the burden of responsibility for education back into the hands of parents. They would decide, individually or collectively, how their children would be educated, in which school and in which language, and given the responsibility which vouchers necessarily entail, they would work to keep costs down as well.

Within Quebec, it is counter-intuitive but true that the provincial government's ultimate goal of assimilating as many children of immigrants as possible into the French language could best be achieved if the province were to relax many of the same restrictions that it imposed in order to boost this assimilation. Whether or not the political leaders in each of the jurisdictions in which actions must be taken have the courage to attempt to achieve their goals by empowering citizens rather than by taking away their freedoms remains to be seen.

CHAPTER TEN

The Dollars and Sense of Official Bilingualism

> True, this escalating budget needed to guarantee expanded language rights is scary; but surely we may draw some joy, on our way to the bilingual poorhouse, in knowing that the bus fare per mile to get there is somewhat cheaper.
> —*Commissioner of Official Languages, Annual Report (1975)*[1]

As PUBLIC DISCOURSE makes perfectly clear, nobody has a clue how much the federal government's official languages policies cost Canada. The federal government claims the total annual cost of official language spending is less than $700 million. Unofficial estimates range upwards into the multi-billions. Federal government estimates are made with rock solid self-confidence, stated in precise figures. The critics of Official Bilingualism usually make no serious claim of being able to produce precise estimates, merely claiming that federal estimates are far too low. This chapter attempts to map out a somewhat more precise measure of the costs, in order to provide a reasoned, fact-based critique of the official numbers produced each year by Ottawa. Amazingly, this has never been attempted before.

The contrast in attitudes between the supporters and critics of federal language-based spending can be clearly seen in comparing the texts of two speeches delivered in 1992 to Edmonton Rotarians. Commissioner of Official Languages Victor Goldbloom gave his audience as precise an estimate of the costs as could ever be desired:

> What about costs? Annual federal expenditures are over $100 billion. One percent of that would be $1 billion. We spend less than that, about $654 million, on Official Languages. $254 million of that is made up of transfer payments from the federal government to the provinces for education. About $335 million goes to services, including language training where needed. That comes to $13 a year for each of us, about 3 and a half cents a day. It seems to me that the break-up of our country would be far more costly than that. . . . [2]

By contrast, Ron Leitch, the president of the Alliance for the Preservation of English in Canada, admitted that the facts available to him made it impossible to do more than to provide vague guesses as to the real costs:

> One must keep in mind that the $654 million annually is only for the

promotional aspect of Official Bilingualism.... In reality Official Bilingualism costs untold millions, because many expenditures are interwoven into ministry budgets so it is next to impossible to be able to determine total costs to the people of Canada.[3]

Leitch's refusal to pretend an ability to be precise is probably more honest than Goldbloom's stab at precision, but it provides no hard numbers, so it carries no weight. Although many Canadians are suspicious that the official numbers are mere window-dressing, they do not trust such vague criticisms. Compounding their suspicion is the periodic appearance of unofficial estimates, freed from any logical connection to the facts, that soar upwards to infinity. A prime example is this letter to the editor, published in a small-town newspaper in eastern Ontario:

> Bilingualism costs between $5 billion and $10 billion per year. This is equivalent to up to 50 percent of all other social services combined and is in addition to the economic penalties suffered by Canadian businesses forced to comply to Consumer and Corporate Affairs translation laws. ...[4]

For those who have a genuine curiosity about the real costs, the problem is that neither the supporters nor the critics of Official Bilingualism have ever attempted a systematic costing of each of the many federal government policies that relate to official languages policy. This chapter attempts to establish the framework for such a costing, and makes a preliminary stab at producing a reasonably accurate cost estimate.

By my estimate, the total annual cost to the Canadian economy of federal language policy is around $4 billion. Of this, $2.7 billion consists of direct federal government expenditures, $300 million consists of provincial spending on language programs resulting from federal initiatives, and slightly over $2 billion consists of private sector compliance costs with federal language regulations.[5]

WHY MOST OF THE EXISTING COST ESTIMATES ARE WORTHLESS

The Official Estimate

The Commissioner of Official Languages, Canada's legally-appointed overseer in French and English matters, has an extensive research staff, powers to investigate and summon witnesses, the mandate to report directly to Parliament, and access to the national media. Thus, unlike the critics of Official Bilingualism, who are mostly underfunded freelancers, the Commissioner is uniquely equipped to bring coherence to the debate on the costs of bilingualism by producing a truly comprehensive tabulation of the costs of federal language policy.

Instead, one Commissioner after another has chosen to simply accept at face value the cost estimates produced by government agencies, despite the fact that these organizations have every political incentive to keep their estimates as low as possible.

Every year, the Treasury Board of Canada, the federal government's financial overseer, issues a report on official languages in federal institutions which contains a well-vetted estimate of the costs of official languages programs. The Commissioner of Official Languages—rather unimaginatively, given his ostensible role as an independent critic—reproduces this estimate without change in his annual report to Parliament.[6]

It is curious and disappointing that the Commissioner simply regurgitates the official figures, since this destroys any credibility his estimates might otherwise have. All manner of expenditures are left off the Treasury Board estimates, including the internal costs to federal departments of complying with the demands imposed by the Commissioner himself. Also excluded from the list are the compliance costs to individuals, corporations and provinces of the bilingualism requirements of federal regulations under a host of laws and of the costs of complying with the language provisions in the *Canadian Charter of Rights and Freedoms*. Transfer payments to provinces and territories for language programs represent the largest single item on the official lists, at $264 million, but this total does not include the provinces' own contributions towards these programs, even though most federal spending in this area takes the form of shared-cost programs.

The problem of inaccurate government estimates is hardly new. It is nearly twenty years since Keith Spicer, the first Commissioner of Official Languages, warned:

> But surely there is merit in keeping more meaningful accounts. Without them, those dealing with language reform will have to continue waffling on the recurring question of costs—hearing, but being unable to contradict convincingly, such deliciously polemical estimates ... as "three billion dollars a year for bilingualism." It would seem more sensible to pull the whole lot of linguistic items together, specifying the purpose of each, tote up the terrifying sum, add on ten per cent for indirect or integrated costs, then publish and defend the thing as a high but necessary price for being Canadian. ...[7]

His advice was ignored, with the result that the cost estimates of all subsequent Commissioners have been useful only as universally-accepted lowball estimates of language costs, which serve as the floor for any serious discussion.

Equally distressing is the use by the two most recent Commissioners of an accounting trick to foster the illusion that languages spending is lower than it is. Invariably, in publications from the Office of the Commissioner, calculations of historical expenditures under federal official languages programs are

Figure 10.1
Historical cost estimates used by the Commissioner of
Official Languages are designed to make costs appear to
be lower than they really are.

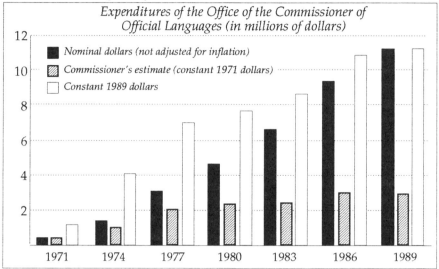

Sources: See *Notes for Figures*

calculated both in current (or 'nominal') dollars, and in constant, inflation-adjusted figures. The trick is that the figures are adjusted downwards to fit a price index based on price levels dating from the beginning of the program, rather than to fit an index based on up-to-date prices.

Thus, for example, a table in a 1989 document entitled *The Office of the Commissioner of Official Languages: A Twenty-Year Chronicle* lists the internal spending of the Office as having grown in nominal terms from $388,000 in 1970-71 to $11.3 million in 1988-89, but as having risen much more modestly in inflation-adjusted dollars from $388,000 to $3.2 million. Mathematically, this is valid, but from the perspective of a reader in 1989, it would have made far more sense to calculate backwards from the present amount and observe that in terms of post-inflation 1989 dollars, spending in 1971 had already reached $1.4 million. Instead, the Commissioner makes the true but arcane observation that in 1989 spending was only a modest $3.2 million if calculated in out-of-context pre-inflationary 1971 dollars.[8]

The current Commissioner, who does not seem to share Keith Spicer's views on accounting, also claims that official languages spending has dropped dramatically over the past decade. In a pamphlet published in 1991, Commissioner Victor Goldbloom maintains that "since the 1977-78 fiscal year official languages spending has declined by 46.5 percent when adjusted for inflation."[9] This remarkable economy measure appears to have been attained mostly

Figure 10.2
The Commissioner of Official Languages claims that since 1978, official language spending has declined by 46.5 % (adjusted for inflation). Here's why...

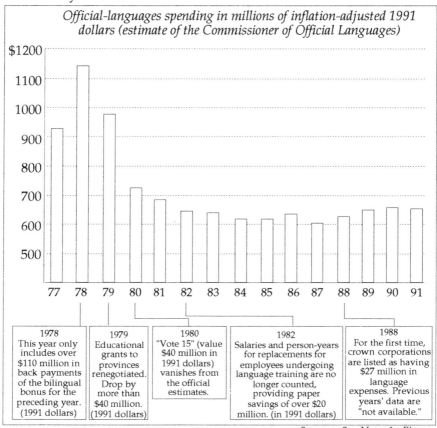

Sources: See *Notes for Figures*

through the arbitrary reclassification of certain categories of language-related expenditures from the official estimates, even though some of these expenses have grown in real terms over the intervening years.

The curious blend of over-estimates and internal inconsistencies that characterize the annual reports of the Commissioner of Official Languages has made his official expenditure estimates virtually worthless.

The Unofficial Estimates

The unofficial estimates made by critics of federal policy also have their problems. Opponents of Official Bilingualism have a tendency to confound spending carried out in the name of the federal government's official languages regime with other types of spending intended to foster national unity. For example, the $70 billion surplus that Quebec has run in federal transfer payments between 1970 and the present sometimes gets lumped into the same category as monies spent on official languages policy. But while it is not unreasonable to categorize the dollars spent on bilingualism as part of Canada's program of unity-based spending, it is invalid to do the reverse. Say what one will, official languages policy is not to blame for Quebec's domination of Canadian milk quotas, the shift of the CF-18 maintenance contract from Winnipeg to Montreal, the transfer of the Canadian space agency from Ontario to Quebec, or the oversize share of patronage pork that Quebec is frequently said to receive.

It is not just anglophones who mistakenly include extraneous items as costs of Official Bilingualism, and federal spending is not the only area where funds with other functions get mistaken for language subsidies. A typical error is made by Daniel Latouche, a professor at the Université du Québec à Montréal's *Institut national de la recherche scientifique*, who writes indignantly:

> Each year we [francophone Quebecers] spend a few hundred millions of dollars on the institutions of the anglophone community, more I might add than all the provinces and the federal government [combined] spend each year for the institutions of French Canada. . . . Some of us do not like it but McGill, the Protestant School Board, the Montreal General Hospital and the Centaur Theatre are part of our heritage and will continue to be so. Even Alliance Quebec is supported by the taxes of francophones.[10]

With the exception of Alliance Quebec, which is a lobby group, these institutions are not purely or primarily concerned with language itself. The amount of provincial money devoted to these institutions is not vastly greater than that which would be spent if the institutions were French, since people do have to be educated and hospitalized in one language or another. In fact, there is substantial evidence to suggest that McGill University is substantially underfunded as a result of deliberate provincial policy.[11] As well, much of the federal money transferred to the province to support English-language education is appropriated instead for other provincial measures, and never makes its way into the education system.[12]

ESTABLISHING THE COSTS: A SECTOR-BY-SECTOR ANALYSIS

The Public Service

The internal cost to the Public Service of operating in both official languages is enormous, and bears no resemblance whatever to official figures. By the Official Language Commissioner's estimate, this cost in fiscal year

1991-92 was $278 million.[13] The real figure appears to be about three times as much—$998 million.

When discussing costs, official languages-related spending within the Public Service should be divided into two categories. In the first category are bilingual and minority-language services which the Public Service provides to Canadian citizens. These costs are enumerated elsewhere in this chapter, and are not included in the total cited above. In the second category are the costs involved in running the Public Service internally in more than one language, which are included in the total costs, and are enumerated below.

Included in this category are such items as the translation of documents, which costs the government $102.4 million[14] annually, as well as bilingual bonuses and second-language training for public servants whose positions *do not* involve serving the public. Language training for public servants who do not serve the public costs $17 million each year, in addition to the $32 million that is spent training public servants who *do* serve the public. As estimated by the Commissioner of Official Languages, the total training-cost figure for all public servants in both categories is only $31.3 million, but this figure is the result of his failure to take into account the $17 million in salaries paid every year to replacement workers who step in for public servants attending language training during office hours.[15] Likewise, the Commissioner's estimates fail to take into account the fact that all language exams are conducted during office hours, consuming 19,000 hours of paid employee time each year, at a total cost of $383,000.[16]

However, these individual costs are best understood as components of a vastly larger cost, which is much harder to calculate. An immense burden of organizational inefficiency is placed on the Public Service by the requirement that it be organized to operate in both official languages in a manner that bears no resemblance whatsoever to the operational model adopted by successful bilingual organizations in the private sector.

At the heart of this inefficiency is the rejection of the private-sector model, under which the work force is divided into French and English unilingual work units which require only minimal contact with each other in the course of daily operations. Instead, every single post in the Public Service has received a linguistic designation which can only be changed with extraordinary difficulty. This designation determines who will be allowed to occupy the post, the language in which it must be supervised, the language in which correspondence will take place, and a variety of other considerations. The disastrous consequences of this system for merit hiring are described in detail in Chapter Eight. Tied closely to the system of bilingual post designations has been an intensive and sustained effort to force tens of thousands of public servants to carry out their job functions in both official languages at once, whether there is a job-related need for this or not.

The impact of this system on the Public Services' overhead costs is enormous, but it is also completely impossible to calculate by direct means. One indicator of costs is offered by University of Moncton Professor of Public Administration Donald Savoie, who writes in his book, *The Politics of Public Spending in Canada*, that the Public Service is strangled by:

> [The complex] accountability relationships between departmental management and other organizations. The result is that there is little room for managers to exert discretion, be flexible, or adapt to special situations. The cost of such procedures and regulations is . . . high, with some suggesting that it accounts for 20 to 30 percent in unnecessary overhead. One official reported: 'I have about 237 person-years in the organization in personnel and administration and a lot more in Finance. And they are there because I have to have very heavy management systems in order to serve the central agencies. But they are largely overhead and the costs of this overhead are much too large . . . but as long as they [central agencies or guardians] are willing to pay for it to meet central agency requirements, then I'm willing to accept that additional cost.'[17]

The twenty-to-thirty percent figure cited by Savoie represents a high estimate, so it is likely that the true total cost of the overhead he describes is somewhat lower. Of course, not all the redundant additional overhead costs in the Public Service are caused by language-related inefficiencies, nor is there even any proof that it is the largest source of redundant overhead. Nonetheless, a very considerable amount of waste can be traced back to this source. It seems reasonable, for reasons which will be explained below, to set this overhead cost at approximately five percent of all Public Service staffing costs, or $951 million per year. This represents only a fraction of Savoie's twenty-to-thirty percent figure.

Because of the complete lack of hard numbers on which to build any estimate of overhead costs, it is necessary to turn instead to a combination of theoretical work on the cost of regulation and anecdotal evidence of high language-related costs. American scholars have made significant strides towards assigning dollar values to the hidden costs of government regulation of the private sector and semi-governmental institutions such as hospitals and universities. As long as the usual caveats about the imprecision of such estimates is not forgotten, their work can be applied to Canada's Public Service.

Researchers at the Center for the Study of American Business at Washington University in St. Louis, Missouri have calculated that on average, twenty dollars in compliance costs are imposed by every dollar of enforcement costs of the regulatory agencies.[18] The cost of regulating official languages in the Public Service is $48 million, which implies a total overhead cost of nearly $1 billion.

There are three types of cost associated with regulation:

- *Direct costs*, also known as 'enforcement costs,' are the budgets of the regulatory institutions ('central agencies' or 'guardians' as Savoie calls them);
- *Indirect costs* include the time and effort that Public Service managers must divert from other objectives in order to ensure they are complying with the demands of the regulators. In the case of the Public Service manager quoted above by Savoie, the time and effort involved in compliance consumes 237 person-years annually. Also involved are the costs of reorganizing workplace environments to avoid attracting the attention or the wrath of the regulators. This requires extensive use of quota hiring to fill individual posts in order to achieve perfectly proportioned ratios of the two linguistic groups within each seniority level and technical specialization of each federal agency;
- *Opportunity costs* include the goals that the regulated institutions might have achieved with the resources which in fact were consumed in fulfilling the regulatory requirements.

It seems likely that in a Public Service environment, the opportunity costs are significantly lower than would be the case in a private, profit-making organization. Public Service agencies have specific mandates to fulfill. During the free-spending 1970s and 1980s, non-compliance with these mandates, whether due to high overhead costs stemming from excessive regulation or to other causes, has been solved by simply increasing the budget of the agency in question. For this reason, opportunity costs can probably be regarded as nonexistent. On the other hand, this attitude of easy money in matters relating to internal bilingualism has led Public Service managers to overfulfill their regulatory obligations in the hope of currying favour with their superiors, secure in the knowledge that language-related cost overruns will always be regarded generously.

Such numbers can only be confirmed in general terms, but there is plenty of anecdotal evidence to suggest that costs are wildly out of control. One example is the federal government's $100 million translation budget, which has bloated to such a point that by now about eighty percent of the costs associated with translations can reasonably be classified as waste. (This example is explored in detail in Appendix A.)

Another example of regulation and compliance-inspired spending is the all-pervasive Public Service obsession with ensuring that neither French nor English is ever treated with lesser priority than the other official language in any circumstance, no matter how petty. This is a dramatic contrast to the fairly laid-back attitude toward the equality of official languages in the public services of other multilingual countries like Switzerland, Malaysia and Singapore. An examination of declassified documents from a few federal departments reveals just how wacky the micro-management of official languages has become.

The office of the Commissioner of Official Languages is just one of the agencies overseeing official languages in the Public Service. It carries out twenty or more in-depth linguistic audits and ninety brief studies of federal agencies in a typical year.[19] It also monitors, on an ad-hoc basis, compliance with a variety of aspects of these regulations, for example, by anonymously phoning government numbers to see if they are answered using approved protocol. If the answering is below par, the department's official languages division is contacted and instructed to correct the situation.

One such event is recorded in several documents obtained under the *Access to Information Act*. On July 18, 1986, an employee from the Commissioner's office twice called a number at the Department of Energy, Mines and Resources. Calling in French at 9:30 a.m., the caller from the Commissioner's office was at one point in his conversation with the receptionist asked this apparently forbidden question: "Vous ne comprenez pas l'anglais?" When the employee called again at 11:22 (again in French), the same receptionist breached protocol for a second time by uttering, "One moment please."

This offence launched an elaborate chain of events: on July 29, a complaint was sent from the Commissioner's office to the director of Energy, Mines and Resources' official languages division. She passed it on to the department's communications division, where an investigation was conducted. Once this was completed, a response was sent back to the official languages division, and a fourth letter summarizing the investigation's findings was sent back to the Commissioner. It reads, in part:

> The incident of last July 18 took place when a new employee ... replaced the regular receptionist during her annual holiday. ... The responsible individual is no longer in our employ. ...
>
> All receptionists are bilingual. Sometimes they have to respond to several calls at the same time and when they get back to someone who is waiting, they have forgotten which language that particular client was using. [Nonetheless] we assure you that we have taken all necessary measures to ensure that this situation *never happens again*.[20]

Another complaint from the Commissioner's office to the same department during the same month in 1986 involved the fact that directory boards on certain floors in an Ottawa office building breached official practice because, in the words of the letter of complaint, they "include the word 'Room' or 'Rm' but not the equivalent in French, 'Pièce.'" Judging from the names listed on the ensuing correspondence, this tempest in a teapot was not resolved until six individuals in the department, in addition to the original recipient of the correspondence, had become involved.[21]

The Commissioner's office is not the only central agency regulating language use in the Public Service. The Treasury Board issues complex directives on language use within the Public Service, designed to achieve an environment in which French can be used interchangeably with English. This is, quite literally, an impossible task, as was demonstrated earlier.

Nonetheless, managers are burdened with innumerable regulations. Typical of the Treasury Board's efforts is a manual on how to chair meetings in which either language may be used at the any time by any participant. The requirements laid out in this manual make it impossible to hold any internal public meeting unless simultaneous translation is available for the meeting's spoken proceedings and written translation is made available for the minutes, agenda, and all working papers that any participant may circulate at the meeting. The only way around these requirements is to hold meetings at which all participants share the same mother tongue. At any ethnically mixed meeting, the full range of translation facilities must be provided, even if every participant is fully bilingual.[22]

The Public Service Commission is a third central agency regulating language in the federal bureaucracy. Typical of the expensive directives that it has imposed is the method that it has imposed for removing unilingual public servants from bilingual posts:

> An employee who is unable to meet the language requirements of his or her position ... is to be transferred ... to another position for which he or she is qualified in all respects.... *Where no appropriate position is available ... the deputy head creates a temporary position* which the employee occupies until he or she is transferred in accordance with his or her Statement of Agreement. The temporary position is at the same group level as the [bilingual] position to which the employee was [previously] appointed. . . . [23]

No statistics are available on the number of unilingual public servants who have been placed in this type of post or on the length of time they have typically held these posts before being transferred to other positions. This expense is, needless to say, not accounted for in official estimates of the cost of Public Service bilingualism.

Because each department contains its own official languages directorate, compliance costs involve responding to their directives as well as those emanating from the Commissioner, the Treasury Board and the Public Service Commission. A typical example of an action initiated by a departmental language directorate comes from the Department of National Defence, where an outdoor French sign was less visible than its English counterpart. The letter of complaint issued by the directorate gives some idea of the expense involved in achieving perfect equality:

> What is now seen from the ground is architecturally pleasant to the eye but unfortunately fails to give both languages equal status. I am convinced that the

designers meant well by putting up lettering of equal style, size and at equal height from the ground to give equal treatment to both Official Languages. And this is commendable. You will agree however that would they have consulted DGOL [Director General of Official Languages] staff and DTTC [departmental terminology experts] before undertaking the project, this situation and the resulting irritant could have been prevented.

As the observation [that the French is less visible than the English] came from within this Headquarters we would prefer not to lodge a formal complaint, but rather seek a resolution of this case "à l'amiable", assuming that corrective action will be taken at a minimal cost and fuss, and at the earliest opportunity to prevent the possibility of receiving a formal complaint from the office of the Commissioner of Official Languages.[24]

In their efforts to avoid running afoul of the Commissioner or the various departmental official languages directorates, individual Public Service managers must go to extraordinary lengths. They must be familiar with hundreds of pages of Treasury Board and Public Service Commission regulations on hiring and promotion. Even if these are followed closely, many of the rules contained in these directives contradict one another, and none state the most important message of all, which is that it is far more important to have a perfectly proportionate balance between anglophones and francophones at every level of seniority than to actually follow the written regulations on hiring and promotion.

The Public Service Commission publishes an annual report to Parliament in which anglophone/francophone percentages are broken down by department, salary range, occupational category, technical specialization and geographical region.[25] Managers make extraordinary efforts to keep their employment as equitable as possible within each of these categories, since career advancement is closely linked to performance on this matter, and it does not help any manager's career to be the least equitable employer in the department.

One recently retired section head described what an enormous relief it had been, in his last few years in the Public Service, to approach the end of his career. At last, with his own future out of his superiors' hands, he could make merit-based hiring and promotion decisions without fear of the consequences.

Equality of outcome of this sort cannot actually be achieved in the real world without the use of preferential hiring practices, but an open use of quotas leaves the manager open to negative publicity of the sort that surrounded the 'Francobank' scandal of the early 1980s when recruits for certain Public Service posts were to be chosen solely from a 'bank' of Francophone talent, to the exclusion of all other applicants.[26]

Considerable effort must be devoted, therefore, to surrounding each hiring decision in reams of unnecessary paperwork and as much obscurantism as possible.

Nonetheless, the public-regulations value of up-to-date detailed information on equitable employment is central to the present organizational structure of the Public Service, so new data is constantly in demand.

To keep data on these matters up-to-the-minute, a huge centralized computer data network, the 'Official Languages Information System' (OLIS) is constantly updated with new information on hirings and promotions. Managers are expected to devote a considerable proportion of their time filling out the paperwork to keep the OLIS data current. This is no minor task; the instruction manual for users of OLIS is 523 pages long.

Figure 10.3[27]
Cost of Internal Bilingualism in the Public Service, 1991-1992:

1)	Direct costs: costs of regulators' salaries and support materials**		$47,551,700
	This total includes:		
	a) Public Service Commission*	$ 5,600,000	
	b) Treasury Board Official Languages Branch	8,200,000	
	c) Commissioner of Official Languages***	4,771,000	
	d) Official languages units within each department and agency	28,980,700	
2)	Indirect costs: Direct costs x 20**		$951,034,000
	This total includes:		
	a) Translation	$101,767,000	
	b) Second-language training and evaluation for persons occupying posts not involved in serving the public**	16,965,000	
	c) Bilingual bonuses paid to persons occupying posts not involved in serving the public	17,605,000	
	d) Other, non-accounted compliance costs*	783,190,748	
	Total:		**$998,585,700**

*not included in official federal estimates of annual language-policy costs.
**official estimates understate this cost.
***To obtain this total, I have assumed that the public-sector regulatory function of the Commissioner of Official Languages includes fifty percent of the Commissioner's $4.3 million complaints and audits budget, fifty percent of his $2.3 million regional operations budget, fifty percent of his $1.3 million policy budget, and one-third of his $2.4 million resource management budget.

Federal Services to the Public

It is not possible to calculate the annual federal cost of providing minority-language services in Canada with a great deal of accuracy, because there are no official estimates of the total costs, and no attempt has ever been made to enumerate the cost within each federal department and agency of providing minority-language services.

Such an enumeration would have to include the cost of providing minority-language service at 2,155 government offices across the country, including training costs, the $800 'bilingual bonus' paid to all qualified incumbents in bilingual positions that serve the public, and (in some but not all cases) the cost of extra staff positions, where it has been necessary to create them in order to provide the services mandated under the *Official Languages Act*. Another presumably small cost factor is the cost of monitoring certain offices in order to determine if there is sufficient demand to declare the office bilingual. It is impossible to place precise dollar values on some of these costs, so it is safer merely to record them as ballpark figures, and in one or two cases, simply to note that costs exist.

Precise dollar values can be assigned to the various services to the public that take the form of federal subsidies. The Promotion of Official Languages Branch of the Department of the Secretary of State spends slightly over $2 million each year on the direct financing of bilingual services in voluntary and non-profit organizations. In 1990, the largest such grant was awarded to Montreal's *World Film Festival*, which received $30,000. Smaller grants were given to 300 other organizations.[28] As well, the Department of the Secretary of State offers a range of translation services to private users: glossaries of specialized vocabularies, a "computerized bilingual data bank," and a "free phone-in service for terminology, proper names and grammatical queries."[29]

In addition, the federal government provides many types of service to the public in which some unmeasured and usually relatively small proportion of total service expenditures are devoted to language-related (particularly minority official-language-related) spending. Normally, no breakdown of this spending is available, so it is impossible to tell what proportion is language-related.

For example, a portion of the $173 million spent each year by the Commissioner of Federal Judicial Affairs is used to provide language training for federal judges and other court officials, and an additional sum has been used for the translation of court documents and transcripts. There is also some evidence to suggest that the total number of federal court judges and other employees has been swelled in order to ensure that new bilingual personnel are hired without causing layoffs of current employees. All of this is being done in order to conform with Section 16 (1) of the *Official Languages Act*. None of it has been costed, and an accurate cost estimate could only be attained by an investigator willing to conduct considerable research, including a thorough review of the payroll and other of the Commissioner's internal documents.

Similar constraints apply to any attempt to learn what proportion of the budgets of the Canada Council, the Canada Film Development Corporation, or the Book Publishing Industry Development Corporation are devoted to projects relating to official languages.[30] It is inconceivable that there would not be some language-related expenses in the $1.29 billion devoted to federal transfers "to provinces, territories, municipalities, other public bodies, organizations, groups, communities, employers and individuals for the provision of training and/or work experience, the mobilisation of community resources and human resource planning and adjustment measures necessary for the efficient functioning of the Canadian labour market."[31]

In most of the cases described above, the proportion of total expenditures being focussed on language-related services is probably pretty small, although the total dollars involved are unlikely to be negligible. But even when it seems obvious that a program of services to the public is devoted primarily to official languages, only detailed investigation will be able to confirm whether or not this is true. It seems like a safe bet to categorize the Department of Employment and Immigration's 'Settlement Languages Program' as being primarily focussed on French and English matters, until further investigation shows that the program has disbursed funds for projects that have nothing to do with official languages, like a $115,000 grant for Afghan women's counselling in Toronto.[32]

Bearing this in mind, the sketchiness of the estimate in the table below will perhaps seem understandable.

Figure 10.4[33]
COST OF FEDERAL SERVICES TO THE PUBLIC (EXCLUDING MEDIA), 1991-1992:

1)	Commissioner of Federal Judicial Affairs (translations, language training, extra hiring of bilingual personnel)*	cost unknown
2)	Grant to the "International Commission of Jurists for its annual programmes on Human Rights for Francophones"*	$ 5,000
3)	Grant to the Institut international de droit d'expression française*	1,500
4)	National Program for the Integration of Both Official Languages in the Administration of Justice	1,005,000
5)	Canada Council (grants to artists and associations which are awarded in whole or in part because of their minority official language status)*	cost unknown
6)	Canada Film Development Corporation (extra expenditures incurred by projects relating to official languages)*	cost unknown
7)	"Contributions for the Book Publishing Industry Development Program" (for publishing projects related, whether by the nature of publisher or subject matter, to official languages)*	cost unknown
8)	"Contribution to governments of Yukon and NWT in respect of programs relating to the use of official languages in areas of territorial responsibility"*	1,985,146
9)	Second-language training and evaluation for persons occupying posts involved in serving the public**	31,603,000

10) Bilingual bonuses paid to persons occupying posts involved in serving the public	32,565,000
Total (excluding unknown costs):	**$68,164,646**

*not included in official federal estimates of annual language-policy costs.
**official estimates understate this cost.

Media-Related Federal Services to the Public

An enumeration of the services provided to the public by the federal government would be incomplete if it did not include all the subsidized media services that the government provides. This includes direct subsidies to minority official-language CBC television and radio stations located deep in the country's unilingual hinterlands, radio frequencies allocated without cost by the Canadian Radio-television and Telecommunications Commission (CRTC) to minority-language private broadcasters, and indirect subsidies in the form of advertising revenues artificially channelled to the minority press by government departments placing unnecessary ads.

Every year, roughly $5 million in federal subsidies are transferred to minority-language newspapers.[34] Normally money is not directed towards the newspapers in the form of direct payments, but is paid instead in the form of advertising revenues for large and unnecessary ads placed by federal agencies. Often, the readership of these newspapers has dwindled to such a point that they can no longer attract private advertising. It is a matter of policy for the federal government to place advertising for no other reason than to provide the revenues to keep these newspapers afloat.[35] Although the purpose of these ads is to subsidize the minority language communities, the expenses involved do not appear on the Commissioner of Official Languages' balance sheet as costs of bilingualism.

As far back as the 1970s, the Department of the Secretary of State was contributing $60,000 per annum in advertising to francophone weeklies outside Quebec, and actively seeking ways to increase this amount. A confidential document from this period contains the following passage, which more or less sums up the federal government's attitude on advertising subsidies:

> The existence of a French press outside Quebec, from Nova Scotia to British Columbia, is a significant indication of the pan-Canadian dimension of *Francophonie*. If all the departments adopted a true bilingualism policy, not only institutional but general, involving the public at large, they would make it a point of honour (like our department) to support the French press outside Quebec and in doing so, would promote its expansion and progress.[36]

One result of the widespread application of this policy is that minority-language newspapers are full of federal government ads not directed towards anybody in particular. In one issue of *L'Express*, a Toronto-based weekly French newspaper, I counted seventeen advertisements placed by nine federal departments and agencies, including one full-page ad placed by Canada Post. *L'Express* is only ten pages long.[37]

The newspapers are only a sideline, however. Broadcasting consumes the lion's share of minority-language media subsidies. In terms of its efforts to reach the remotest and most isolated members of Canada's official-language minorities, the CBC has far surpassed even the heroic efforts of Canada Post, which were described in Chapter Six. By its own estimate, over ninety-nine percent of the members of each linguistic community have direct access to FM and AM radio in their own language, and television broadcasts are available in both languages from coast to coast.[38]

The commitment to blanket coverage has some odd results. Of the eight television stations in CBC's French-language network, six are located outside Quebec, as are more than half the 174 French-language rebroadcasters operated by the network. This pattern of substantial over-representation is repeated for the radio network, and for the CBC's English-language facilities.[39] It means that about half of the corporation's budget for broadcasting and transmission (as opposed to the much larger programming budget) is effectively a subsidy for some rather numerically small minority populations.[40] On this basis, it is possible to use the CBC's published budget figures to determine that roughly $80 million is spent by the corporation each year on servicing Canada's minority communities.[41]

There are additional categories of media-related expense that are easy to overlook. One of the more straightforward is the $5 million earmarked in 1987 by the Secretary of State to support the establishment of community radio stations for francophones outside Quebec.[42] Seven stations were established with the aid of this money. Similarly, the French-language TV5 television network was the recipient of a $7 million start-up grant from the federal government in 1987, allowing it to establish Canada's second coast-to-coast French-language television network.[43] TV Ontario's French-language service, *La chaîne*, is the recipient of nearly $6 million every year in combined federal-provincial government grants.[44]

But probably of much greater significance, in terms of real costs, is the fact that minority-language radio and television broadcasters, including those established with the help of federal grants, are regularly issued radio frequencies by the CRTC. This step was necessary, for example, before the TV5 network could gain slots on crowded airwaves nationwide.[45] TV Ontario was able to gain sufficient space to broadcast two network signals in each of its local markets—one in English, one in French.[46]

In crowded markets, most radio frequencies are already occupied, so space must be made by elbowing existing majority-language broadcasters aside. If there were a free market in radio frequencies, they would be bought and sold among broadcasters themselves, often at considerable expense. But in Canada, the airwaves are public property, and even the Department of Communications has no idea how much they are worth.[47] The cost of assigning airwaves to minority official-language broadcasters who will provide a product for which there is no market demand, and thereby keeping other, more popular broadcasters off the market, therefore imposes a totally uncalculated and unknowable cost on the public.[48]

Usually, this process takes place in silence. Sometimes, however, a popular station is forced out of the market to make way for a minority-language broadcaster. When this happens, it invariably raises howls of public protest. Hubert Guindon, the well-known Montreal-based sociologist, observes that when this was tried in Toronto:

> [It gave widespread public] credibility at the local level to the shibboleth "French power." The French are so "powerful" that they can take away a popular English station and make it a French one in an area where few people would ever meet a French Canadian, or would realize it if they did, for most francophones in Toronto speak English as well.[49]

Likewise, when the CRTC

> moved to grant an English radio and cable TV station in the heart of the Saguenay-Lac St Jean area, [the] local population defined the situation in the same manner. While 'English power' is not nearly so new a slogan and much more of a social and economic fact, it was perceived as an illustration of that power and as an attempt by the state to further the assimilation of the Québécois.[50]

Some indication of the extent to which this phenomenon takes place and hence of the cost of the free provision of band widths can be ascertained from the fact that there is a lobby group, *l'Alliance des radios communautaires du Canada*, which offers, exclusively to French-language radio broadcasters located outside Quebec, services in the process of seeking permits from the CRTC. The organization, which also offers a variety of other start-up services to *hors-Québec* French broadcasters, has twenty-three member stations, including two in the Northwest Territories and one in Newfoundland.[51]

Figure 10.5[52]
COST OF MEDIA-RELATED FEDERAL SERVICES TO THE PUBLIC, 1991-92:

1)	Advertising in minority official-language newspapers*	$5,050,000
2)	50% of CBC distribution activity expenses nationwide*	80,000,000
3)	Subsidy to minority official-language community radio	500,000

4)	Subsidy to TV 5*	2,445,000
5)	Free use of public property (airwaves)*	cost unknown
Total (excluding cost of free use of airwaves):		**$ 87,995,000**

*not included in official federal estimates of annual language-policy costs.

Federal Regulations Governing Language Use in the Private Sector

Federal regulation of the private sector is the most expensive, and also the best hidden of all areas of federal language policy. There is no official budget for private sector bilingualism. Nonetheless, as shown in Chapter Nine, the complete isolation of the Canadian consumer market from the rest of the world, as a result of the bilingualism provisions of the *Consumer Packaging and Labelling Act*, has the effect of imposing an annual $2 billion burden on Canadian consumers in the form of higher prices for packaged products.

The Act also imposes more heavily on Canada's poor than on the wealthy, because the items for which packaging represents the highest proportion of the total price paid by the end user tend to be basic necessities such as packaged foods, toiletries and household cleaning supplies. Almost nothing is added by the Act's bilingualism rules to the price of such luxury products as cars and consumer electronics.

Additional costs are imposed on the private sector by the regulatory presence of the Commissioner of Official Languages, who devotes about $5.8 milllion of his $13 million budget to monitoring the activities of private companies subject to federal regulation. His most prominent activities in this area have been highly public lawsuits against Air Canada over its advertising practices and VIA Rail over its provision of bilingual service.[53]

Because compliance costs are virtually impossible to measure by direct means, it is safer to use the 1:20 direct cost to compliance cost ratio favoured by the economists at the Center for the Study of American Business. On this basis, the annual total of all indirect and opportunity costs imposed by the Commissioner's regulation of the private sector is in the neighbourhood of $116 million.

Figure 10.6 [54]
COST OF FEDERAL SUPPORT OF BILINGUALISM IN THE PRIVATE SECTOR:

1)	Budget of Commissioner of Official Languages for activities related to the regulation of bilingualism in the private sector*	$ 5,797,000
2)	Compliance costs with this regulation (direct regulatory costs x 20)**	115,940,000
3)	Compliance costs with the *Consumer Packaging and Labelling Act***	2,000,000,000
Total:		**$2,121,737,000**

*To obtain this total, I have assumed that the private-sector regulatory function of the Commissioner of Official Languages includes fifty percent of the Commissioner's $4.3 million complaints and audits budget, fifty percent of his $2.3 million regional operations budget, and one-third of his $2.44 million resource management budget.
**not included in official federal estimates of annual language-policy costs.

Education Programs

Each year the federal department of the Secretary of State signs funding agreements with all provincial and territorial governments. These agreements establish the dollar amount of "federal contributions towards the extra costs incurred by provinces and territories for projects and activities undertaken to offer educational services in the official language of the minority (English in Quebec, French elsewhere) and in the second official language at all levels of the school systems."[55]

The official estimate pegs the annual cost of language education programs in Canada at $264 billion[56] but this estimate is completely meaningless, for two reasons. First, estimates from the Office of the Commissioner count as a cost of official languages policies all monies spent by Ottawa on minority official language education, even if these dollars would have been spent in the same manner whether or not Canada had embraced Official Bilingualism.

A good example of funds being miscategorized in this way is the $19,887,474 that the federal government transferred to New Brunswick in fiscal year 1991-92 for French-language education.[57] This transfer is listed as a cost of Official Bilingualism. But it is difficult to believe that much of this money should be categorized as an additional expense imposed by Official Bilingualism. After all, the vast majority of New Brunswick's French-language schools are located in areas of the province where it is English that is the minority language, and where French was the language of education long before bilingualism had become federal policy.

On the other hand, the official estimates ignore the fact that the federal government's contribution is only part of the total cost of minority-language education. The provinces also make substantial contributions which by any objective standard are as much a part of Canada's total language-related spending bill as any federal dollars. In some cases, these provincial funds are spent in order to conform with the additional educational expenditures mandated under Section 23 of the *Charter of Rights and Freedoms*.

The provinces spend even larger sums providing French second-language education, even in areas of the country far from Canada's centres of French culture. In these regions, it is unlikely that French would ever be a useful job skill for any youngster, were it not for the bilingualism requirements that Ottawa has placed on careers within the civil service, the RCMP, crown corporations, and the military. Therefore, the spread of French second-language programs across the country owes much to the federal emphasis on bilingualism as a requirement for personal success. Ottawa's willingness to initiate shared-cost programs in French-second language (FSL) and French immersion programs has also played a role in the expansion of French classes.

In order to determine these costs, it is necessary to study in detail provincial expenditures on education in matters relating to language. Fortunately, this task is made much simpler by the existence of a series of background documents attached as appendices to the educational subsidy agreements that Ottawa signs with each of the provincial and territorial governments every five years. These appendices provide itemized breakdowns of the expenses involved in conducting education in more than one language. What's more, the expenses are neatly arranged to show which are additional expenses that would not be incurred if education systems were run in one language only.

This does not mean that the figures provided by the agreements can be taken at face value. Some of the numbers provided by provincial departments of education are highly suspect. Quebec's education ministry, for example, maintains that it could save almost half a billion dollars every year if it did not have to educate its English-speakers in English, and if it were under no obligation to teach English as a second language to francophone children.[58]

A closer inspection of the evidence provided in the text of the appendices to back up this assertion reveals some curious items. The province's three English-language universities are assumed to be enormous burdens on the educational system, which could be eliminated if they were shut down and the students redistributed to French-language universities. The argument is made that in a unilingual French-language network of universities:

> Canadians from other provinces studying in Quebec's English-language universities would not be as numerous. . . . Our supposition is that their numbers would be proportionate to those Canadians from other provinces currently studying in the French network. Thus, in a unilingual French network in 1989-1990, there would have been 7,318 fewer Canadian students from other provinces, allowing for a savings of $38.7 million.[59]

The $38.7 million savings would be real, from Quebec's point of view, but it is unlikely that the simple act of shutting down McGill University and a couple of other institutions would cause several thousand English Canadians to permanently abandon their plans for post-secondary education. With their options in Quebec shut down, they would simply attend university in other provinces, at about the same cost. It is difficult to see how this is a language-related cost at all.

Similarly, the provincial government makes the rather remarkable argument that English second-language education for students in the French-language school system costs the province $232 million in extra expenses, but that

French second-language education for students in the English-language school system costs nothing at all.[60]

Such foibles can be corrected, however, as long as one is careful in one's reading of the appendices. Taken together, they show that minority-language education in Canada costs about $235 million annually and that second-language education in French for English Canadians and English for French Canadians costs about $208 million each year. These costs are additional to those which would exist in a series of unilingual provincial education systems, and exclude the cost of second-language education in those parts of the country where second-language skills are a clear economic asset—and therefore would be part of any well-rounded education, whether or not Official Bilingualism existed. This means that the cost of ESL for francophones in Quebec is not included in this total, nor is the cost of FSL for anglophones in eastern Ontario, northern New Brunswick or Quebec. Likewise, the cost of most Montreal English-language schools and the entire cost of the English-language universities has been left out of the equation, since these institutions predate official languages spending and would exist in the absence of Ottawa's intervention. A final category of spending excluded from this total is the money for French-language education in those parts of eastern Ontario and northern New Brunswick where French is the language of the local majority.

Figure 10.7
ADDITIONAL EDUCATIONAL COSTS ASSOCIATED WITH FEDERAL OFFICIAL LANGUAGES POLICY:

Prov.	English Second Language	French Second Language	English Minority Education	French Minority Education
Nfld	0	$ 3,899,437	$0	$ 1,723,489
PEI	0	1,406,410	0	5,559,872
NS	0	2,376,073	0	10,398,028
NB	0[61]	6,500,000[62]	0	15,496,763[63]
Que	0[64]	0[65]	73,100,000[66]	0
Ont	0	124,200,000[67]	0	97,486,490[68]
Man	0	10,435,297	0	8,868,348
Sask	0	18,501,849	0	3,721,078
Alta	0	22,227,761	0	6,882,394
B.C.	0	20,327,137	0	10,786,974
Yuk	0	435,366	0	659,000
NWT	0	623,479	0	461,270
Total	0	$210,936,009	$ 73,100,000	$162,043,706

Federal Subsidies of Quebec's Language Policies

In theory, there is no direct connection between the language policies of Ottawa and those of Quebec. In practice, however, as was shown in Chapter Seven, the federal government has permitted Quebec to use the pre-existing system of intergovernmental equalization payments to ease the economic impact of Bill 101, which had the effect of driving out many of Quebec's most economically productive citizens.

Pierre Arbour, a former senior manager at Quebec's *Caisse de dépôt et placement*, has calculated that between 1976 and 1986, Bill 101 cost the Quebec government $10 billion in lost income tax revenues alone from anglophones departing the province.[69] Of this, roughly twenty percent was returned to the province by the federal government in the form of equalization payments.[70] Federal payments to the Quebec government in support of Bill 101 are thus one of the largest items on Ottawa's annual list of language-related expenses.

Another major subsidy to Quebec's language policy comes in the form of transfers from the federal Department of Employment and Immigration to the province "as financial compensation to accompany the federal withdrawal from reception and integration services to immigrants as per Section 26 of the Canada-Quebec Accord related to immigration and temporary admission of aliens." In 1991-1992, $75 million was transferred in this manner. By contrast, only $72.9 million was spent by the federal government for similar programs in all other provinces combined, where it had not withdrawn from this aspect of immigration. On this basis, it is safe to regard this expenditure as part of federal efforts to support Quebec language policy.[71]

A much smaller amount is transferred each year to the Quebec government for "cultural infrastructure," pursuant to an agreement signed between the two governments. In 1991-92, $8.2 million was transferred in this manner. Similar agreements exist with all provinces, and it would be incorrect to assume that all such funds go to language-related matters. However, $5.6 million, or around two-thirds of the total transferred for cultural infrastructure, is used directly by the Quebec Ministry of Cultural Affairs, rather than as direct funding for museums and similar pieces of physical infrastructure. This is different from most provinces, where physical infrastructure consumes almost all of the transfers. Some portion of this $5 million presumably is spent on language-related matters, although further research will be needed if a more accurate breakdown is to be obtained.[72]

Figure 10.8
COST OF FEDERAL SUPPORT OF QUEBEC LANGUAGE POLICIES, 1991-92:

1) Portion of Equalization payments received by Quebec that is attributable to the anglophone exodus* $200,000,000
2) Transfer for "reception and integration" of immigrants* 75,000,000

3) 50%[73] of transfer to Ministry of Cultural Affairs under
    "cultural infrastructure" agreement*   5,628,300
Total: **$280,628,300**

*not included in official federal estimates of annual language-policy costs.

Advocacy and Community Groups

One of the most important expenses associated with Official Bilingualism is the transfer of millions of dollars each year from the federal treasury to French-language activist groups located outside Quebec and English-language groups in Quebec. These groups use the funds partly for community activities, such as regional newsletters, but mostly for lobbying and publicity activities in demand of more extensive rights and privileges for the communities they represent. This creates the odd situation of associations which receive the lion's share of their funding from the federal government using much of that money to publicly condemn the same government for its ungenerous treatment of the communities which the associations claim to represent. This spectacle is made even more bizarre by the fact that most community members do not care enough about the associations' activities to become involved or to donate money.

Official reports refer to disbursements to these groups as "grants to organizations representing official-language minority communities, non-federal public administrations and other organizations, for the purpose of furthering the use and promotion of the official languages." In 1992, the federal government transferred $31.9 million to activist and community groups in the form of "grants," and a further $15.2 million in the form of "contributions."[74]

Another federal expense which ought logically to be classified under the heading of "advocacy and community groups" is that share of the funding for the Commissioner of Official Languages which is devoted to the Commissioner's own advocacy of minority-rights. The Commissioner's office engages not only in the function of regulating the Public Service, as noted earlier in this chapter, but also in supplying the public with information on official languages, and in representing the interests of official-languages minorities to Parliament. Almost all of the information published by the Commissioner for public consumption takes the form of partisan defences of the present linguistic regime or demands for greater sums of money to be spent. The booklet *Some Basic Facts*, which was widely distributed to classrooms across Canada in the early 1990s, is a good example of this, as is the Commissioner's quarterly magazine, *Language and Society*.[75] Representations to Parliament are made through the Commissioner's well-publicized *Annual Report*, and also through the Commissioner's unwritten right to hold a seat on the Standing Joint Committee of Parliament on Official Languages.

Another program, axed by then-Justice Minister Kim Campbell in 1992 and then restarted in the course of the 1993 federal election campaign, is the Court Challenges Program. This program was used to finance various legal challenges on behalf of minority or 'victim' groups, with the intent of building case law in their favour. No language-related expenditures were made under this program during this eighteen-month interregnum, so no expenses are recorded in Figure 10.7, which records 1992 costs. In the past, however, the program has contributed significantly to a variety of language-related court challenges designed to extend minority official-language rights through judicial activism.[76] Typically, such challenges cost $35,000 per appeal, and over $100,000 if they made it all the way to the Supreme Court of Canada.[77]

Figure 10.9 [78]
COST OF FEDERAL SUPPORT OF ADVOCACY GROUPS, 1992:

1)	"Grants" to 67 organizations representing francophones residing outside Quebec*	$29,444,725
2)	"Contributions" to two organizations representing francophones residing outside Quebec	14,530,465
3)	"Grants" to 10 organizations representing anglophones residing in Quebec*	2,484,500
4)	"Contributions" to two organizations representing anglophones residing in Quebec	695,000
5)	Budget of Commissioner of Official Languages for activities related to advocacy of official language minority rights**	2,611,000
Total:		**$49,765,690**

*To obtain this total, I have assumed that the $165,000 granted to the Federation of Canadian Municipalities is divided equally between efforts to promote the well-being of francophones outside Quebec and anglophones inside Quebec.

**To obtain this total, I have assumed that the advocacy function of the Commissioner of Official Languages includes fifty percent of the Commissioner's $1,290,000 policy budget, fifty percent of his $2,315,000 regional operations budget, and one-third of his $2,440,000 resource management budget.

TOTALLING THE BILL: THE CUMULATIVE COST OF BILINGUALISM: 1969-1992

Once the main categories of expense have been determined, it is possible to determine the total expenses associated with federal laws in each of the years since Official Bilingualism was entrenched in law in 1969, and to determine the total cumulative impact of these expenses.

Some of the impact has taken the form of federal government spending. To

Figure 10.10
Annual cost of various federal language programs, 1972 - 1992

Fiscal Year Ending	Internal P.S. Language	Non-media services to the pubic	Media-related services to the public	Regulation of private sector (regulatory agency costs only)	Education costs (federal payments only)	Federal support of Quebec language policy	Support of advocacy groups	Annual Total
1972	253,524,580	17,305,888	22,340,491	1,016,195	79,596,000	0	2,000,000	375,783,154
1973	273,260,020	18,653,053	24,079,571	1,095,300	79,596,000	0	3,100,000	399,783,944
1974	302,863,190	20,673,800	26,688,191	1,213,958	79,596,000	0	800,000	431,835,139
1975	335,502,580	22,901,804	29,564,362	1,344,758	79,596,000	0	3,600,000	472,509,531
1976	360,551,420	24,611,667	31,771,657	1,445,187	79,596,000	0	3,300,000	501,275,931
1977	389,395,530	26,580,600	34,313,389	1,560,803	162,934,000	0	5,545,000	620,269,322
1978	424,312,090	28,964,046	37,390,223	1,700,757	222,164,000	200,000,000	10,503,000	925,034,116
1979	463,023,393	31,606,562	40,801,496	1,855,925	217,498,000	200,000,000	12,970,000	967,755,376
1980	510,085,380	34,819,032	44,948,533	2,044,560	175,598,000	200,000,000	13,649,000	981,144,505
1981	573,087,000	39,119,597	50,500,212	2,297,087	178,598,000	200,000,000	16,899,000	1,060,500,893
1982	635,329,560	43,368,348	55,985,004	2,546,573	181,269,000	200,000,000	19,899,000	1,138,397,485
1983	671,764,230	45,855,422	59,195,613	2,692,612	176,095,000	200,000,000	22,899,000	1,178,501,877
1984	701,367,400	47,876,170	61,804,233	2,811,270	182,161,000	200,000,000	22,899,000	1,218,919,073
1985	728,693,400	49,741,475	64,212,191	2,920,800	204,377,000	200,000,000	23,225,000	1,273,169,866
1986	759,055,630	51,814,037	66,887,699	3,042,500	214,306,000	200,000,000	27,349,000	1,322,444,866
1987	790,682,295	53,972,956	72,119,687	2,977,166	216,541,000	200,000,000	27,138,000	1,363,431,104
1988	825,347,550	56,339,203	75,174,319	3,366,666	216,541,000	200,000,000	31,638,000	1,408,406,738
1989	857,949,640	58,564,661	78,047,203	3,663,833	235,845,000	200,000,000	43,190,000	1,477,260,337
1990	901,207,610	61,517,502	81,859,079	4,128,833	250,607,000	200,000,000	43,790,000	1,443,110,024
1991	944,662,070	64,483,755	85,688,270	4,128,833	253,939,000	280,628,300	45,190,000	1,678,720,334
1992	998,585,700	68,164,646	87,995,000	5,797,000	253,939,000	280,628,300	45,190,000	1,740,299,646

Sources: See Notes for Figures

the extent that this additional spending boosted each year's federal deficit above the level that otherwise would have been set, this spending finds its present-day manifestation in the form of a sizable proportion of the federal debt (i.e., the accumulated deficit). To the extent that federal shared-cost programs, or federally-initiated laws like the *Charter of Rights*' Section 23 led to provincial deficit spending, the manifestation is found in the various provincial debts.

Wherever federal laws and regulations caused private-sector actors, rather than governments, to spend on language matters, the manifestation of these costs is found not in debts but in the accumulated result of years of reduced investment in the Canadian economy. Money that was diverted over the years to fund compliance with various federal regulations is money that could not be invested; in economic terms, it may be thought of as having been converted from investment capital into a form of consumer good, mostly in the form of bilingual labels and packages. The result of this diversion was a slower rate of economic growth in each of the years in which the relevant laws have been in force, and a lower total Gross National Product today.

The *Consumer Packaging and Labelling Act*, for example, has affected the growth of the Canadian economy precisely as the American regulatory jungle has affected the United States economy. Prominent American economist William Niskanen explains how the U.S. has been affected:

> Several studies based on macroeconomic data . . . suggest that one-tenth to one-quarter of the reduction in productivity growth in the late 1970s was attributable to the increase in regulation in that period. Several recent studies suggest that the combination of conditions that lead to the unusually high employment of lawyers in the United States may reduce U.S. GNP by about 10 percent.[79]

Unfortunately, it will be impossible to place even an approximate figure on the permanent loss of economic growth attributable to the opportunity costs associated with regulatory compliance until substantially more research has been done. This work is beyond the scope of the present study, so it is only possible to note here that the annual $2-billion cost to Canadian consumers of complying with the *Consumer Packaging and Labelling Act* has been a burden on their personal budgets since 1974. From their perspective, this single piece of legislation has had the effect of diverting $40 billion out of their pockets over the past twenty years.

If the long-term impact of private-sector opportunity costs can only be hinted at, the opposite is true of the direct impact on the debt of federal and provincial deficit spending on official-languages programs initiated in Ottawa. Once the amount spent in each year has been calculated, it can be added to the government deficit for that year, then multiplied by the interest rate paid on government debt that year. The total of the spending plus the interest is then

THE DOLLARS AND SENSE OF OFFICIAL BILINGUALISM   249

Figure 10.11
Federal Official Languages spending and the debt

Year	Official Estimate language costs (000)	Real language costs	Cumulative additons to the national debt	Average interest on federal debt %	Total federal debt
1974	185,825	431,835,139	431,835,139	6.47	18,128,000,000
1975	227,501	472,509,531	935,609,534	7.24	19,275,000,000
1976	310,425	501,275,931	1,510,237,252	7.84	23,269,000,000
1977	375,185	620,269,322	2,244,227,439	7.53	29,586,000,000
1978	509,630	925,034,116	3,346,331,100	7.89	39,622,000,000
1979	475,460	967,755,376	4,613,583,109	8.95	55,807,000,000
1980	390,422	981,144,505	6,077,308,407	10.46	68,565,000,000
1981	415,620	1,060,500,893	7,848,854,384	11.70	81,263,000,000
1982	448,184	1,138,397,485	10,088,446,139	14.03	94,869,000,000
1983	456,908	1,178,501,877	12,390,800,916	11.14	119,522,000,000
1984	454,586	1,218,919,073	14,921,905,806	10.59	157,011,000,000
1985	496,462	1,273,169,866	17,882,743,219	11.31	191,448,000,000
1986	505,534	1,322,444,866	21,111,488,512	10.66	233,496,000,000
1987	504,640	1,363,431,104	24,446,732,643	9.34	264,101,000,000
1988	541,538	1,408.406,738	28,204,470,388	9.61	292,184,000,000
1989	589,612	1,477,260,337	32,733,454,421	10.82	320,918,000,000
1990	626,152	1,443,110,024	37,842,711,340	11.20	357,961,000,000
1991	653,668	1,678,720,334	43,578,170,329	10.72	388,429,000,000
1992	660,721	1,740,299,646	49,179,495,867	8.86	423,072,000,000

Sources: See *Notes for Figures*

Figure 10.12
Impact of federal Official Languages spending on the debt

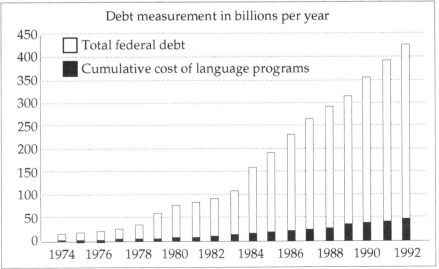

Sources: See *Notes for Figures*

added to the deficit for the following year, along with the new year's language-related deficit spending. The two-year total must then be multiplied by that year's interest rate, and so on, for every year in which Ottawa has recorded a deficit.

This procedure works well for all spending from 1974 onwards. In 1973 the federal government ran its last-ever budget surplus, so it is not really legitimate to add the first five years of spending on Official Bilingualism (1969-1973) to the debt.

On this basis, the total cumulative cost of federal languages policy from the beginning of the Trudeau years to today has been the addition of $49 billion to the federal debt, billions more to various provincial debts, and a permanent loss to Canadian consumers of $40 billion worth of consumption.

SUMMARY

To say that federal languages spending is expensive is an understatement. In every area of language policy, the federal government has either placed huge burdens on the Canadian economy or it has assumed them directly, thereby placing huge burdens on Canadian taxpayers.

This does not mean that all language-related spending should be stopped, which would be unconstitutional, and also unconscionable. But if the measures proposed earlier in this book were to be enacted, the savings in education costs, service costs, regulatory costs, the costs involved in running the Public Service in both languages and the costs of regulating language use in the private sector could be in the billions annually. Canadians could save upwards of half, and perhaps more than two-thirds, of the money currently devoted to feeding the Official Bilingualism monster. Yet the very real benefits that the public derives from official languages programs would be retained.

There would be an additional benefit. The current mishmash of language-related programs was adopted not so much out of goodwill towards minorities but because of the fear that if Canada did not, as a unit, provide an immediate and vigorous response to the issues of most concern to Quebec, the province might leave Confederation. Today, nothing holds Quebec as tightly to Canada as the belief that there is more prosperity inside a united Canada than outside a divided one. Every measure of economic inefficiency in federal policy weakens this key link, and every policy that enhances growth or prosperity strengthens it. Savings of the magnitude available in official languages policy will not easily be found elsewhere. It would be a shame to weaken national unity because we are afraid to look at revising policies that were originally designed to strengthen it.

Conclusion

> You will also be asked to consider measures relating to ... citizenship, to national symbols, to culture agencies. ... Some of these proposals involve the righting of wrongs and others the opening of opportunities long denied. Together they exemplify the essential connection between justice and national unity.
>
> —*Speech from the Throne, first Trudeau government (1968)*

OFFICIAL BILINGUALISM has come as close as any policy in the history of Canada to accomplishing the opposite of its intended objectives. Founded with the intention of uniting the country, it has at best failed to limit the allure of Québécois nationalism, and at worst it has driven Canadians further apart. Designed to correct historic wrongs, it has created new injustices. Intended to help create a new national identity in which all Canadians could share, it has become instead a symbol of sectionalism, elitism and division. Even the simple goal of bringing rationality and coherence to Canada's language laws has been lost, as the federal government has adopted mutually contradictory stands on various aspects of language policy.

The policies that collectively go by the name 'Official Bilingualism' are the outgrowth of two phenomena that swept Canada in the 1960s. The first of these was the rising self-confidence and self-awareness of French-speaking Canadians. The second phenomenon was the English Canadian realization that with their imperial past within the British Empire now fading and no longer a source of identification, there was distressingly little to distinguish persons living north of the forty-ninth parallel from the citizens of the great republic to the south.

It was during this decade that philosopher George Grant compared the ways in which French-speaking and English-speaking Canada were reacting to the threats that each feared might lead to its own extinction. In Quebec, he noted, there was the burst of self-affirmation and self-discovery known as the Quiet Revolution. In English Canada, there was confusion, uncertainty and self-doubt. Grant wrote, "Indigenous cultures are dying everywhere in the modern world. ... The French on this continent will at least disappear from history with more than the smirks and whimpers of their English-speaking compatriots—with their flags flying and, indeed, with some guns blazing."[1]

What Grant did not imagine was that the country could be set on an entirely new course by the emergence of a new ideology that would profess to answer at a single blow the utterly different concerns of English and French Canada.

With the national agenda dominated by the contrasting moods of the two language groups, it is no wonder that charismatic newcomer Pierre Trudeau was able to sweep the country off its feet in the election of 1968. His credo of Official Bilingualism seemed to answer the hopes and fears of both language communities at the same time. For French speakers, there would at last be official recognition of their language's equality with English. For English Canadians, there was the promise that the bilingual, multicultural character of the restructured Canada would provide the country with a much-needed sense of identity. Simultaneously, it was explained to anglophones, Quebec would be dissuaded from seceding, and the full participation of francophones in the country's future would provide the magic ingredient that would allow all Canadians to share in a self-confident new collective identity.

The keystone of the whole policy would be its emphasis on linguistic justice. Under Official Bilingualism, existing injustices would be ended and past wrongs would be righted.

Canada's official languages programs were thus initially conceived as a means of simultaneously forestalling Quebec independence, defining a sense of Canadian collective identity, and introducing justice to an area of policy that traditionally had been the source of endless injustices. The means by which this would be accomplished would permit the rise of new forms of cultural interaction which would make Canada a model for the post-nationalist world of the future.

At least this was the theory behind Official Bilingualism. Unfortunately, like so many other policies intended to accomplish a series of subtly connected and interdependent goals, Official Bilingualism was too clever by half. Filled with too many disparate elements, it has failed to achieve any of its objectives. Quebec's sense of itself did not rub off on the rest of the nation, and Ottawa's efforts to convince Quebecers that federal language policy could answer all the questions being sought in independence has produced no clear-cut victory for federalism. What's more, old injustices in policies like Public Service hiring were merely replaced by new ones.

And, of course, there is a price tag associated with the grab-bag of language policies that have been growing and evolving since the 1960s. Official Bilingualism has been far more expensive in dollars and cents than anybody had imagined it would be, and has produced far more resentment than goodwill. The failure of Official Bilingualism to achieve its objectives was summed up by Hubert Guindon in 1978, when he warned that:

Local resentment would still be a reasonable price to pay were the [federal government's] objective to be met. Should the resentment be temporary and the long-term objectives ensuring national unity be achieved, historians would certainly describe such persistence as an example of statesmanship. Unfortunately, it is increasingly evident that its main objective, creating a bilingual and bicultural Canada "a mari usque ad mare" by ensuring the viability of French communities outside Quebec, is an illusion. In such a case, persistence obviously becomes political irresponsibility.[2]

Political responsibility means admitting that the policies adopted in 1969 were sociologically and politically naïve to begin with and that they have been twisted into incoherence by revsions that have been made to them since that date. It means admitting that the state is not capable of doing all that the idealists of the 1960s thought it could, to mould society or redirect the flows of assimilation and linguistic integration. This in turn means that responsibility involves making the goals of language policy more modest: not to redefine the Canadian identity, but to provide an institutional backdrop that will not interfere with the efforts of Canadians to develop their own collective loyalties; not to offer services in order to halt the geographic polarization of English and French, but to provide aid and comfort to those minorities that are genuinely in need of services in their own language; not to use the federal Public Service as a vast vanguard of bilingual employment, but to provide fairness in hiring and promotion for members of both linguistic communities, and so on.

Responsibility also means re-examining the first principles on which official languages policy should be based. In this book I have suggested that Canadian language policy should be based on a pragmatic, utilitarian conception of justice. Its sole focus should be on providing equality of treatment to all Canadians, whether they are members of the French majority in Quebec, the English majority elsewhere, or either of the country's two minorities. This requires a delicate balance of rights and obligations, so that the privileges enjoyed by one of these classes of citizens do not turn into millstones to be borne by all the others.

Canadians are fortunate to have an impressive body of scholarship on the alternatives available to the country in each area of language policy. Much of what has been discussed and advocated in this book is neither new nor original. In particular, there are the recommendations of the Royal Commission on Bilingualism and Biculturalism, which are much praised in policy-makers' rhetoric, but which have been almost entirely ignored in practice. The solutions proposed by the Royal Commissioners are in some cases out of date, but they represent a school of thought that is practical and moderate—in other words, thoroughly Canadian. After years of pursuing chimerical notions, we could do worse than to re-examine their findings and put their principles (if not always their precise recommendations) into practice.

APPENDIX A

Federal Translation Costs: A Study in Waste

> Whatever activity government engages in tends to cost roughly twice as much as the same activity carried out by private entities.
> —*Milton Friedman*[1]

In chapter ten, I make the claim that the additional internal costs that the current regime of Official Bilingualism impose on the federal bureaucracy have increased the general cost of transacting business by about five percent, or $951 annually.

Such a bold assertion requires not only a reasoned defence (which I believe that discussion provides), but also an effort to apply it in a systematic way to at least part of the Public Service. This appendix is an attempt to illustrate that the estimate of five percent is not excessive, by means of a closer examination of a facet of the Public Service where the costs imposed are far in excess of five percent.

Hidden away in the bowels of the Canadian bureaucracy is a small army of bilingual scribes, diligently translating hundreds of millions of words each year for the internal use of the various arms and agencies of the Public Service of Canada. Obscured from public scrutiny by the sheer magnitude of the beast it serves, the translation bureaucracy has grown wildly out of control.

It is difficult to accept that such extraordinarily high costs are solely the result of ineptitude or mismanagement. A far greater role in the development of these costs has probably been played by the dominant ideology of the past quarter century, which has held that national unity can only be preserved by the maintenance of the broadest possible range of federal services, regardless of the costs involved. The belief that no price is too high to pay for the unity of one's country has mutated, among some policy-makers and administrators, into the conviction that spending more money on the promotion of official languages is invariably virtuous for its own sake, whether or not anything concrete is actually accomplished by the extra expense. In a sense therefore, the excesses and waste of the Translation Bureau are a metaphor for the unnecessary spending that takes place in all areas of policy relating to official languages.

There are two ways in which money is wasted on translations. First, federal government translations cost several times as much, per word, as do translations made by private contractors. Second, at least half of all translations made by the government are unnecessary, since it does not matter to Canadians whether internal government documents and correspondence exist only in one official language or the other, as long as the government can still govern effectively.

Cost Per Word

Treasury Board estimates indicate that translations within the Public Service cost $122 million in fiscal year 1991-92.[2] Of this amount, over eighty percent was spent by the federal government's notoriously inefficient Translation Bureau, an organization which seems to have decided that its corporate mission is to prove the accuracy of Milton Friedman's axiom about the cost of government activities, quoted at the beginning of this appendix.

The scope of this mini-bureacracy is described in an article published in 1985 in the language commissioner's magazine, *Language and Society*, in which Jean Delisle, an associate professor at the University of Ottawa, proudly points to the elephantine proportions of the Bureau:

> Riddle: Name the giant that has 900 translators, about 100 interpreters, a similar number of terminologists and managers and a support staff of 550 serving 150 client organizations . . . a computer that translates over 8 million words each and every year; dozens of word processors with video display screens; a computerized terminology bank that boasts 1.5 million entries; seven Grapho-Braille terminals enabling visually handicapped users to access this electronic dictionary and over 400 data bases, 16 word counters; and regional offices located across the country from Chilliwack, British Columbia to Halifax. . . . The answer, as you have probably guessed, is the Government of Canada's Translation Bureau.[3]

Blind to the implications of his article, Delisle includes charts showing that the Bureau's workload had increased from 89 million words in the fiscal year 1968-69 to 300 million in 1983-84 and that in the same period, its budget had grown from $6 million to $82 million.

A quick calculation reveals this as showing that the per-word translation cost has risen from 6.7 cents per word in 1969 to 27.3 cents per word in 1984. Even after fifteen years of inflation are factored in, this is a drop in efficiency of twenty-five percent.

In 1991, the Bureau translated 313 million words—roughly one million pages of single-spaced typewritten text. This was done at an average direct cost of 27.3 cents per word, as compared to typical private sector costs of 14.4 cents per word.[4] Further indirect costs such as personnel management, office rental expenses, and equipment costs pushed the total price per translated word to 41.6 cents.[5] Moreover, the Auditor-General has produced embarrassing evidence that seventy-five percent of the translators employed by the Bureau in

1991 were still incapable of meeting efficiency goals of 200 words per hour that had been set seven years earlier, following an earlier unfavourable report on their efficiency.

This would give the Translation Bureau a strong claim to the title of the most inefficient organization in the entire federal apparatus were it not for the fact that translations produced by the Canadian military are even more expensive by a factor of nearly 100 percent. By the Department of National Defence's own estimate, the average cost for translating military documents in the five-year period ending in 1995 will be an amazing 73.7 cents per word, or $220 per page—fully five times as expensive as the rate charged by private translators. The total cost for translations in this department alone is projected to run to $73 million over this five-year period.[6]

Unnecessary Translations

The problem of unnecessary translations is at least twenty-five years old. In its reports, the B&B Commission often expressed its dismay at the practice of making unneeded translations.[7] In the 1960s, most unnecessary translations were made from French to English. Today the reverse is true, but the scale of the problem is far worse than it was a quarter-century ago. It is currently federal policy to translate all "work instruments" including all technical manuals, into both official languages.[8] In practice this leads to a flood of one-way translations into French, because most technical documentation for computers, software and machinery is written in English.

The most famous recent example of the high costs involved in translating technical documents involves the 500,000-page technical manuals for two new frigates currently under construction. In 1991, columnist Diane Francis reported in the *Financial Post* that a full translation of these manuals would cost $100 million. Francis quoted a defence department spokesman as stating that the first 100,000 pages had already been contracted out for translation at a cost of $20 million, and extrapolated her figures from this.[9]

Francis' article provoked an immediate, angry response from *Language and Society*, which published an article claiming that "a check with National Defence and the Department of Supply and Services showed that [Ms. Francis'] interpretation of the information was erroneous. The cost of translation, according to estimates, might reach $43.5 million by the time work is completed." For the benefit of readers who could not bring themselves to accept that $43.5 million is a bargain, the article went on to argue that compared to the total cost of the frigates, the manuals would be inexpensive: "Frigates have their uses, but no one ever said they were cheap."[10]

Nor, it would seem, are they included in the government's official cost estimates. There is no trace of the cost of translating the frigate manuals in the Treasury Board's total cost figures for Canadian bilingualism. Instead of being placed on the ledgers as a translation expense, the translation of the manuals appears to have been counted as part of the overall cost of the ships.

This seems to be a fairly standard accounting practice in the Department of National Defence. When the department purchased four DeHavilland Dash-8 aircraft in the 1980s, the contract of purchase instructed that translated manuals be included, at an additional cost of $10,000.[11] There is no hint of a cover-up in this accounting, since costs can be registered only once on the government's books. But this does not change the fact that significant translation costs do not show up on the official estimates.

The frigate manuals represent only a tiny fraction of the total potential costs of translating technical materials. Testifying in 1989 before Parliament's Standing Joint Committee on Official Languages, Lieutenant-General James Fox indicated that DND had a backlog of four million pages of technical documentation in need of translation. To update this at current Translation Bureau rates would involve an expenditure of just under half a billion dollars.[12]

Fortunately for the Canadian treasury, DND has never been given the resources necessary to carry out this vast undertaking. Instead, by agreement with the Treasury Board, the department has limited itself to translating only 330,000 pages of the backlog over the four-year period between 1991 and 1995 at a total cost of $73 million.[13]

Following the publication of Diane Francis' embarrassing article, DND set up a ministerial committee to examine its translation problems. The report, published in 1992, paints a picture of organizational chaos and misplaced priorities on an almost unimaginable scale. The committee reported that in some cases the translation backlog was so severe "that it would be fifteen or more years before some courses could be offered completely in French due to the amount of material in the translation queue."[14]

In other cases, technical translations were made fairly promptly but were ignored by the technical personnel for whom they had been intended. The committee reported that at the Air Force base at Bagotville, Quebec:

> French was very much the working language. However, all the technical terms were referred to by their English names. The purist, we suppose, would turn somersaults. But the technicians were clearly a happy, well-motivated and proud group of men and women. Did they feel terms in French should be substituted? The question elicited shocked looks. Did we have any idea how many terms one had to know in a complex system like the CF-18? But, we countered, what about the young technicians who had been taught terms in French; would they not prefer to use and expand their French technical vocabulary? Such a young technician responded that he would have to know the terms in both languages (making his lot harder than his colleague's in Cold Lake) because squadrons have to be able to operate together. . . . Technicians,

although working in French orally, referred to the English text even when French and English were presented side by side on the same page.[15]

Observing that the decision to translate all technical documentation seems to be based more on ideology than on practical considerations, the Committee proposed that all technical documentation should remain untranslated unless it is actually needed. To ensure that this does not lead to discrimination against francophones, the decision to translate or not should be left to a francophone officer. As the report explains:

> The translation test should be: will translated material be used? Who should make such a decision? It seems to us it is best made by a francophone officer who is close to the potential user [and] who is sensitive to the degree which French is used as the language of work. . . . [16]

The Committee's single recommendation on the subject of translations makes such good sense that one can only hope it will be followed in all departments of the federal government.

How to Reduce Translation Costs

Federal translation costs could be cut to a fraction of their present level if two conditions were met. First, Public Service restructuring should allow more documents to serve their entire life cycle without passing from the hands of unilingual anglophones to unilingual francophones, or the reverse. This would greatly reduce the volume of translations needed. Second, all translations of non-secret documents should be done by privately contracted translators instead of the overpriced underperformers of the Translation Bureau.

The need for translations of documents would be far less than it presently is had the federal government, in the late 1960s, chosen to follow the Public Service staffing recommendations of the Royal Commission on Bilingualism and Biculturalism. In particular, the creation of vertically-integrated French-language work units and English-language units within the Public Service would have greatly reduced the number of documents flowing from public servants using one official language to public servants using the other.

The most rapid period of expansion for the Translation Bureau took place between 1969 and 1974, in the wake of the passage of the first *Official Languages Act*.[17] The new Act greatly increased the number of bilingual posts and seems to have driven up the demand for bilingual documents as well.[18] Since there are strong arguments in favour of abandoning the bilingual post system and returning to the language-based units recommended by the B&B Commission on the grounds that it would be a fairer system both for unilingual anglophones and for unilingual francophones, lower numbers of expensive translations would be a beneficial side-effect.

A Flood of Unnecessary Translations

> Recent studies have indicated a lack of rigour in the implementation of these policies and guidelines. Many written communications are automatically translated into the second official language without knowing whether there is a need for the document to be translated.
>
> —*Treasury Board circular (1981)*[19]

If the federal government were to adopt the French- and English-language unit system, the volume of translations in the federal government would probably be cut in half.

The further expedient of firing or reassigning everybody in the Translation Bureau and shutting down this incontinent institution would have the effect of transferring the remaining translation work to Ottawa's legions of fast and efficient private sector translators. In a single blow, it would cut the cost of government translations in half. For translations done in-house by the military, the savings in per-word costs could be as high as eighty percent. Total savings from a combination of reduced translation volume and lower per-word costs could realistically be expected to approach three-quarters of the money currently spent on translations, with no loss at all in quality or speed.

Translations are an extreme example of inefficiency and waste; it would be foolish to suggest that the savings available simply by ending duplication and waste elsewhere in Canada's vast network of language-related expenses would come anywhere close to approaching the levels attainable in translations. But it is important to realize that there are tens of millions of dollars out there being wasted, in practice, because of a simple unwillingness to treat bilingualism-related questions as normal matters of economy. Canadians are poorer as a result.

Footnotes

INTRODUCTION

1. Christian Dufour, *A Canadian Challenge: Le Defi Québécois*. Lantzville, British Columbia and Halifax: Oolichan Books and the Institute for Research on Public Policy, 1990, p. 149.
2. Leslie Green and Denise Réaume, "Bilingualism, Territorialism, and Linguistic Justice." *The Newsletter of the Network on the Constitution*, Vol. 1, No. 3, July 1991, p. 11.
3. Mother-tongue figures for the city of Montreal (not the much larger Montreal Urban Community or Census Metropolitan Area).

1. LANGUAGE AND JUSTICE

1. Green and Réaume, "Bilingualism, Territorialism," p. 10.
2. Lucien Bouchard was a cabinet minister under Brian Mulroney at the time (1988). It is possible that his views have since shifted.
3. Jean Laponce, *Languages and their Territories*. Toronto: University of Toronto Press, 1987, p. 70.
4. On this point, Jean-Luc Migué writes:

    The first proposition that economic theory has established with respect to language is that multilingualism increases transaction costs between economies or between groups or individuals within one economy. The exchange of products, services and factors of production—and particularly of technology and professional services—entails communication between traders. The fact that traders speak different languages requires that one or both of the two parties concerned invest in learning a second language. The real cost of multilingualism lies in this investment. Multilingualism can thus be analysed as being equivalent to transportation costs.

    (See Jean-Luc Migué, *Nationalistic Policies in Canada: An Economic Approach*. C.D. Howe Institute, p. 30.)

5. Ernest Gellner, speaking in an interview recorded for the CBC Radio program *Ideas*. See "Nationalism: The Modern Janus." Transcript for *Ideas*, Canadian Broadcasting Corporation, ID 9291, pp. 3-4.
6. Jacques Leclerc, *Langue et Société*. Laval, Quebec: Mondia Editeurs, 1986, p. 29.
7. F.L. Morton, "The Language Conflict is About Power, not Poetry." *Alberta Report*. Edmonton. May 15, 1989, p. 16.
8. These are well-established philosophical concepts. As used here, they are based loosely on the concepts of "negative freedom" and "positive freedom" discussed by the British philosopher Thomas Hill Green in his essay, "The Senses of Freedom." See John Rodman (ed.), *The Political Theory of T.H. Green: Selected Writings*. New York: Appleton-Century-Crofts, 1964, pp. 75-90.
9. Census figures for 1960 indicated that two-thirds of white South Africans were bilingual in the two official languages. This figure received wide circulation in Canada during the language debates of the 1960s. Source: B&B Commission, *Report*, Vol. 1, p. 81.
10. All Swiss demographic data is from K.D. McRae, *Conflict and Compromise: Switzerland*. Waterloo, Ontario: Wilfrid Laurier University Press, 1983, pp. 55-56. The five largest minority populations in Switzerland in 1980 were: 1) the 89,000 Italians of Zurich; 2) the 48,000 Germans of Vaud; 3) the 37,000 Italians of Vaud; 4) the 32,000 Germans of Geneva; and 5) the 32,000 Italians of Geneva.
11. This figure includes immigrants and aboriginals who speak a non-official language at home, but are also capable of speaking one official language (English).
12. The figures for Manitoba in 1870 are imperfect, since no census was conducted at the time, but it is generally agreed that French-speakers formed a narrow majority at the time.

FOOTNOTES

13 See Statistics Canada, *Home Language and Mother Tongue: The Nation*. Ottawa: Minister of Industry, Science and Technology, 1992.
14 Commissioner of Official Languages, *Annual Report 1975*. Ottawa: Minister of Supply and Services, 1976, p. 19.
15 Peter Brimelow, *The Patriot Game: Canada and the Canadian Question Revisited*. Stanford: Hoover Institution Press, 1986, p. 95.
16 Pierre Trudeau, "The New Treason of the Intellectuals." First published in French in *Cité Libre*, April 1962. Republished in a translation by Patricia Claxton, in *Federalism and the French Canadians*. Toronto: Macmillan, 1968, pp. 151-181. The quote is taken from pp. 178-179.
17 Elsewhere in the same essay his position is somewhat less extreme, but he still comes down more heavily on the side of the personality principle than any other author:

"[W]henever there is a sufficient number of French-speaking people to form a school (or university), these people must have the same rights as English Canadians in the matter of taxes, subsidies, and legislation on education. Of course the concepts of 'sufficient number' and 'equal rights' will have to be defined judicially or administratively; but both judges and administrators will have as a guide the fact that these concepts have been applied for the past hundred years in remote areas of Quebec wherever there lived a 'sufficient number' of English-speaking Canadians."

The key to understanding this passage is recognizing that during the early industrial era in Quebec (which was ending about the time that Trudeau was rising to prominence) there had been a class of English-speaking engineers and technicians scattered across the province as a technical and managerial elite at the province's mines, factories and mills. Despite the fact that this minority represented no more than a tiny fraction of the population in any of the province's industrial towns, it was always given the right to levy its own school taxes and set up its own schools. Trudeau was, in other words, anticipating that the "sufficient number" measure would include communities with only a few dozen school-age children. This belief was reflected in the wording of the most important pieces of language legislation passed while Trudeau was prime minister. It is found in the 1969 *Official Languages Act* and again in Section 23 (3) of the *Canadian Charter of Rights and Freedoms*, and has apparently achieved the goal intended for it; court interpretations of Section 23 (3) have had the effect of forcing reluctant provincial governments to extend minority-language schooling to some very small minority populations. See "Quebec and the Constitutional Problem," translated by Joanne L'Heureux and published in Pierre Trudeau, *Federalism and the French Canadians*, p. 50.
18 *Ibid.*, pp. 48-49.
19 *Ibid.*, p. 174.
20 *Ibid.*, p. 163.
21 Pierre Trudeau. Testimony at preliminary hearing, Royal Commission on Bilingualism and Biculturalism. Thursday, November 7, 1963. Typed transcript of the hearing. National Archives of Canada, Record Group 33: Royal Commissions, Series 80: Royal Commission on Bilingualism and Biculturalism, Volume 110, pp. 209-210. My translation. The original typescript appears never to have been proofread or revised and contains numerous errors. I have corrected two in this quote: "dix" is used instead of "deux," and the words "no longer worth paying the price" ("s'il ne faut plus payer le prix") have been transcribed as a positive rather than a negative statement—which renders the sentence nonsensical—without noting them in the text with the usual 'sic' notation, since these errors are clearly the fault of a typist, rather than of Trudeau himself.
22 Canada, *A National Understanding: The Official Languages of Canada*. Ottawa: Minister of Supply and Services, 1977, pp. 41-42.
23 Leslie Green and Denise Réaume, "Bilingualism, Territorialism and Linguistic Justice." *The Network*. July 1991, p. 10.
24 George Galt, "Can't Live With Them, Can't Live Without Them." *Saturday Night*, June 1991, p. 11.
25 See The Task Force on National Unity, *A Future Together: Observations and Recommendations*. Ottawa: Minister of Supply and Services, January 1979, pp. 51-53.
26 A good example of first-ministerial lack of enthusiasm came at the St. Andrew's premiers' conference in August 1977. The premiers rejected an offer from René Lévesque to complete reciprocity agreements with Quebec regarding the extension of minority-language schooling privileges in that province to children of parents who had been educated in English in another province, as long as that province itself was offering minority language schooling facilities at a certain level of accessibility.

262 LAMENT FOR A NOTION

Lévesque's proposal, which fits entirely within the bounds of territorialism, was made with publicity purposes in mind, rather than as a strictly serious offer, because he was confident that it would be universally rejected.

27 Conrad Black, *Duplessis*. Toronto: McClelland and Stewart, 1977, p. 578.
28 Ramsay Cook, *Canada and the French-Canadian Question*. Toronto: Macmillan, 1967, p. 71.
29 Don Braid and Sydney Sharp, *Breakup: Why the West Feels Left Out of Canada*. Toronto: Key Porter, 1990, pp. 115-116.
30 Pierre Trudeau, "Trudeau Speaks Out." *Maclean's*. September 28, 1992, p. 25.
31 Quote is taken from the English translation of Georges Mathews' *L'Accord*, to which the publisher assigned the toned-down title, *Quiet Resolution: Quebec's Challenge to Canada*. Toronto: Summerhill, 1990, p. 29.
32 The total expenses of the commission exceeded $3 million, far greater than those of any previous royal commission. See Donald Horton, *André Laurendeau: French Canadian Nationalist 1912-1968*. Toronto: Oxford University Press, 1992, p. 213. For the number of researchers and other support workers, see p. 251.
33 Pearson was not alone in his ignorance, as the royal commission itself noted in the preface to its first volume:

> From the outset we recognized the need to undertake a great deal of research, because practically none of the questions raised by the Commission's terms of reference had been systematically investigated before. The Public Service, education, and the mass media have certainly been studied as separate subjects, but seldom in the light of Canada's languages and cultures. There was scattered and piecemeal information available on these topics, but very often the most elementary facts were still unknown—for example, the number of English- and French-speaking people working for the federal government.
> (Royal Commission on Bilingualism and Biculturalism: *Report*, Vol. 1. Ottawa: Queen's Printer, 1967, p. xvi.)

34 When the commission's interim report was published in 1965, Laurendeau noted that its findings made the prime minister uncomfortable. He wrote in his diary, "I got the impression that [Pearson] found our analysis lucid, but he's not unaware that this lucidity may cause him some problems." Diary entry for February 11, 1965, quoted in Donald Horton, *André Laurendeau*, p. 219.

Had the commission produced the report that Prime Minister Pearson evidently expected to receive, it would have been fairly collectivist in tone, stressing group rights and individual duties, rather than the rights of individuals and the duty of collectivities. The commission's terms of reference, were couched in old-fashion terms of 'race' and leave the impression that they could have been penned by one of Britain's more benign turn-of-the-century imperialists, when ethnic groups were called races, and each one was imagined to have unique and permanent characteristics which it could use to further the well-being of humanity.

At the core of the terms of reference was this mandate:

> To inquire into and report upon the existing state of bilingualism and biculturalism in Canada and to recommend what steps should be taken to develop the Canadian Confederation on the basis of an equal partnership between the two founding races, taking into account the contribution made by the other ethnic groups to the cultural enrichment of Canada and the measures that should be taken to safeguard that contribution....
> (B&B Commission, *Report*, Vol. 1, p. xx.)

In interpreting the terms of reference, the commissioners moved carefully towards an individualist interpretation. They started by rejecting the concepts of English and French races: "There is no such thing as an English or a French 'race,'" their report states. They warned that this created the picture of a "kind of hereditary aristocracy composed of two founding peoples, perpetuating itself from father to son, and a lower order of other ethnic groups, forever excluded from spheres of influence." (B&B Commission, *Report*, Vol. 1, pp. xxii, 9.)

35 B&B Commission, *Report*, Vol. 1, p. xxviii.
36 *Ibid.*
37 *Ibid.*, p. xxx.
38 *Ibid.*, pp. 105-117.
39 Leclerc, *Langue et Société*, p. 274.

40 Lucien Bouchard, quoted in Jennifer Robinson, "Who Speaks for the Anglos?" Montreal *Gazette*, August 6, 1988, p. B1.
41 *Ibid.*
42 Leclerc, *Langue et Societé*, p. 182.
43 Stéphane Dion, "Explaining Quebec Nationalism." R. Kent Weaver (ed.),*The Collapse of Canada?* Washington: The Brooking Institute, 1992.
44 Reginald Whitaker, "Quebec's Use of the Notwithstanding Clause was Right." Paul Fox and Graham White (eds.), *Politics: Canada*. Toronto: McGraw-Hill Ryerson, 1991, p. 89.
45 Svend Robinson, Letter to Tony Kondaks. June 1, 1989. My thanks to Tony Kondaks for permission to quote from this document.
46 Horatio Hockin, from a 1927 debate in the House of Commons. For a review of this debate, including Henri Bourassa's response, see Ramsay Cook, *Canada and the French-Canadian Question*, pp. 38-39.
47 Reed Scowen, *A Different Vision*. Don Mills: Maxwell Macmillan Canada, 1991, p. 75.

2. LINGUISTIC INTOLERANCE AND DEMOGRAPHIC DECLINE

1 Sheila McLeod-Arnopoulos and Dominique Clift, *The English Fact in Quebec*. Montreal: 1980, McGill-Queen's University Press, p. xiii.
2 Canada's very earliest language laws were passed in the 18th century by royal governors who were remarkably tolerant towards their mostly French-speaking subjects. French was, at the time, the language of science, the arts, and diplomacy, to say nothing of polite society throughout Europe. It was probably for this reason, as much as out of any sense of tolerance, that the first British governors of Quebec used French not only as the language of relations with the habitants, but also for their correspondence and personal work.

   The use of French by Governors Murray and Carleton is described in McLeod-Arnopoulos and Clift, *The English Fact in Quebec*, pp. 52-54.
3 As a caveat, it should be noted that this rule applies only to linguistic communities that believe themselves to have a realistic chance of surviving (although often this belief persists long after outside observers have concluded that no practical means of saving the linguistic minority exists). When this hope has been abandoned even by the community members themselves, they abandon any attempts to use government measures to save their language and focus instead on assimilating peacefully. It appears that the attention of groups in this desperate linguistic situation tends to focus on retaining those non-linguistic aspects of culture which they consider to be the most important aspects of the ancestral culture. Typically, these focus points of cultural retention include work attitudes, family values, and religion. The ancestral language is assigned a lesser relative level of importance than these other elements of culture.
4 Ronald Rudin, *The Forgotten Quebecers: A History of English-speaking Quebec 1759-1980*. Quebec City: Institut québécois de recherche sur la culture, 1985, p. 55.
5 At the conclusion of the Revolutionary War, Loyalist settlers flooded northwards, but were redirected west into what would become Ontario and east into what would become New Brunswick. Following a policy of separating Canada's English- and French-speaking populations, the colonial authorities refused to permit Loyalist settlement in lands touching upon seigneuries. Settlement in areas bordering the United States was also forbidden, for security reasons. When some settlers attempted to homestead on the edge of Lake Missisquoi just north of Vermont in what would eventually become the Eastern Townships, their houses were razed by order of the Governor.
6 Ronald Rudin, *The Forgotten Quebecers*, p. 54.
7 Marc V. Levine, *The Reconquest of Montreal: Language Policy and Social Change in a Bilingual City*, Philadelphia: Temple University Press, 1990, p. 8.
8 Rudin, *The Forgotten Quebecers*, p. 179.
9 Richard Joy, *Languages in Conflict*. Toronto: McClelland and Stewart, 1972, p. 32.
10 Denis Monière, *Ideologies in Quebec: The Historical Development*. Toronto: University of Toronto Press, 1981, pp. 76-77. The Quebec *Gazette* was published briefly, starting in 1764, and the Montreal *Gazette* (the ancestor of today's Montreal *Gazette*), from 1785 to 1793. But the influence of these newspapers was limited.
11 *Le Canadien* is quoted in Mason Wade, *The French Canadians: 1760-1967*. Toronto: Macmillan, 1968, Vol. 1, p. 117.

12 See population figures in Rudin, *The Forgotten Quebecers*, p. 28.
13 Fernand Ouellet, "Lower Canada." *The Canadian Encyclopedia*, Vol. 2. Edmonton: Hurtig Publishers, 1988, p. 1248.
14 Quoted in Mason Wade, *The French Canadians*, p. 142.
15 Montreal *Gazette*, October 27, 1832. *Ibid.*, p. 141.
16 Chambre d'assemblée, Bas-Canada, *Les 92 résolutions proposées à la chambre par Bédard*. February 21, 1834. Original document. National Library of Canada. Catalogue No. FC2921.B3.Fol. Resolutions No. 3, 4, 25, 34, 36, 46, 52, 55, 75, 76, 77 and 83 hint at ethnic tensions, although an effort was clearly being made to avoid taking an overtly anti-English line, since the resolutions were meant to be a negotiating tool as well as a statement of principle.
17 Jean-Paul Bernard, *Les Rébellions de 1837-38*. Montreal, 1983, p. 323. The French and English communities did not polarize completely in 1837 and 1838. Some of the leaders of the rebellion, including Robert Nelson, the self-proclaimed president of the Republic of Lower Canada, were English speakers. Some Irish Catholics rallied to the side of rebels on the basis of a common religion and a common hatred of the British. Nonetheless, the distance between the two language communities was great. English speakers were involved in some mass events of their own during the rebellion, most notably a series of 'Great Loyal Meetings,' which attracted crowds of up to 7,000 people in Montreal and Quebec City.
18 P.A. Buckner, "Rebellions of 1837." *The Canadian Encyclopedia*, Vol. 3, p. 1833. The extent to which economic concerns were predominant over ethnic conflicts has been the subject of a long-standing debate among historians. Donald Creighton's influential reinterpretation of the rebellion in his book *The Commercial Empire of the St. Lawrence 1760-1830*, (Toronto: 1937) was the first to suggest the supremacy of economic factors in the conflict. Earlier works tended to stress the ethnic conflict exclusively, while later accounts like Mason Wade's *The French Canadians* (Toronto, 1968), have often seen the rebellion as caused by a combination of ethnic and economic tensions.
19 Joy, *Languages in Conflict*, p. 51.
20 Laurier is quoted in H. Blair Neatby, *Laurier and a Liberal Quebec*. Ottawa: The Carleton Library, 1973, p. 215.
21 Joy, *Languages in Conflict*, p. 93. The population of urban francophones increased from 185,000 in 1871 to 474,000 in 1901.
22 Jean Hamelin and Yves Roby, "L'Evolution économique et sociale du Québec." *Recherches sociographiques*, 10 (1969), pp. 157-169.
23 Quoted in Mason Wade, "The French Parish and Survivance in Nineteenth Century New England." *The Catholic Historical Review*, Vol. 36, *July 1950, p. 173*.
24 Quoted in Robert Le Blanc, "The Francophone 'Conquest' of New England: Geopolitical Conceptions and Imperial Ambition of French-Canadian Nationalists in the Nineteenth Century." *American Review of Canadian Studies*, 1985, Vol. 15, No 3, p. 293. My translation.
25 The article (from the March 8, 1849 issue of the Stanstead *Journal*) reads:
> In twenty years (think of that, reader) this beautiful country, now mostly owned and inhabited by Anglo-Saxons, will be covered with the inhabitants of the banks of the St. Lawrence, as was the devoted land of Egypt with frogs, in the days when the children of Israel 'went a gipsying' in the wilderness. And like those same Israelites, the inhabitants of these Townships will take up their line of march for the "Far West," in long and solemn procession, the old, the middle-aged and the young, with such 'gear' as their 'invaders' shall see fit to allow them. . . . And those few who remain soon become so enamored of the delightful habits and customs of the country, that they will embrace their usages, religion and language! Then also will be seen flourishing monasteries and nunneries, and the places were men have been wont to worship God according to the dictates of their own consciences, will be filled by 'stoled priests,' and the altars of incense. Then will be revived all the ancient glories of the 'Nation' before the conquest, and the face of these 'benighted Townships' will 'blossom' like the rest of French Canada.

(Quoted in J.I. Little, "Watching the Frontier Disappear: The English-speaking Reaction to French-Canadian Colonization in the Eastern Townships, 1844-90." *Journal of Canadian Studies*, Winter 1980-81, pp. 94-95.)
26 *Ibid.* p. 97.
27 A more thorough account of the story may be found in Bernard Epps, *The Outlaw of Megantic*. Toronto: McClelland and Stewart, 1973.

28 Little, "Watching the Frontier Disappear," p. 104.
29 *Ibid.*, p. 108.
30 Persons of French origin represented 9.8 percent of P.E.I.'s population in 1881, 10.8 percent in 1891, 13.6 percent in 1901, 13.8 percent in 1911, and 13.5 percent in 1921. No figures exist for 1871, since the Island was not then part of Canada and did not collect statistics on language origin. Persons of French origin represented 15.8 percent of New Brunswick's population in 1871, 17.6 percent in 1881, 19.2 percent in 1891, 24.1 percent in 1901, 28.1 percent in 1911, and 31.2 percent in 1921. Source: *Canada Yearbook*, various years.
31 Another measure of Acadian opposition was their withdrawal of their children from school. During the period between the passage of the Act in 1871 and the announcement of a compromise restoring many rights four years later, the number of students in mainly French-speaking Gloucester County dropped by over 1,000. In Madawaska County, there were no public schools at all by May 1875. See Katherine F.C. MacNaughton, *The Development of the Theory and Practice of Education in New Brunswick 1784-1900*, Fredericton: University of New Brunswick, 1947, p. 200.
32 B&B Commission, *Report*, Vol. 2, p. 44.
33 Details of the compromise are described in MacNaughton, *Education in New Brunswick*, pp. 220-221.
34 For example, in 1910, when he was faced with the possibility that Ontario's English-speaking Protestant majority might attack the province's entire separate school system because of the insistence of Franco-Ontarians that they receive an education in their own language, Francis Fallon, the Irish Archbishop of London, declared that it was his intention "to wipe out every vestige of bilingual teaching, in the public schools of this Diocese." Bishop Fallon is quoted in the B&B Commission, *Report*, Vol 2, p. 49.
35 Quoted in Jonathan Schull, *Laurier, The First Canadian*. Toronto: Macmillan, 1965, p. 227.
36 See the description of the Lake St. Clair colony in the 18th century in Robert Choquette, *L'Ontario français, historique*. St-Laurent, Quebec: Editions Etudes Vivantes, 1980, p. 39.
37 As the *Constitutional Act* of 1791 was being prepared, there was an abortive proposal to make the Windsor region an enclave of Lower Canada.
38 In Ontario, the fearful reaction against the expanding francophone minority would eventually take the form of laws restricting the right of children to be educated in French, because public education had come to be perceived as the most effective method of linguistic manipulation open to government. For this reason, the relaxed attitude that prevailed in Ontario throughout most of the 19th century can best be illustrated by showing the considerable tolerance that prevailed in public education.

For example, in replying on April 24, 1857, to the trustees of School Number 3 in Charlottenburg Township in Eastern Ontario, Dr. Egerton Ryerson, the Superintendent of Education of Canada West, wrote:
> I have the honour to state in reply to your letter of the 16th that as French is the recognized language of the country, as well as English, it is quite proper and lawful for the trustees to allow both languages to be taught in their school to children whose parents may desire them to learn both.

When Ryerson wrote this, persons of French ancestry made up less than four percent of the population of Canada West, and English was the majority language in every county in the province. The Census of 1861 revealed no marked changes in Canada West's population patterns, and the rights of the Province's French-speaking minority seemed so secure that nobody, French or English, judged it necessary to protect francophone educational rights (as distinct from Catholic rights) when the *British North America Act* was drafted.
39 Prescott County, east of Ottawa.
40 T.J.B. Symons, "Ontario's Quiet Revolution," in R.M. Burns (ed.), *One Country of Two?* Montreal: McGill-Queen's University Press, 1971.
41 Census of Canada, 1931; *Canada Year Book 1990*. Ottawa: Minister of Supply and Services, 1989, pp. 2-26.
42 D'Alton McCarthy, *Commons Debates*, 1890, Vol. 1, No 51. This and many other similar statements made by McCarthy have been compiled by J.R. Miller in his article, "'As a Politician He is a Great Enigma': The Social and Political Ideas of D'Alton McCarthy." *The Canadian Historical Review*, Vol. 58, No. 4, 1977, pp. 399-422.
43 As well, the legislation was twice rejected by the St-Boniface County Court as *ultra vires* (in 1892 and in 1909). However, the Manitoba authorities chose to ignore these decisions, perhaps on the

basis that higher courts had accepted the constitutionality of the laws. See André Braën, "Bilingualism and Legislation." Michel Bastarache, (ed.), *Language Rights in Canada*. Montreal: Les éditions Yvan Blais, 1987, p. 86.

44 Armand Lavergne stated, in the provincial assembly: "If the Germans are persecutors, there are worse than persecutors at our very gates. . . . I ask myself if the German regime might not be favourably compared with the Boches of Ontario." Quoted in Ramsay Cook, *Canada and the French-Canadian Question*, p. 37.

45 An average of 207,000 immigrants per year had arrived in Canada between 1901 and 1914 (as compared to an annual average of 48,000 between 1867-1901). The assimilation trends were shown clearly in the 1921 census. Source for immigration statistics: Reginald Bibby, *Mosaic Madness: The Poverty and Potential of Life in Canada*. Toronto: Stoddart, 1990, p. 27.

46 Figure for 1901: ethnic origins. Figure for 1961: mother tongue.

47 Stéphane Dion, "Explaining Quebec Nationalism." p. 78.

48 Trudeau, *Federalism and the French Canadians*, p. 18.

49 For example, see Dion, "Explaining Quebec Nationalism," p. 91.

50 Gary Caldwell, "Anglo-Quebec: Demographic Realities and Options for the Future." Richard Bourhis (ed.), *Conflict and Language Planning in Quebec*. Avon, England: Multilingual Matters, 1984, p. 209.

51 William Tetley, The Liberal candidate, won the 1968 by-election. He recounts the story of Bertrand's machinations in "The English and Language Legislation: A Personal History." Gary Caldwell and Eric Waddell (eds.), *The English of Quebec: From Majority to Minority Status*, pp. 384-5.

52 These figures—29.7 births per 1000 population and 13.8 births per 1000 population are for 1957 and 1972 respectively. Cited in Bernard Bonin, "Pendant que d'autres pays étouffent, le Québec fait face à une croissance trop lente." *Le Devoir*, Montreal: September 27, 1974, p. A5.

53 Jacques Henripin, "Faut-il tenter d'accroître la fécondité au Quebec?" *Bulletin de l'association de Démographes au Québec*. Montreal: November 1974, p. 92 ff.

3. VICTORY OF ASYMMETRY

1 *Parliamentary Debates on the Subject of the Confederation of the British North American Provinces*. Third Session, Eighth Provincial Parliament of Canada. Quebec City: Hunter, Rose and Co. Parliamentary Printers, 1865, p. 236. Italics added.

2 Peter Brimelow, *The Patriot Game*, p. 90.

3 The political record of the Court Challenges Program is examined in Ian Ross Brodie, *Interest Groups and the Charter of Rights and Freedoms: Interveners at the Supreme Court of Canada*. Unpublished Masters' thesis. University of Calgary, Department of Political Science, 1992, pp. 80-112.

4 On page 13 of his 1988 *Annual Report*, now-retired Commissioner D'Iberville Fortier writes:
> Few informed observers could deny that the French language, which is in a minority position in Canada and still more so in North America, is seriously threatened. It is threatened from within with regard to its quality, and from without with regard to its ability to compete. That is why the "language issue" is so acute in Quebec, the principle centre of the French language on this continent. In point of fact, Quebec is also the most bilingual province in Canada. Francophone Quebecers rightly feel that Quebec has traditionally shown more generosity towards its linguistic minority than was required of it by constitutional or legislative provisions. This we have often stated in the past.

Current Commissioner Victor Goldbloom also finds little to object to in the present arrangements in Quebec:
> I think it is important to do two things. One is to make sure that we have a complete picture, that we know that in addition to Bill 178 there is also Bill 142, adopted about three years ago, which guarantees the availability and accessibility of health care and social services in English for English-speaking Quebecers. This has been reinforced in Bill 120, just adopted during the summer, which is a restructuring of the health care and social services system. I think what is happening within Quebec society is a greater realization of our interdependence.

(From a speech delivered to the annual meeting of Canadian Parents for French, October 19, 1991.)

5 Dufour, *A Canadian Challenge*, pp. 99-100.

6 Fédération des francophones hors Québec, *The Heirs of Lord Durham*. Ottawa: Fédération des francophones hors Québec, 1978, p. 17.
7 Commissioner of Official Languages, *Annual Report 1975*. Ottawa: Minister of Supply and Services, 1975, p. 15.
8 The population statistics cited here are first official language spoken figures from the 1991 census, which reflect the language preferences of immigrants whose mother tongue is neither English nor French. For those immigrants who indicate that both French and English are first official languages, half have been awarded to each language group. See Statistics Canada, *Population Estimates by First Official Language Spoken, 1991*. Catalogue no. 94-320.
9 For Ontario and New Brunswick, the figures are census data for the decennial census preceding the date on which legislation was passed. For Manitoba, the 1891 census was used. All figures cited are 'racial origins' data, except the 1941 figure for Acadians, which is a mother tongue statistic.
10 In the 1931 census, persons with English mother tongue represented 14.9 percent of Quebec's population. If mother-tongue groups likely to assimilate mostly into English (such as Germanic, Nordic, and Slavic languages) are added to the total, the percentage rises to just under twenty percent.
11 For a detailed discussion, see André Bernard, "L'abstentionnisme des électeurs de langue anglaise du Québec." *Le Processus Electoral au Québec: Les Elections Provinciales de 1970 et 1973*. Montreal: éditions Hurtubise HMH, 1976, pp. 155-166.
12 See Maurice Pinard and Richard Hamilton, "The Independence Issue and the Polarization of the Electorate: The 1973 Quebec Election." *Canadian Journal of Political Science*, Vol. 10, No. 2, June 1977, p. 226.
13 Quebec. Directeur-général des élections du Québec, *Rapport des résultats officiels du scrutin: Référendum du 20 mai 1980*. Quebec City, 1980, pp. 179-184.
14 *Ibid.*, p. 19.
15 Election statistics are cited in Maurice Pinard and Richard Hamilton, "The Parti Québécois Comes to Power: An Analysis of the 1976 Election." *Canadian Journal of Political Science*. Vol. 11, No. 4, December 1978, pp. 768, 775. The Liberals won only 33.8 percent of the popular vote, while minor parties and independent candidates won 24.8 percent.
16 Poll cited in Maurice Pinard and Richard Hamilton, "The 1973 Quebec Election," p. 757. It is also interesting to note that language had scarcely been an issue among francophones on election day. Two polls conducted at the time of the 1976 election showed that French-speakers were only marginally in favour of restrictive language legislation. Fully forty-one percent of francophones favoured either making the province's existing language legislation less restrictive or abolishing it altogether, while another sixteen percent had no opinion on the language issue. Francophone voters swept the Parti Québécois into power based on the fact that it promised good government. The fact that its platform included the most restrictive language laws the province had ever seen was almost irrelevant.
17 Directeur-général des élections du Québec, *Rapport des résultats officiels du scrutin du 13 avril 1981*. Quebec City, 1981, pp. 29-31, 45.
18 Georges Mathews, *Le choc démographique*. Montreal: Boréal Express, 1984, p. 85. My translation.
19 Scowen, *A Different Vision*, p. 102.
20 Directeur-général des élections du Québec, *Rapport des résultats officiels du scrutin de 25 septembre 1989*. Quebec City: Editeur officiel du Québec, pp. 758, 935.
21 Trudeau, *Federalism and the French Canadians*, p. 69.
22 For an excellent discussion of the weak federal responses to the educational crises in New Brunswick, Manitoba, and Ontario, see Laurier Lapierre, *Federal Intervention Under Section 93 of the BNA Act. Report submitted to the Royal Commission on Bilingualism and Biculturalism*. Ottawa: mimeograph, May 1966.
23 H. Blair Neatby, "Mackenzie King and French Canada." *Journal of Canadian Studies*. Vol. XI, No. 1, February 1976, p. 9. Neatby quotes King as writing in his diary that the padlock law "really should not, in the name of Liberalism, be tolerated for one moment."
24 *Ibid.*, p. 12.
25 All election statistics are from *Ibid.*, p. 3.
26 Conrad Black is of the opinion that this matter was "perhaps the last straw in Quebec's indulgence of the Bennett government." Conrad Black, *Duplessis*, p. 95.
27 McLeod-Arnopoulos and Clift, *The English Fact in Quebec*, p. 73.

28 *Ibid.*, p. 71.
29 Trudeau is quoted in Peter Brimelow, *The Patriot Game*, p. 90.
30 See the speech of René Matte (a Créditiste MP from Quebec) in the House of Commons. *House of Commons Debates*, November 21, 1975, p. 9331.
31 Detailed calculations of the total cost of transfers to provinces have been compiled by Robert Mansell of the University of Calgary. These figures are reviewed in Kenneth Whyte, "Prime Beef." *Saturday Night*. October 1991, pp. 70-71, 89-91. The federal finance department's own figures confirm this. In 1977-78 to 1986-87, a total of $43.4 billion in equalization was paid out, of which $23.6 billion went to Quebec. See Federal-Provincial Relations Division, Department of Finance, *The Equalization Program: Nature and purpose of program, explanation of how payments are calculated, special program characteristics, use of program outputs to calculate indices of fiscal capacity and historical summary of program entitlements, 1957-58 to 1992-93*. Ottawa: mimeograph, November 1992, p. 17.
32 See Dalton Camp, "The Plot to Kill Canada." *Saturday Night*, June 1991, pp. 16-17.
33 The influence of the Reform Party on the election results in British Columbia has been summarized as follows:

> The Reform Party ... ran 30 of a possible 32 candidates. In 17 of the constituencies, the Reform Party—along with other right-wing fringe parties—established the potential to affect the electoral outcome. In at least half a dozen of these seats, they significantly altered Conservative fortunes ... In five seats (Kootenay East, Okanagan-Similkameen-Merritt, Saanich-Gulf Islands, Surrey North, and Victoria) they clearly altered the results. The effect was the election of five NDP MPs. (D. Munroe Eagles, James Bickerton, Alain-G. Gagnon and Patrick Smith, *The Almanac of Canadian Politics*. Peterborough, Ontario: Broadview Press, 1991, p. 583.)

34 In other words, the size of the margin between the winning Conservative candidate and his or her nearest rival, rather than the percentage of the total vote garnered by the Conservative. The precise figure is 23.9 percent. Figures are drawn from *Ibid.*, pp. 521-577.
35 Mulroney is quoted in Mordecai Richler, *Oh Canada! Oh Quebec!: Requiem For a Divided Country*. Toronto: Penguin Books, 1992, p. 32.
36 See the population projections in Canada, Minister of Health and Welfare, *Charting Canada's Future*. Ottawa: Minister of Supply and Services, 1989, p. 3.
37 Mathews, *Chocdémographique*, p. 151. In fact, his calculations were a little off. As of the 1991 election, there were 295 seats. This left Quebec with 25.4 percent of the total.
38 Text of the "Langevin Accord" (legal wording of the Meech Lake Accord, approved by the prime minister and premiers at Parliament's Langevin Block on June 3, 1987). The wording of the original agreement, signed at Meech Lake a month earlier, is slightly different. See David Milne, *The Canadian Constitution: From Patriation to Meech Lake*. Toronto: Lorimer, 1989, pp. 286-287, 291.
39 See Graham Fraser, "Immigration Deal Transfers Powers." *The Globe and Mail*, Toronto: December 24, 1990, p. A1.

4. THE LIMITS OF LANGUAGE POLICY

1 Yvan Allaire, "De L'utilisation abusive des statistiques." *Le Devoir*. Montreal: August 2, 1974, p. A4.
2 Public Service Commission, "Staffing Support Information." Ottawa, 1990, p. 86.
3 Laponce, *Languages and Their Territories*, p. 63.
4 Thomas Sowell, *Ethnic America*. New York: Basic Books, 1981, p. 286.
5 Leclerc, *Langue et Société*, p. 177. My translation.
6 Leclerc predicts that all but 450 of the world's thousands of languages will be extinguished in the forseeable future. *Ibid.*, p. 198.
7 These are Algonquin-Cree (47,975 speakers), Inuktitut (16,780 speakers), Algonquin-Ojibway (11,895 speakers), and Athabaskan (7,895 speakers). Figures are for persons using these tongues as their language of principle use at home. See Gordon Priest, "Aboriginal Languages in Canada." *Language and Society*, Winter 1985, pp. 16-17.
8 Pessamessa is quoted (in French) in Jacques Leclerc, *Langue et Société*, p. 182. My translation.
9 Raymond Breton, "Institutional Completeness of Ethnic Communities and the Personal Relations of Immigrants." *American Journal of Sociology*, Vol. 70, 1964, pp. 200-201.
10 *Ibid.*, pp. 193-205.

FOOTNOTES

11 Laponce. *Languages and Their Territories*, p. 69. Scholars do not agree on the exact number of living languages in existence worldwide. Laponce suggests 2,000. Other estimates range as high as 6,000. See Jacques Leclerc, *Langue et Société*, p. 123.
12 *Ibid.*, p. 159.
13 B&B Commission, *Report*, Vol. 1, p. xliii.
14 Cited in Laponce, *Languages and Their Territories*, p. 56.
15 Figures for numbers of persons claiming French ancestry are from *Canada Yearbook 1990*, pp. 2:28-2:30. For each of the western provinces, the total number of persons claiming French ancestry only was added to half the total number of persons claiming French plus British or French plus 'Other' ancestry.
16 See Richard Joy, *Languages in Conflict*, p. 118; Statistics Canada, *Population and Dwelling Characteristics—Census Divisions and Subdivisions: Ontario*. Ottawa: Minister of Supply and Services. 1987, p. 451.
17 Gill, "Language policy in Saskatchewan, Alberta and British Columbia,"ARCS, Spring '85, p. 31; Catherine Lengyel and Dominic Watson, *La situation de la langue française en Colombie-Britannique*. Quebec City: Editeur officiel du Québec,1983, p. 18.
18 Joy, *Languages in Conflict*, p. 26.
19 Leclerc, *Langue et Société*, p. 180. My translation.
20 *Ibid.*, p. 160. My translation.
21 Laponce, *Languages and Their Territories*, p. 115.
22 *Ibid.*, p. 72. William Mackey of Laval University has charted the relative strength of various languages as choices of scientific publication, from 1880 to 1980. Although English dominated in 1880, with over thirty percent of all scientific publications, by 1900 it was in third place at around thirty percent, behind French (forty percent) and German (around twenty-three percent). English did not re-establish its dominance as a scientific language until 1930. See William Mackey, "La Mortalité des Langues et le Bilingualisme des Peuples." *Anthropologie et Sociétés*. 1983, Vol. 7, No. 3, p. 11.
23 Jeremy Boissevain, *The Italians of Montreal: Social Adjustment in a Plural Society*. Background Study No. 7 for the Royal Commission on Bilingualism and Biculturalism. Ottawa: Information Canada, 1970, p. 60.
24 Rudin, *The Forgotten Quebecers*, pp. 90-91.
25 Ronald Rudin provides a brief but excellent review of the relationship between economic development and the decline of English in the Gaspé. See *Ibid.*, pp. 183-185.
26 B&B Commission, *Report*, Vol. 2, p. 56. The Royal Commission also commissioned a working paper which examined the services offered to English speaking students in greater detail. See Jean-Yves Drolet. *Etude des conditions faites aux étudiants anglophones dans des régions du Québec où la population Canadienne-anglaise est peu nombreuse*. A working paper prepared for the Royal Commission. Ottawa: mimeograph.
27 Source: Special data run of 1991 home language statistics by county, prepared by Statistics Canada. (Figures are for the census districts of Pabok and La Côte-de-Gaspé).
28 Joy, *Languages in Conflict*, p. 32.
29 Peter Mentzel, "Nationalism." *Humane Studies Review*, Vol. 8, No. 1, p. 14.
30 *Ibid.*
31 Leclerc, *Langue et Société*, p. 179.
32 Laponce, *Languages and Their Territories*, p. 60.
33 Joy, *Languages in Conflict*, p. 13; Hugh Thorburn, *Politics in New Brunswick*. Toronto: University of Toronto Press, 1961, pp. 32-35.
34 In Gloucester County at the time of the 1991 Census, 41.5 percent of the francophone population (as measured by home language) was capable of speaking English. Source: Statistics Canada, special run of home languages and languages spoken data, compiled by county.
35 In 1911, 42,599 persons in Prescott County and Russell County reported themselves to be of French origin, while 19,919 reported themselves as members of other groups. Source: Dominion Bureau of Statistics, *Census of Canada 1911: Areas and Population by Provinces, Districts, and Sub-Districts*. Ottawa: King's Printer, 1913, p. 336.

In 1991, 44,527 persons in Prescott and Russell United Counties used French as their home language, while only 20,367 used English. Source: Statistics Canada, special run of home language data, compiled by county. Slight changes to the county boundaries between the two census dates

5. ASSIMILATION AND THE FAILURE OF FEDERAL ACTION

1. Jacques Leclerc, *Langue et Société*, p. 269. My translation.
2. Richard Joy, *Languages in Conflict*, pp. 135-136.
3. In conversation with me in summer 1992, Richard Joy described the process of self-publishing as "slow death." Although *Languages in Conflict* eventually became well-respected in the academic community and Joy was able to find publishers for two additional books of language demographics (as well as a second edition of *Languages in Conflict*), he was still able to give me a fresh, unused copy of the original edition, a full quarter-century after it had been published.
4. Victor Goldbloom, *Speech to the Downtown Rotary Club of Edmonton*, January 30, 1992. Mimeograph, p. 2.
5. Montreal *Gazette*, March 26, 1991.
6. Statistics Canada, *Home Language and Mother Tongue: The Nation*. Ottawa, 1993, p. 172.
7. In total, 2,280,000 Canadians speak a language other than their mother tongue in the home. This includes 2,070,000 who have adopted English, 142,000 who have adopted French, 62,000 who have adopted a non-official language, and 7,000 who have adopted both English and French. Source: Statistics Canada. *Home Language and Mother Tongue: The Nation*, pp. 220-224. *These figures were obtained by using a table which cross-tabulates mother tongue statistics with home language statistics.*
8. B&B Commission, *Report*, Vol. 1, pp. 17-18.
9. Statistics Canada, *Home Language and Mother Tongue: The Nation*, p. 10.
10. Hubert Guindon, "The Modernization of Quebec and the Legitimacy of the Canadian State." *Canadian Review of Sociology and Anthropology*, Vol. 15, No. 2, 1978, p. 236.
11. The first demographer to note this fact was Richard Joy; one of the most important contributions of his book *Languages in Conflict* was its analysis of language trends for regions within provinces.
12. Donald Cartwright, "Accommodation Among the Anglophone Minority in Quebec to Official Language Policy: A Shift in Traditional Patterns of Language Contact." *Journal of Multilingual and Multicultural Development*, Vol. 8, Nos. 1 and 2, 1987, p. 188.
13. *Ibid.*
14. Figure extrapolated from Perry Garfinkel, "Madawaska: Down East with a French Accent." *National Geographic*, September 1980, p. 380.
15. This includes all persons for English is the home language, plus all those for whom a non-official language is the home language and English is the first official language spoken.
16. Special tabulation of home language and language spoken statistics, Statistics Canada, 1991 Census. As well, there are several less populous areas which might arguably be described as part of the English-speaking heartland, but which strike me, by the standards of the rest-stop test, to be linguistic islands. They are:

    - Quebec's Eastern Townships, which contain 56,730 anglophones, pressed against the border with New York and Vermont. The English-speaking population of the region is in slow decline, suggesting the proximity to the U.S. is not enough to keep the English language alive in the long term;
    - Quebec's Gaspé Peninsula, which contains 4,000 anglophones, cut off by hundreds of kilometres of bad roads from the English-speaking regions of New Brunswick.

    Source for population statistics: Statistics Canada, special run of home language data for selected census districts in New Brunswick, Ontario and Quebec. 1991 Census Data.

17. Outside the counties of eastern and north-eastern Ontario and northern New Brunswick that contain sizable francophone populations, there are only 198,000 francophones (as measured by home language) in all of English Canada. By contrast, there are 364,000 persons in these nine provinces who speak Chinese at home, and 171,000 who speak Italian. The total population of the English-speaking provinces, excluding the parts that have francophone majorities or large francophone minorities, is 18,904,000. Sources: Statistics Canada (1991 Census), *Home Language and Mother Tongue: The Nation*, pp. 12-43; Statistics Canada, Special tabulation of 1991 census data on home language by county for Ontario, New Brunswick and Quebec.

FOOTNOTES

18 Figures for use of Chinese and Italian are stated in Statistics Canada, *Home Language and Mother Tongue: The Nation*, pp. 44-63.
19 For example, see Jacques Brossard, *L'accession à la souveraineté et le cas du Québec*. Montreal, Les presses de l'université de Montréal, 1976, pp. 187, 490-492.
20 Statistics Canada, *Knowledge of Languages: The Nation*. 1991 Census, Ottawa, 1993.
21 Quoted in Joy, *Canada's Official Language Minorities*, p. 20.
22 Toronto, with 28,000 francophones (measured by mother tongue), has by far the largest French-speaking population of any English Canadian city. Yet only twenty-three of metropolitan Toronto's hundreds of census tracts had as much as a five percent concentration of francophones, and none with more than 7.5 percent. Source: Ontario, Ministry of Citizenship, *Mother Tongue Atlas of Metropolitan Toronto*, Vol. 3. Toronto: Ministry of Citizenship, 1989.
23 See Table 3, "Population by Home Language, for Census Metropolitan Areas 1991," in Statistics Canada, *Home Language and Mother Tongue—The Nation*. Ottawa, 1993. Population figures include all census metropolitan areas outside Quebec except Ottawa-Hull and Sudbury, since parts of these cities are part of Canada's French-Canadian heartland.
24 This figure was obtained by subtracting the francophone populations of English Canada's census metropolitan areas from the 198,000 total who do not live in counties that I have included as part of the Quebec-based heartland. Single and multiple responses were counted. Sudbury, Ottawa and Winnipeg were not included among the cities counted (Ottawa and Sudbury are part of the French-language heartland and Winnipeg contains St. Boniface, which must be regarded as a traditional French settlement).
25 Catherine Lengyel and Dominic Watson write, "The first to labour in the rich delta of the Fraser River or to plant the first crop in the . . . Okanagan, these [French Canadian pioneers] formed at the time a numerous and homogeneous group representing 60 percent of the population in British Columbia in the 1850's." See their book, *La situation de la langue française en Colombie-Britannique*. Quebec City: Conseil de la langue française, 1983, p. 11. My translation. Vol. 2 of the Fédération des francophones hors Québec publication, *Les Héritiers du Lord Durham*, includes this note: "1838: More than 60 percent of the white population of British Columbia was French Canadian, out of a population of 6,900 souls. (This includes the territories of British Columbia, Oregon and Washington)". See p. 11. My translation.
26 See Robert Gill, "Federal and Provincial Language Policy in Ontario and the Future of the Franco-Ontarians." *American Review of Canadian Studies*, Spring 1983, pp. 24-28. See also Statistics Canada, *Home Language and Mother Tongue: The Nation*, Ottawa, Ministry of Industry, Science and Technology, 1993, p. 55.
27 Robert Gill, "Federal, Provincial, and Local Language Legislation in Manitoba and the Franco-Manitobans." *American Review of Canadian Studies*, Vol. 12, No. 1, Spring 1982, p. 42.
28 Yasuo Wakatsuki, "Japanese Emigration to the United States, 1866-1924." *Perspectives on American History*, 1979, p. 465.
29 Eighty-six percent of local residents used French at home, fifty-four percent of hours spent listening to the radio were devoted to English programming, and seventy-three percent of television viewing was done in English. Jolicoeur's study is cited in Richard Joy, *Canada's Official Language Minorities*, pp. 10-11.
30 Statistics Canada, *Knowledge of Languages: The Nation* (1991 Census), p. 125.
31 Statistics Canada, *Knowledge of Official Languages*, (1991 Census), pp. 14-21.
32 Argenteuil, Arthabaska, Bonaventure, Brome, Compton, Drummond, Gaspé, Gatineau, Hull, Huntingdon, Megantic, Missisquoi, Montreal, Pontiac, Richmond, Shefford, Sherbrooke, Stanstead, and Wolfe counties.
33 Sellar is quoted in Rudin, *The Forgotten Quebecers*, p. 189.
34 Pontiac County, northwest of Ottawa.
35 Donald Cartwright has observed that the proximity of the border counties along the southern edge of the Eastern Townships to the United States may have an impact on the language dynamics of the region, and particularly on the surprisingly high rates of unilingualism among anglophones. See Donald Cartwright, *Official-Language Populations in Canada: Patterns and Contacts*, Occasional Paper No. 16, The Institute for Research on Public Policy, July 1980, pp. 32-33.

36 These figures exclude Pontiac and Gatineau counties in West Quebec, and Brome, Huntingdon and the Eastern Townships. Source: Special run of unpublished 1991 census data, prepared on request by Statistics Canada.
37 Measured by mother tongue. See Treasury Board, *Impact of Official Languages Regulations*, Section D, pp. 30, 39.
38 Statistics Canada. *The Daily*. September 15, 1992. Catalogue #11-001E, p. 13.
39 Joy, *Canada's Official Language Minorities*, p. 23.
40 Joy, *Languages in Conflict*, p. 65.
41 Richard Joy reports that the circulation of *La Liberté et le Patriote* was 8,000 in the late 1960s. See *Languages in Conflict*, p. 67. In 1993, it has 4,500, according to figures provided by the newspaper in response to a telephone call placed by my research assistant.
42 Claude Arpin, "Newspaper Reflects Diminishing Anglo Numbers," in the *Gazette*, Montreal, April 7, 1993, p. A4.
43 Robert Gill, "Language Policy in Saskatchewan, Alberta, and British Columbia and the Future of French in the West." *American Review of Canadian Studies*, Spring 1985, p. 27.
44 I have been unable to locate an original copy of the *New York Commercial Advertiser*. This quotation is a translation of a French translation by Edouard Hamon of the English original, from his book, *Les Canadiens-Français de la Nouvelle-Angleterre*. Quebec City: Editions N.S. Hardy, 1891, p. 152.
45 Franklin Roosevelt, Letter to Mackenzie King, May 18, 1942. Reproduced in Jean-François Lisée, *In the Eye of the Eagle*. Toronto: Harper and Collins, 1990, p. 279.
46 Out of over 170 cities and towns in the six New England states in which Father Edouard Hamon recorded French-Canadian populations of at least twenty-five (and normally upwards of several hundred) in 1890, French Canadians formed a majority in only twenty. Of these, twelve were located in Maine's Madawaska Valley, which borders upon New Brunswick and Quebec. In this valley, French survives as the language of daily use to this day.

As for the rest of New England, the absence of more than a handful of municipalities in which French was the majority language made its long-term survival difficult, once the reinforcement stopped coming. The only really large centre in New England in 1890 with a French-speaking majority was Fall River, with a francophone population of just under 17,000. Even in Lowell, Massachusetts—the best-known of the *petits-Canadas*—French-speakers formed only one-fifth of the local population. All in all, less than 60,000 of the 306,000 French Canadians that Father Hamon calculated to be living in New England in 1890 lived in communities where French was the majority language. Of these, 15,000 lived in the Madawaska region. Source: All figures are derived from Edouard Hamon, *Les Canadiens-Français de la Nouvelle-Angleterre*, pp. 179-450. See especially pp. 243, 264, 277, 302, 315, 325, 331, 402, 412, where the French-majority parishes are described.
47 The 1900 Census classed 851,000 residents of the United States as being of French-Canadian origin (a figure which included only immigrants and the children of immigrants; subsequent generations are not identified). As the total number of persons shown by the 1901 Census of Canada as being of French origin was only 1,649,000, it is clear that the southward migration of the 19th Century had affected well over one-third of the descendants of the original French colonists. See Richard Joy, *Languages in Conflict*, p. 69.
48 Eric Waddell, a professor of geography at Laval University, writes, "The urbanization of French Canadian society at the turn of the century occurred essentially in the textile towns of New England, and hence in another political realm unscarred by the continuing struggle for power between two 'founding peoples.'" See Eric Waddell, "Language, Community and National Identity: Some Reflections on French-English Relations in Canada." Alain-G. Gagnon and James Bickerton, *Canadian Politics: An Introduction to the Discipline*. Peterborough: Broadview Press, 1990, p. 614.
49 This point is made by Mason Wade in "The French Parish and *Survivance* in Nineteenth-Century New England." *The Catholic Historical Review*, Vol. 36, July 1950.
50 Edouard Hamon, *Les Canadiens-Français de la Nouvelle-Angleterre*, pp. 126-127.
51 Joy, *Languages in Conflict*, p. 70.

52 Yolande Lavoie, "Les mouvements migratoires des canadiens entre leurs pays et les États-Unis au XIXé et au XXé siècles: étude quantative." *La population du Québec: études retrospectives.* Montreal: Boréal Express, 1973, p. 78.
53 See Kenneth Buckley, "Population and Migration." M.C. Urquhart (ed.), *Historical Statistics of Canada.* Toronto: Macmillan, 1965.
54 Raymond Breton, "Institutional Completeness of Ethnic Communities and the Personal Relations of Immigrants." *American Journal of Sociology*, Vol. 70, 1964, p. 204.
55 This observation is made in George Tombs, "Franco-Americans Grapple with Assimilation." Montreal *Gazette*, August 13, 1988, p. B5. Also, for a brief portrait of the current state of French Canadian culture in New Hampshire, see Janet Rae Brooks, "Quebec's Abandoned Confrères." *The Globe and Mail*, June 20, 1992, p. D2. A 1987 study prepared for the Quebec government's Conseil de la langue française maintains that by the year 2000, only a quarter of a million Americans will still be using French as a daily language. Since this number includes nearly 200,000 French-speaking immigrants from Europe and elsewhere, the logical conclusion is that at most 50,000 native-born Americans in the entire country will be using French. This small total must be shared between Louisiana and New England, which gives some idea of the thoroughness of the assimilation that closed borders can bring. See Calvin Veltman, *L'Avenir du Français aux États-Unis.* Quebec City: Conseil de la langue française, 1987, p. 225.
56 Perry Garfinkel, "Madawaska: Down East With a French Accent." *National Geographic*, September 1980, p. 386.
57 Source: Edouard Hamon, *Les Canadiens-Français de la Nouvelle-Angleterre*, pp. 179-450.

6. SPEAKING IN TONGUES

1 Conseil de la langue française, *Le projet de la loi C-72 relatif au statut et à l'usage des langues officielles au Canada.* Quebec City: mimeograph, 1988, p. 17. My translation.
2 Examples from Manitoba and Ontario give some idea of the strong emotions that debates over the extension of minority-language services can raise. In the early 1980s, when the provincial government of Manitoba tried to introduce full bilingual services in areas of provincial jurisdiction, nearly 700,000 Manitobans signed petitions calling for the proposed legislation to be abandoned. Over 200,000 people voted in plebiscites held on the issue in twenty cities and towns, including Winnipeg, and condemned the proposed law by a margin of four to one. Source: Russell Doern, *The Battle Over Bilingualism*, p. 2. A few years later, when the government of Ontario passed a law introducing French-language services in all towns with ten percent francophones, 112 Ontario municipalities— twelve percent of all the towns and cities in the province—adopted laws declaring themselves unilingual. See Grant Purves, "Official Languages in Canada." Library of Parliament, Research Branch. *Current Issue Review* 86-11E, April 18, 1986, revised November 17, 1990, p. 7.
3 Quoted in Commissioner of Official Languages, *Special Report to Parliament Pursuant to Section 67 of the Official Languages Act, on the Tabling of Draft Regulations and in Particular of Regulations on Communications With and Services to the Public*, October 23, 1990, p. 13.
4 One example of the extreme concern with equity can be found in the minutes of the Standing Joint Committee of Parliament on Official Languages, for May 2, 1991, p. 32:16, in which the Committee states, in a report on a proposed draft of regulations to be adopted under the new Act: "The proposed Regulations would cover ninety-two percent of francophones outside Quebec and ninety-six percent of anglophones inside Quebec, which strikes us as an acceptable outcome given the dispersion of the francophone minorities outside Quebec." The concern of the committee seems to have been strongly focussed on getting the percentage of francophones as close to that of anglophones as possible (more, one must assume, for public relations reasons than for any practical reason relating to the objective needs of the minority communities).
5 In order to obtain the complete listing of regions covered by bilingual services contained in the Treasury Board document, *Impact of Official Languages Regulations on the Federal Electoral Districts* (Ottawa: mimeograph, 1991), it was necessary for my research assistant to file a request under the *Access to Information Act*. This does not mean that the document was a state secret, merely that it was so obscure and well-hidden that no member of the public or media had ever previously known to ask for it. (Under the Act, classified status is lifted as soon as one successful request for access has been filed.) As far as I am aware, this document is the only complete listing of bilingual service areas.

This means, among other things, that upon receipt of this study, I became the only private citizen in this bilingual country to actually know which parts of the country were legally bilingual!

6   Charles Castonguay, "Why Hide the Facts? The Federalist Approach to the Language Crisis in Canada." *Canadian Public Policy*, Vol. 5, No. 1, Winter 1979, p. 6.
7   See Conrad Black, *Duplessis*, p. 95.
8   Finland is not the only jurisdiction in the world to successfully use this system. The Swiss canton of Berne is linguistically divided between a francophone population that predominates in the northwest and a germanophone population that predominates everywhere else. In the northwest, services are offered in French only, and in the rest of the canton, in German only. In the small city of Bienne/Biel, which sits astride the linguistic frontier, government services are available in both languages. Three other Swiss cantons (Valais, Fribourg and Grisons) have adopted the Finland model of territorial bilingualism for internal use. Even Belgium has made the national capital (Brussels) a bilingual region, in violation of the territorial imperative to which the country claims to adhere rigorously.
9   B&B Commission, *Report*, Vol. 1, pp.107-108
10 The figures quoted here are not cited in the report (which provides no totals since the precise totals shown there were meant only to be a rough example of what could be done, not a concrete recommendation), but instead are compiled directly from the 1961 Census.
11 Marisa Akow, "The Unofficial Official Languages Act." Commissioner of Official Languages, *You Put it in Words*. Ottawa: Minister of Supply and Services, 1986, p. 11.
12 Kenneth McRae, "Bilingual Districts in Finland and Canada: Adventures in the Transplanting of an Institution." *Canadian Public Policy*. Vol. 4, No. 3, Summer 1978, p. 339. More recently, the same sort of anger has been incited by the exactly parallel situation caused by Ontario's French-language service law, Bill 8. Commenting on the law, an article in the January 1990 newsletter of the Alliance for the Preservation of English in Canada reports, "Members will recall that Bill 8 makes provision for other areas to be designated [bilingual] but th*ere is no provision for areas, where the French population falls below the required 10% or 5,000 people, to be deleted or redesignated."* (Italics in the original). Strictly speaking, bilingual regions can be designated unilingual, but this requires a vote of the legislature, rather than the simple order-in-council needed to create a bilingual designation.
13 See Bilingual Districts Advisory Board, *Recommendations of the Bilingual Districts Advisory Board*, Ottawa: Information Canada, March 1971, pp. 33, 61, 75-76.
14 As an explanation for declaring all of Quebec a single very large bilingual district, the Board wrote:
> The province of Quebec is a very special case. The reverse of what occurs in the other provinces of Confederation obtains here.... [T]he English of Quebec, while a minority within their own province, belong to the majority in Canada.... Citing statistical forecasts, some have even claimed that, in Quebec, it is the French language and not English which is being threatened, if not seriously compromised.
>
> On the other hand, as much through generosity as through necessity, Quebec has blazed the trail in the field of bilingualism and the authorities have been careful to give full rights to both official languages wherever this seemed proper and practical.... Conscious of this historical record and of a firmly established tradition dating back over a century, the Board ... decided to recommend for federal purposes the establishment of a single bilingual district comprising the whole of the province of Quebec.
>
> (*Ibid.*, pp. 43-44.)

15 McRae, "Bilingual Language Districts." *Canadian Public Policy*. p. 342.
16 Although some of the smaller districts proposed in the 1971 report had been dropped.
17 Bilingual Districts Advisory Board, *Report*. Ottawa: Information Canada, 1975, p. 41.
18 *Ibid.*, p. 109.
19 *Ibid.* Minority report of Adélard Savoie, p. 219.
20 *Ibid.* Minority report of Eleanor Duckworth, p. 225.
21 The Parliamentary debate that took place on the day the second report was released provides an instructive view of the conflict between the Trudeau view of coast-to-coast bilingualism and the emerging asymmetrical view. Trudeau himself was not present in the House of Commons, and the government's point of view was expressed instead by C.M. Drury, the acting president of the Treasury Board. Drury explained that the government considered the report's proposals for Canada's nine English-majority provinces to be acceptable, but that the proposals for Quebec itself were not. He served notice that bilingual districts might be created not only in Montreal, but also in

Sherbrooke, Rouyn-Noranda, and Schefferville. House of Commons Debates, November 21, 1975, p. 9327.
22 The debate over the bilingual districts continued outside Parliament. In 1976, University of Ottawa mathematician Charles Castonguay published a paper in the *Journal of Canadian Studies* calling for the creation of bilingual districts designed solely to aid Canada's French-speaking minorities. Castonguay's paper is arguably the clearest and most detailed explanation ever made of the principles behind the (as yet unnamed) ideology of asymmetrical bilingualism. Like Trudeau, Castonguay rejected the recommendations of the Bilingual Districts Advisory Board, but for a very different reason. Castonguay stated that he believed the Board had been correct to focus on using bilingual districts as a means of bolstering the strength of minority languages and thereby to halt the forces of assimilation, rather than simply as a tool to provide greater comfort to the minorities. However, he argued that these efforts would be counterproductive within the big picture, if identical sets of minority-language services were provided to English-speakers in Quebec and French-speakers elsewhere. This is because of the unequal sizes and relative strengths of the two languages. French, he noted, is in a peripheral position in the English-majority provinces, and has no power to draw new adherents. Therefore, the most that could be accomplished through the creation of the twenty-five bilingual districts outside of Quebec would be to slow or perhaps halt the assimilation of this minority, which totalled (according to the 1971 census) only 675,000 individuals. On the other hand, the same census had shown English to be the home language of fully 900,000 Quebecers, and had revealed that even within Quebec's borders, there were some native French-speakers who had converted to the use of English in the home. To add to the assimilative powers of this minority by guaranteeing the provision of services in English, Castonguay argued with impeccable logic, would undermine the stated goal of Federal languages policy, by speeding, rather than slowing the overall processes of assimilation within Canada as a whole. He states:

> The principle of equality commands us, therefore, to create no bilingual districts at all in Quebec for the time being. The possibility remains that they could be created in the future, when a new linguistic equilibrium has been created in Canada, which is to say, when a future census shows that in a region of Quebec the English minority has stopped profiting at the expense of French from linguistic transfers between the two groups.
>
> (See Charles Castonguay, "Pour une politique des districts bilingues au Québec." *Journal of Canadian Studies*, 1976, p. 58.)

In the meantime, Castonguay argued, bilingual districts should be established only in the border regions of Ontario and New Brunswick, where French-speakers represent a substantial but threatened minority. Paradoxically, the best way for the federal government to achieve the goal of complete equality between Canada's two official languages would be to guarantee different rights to each of them.
23 Treasury Board circular 1982-6. Treasury Board File No. 4500-00, January 29, 1982, Annex "A".
24 The 'exclusion' or 'inclusion' of Montreal as a bilingual district had always been a little bit of a semantic game. The Bilingual Districts Advisory Board had maintained that designating Montreal bilingual was not necessary because the city could still receive services in English under the "sufficient demand" clause of the *Official Languages Act*. "Sufficient demand" protection was precisely what the listing in Treasury Board Circular 1982-6 guaranteed. However, with the first tier of minority protection (bilingual districts as defined under Section 9.1 of the *Official Languages Act*) now abandoned, the second-tier protection of section 9.2 now represented full federal protection, so the stigma of second-class status was lifted.
25 Section 22 of the Act reads:

> Every federal institution has the duty to ensure that any member of the public can communicate with and obtain services ... in either language ... in Canada or elsewhere, where there is sufficient demand for communications with and services from that office of facility in that language.

Having failed to clarify the language of the Charter, the *Official Languages Act* proceeds, a few paragraphs further on, to give the government the right to arbitrarily determine where and when minority-language services will be provided:

> The Governor in Council may make regulations
> (a) prescribing the circumstances in which there is significant demand for the purpose of paragraph 22(b) or subsection 23(i);
> (b) prescribing circumstances not otherwise provided for under this Part in which federal institu-

276　LAMENT FOR A NOTION

    tions have the duty to ensure that any member of the public can communicate with and obtain available services from offices of the institution in either official language.
    [Section 32(1), paragraph (a) and (b)]
26 The full text of the Act on this point reads as follows:
    In prescribing circumstances under paragraph (1)(a) or(b), the governor in council may have regard to
    (a) the number of persons composing the English or French linguistic minority population of the area served by an office or facility, the particular characteristics of that population and the proportion of that population to the total population of that area;
    (b) the volume of communications or services between an office or facility and members of the public using each official language; and
    (c) any other factors that the Governor in Council considers appropriate.
    [Section 32 (2)]
27 See Official Languages Branch of Treasury Board, *Regulations on Services to the Public: a Description of the Treasury Board Secretariat's Preferred Approach*. Ottawa: October 2, 1987, mimeograph, p. 5. Italics in the original.
28 *Ibid.*, pp. 5-8.
29 See Treasury Board, Impact of Official Languages Regulations on the Federal Electoral Districts. Ottawa: mimeograph, 1991. In particular, note Section D, which records the impact of the proposed regulations on small towns and rural areas.
30 See the explanatory text published with the 1992 regulations, which discuss the rejection of the "potential demand" approach. See *Canada Gazette*, January 1, 1992, p. 256.
31 To obtain these figures, the minority population was assigned all persons who claim to speak the minority official language as their sole home language, and half of those who claim to speak both English and French as home languages. Source: Statistics Canada, *Home Language and Mother Tongue: The Nation*.
32 *Canada Gazette*, January 1, 1992, p. 257.
33 I have gone to considerable effort to make an accurate estimate of the number of federal offices which have been designated bilingual by the 1992 regulations, but this number is still only a (conservative) estimate. To obtain this number, I added all the federal offices listed in *Impact of Official Languages Regulations on the Federal Electoral Districts*, Sections C.1, C.2 and D. As well, I have obtained mimeographed documents from the media relations branch of Canada Post corporation, which make it possible to count the number of post offices in each census metropolitan area which are legally obliged to provide bilingual counter service. As a rule, Canada Post overfulfills its requirements (e.g.: it has twelve bilingual outlets in Toronto, even though only ten are mandated). The numbers I have used are the *mandated* figures, since it is my intention to examine federal regulations on service to the public, not Canada Post's compliance record. The totals are as follows:
•   Census metropolitan areas with Official-Language minority populations (as measured by mother tongue) of at least 5,000:

City	Offices	Post Offices
Ottawa-Hull	112	154
Halifax	47	2
Saint John	27	2
Montreal	53	103
Quebec	33	3
Sherbrooke	19	3
Toronto	51	10
Hamilton	19	2
St. Catharines-Niagara	9	3
Windsor	21	3
Sudbury	19	9
Winnipeg	58	5
Calgary	42	4
Edmonton	48	4

Vancouver	56	4
Total offices =	614	309

- Census metropolitan areas with official language minority populations (as measured by mother tongue) of less than 5,000):

City	Offices	Post Offices
Oshawa	4	1
Kitchener	4	1
London	4	1
Victoria	4	1
Saskatoon	4	1
Thunder Bay	4	1
Regina	4	1
Trois-Rivières	3	1
Chicoutimi-Jonquière	3	1
St. John's	4	1
Total offices =	38	10

- Census subdivision with total populations under 100,000, which qualify as areas of significant demand: 1,184 federal offices, including all relevant postal outlets.

The total number of mandated bilingual federal offices in Canada: 2,155.

34 *House of Commons Debates*, July 6, 1988, pp. 17, 185.
35 There were 946,255 francophones (as measured by mother tongue) living outside Quebec in 1991. Of these, 801,690 were bilingual. There were 15,570,735 anglophones (as measured by mother tongue) living outside of Quebec in 1991. Of these, 987,385 were bilingual. Source: Statistics Canada: *Knowledge of Languages: The Nation*, pp. 24, 45. Only single-response mother tongue figures were used for this calculation.
36 Among holders of bilingual positions, francophones are over-represented in every region of the country: fifty-two percent of bilingual posts in the National Capital Region, sixty-four percent in New Brunswick, thirty-eight percent in the West and North, forty-two percent in those parts of Ontario outside the National Capital Region, and forty-four percent in overseas positions. Even in Quebec, which is the one part of Canada where bilingual anglophones outnumber bilingual francophones as a proportion of their respective populations, francophones are overrepresented, holding ninety-two percent of all posts designated bilingual. Source: Public Service Commission of Canada, Brief to the Legislative Committee on Bill C-72 on the Status and Use of the Official Languages of Canada. Ottawa: April 19, 1988, mimeograph, p. 6.
37 These comments are part of a presentation made to the Quebec government's Bélanger-Campeau Commission. Quoted in Richard Fidler, (ed.), *Canada Adieu? Quebec Debates its Future*. Lantzville, British Columbia and Halifax: Oolichan Books and the Institute for Research on Public Policy, 1991, p. 274.
38 Paul Bunner, Philip Day, "Halting Bilingualism's Creep," *Alberta Report*. Edmonton: February 22, 1988, p. 13.
39 Standing Joint Committee of Parliament on Official Languages, *Minutes*. February 10, 1987. pp. 6:12, 6:28. In privately-run postal outlets, the language requirements are equally restrictive, but staffing arrangements are obviously not constrained by collective bargaining considerations.
40 *Ibid.*
41 See Treasury Board, *Impact of Official Languages Regulations*, Section D, p. 129.
42 In 1992, 20,885 Saskatchewan residents reported French as their sole mother tongue. Only 6,350 reported French as their sole home language. See Statistics Canada, *Home Language and Mother Tongue: The Nation*, pp. 11, 190.
43 Statutes of Canada, 1960, 8.9, Eliz II, C. 44, s. 2 (g).
44 *Official Languages Act*, 1969. 17-18 Eliz II, Chapter 54. s. 2.
45 Strictly speaking, this ruling applied to Section 19 (2), not Section 19 (1). However, the wording of the two sections is identical except that 19.2 refers to "any court in New Brunswick." It was clear that the ruling applied to federal courts as well.

46 The relevant section of the *Criminal Code* is 530 (1) (e). This section may not apply in Quebec, due to a conflict with Section 133 of the BNA Act. For a brief description of the conflict, see Commissioner of Official Languages, *Annual Report*, 1991, pp. 19-20.
47 Ontario is the least bilingual of the three provinces. Yet legal forms have been available in French in Ontario since 1975. Translations of Ontario statutes have had legal status in provincial courts since 1978. Since 1980, defendants in any part of Ontario have had the right to a criminal trial in French. Civil trials have been conducted in French in all parts of Ontario with significant minority populations since 1982. For further details of judicial rights in this province, see Robert Gill, "Federal and Provincial Language Policy in Ontario and the Future of the Franco-Ontarians." *American Review of Canadian Studies*, 1983, Vol. 13, No. 1, pp. 14-15.
48 Michel Bastarache, "Bilingualism and the Judicial System" *Language Rights in Canada*, p. 141. Although I disagree with the tone of this remark, I should note that it is very much out of keeping with the rest of the article from which it is taken, which is probably the best, most detailed account of the history of official-language use in the Canadian court system (for the period preceding the implementation of the 1988 *Official Languages Act*).
49 See Robin Brunet, "A Choice at any Cost." *Alberta Report*, October 7, 1991, pp. 40-41. The trial of André Rivest took place in 1991, after the *Official Languages Act* had been proclaimed, but before its provisions regarding bilingual court officers had come into effect.
50 A leaked 1988 Justice department analysis of Bill C-72 (*The Official Languages Act*) concluded that under the new law, "Every court would have the duty to ensure that judges and other presiding officers can understand proceedings without simultaneous translation." See Paul Bunner and Philip Day, "Halting Bilingualism's Creep." *Alberta Report*, February 22, 1988, p. 11. The same obligations are imposed on provincial courts by Section 94 of the *Official Languages Act*, but the imposition is contingent on the approval of the government of the province in question.
51 Several examples are offered on p. 20 of the Commissioner of Official Languages, *Annual Report 1991*. Ottawa: Minister of Supply and Services, 1992.
52 Charles Castonguay, "Pour une politique des districts bilingues au Québec." *Journal of Canadian Studies*, August 1976, p. 50. My translation.
53 Lengyel and Watson, *La Situation de la langue française en Colombie Britannique*, p. 30.
54 Treasury Board of Canada Secretariat, *Good Morning ... Bonjour*. Ottawa: Communications Division, Treasury Board, 1988, p. 25.
55 *Ibid.*, pp. 23-24. My italics.
56 *Toronto Sun*, June 12, 1991. Nationwide, 600 Revenue Canada employees participated in the paid-to-practice program.
57 Mordecai Richler, "Language Problems," p. 16. The idea that minority-language services must be provided to "the travelling public" in even the most linguistically homogeneous regions is summed up on page 13 of the pamphlet "Some Basic Facts," published by the Commissioner of Official Languages: "Even in areas such as Saskatchewan or Saguenay/Lac-Saint-Jean, where official language minority communities amount respectively to 24,000 francophones (2.3%) and 9,000 anglophones (2.2%), the needs of the travelling public must also be kept in mind."
58 Canada. "Official Languages (Communications with and Services to the Public) Regulations." *Canada Gazette*, Part 2, January 1, 1992, 5 (2) (b).
59 Source: Mimeographed lists of bilingual post office locations as of December 1992, compiled for internal use by Canada Post. No document title. Provided to me upon request by Canada Post Corporation, Media Relations Branch.
60 There are fifty-two federal departments and agencies in Toronto offering French-language services at one or more locations, according to the Treasury Board document *Impact of Official Languages Regulations on the Federal Electoral Districts*. Ottawa: mimeograph, 1992. Section 'C.'
61 *Canada Gazette*, January 1, 1992, pp. 241-253.
62 This observation is made in Richard Joy, *Canada's Official Languages: The Progress of Bilingualism*. Toronto: University of Toronto Press, 1992, p. 17.
63 Federation of Canadian Municipalities, *At Your Service ... in Both Official Languages: A Guide to the Delivery of Municipal Services in English and French*. Ottawa: Federation of Canadian Municipalities, 1987, p. 3.
64 Joy, *Canada's Official Languages*, p. 117.
65 The Gendron Commission. See Scowen, *A Different Vision*, p. 131.

66 See, for example, Rudy Le Cours, "Bourassa: créer des districts bilingues en étendant la loi 101." *Le Devoir,* November 29, 1986, p. A2.

7. PASSING THE BUCK
1 Quoted in George Radwanski, *Trudeau.* Toronto: Macmillan, 1978, p. 96.
2 Gouvernement du Québec, Ministère des finances, *Comptes publiques 1991-1992.* Quebec City: Ministère des finances, December 1992, pp. 1-46.
3 Some of the more bizarre regulations are described in Emmanuel Didier, "Private Law of Language," Michel Bastarache, *Language Rights in Canada.* Montreal: Les Editions Yvon Blais, 1987. The rubber stamps, warehouse forms and magazine subscriptions are mentioned on pp. 372-373.
4 *Ibid.,* pp. 319-439.
5 See January 1, 1992 Regulations, Section 12 (1). Section 12 (2) covers services provided by means of pre-printed instructions.
6 Chris Wood, "New Bilingual Rule Brings Airport Turbulence." *Financial Post,* May 7, 1983, p. 7.
7 This passage from a letter from D.C. McAree to leaseholders at Toronto International Airport is quoted in Morton Shulman, "Bilingual Clerks? Baloney." Toronto *Sun,* May 30, 1982, p. 22.
8 *Ibid.*
9 Canadian Press, "Teed-off Residents Sink Bilingual Golf Course Idea." *The Gazette,* Montreal, March 2, 1989, p. A2.
10 Brimelow, *The Patriot Game,* p. 87.
11 Grant Purves, "Official Bilingualism in Canada." *Current Issue Review* 86-11E. Library of Parliament Research Branch, Ottawa, November 17, 1990.
12 Colette Duhaime, "Privatized Airports: Will They Concern Themselves With Language?" *Language and Society,* Spring 1991, p. 30.
13 *Ibid.*
14 Marjorie Nichols, "The Language of Privatization," in *Language and Society,* Winter 1987, pp. 5-6. The Commissioner of Official Languages was still pursuing Petro-Canada four years later. See Colette Duhaime, "Petro-Canada should continue to be subject to the Official Languages Act." *Language and Society,* Spring 1991, p. 31.
15 Nichols, "The Language of Privatization," p. 5.
16 Duhaime, "Privatized Airports," p. 30.
17 Figures are taken from the 1985-1991 *Annual Reports* of the the Public Service Commission (Ottawa: Minister of Supply and Services). The titles of the tables from which these cumulative totals are compiled are "Layoff, Category, Sex and Language Group" (figures from the table in the 1985 report extend the figures back to 1979).
18 To establish the percentage of the relevant official-language minority communities that subscribe to the subsidized newspapers, I have added up the paid circulation of each of the small-circulation minority-language newspapers in Canada, multiplied this by the readership that each individual copy is likely to enjoy (2.1 readers per average paid subscription, according to the Audit Bureau of Circulation), and divided this figure by the number of individuals who claim the relevant minority official language as their mother tongue. Mother tongue was used rather than the more accurate home language figure because it is mother tongue that is at the centre of all federal government claims to service the official language minorities. Sources for circulation figures: Quebec Community Newspaper Association, *Rate Sheet No. 11.* Ste-Anne-de-Bellevue, Quebec, January 1993; Association de la presse francophone hors Québec, Opérations publicitaires et services de communications, *1993 Rate Card,* Ottawa: 1993. Both publications cite both total circulation and paid circulation. I have counted only paid circulation, since unpaid circulation is a suspect measure for any publication that is basing its advertising rates for a captive market of obligatory advertisers on total circulation numbers. So long as the advertisers have no power to call into question the utility of the free distribution, there is an obvious incentive to boost the circulation of free copies, even if most of them go straight into the garbage can at the recipient's end. On this basis, I counted 51,979 paid subscriptions (i.e., 109,156 readers) for the French-language newspapers outside Quebec, and 64,790 paid subscriptions (i.e., 136,059 readers) for the English-language newspapers inside Quebec. These figures exclude all large-circulation minority-language newspapers such as the *Montreal Gazette,*

280   LAMENT FOR A NOTION

Ottawa's *Le Droit*, and Montreal's *Suburban*. Speciality publications like *The McGill Daily* were also excluded.

19 Establishing the cost to federally-regulated private advertisers cannot be done by direct means, since budgets are not kept for advertising in the minority press. The total of $1.96 million was established by (1) taking the number of lines of advertising placed by federally-regulated businesses in a typical issue of *L'Express* (Toronto) and the *Chronicle-Telegraph* (Quebec City) and averaging them, then assuming that this average is applicable to all minority newspapers; (2) multiplying the number of lines by the per-line advertising cost for each newspaper (excluding the Montreal *Gazette* and Ottawa's *Le Droit*); (3) multiplying this total, in the case of each newspaper, by the number of issues; (4) adding these totals together. Sources for circulation figures and per line ad rates: Quebec Community Newspaper Association, *Rate Sheet No. 11*, Ste-Anne-de-Bellevue, Quebec, January 1993; Association de la presse francophone hors Québec, Opérations publicitaires et services de communications, *1993 Rate Card*, Ottawa, 1993. The *Gazette*, the *Suburban*, the Montreal *Monitor*, the Montreal *Downtowner* and *Le Droit* were not counted because they are large-circulation papers with sufficient readership that ads placed in them cannot be regarded as mere subsidies.

20 See George Koch, "Come Fly With Fortier." *Alberta Report*, November 5, 1990, p. 18.

21 Dorothy Guinan, "The Chronicle-Telegraph: Quebec City's English Newspaper." *Language and Society*, Fall 1991, p. 32.

22 *The Chronicle-Telegraph*, Quebec City, April 22, 1992.

23 Home language figures are from Statistics Canada, *Home Language and Mother Tongue: The Nation* (1991 Census), p. 44. Figure on unilingual anglophones is from Statistics Canada, *Knowledge of Languages: The Nation* (1991 Census), p. 11.

24 Mark Kennedy, "What Price Bilingualism? Estimates Vary so Widely, There's No Bottom Line." The *Citizen*, Ottawa: March 23, 1991, p. B5.

25 Certain products imported in small quantities for which the packaging is only in ethnic languages are exempted from the normal bilingual rules. Certain other exemptions are also granted by the regulations under the Act.

26 Sarah Scott, "Scrap Bilingual Cereals: Jeanniot." Montreal *Gazette*, April 26, 1991, p. A2.

27 Michael Jenkinson, "Ottawa Moves Towards Deregulating Metric Sizes." *Alberta Report*, April 5, 1993, p. 20.

28 In a more spectacular example, a retail producer described to me how he had marketed a 375 gram jar of mustard from France with a 250 gram label.

29 The November 27, 1989 edition of *Automotive News* carried the story of Ford of Canada's decision not to import its made-in-Australia Capri Roadster: "Ford cited the costs associated with preparing the car for sale in two languages (French and English) ... vs. the small number of potential sales."

30 Robert Matas, "Store Owners Forced to Say Au Revoir." *Globe and Mail*, May 7, 1991, p. A5.

31 Pierre Arbour, *Québec Inc. et la tentation du dirigisme*. Montreal: L'Étincelle éditeur, 1993, p. 162.

32 Roger Miller, "The Response of Business Firms" in Richard Bourhis (ed.), pp. 127-129.

33 Thomas Courchene, "Avenues of Adjustment: The Transfer payment System and Regional Disparities." *Canadian Confederation at the Crossroads*. Vancouver: Fraser Institute, 1978, p. 163.

8. THE LORD OF THE FILES

1 "Thanks, but no thanks, Maz." An editorial in the Edmonton *Journal*, March 12, 1993.

2 In 1988, there were 565,398 employees in the Statistics Canada 'universe' of federal employees. This total includes public servants, employees of crown corporations, officers and civilian employees of the RCMP, and military personnel. See Paul Thomas, "The Administrative Machine in Canada." Paul Fox and Graham White, *Politics: Canada*. Seventh edition. Toronto: McGraw-Hill Ryerson, 1991, p. 469.

3 In 1974, 18.8 percent of posts in the Public Service were open to unilingual francophones (i.e., they were classified either "French essential" or "English or French essential," meaning that anybody could hold the post, as long as he or she was capable of speaking one of Canada's official languages. By 1992, only 11.7 percent of posts were still classified as belonging to one of these two categories. Source: Letter from Treasury Board of Canada, June 2, 1993 in response to a request made under the Access to Information Act. Treasury Board file no: 135-9394-0010.

4 Kenneth Kernaghan, "Representative Bureaucracy: The Canadian Perspective." *Canadian Public Policy*, Vol. 21, 1978, p. 501.
5 Treasury Board, *Official Languages Annual Report, 1990-91*, p. 44.
6 *Ibid.*, p. 47.
7 Throughout the 1980s, the percentage of francophones recruited in all scientific categories of the Public Service closely parallelled the numbers graduating from Canada's universities. Official Languages Branch, Treasury Board Secretariat, *Anglophones and Francophones in the Scientific and Professional Categories of the Public Service of Canada*, Ottawa: mimeograph, 1991, pp. 12-13. Between 1978 and 1991, the representation of francophones in Public Service management positions has increased from eighteen percent to twenty-two percent. In scientific and professional posts it has increased from nineteen to twenty-three percent, and in technical positions it has increased from eighteen percent to twenty-one percent. See Treasury Board, *Official Languages Annual Report, 1990-1991*. Ottawa: Minister of Supply and Services, 1991, p. 46
8 *Ibid.*, p. 45.
9 V. Seymour Wilson and Willard Mullins, "Representative Bureaucracy: Linguistic/Ethnic Aspects in Canadian Public Policy." *Canadian Public Administration*, Vol. 21, 1978, p. 535. Emphasis is mine.
10 Steve Vanagas, "Redefining Merit." *British Columbia Report*, July 12, 1993, p. 10.
11 Lester Pearson, *House of Commons Debates*, April 6, 1966, p. 3915.
12 The ruling is described in Erna Paris, "Guilt, Anxiety and Bilingualism in the Civil Service." *Saturday Night*, March 1972, p. 17.
13 Professional Institute of the Public Service of Canada, *Survey of Official Languages: Final Report*. Ottawa: mimeograph, 1991, p. 4.
14 For respondents of both language groups, total responses were as follows:
   1) 28.8 percent of respondents felt that the federal government's language-based hiring and promotion practises had already had a negative effect on their own advancement opportunities. Only 8.1 percent reported a positive impact on their own careers;
   2) 41.8 percent of respondents felt their personal future advancement opportunities would be harmed by the federal policy requiring bilingual positions in the management category to have at least a 'B' level of proficiency (substantial proficiency) in both official languages. On the other hand, only 12.6 percent felt that their future advancement opportunities would be enhanced by the policy;
   3) 40.1 percent felt that their personal advancement opportunities would be harmed by a newly-introduced policy, requiring departments to raise the language proficiency standards for incumbents in bilingual Executive Group positions in bilingual regions of the country from 'B' to 'C' (native-like proficiency) by 1998. Only 8.1 percent expect to benefit from this new policy;
   4) 34.7 percent of respondents reported that they had on one or more occasions passed up the opportunity to apply for certain posts for which they felt they were otherwise qualified, because of linguistic job requirements that they could not meet. See Professional Institute of the Public Service of Canada, *Survey of Official Languages: Final Report*. Ottawa: mimeograph, 1991, pp. 84-88.
15 *Ibid.*
16 *Ibid.*
17 58.8 percent of positions are designated English essential, 6.5 percent are designated French essential, and 5.5 percent are designated as open to either French or English applicants. Source: Commissioner of Official Languages, *Some Basic Facts*, p. 16.
18 Sources: Letter from Treasury Board of Canada, June 17, 1993, in response to a request for information under the *Access to Information Act*. Treasury Board File No. 135-9394-0010; Victor Goldbloom, speech to the Chamber of Commerce, Laval, Quebec, May 28, 1992, mimeograph, p. 6.
19 The current Commissioner of Official Languages, Victor Goldbloom, has been outspoken in identifying this as the root problem. See his comments in Chantal Hébert, "Une épidémie de 'Bilinguité' payante pour les fonctionnaires." *Le Devoir*, May 6, 1992, p. A3.
   A little rummaging through documents obtained via the access to information law shows the mechanism by which bilingual incumbents cause their jobs to be redesignated bilingual. A typical case is that of an electronic technician's job (position GS50-00797 in the Department of Energy, Mines and Resources). An anonymous complaint was received by the Office of the Commissioner of Official Languages, that the post should be made bilingual, because part of its work is carried out in the National Capital Region. This complaint was almost certainly launched by the incumbent in the job himself, under cover of the anonymity guaranteed to all complainants by the Commissioner.

Several inter-departmental memos had to be launched and a small investigation conducted before the matter could be resolved. Sources: Letter from Raymonde Gour-Tanguay to A. G. Damley, November 5, 1986; letter from Gilberte Tardife to Raymonde Gour-Tanguay, November 6, 1986.
20 Victor Goldbloom, speech to Laval Chamber of Commerce, p. 6.
21 Treasury Board Circular 1977-46 (p. 59) contains the following provision: "Because either/or positions could be staffed with employees who have either English or French as their first official language, whenever an either/or position is identified, any position which is in communication with that position in performing its duties must be identified as bilingual. For similar reasons, any supervisory position with one subordinate either/or position must be identified as bilingual."
22 Jack Aubry, "Numbers Game." Ottawa *Citizen*, March 23, 1991, p. B4.
23 This exchange is excerpted from the minutes of a meeting of Parliament's Standing Joint Committee on Official Languages (February 10, 1987). This sort of pressure is typical. Joe Pelisek, an official with the Professional Institute of the Public Service, reports that even though the Treasury Board has produced guidelines stating that jobs should be redesignated bilingual only when there is a demonstrable need, "managers have ignored those rules and are declaring positions bilingual whether they are needed or not.... Many managers believe they will be looked upon favourably by senior officials if they have more bilingual staff." (Pelisek's comments are paraphrased in David Pugliese, "Union Urges Bilingual Cuts." Ottawa *Citizen*, December 9, 1992, p. A6). The results of this sort of pressure are predictable: nearly every department and agency works hard to promote more francophones if they are under-represented and is careful not to let their numbers drop, if they are over-represented. Consider, for example, the findings of a 1979 report reviewing the linguistic hiring practices of fifty federal government departments and agencies. Despite an overall balance in the proportion of anglophone and francophone employees in the aggregate hiring figures of all departments combined with some departments having a higher-than-equitable proportion of anglophones and others having a higher-than-equitable proportion of francophones, the report noted a decidedly one-sided trend. Twenty of the departments and agencies planned to work actively to increase francophone representation, while the remaining twenty intended to either maintain existing ratios or make selective increases in their hirings of francophones. Under-representation of anglophones was completely ignored. See Treasury Board, *Language Reform in Federal Institutions*. Ottawa: 1979, mimeograph, p. 21.
24 *Public Service Employment Act*. Sections 10 and 12. See also Treasury Board, *Scientific and Professional Categories*, p. 4.
25 Treasury Board Secretariat, *Information Session for the Preparation of Letters of Understanding on Official Languages*. Ottawa: mimeograph, November 1989, p. 10.
26 Percentage figures for francophone and anglophone representation in departments of the federal civil service for September 1964 are cited in the B&B Commission *Report*, Vol. 3A, p. 210.
27 *Ibid.*, p. 212.
28 *Ibid.*, p. 214.
29 The B&B Commission *Report* is quite specific in stating that no deliberate anti-French discrimination took place in Public Service hiring and promotion. See the Commission's *Report*, Volume 3A, p. 252. Although the Commissioners did not elaborate greatly on this matter, the accuracy of their analysis of the problems facing French-speakers in an environment dominated by English has since been confirmed and extended by independent research. A 1981 study on languages of work, published by Montreal's Institute for Research on Public Policy, shows that in jobs requiring teamwork, it is important for workers to be able to overhear and understand conversations in which they are not directly involved. The passive accumulation of information overheard in this manner serves as the key means by which workers are able to learn of new or peripheral information that will allow them to complete their jobs effectively. Sanford Borins summarizes this research in his book on bilingualism among air traffic controllers: "Anyone who speaks a second less than perfectly knows that he is more effective when speaking directly to the other party, when there is no background noise, or more generally, when the ratio of signal to noise is high. What distinguishes our mother tongue is that we can function more effectively in it at very low signal-to-noise ratios." Sanford Borins, *The Language of the Skies: The Bilingual Air Traffic Control Conflict in Canada*. Kingston and Montreal: McGill-Queen's University Press, The Institute of Public Administration of Canada, 1983, p. 223.
30 B&B Commission, *Report*, Vol. 3A, p. 254.

31 Quebec has retained a fully unilingual Public Service, which is basically no different than the unilingual model that the Canadian government employed between the introduction of merit hiring in 1918 and the introduction of bilingual post designations in the 1970s. The main difference between the language regime presently employed by the Quebec government and the one abandoned by Ottawa is, of course, that French is the exclusive working language of the provincial Public Service. The unoriginality of the Quebec model means that there is not a great deal that the federal government can learn from Quebec. But the existence of a parallel example of a unilingual Public Service within Canada, organized on a merit basis, does give a chance to conduct an experiment regarding the foundation-stone of the B&B Commission's proposals regarding Public Service reform. The Commission maintained that the reason that francophones were under-represented in the federal civil service was that most of them, including most who were bilingual, were unable to compete in an English-speaking environment because their skills in English were almost never up to the standard of native English-speakers.
32 Public Service Commission of Canada, *Brief to the Legislative Committee on Bill C-72 on the Status and Use of the Official Languages of Canada*. Ottawa, April 19, 1988, mimeograph, p. 2.
33 Public Service Commission/Treasury Board, *Circular 1977-46*, p. 52.
34 Here is a typical expression of the attitude that the injustices imposed by the bilingual quota system are an acceptable price for the increased pace of reform (from a 1977 document justifying high quotas imposed in 1973): "The situation in federal institutions at that time *justified measures which would accomplish substantial progress in a short period of time*. The measures adopted by the government were those that were necessary when there is a significant gap to close and inequalities to be corrected; they were uniform and standard, applied at the same time and in the same way in all departments, and the policy guidelines and implementation procedures were under the control of central agencies. *The Government felt that there was a need, at the time, for both continuity and comprehensiveness in implementation.*" See Treasury Board and Public Service Commission, *Revised Official Languages Policies in the Public Service of Canada*. Ottawa: 1977, mimeograph, p. 7. My italics.
35 The only mention of the Public Service in the *Official Languages Act* (other than peripheral references in sections dealing with services to the public) is in Section 40 (4) which confirms the authority of the Public Service Commission to make appointments to posts serving the public, and stresses that the merit principle as defined in the *Public Service Employment Act* will apply to such posts. The directives to the Public Service during the 1968-1973 period regarding equitable employment for francophones and anglophones are remarkably sparse. Treasury Board Circular 1973-88 (issued June 30, 1973) lists the relevant documents as being two Treasury Board circulars (1970-95 and 1971-21), a constitutional paper titled "Federalism for the Future" (1968), and a statement by Prime Minister Trudeau in the House of Commons (June 23, 1970). See Treasury Board Circular 1973-88, p. 4.
36 One possible reason for choosing not to issue explicit guidelines is hinted at in the exchanges that took place in the House of Commons in May and June 1973, as the House prepared to adopt a resolution on bilingualism in the Public Service. Robert Stanfield, the opposition leader, suggested that staffing rules should be included in an amendment to the *Official Languages Act*. Government MPs argued that the complexity and uncertainty of the circumstances in which the rules were being implemented made necessary the adoption of flexible rules, easily subject to change.
37 B&B Commission, *Report*, Vol. 3A, p. 258.
38 *Ibid.*, p. 277.
39 *Ibid.*
40 *Ibid.*
41 Trudeau is quoted in Brimelow, *The Patriot Game*, p. 86.
42 Journalist Richard Gwyn offers this explanation:
> On the day after the *Official Languages Act* was passed, the Calgary *Herald* came right to the point: "For the more rewarding jobs, bilingualism is being made practically necessary." Initially, these "rewarding" jobs meant just the top ones at Ottawa; inevitably, though, it would soon mean all the middle-rank jobs that fed the top; then jobs in the "para-government," all the way from the Canadian Manufacturers' Associations to the Canadian Labour Congress, on down the line to jobs in all companies which had dealings with francophones, and to some provincial government positions. Eventually, unilingualism could mean a life sentence to job immobility. Trudeau knew this all along. He fibbed about it as a necessary means to an end.
> (Richard Gwyn, *The Northern Magus*, p. 223.)

43 Some very limited experimentation with language-based work units did take place in the early 1970s. A one-year experiment with the units was commenced on June 23, 1971 and terminated on October 29, 1971 when plans for 475 such units with 29,000 employees were announced. The plan seems never to have been fully implemented. See V. Seymour Wilson, 'Language Policy.' G. Bruce Doern and V. Seymour Wilson (eds.), *Issues in Canadian Public Policy*. Toronto: Macmillan of Canada, 1974, pp. 273-274; Treasury Board Circular 1970-95, September 14, 1970. The House of Commons resolution of June 1973 regarding Public Service quota hiring sets out explicit rules for quota hiring, but also pays lip service to French language units.

One of the problems with these experiments was that the units were largely used as a training ground for unilingual anglophones learning French, rather than as French-only work environments. This may have doomed them from the start, as Créditiste M.P. René Matte warned in the House of Commons in 1970: "We do not object to helping anglophone participants learn French, but if French units are designed for that purpose, nothing will change." See *House of Commons Debates*, June 23, 1970, p. 8494.

Language-based units, now renamed "Units working in French" were again proposed in 1975, but the proposal again proved abortive. See Treasury Board Circular 1975-111, September 25, 1975; Jacques Robichaud, "Le bilinguisme dans l'administration fédérale du Canada (1969-1982)," *Les cahiers de Droit*, March 1983, p. 124. A final stab at producing something vaguely like French-language units was made in 1977, when a Treasury Board circular made the vague and modest proposal that departments and agencies "increase the number of opportunities for working in French through increasing the number and percentage of French-essential positions." As the figures on the declining number of such posts over the past two decades confirms, this policy was never adopted. See Treasury Board Circular 1977-46, p. 48.

44 Treasury Board Circular 1971-21, March 9, 1971 imposes the following quotas of bilingual personnel, to be filled by 1975: executive category 60%; administrative and foreign service category 50%; administrative support 35%; scientific and professional categories 15%; technical category 15%; operational category 15%. See pp. 3-4.
45 Sandra Gwyn, "Speaking the Unspeakable, Bilingually." *Saturday Night*, July-August 1976, p. 11.
46 René Lévesque is quoted in V. Seymour Wilson, "Language Policy," G. Bruce Doern and V. Seymour Wilson (eds.), *Issues in Canadian Public Policy*, p. 265.
47 Erna Paris, "Guilt, Anxiety, and Bilingualism in the Civil Service." *Saturday Night*, March 1972, p. 18.
48 Gérard Pelletier, "1968: Language Policy and the Mood in Quebec." Thomas Axworthy and Pierre Trudeau (eds.). *Toward a Just Society: The Trudeau Years*. Toronto: Viking, 1990, p. 223.
49 Treasury Board Circular 1973-88 (June 29, 1973), p. 16. Most of the elements of the circular were covered in advance by a statement issued on December 14, 1972 by Treasury Board President Bud Drury.
50 Language Reform in Federal Institutions, p. 14.
51 Sandra Gwyn, "Speaking the Unspeakable," p. 13.
52 *Ibid.*
53 *Ibid.*, p. 11. Amusingly, the Treasury Board insisted that the training system, imposed in 1973, had been successful—even as it was busy dismantling the 1973 reforms. In 1977 it reported that "the proportion of bilingual positions that are occupied by bilingual incumbents has risen from forty percent in May, 1974 to eighty percent in September 1977." (See "Revised Policies," 1977). These figures reflected only the number of individuals who had completed language training, ignoring the fact that for most the training had produced no visible skills.
54 *Ibid.* p. 11.
55 Remarkably, this policy outcome had been predicted as early as 1974, when V. Seymour Wilson warned, "A reading of the guidelines makes it clear, for example, that one of the possible implications of strictly adhering to them is the curtailment of French-Canadian recruits to the Public Service, a possibility which would be altogether counter-productive to the government's language policy." V. Seymour Wilson, "Language Policy," G. Bruce Doern and V. Seymour Wilson (eds.), *Issues in Canadian Public Policy*, p. 272.
56 See Pierre Foucher, "The Right to Receive Public Services in Both Official Languages." Michel Bastarache (ed.), *Language Rights in Canada*. Montreal: Les Editions Yvon Blais, 1987, pp. 244-247.

57 Since the passage of an obscure Treasury Board directive in 1981, it has been the rule that any position designated bilingual will automatically be upgraded to 'bilingual-imperative' status if filled by a unilingual employee who fails to become bilingual after three years on the job. The reason for this, Treasury Board circular 1981-29 states, is that the continued occupation of a bilingual post by a unilingual incumbent beyond the initial three years period would "either jeopardize the unit's capacity to fulfil its linguistic operational responsibilities or call into question the need for bilingualism in that position."

At first blush, this seems to be reasonable enough. However, regulations provide no mechanism by which the bilingual status of the position can be 'called into question.' If the need for bilingual status for a post really is questionable, then the logical approach would be to *review* its status, rather than to automatically declare it bilingual-imperative. Following this review, posts found to be genuinely in need of a bilingual designation could then be bumped up to imperative status. Those not in need of a bilingual designation could be down-graded to either English-essential status, French-essential status, or 'either/or' status. The need for a regularly scheduled, objective post-by-post assessment of this sort was made by the B & B Commission in 1969, and ignored by the Trudeau government. Instead, since 1981 many posts which do not need to be staffed by a bilingual person are ratcheted upwards to imperative status, where only members of the bilingual elite can ever hope to fill them.

Since 1989, there has been only one way to redesignate bilingual posts as unilingual. If an incumbent in a bilingual post fails to meet the language requirements of his or her post, the post may under some circumstances be redesignated unilingual. However, before this happens, "the employee interested in recovering the bonus" will be given the chance "to discuss with their supervisor the means to achieve this goal. A special training program at government expense, has been designed for that specific purpose...." Given that a post is likely to be redesignated unilingual only if the incumbent fails a Language Knowledge Examination and then refuses the free training to gain the skills necessary to recover his or her $800 annual bilingual bonus, it is unlikely that this procedure produces a large number of redesignations. See Department of Finance/Treasury Board, Circular 1989-38(P), pp. 1-2.

58 As of March 1992, 70.4 percent of appointees to bilingual-imperative posts were francophones, as opposed to 61.5 percent of appointees to bilingual-essential posts staffed on a non-imperative basis. Source: Letter from C.J. Ferguson, Access to Information and Privacy Coordinator, Treasury Board of Canada, to Stephanie Mullen, June 17, 1993. Treasury Board File No. 135-3394-0014.

59 The fundamental flaws of Canada's Public Service language regime are encapsulated and codified in the 1988 Act. As outlined in the 1988 *Official Languages Act*, federal regulations on bilingualism in the Public Service are designed to attain three goals:

1) to ensure that members of the public can receive services in both official languages where numbers warrant;

2) to permit public servants to work in the official language of their choice, as long as they reside in one of a fairly limited number of "bilingual regions" in eastern Ontario, west Quebec, the Gaspé, and New Brunswick; and

3) to ensure that the proportion of French-speakers and English-speakers in the Public Service reflects Canada's linguistic make-up. This proportionate level of representation is to be achieved in the overall composition of the Public Service and also at all levels of seniority and in all fields of operation. The Act instructs that this must be done without infringing upon "the merit principle" in hiring and promotion. *Official Languages Act*, 1988, Section 38(3).

As enumerated here, there is nothing in the Act that would be found really objectionable. The first of the goals is universally recognized as being just and fair.

The Act's second goal of permitting both language groups to work in their mother tongue within the Public Service is also widely recognized as reasonable. If Canadians do not want to discriminate against unilingual French-speakers, it is necessary to provide an environment in which French-speaking public servants can have equitable opportunities for advancement, while working exclusively in French. However, the bilingual regions concept is an extraordinarily clumsy method of reaching this goal.

Under the present language regime, the principle of permitting individuals to work in their language of choice in these regions has become so distorted that virtually all supervisory personnel in these regions are required to be bilingual. Since Canada's Public Service is unusually geographically concentrated around the national capital, this means that most supervisory posts are located in bilingual regions. Section 36(3)(ii) of the *Official Languages Act* states that senior management as a whole in all "bilingual regions of the Public Service," as well as in offices outside Canada and in all head offices of government departments and agencies, should be able to function in both official languages. The bilingual regions policy therefore cuts off most avenues of advancement to supervisory positions for unilingual speakers of either official language, in a way that would not happen under the French-language unit and English-language unit system.

The third goal is self-contradictory. It is impossible to produce a perfect linguistic mix at every level of every department in the entire Public Service of Canada without violating the merit principle and hiring at least some employees on the basis of linguistic talent alone.

60 Vincent Della Noce. Comments made while questioning a witness at the Standing Joint Committee of Parliament on Official Languages. Minutes of the Committee, February 12, 1985, p. 2:38.
61 Royal Commission on Government Organization (Glasscoe Commission), *Report*, Vol. 1. Ottawa: The Queen's Printer, 1962, p. 267.
62 An experimental program had been launched a year earlier in the Department of Northern Affairs and Natural Resources. See B&B Commission *Report*, Vol. 3A, p. 161.
63 G.G.E. Steele, "Bilingualism in the Canadian Public Service," an address to the National Conference, Civil Service Federation Convention, August 25, 1965. *Civil Service Review*, 38, No. 3, Ottawa, 1965, p. 68.
64 Public Service Commission, *Staffing Support Information*. Ottawa, 1990, p. 86.
65 There are 2,000 working hours in a year of forty-hour work weeks.
66 Public Service Commission, *Annual Report:Statistics*, 1991, p. 74.
67 Fédération des francophones hors Québec, *The Heirs of Lord Durham*, p. 72.
68 Since it has proved impossible to provide second language training for every civil servant, the government has had to introduce a form of rationing, which is tastefully referred to as 'screening.' One internal document describes the screening process this way: "screening is designed to limit student intake to those personnel with sufficient second language ability to reach the functional level within the available training hours...." Department of National Defence and Treasury Board, *Letter of Understanding*, p. 35. No individual can qualify for second language training without first passing a test designed to determine his natural ability to learn languages. Individuals are given a brief introduction to a language with which they are certain to be completely unfamiliar (Kurdish is the language currently used) and then tested on their retention of what they have learned. Failing this test eliminates the possibility of qualifying for one of the limited number of second-language training slots.

Persons who have failed to pass the Kurdish language test can still choose to learn French or English at their own expense during their own spare time, and many do choose to follow this expensive and time-consuming course. Night classes at Ottawa's high schools and universities are jammed with civil servants. But this training is no guarantee that a unilingual public servant will be able to apply for one of the ever-growing number of bilingual-essential posts. Managers are, as a rule, reluctant to place unilingual applicants with low language learning ability into bilingual posts, since a failure to become bilingual in three years will result in the embarrassment and hassle of seeing the position up-graded to "bilingual-imperative" as a result of their own failure to staff it with a person capable of becoming bilingual.
69 Public Service Commission, *Annual Report: Statistics*, 1991, p. 74.
70 Figures on unilingual public employees were obtained from these sources: Public Service Commission *Annual Report, Statistics*, 1991, p. 8 (which shows the 'Treasury Board universe' as containing 234,334 persons); President of the Treasury board, *Official Languages in Federal Institutions*, p. 34 (which shows that 55,257 public servants are employed in bilingual posts and meet the language requirements of their jobs); Marc Thérien, "Progress of Official Languages at the federal level." *Language and Society*, Summer 1989, pp. 12-34. (Thérien states that 13,000 bilingual employees fill unilingual positions.)
71 Laponce, *Languages and Their Territories*, p. 156.
72 Gordon Robertson, "Principle and the Art of the Possible." *Language and Society*, Summer 1983, p. 13.
73 A Treasury Board Secretariat survey in 1987 determined that francophone public servants spend sixty-one percent of their time at work in English, communicate with their immediate supervisor in

FOOTNOTES 287

English sixty-four percent of the time, use English sixty-six percent of the time when participating in internal meetings, and draft sixty-nine percent of documents in English. Source: Treasury Board Secretariat, *Survey on the Use of Both Official Languages*. Ottawa: unpublished mimeograph, 1987. Unnumbered page.

74 Source for 1965 figures: B&B Commission *Report*, Vol. 3A, p. 122. I have used the Report's figures for skill in writing in the second official language, rather than for other categories of linguistic skill (speaking, reading, understanding spoken conversation) because it is the most difficult skill, on which respondents were most likely to be harsh and realistic in their self-assessment (the figures for 1965 are responses to a survey). Source for 1991 figures: Professional Institute of the Public Service, *Survey of Official Languages: Final Report*, p. 69.
75 Department of National Defence and Treasury Board of Canada, *Letter of Understanding*, June 10, 1991, p. 27.
76 Dion's comments are quoted in Kenneth McRoberts and Dale Posgate, *Quebec: Social Change and Political Crisis*. Toronto: McClelland and Stewart, 1980, p. 136.
77 Christopher Beattie, *Minority Men in a Majority Setting: Francophones in the Canadian Public Services*. Ottawa: Carleton University Press, 1975, pp. 12-13.
78 Peter Brimelow seems to have been the first observer to identify this problem. See *The Patriot Game*, p. 96.
79 Borins, *Language of the Skies*, p. 221.
80 B&B Commission, *Report*, Vol. 3A, p. 266.
81 *Ibid.*, p. 267.
82 *Ibid.*
83 *Ibid.*
84 *Ibid.*, p. 277.
85 Commissioner of Official Languages, *Annual Report*, 1975, p. 15.
86 Morrisson's findings are cited in Yvan Allaire and Roger Miller, *Canadian Business Response to the Legislation on Francization in the Workplace*. Montreal: C.D. Howe Institute, 1980, p. 18.
87 Source: Testimony of Bill McKnight to the Standing Joint Committee on Official Languages. See the Committee's Minutes for December 12, 1989, p. 7:31.
88 In total, there are seventy-four French Language Units (FLUs) and 561 English Language Units (ELUs) within the Canadian Forces, and 738 'bilingual units' (BLUs) in which communications take place in both official languages. (Source: Department of Defence and Treasury Board, *Letter of Understanding*, p. 18.) The linguistic designation of each unit as an FLU, an ELU or a BLU should, under the Canadian Forces official languages model introduced in 1972 at about the same time the rest of the Public Service was adopting the present language regime of individual post designation, rest entirely upon "functional criteria independent of their geographic location." (Source: *Ibid.*, p. 17-19).

   The creation of many bilingual posts in the officer corps has cut off advancement opportunities for unilingual servicemen and women. In the military, 2,731 supervisory positions are designated bilingual. Only 372 (or forty-two percent) of the officers meet the linguistic requirements for these positions, and even less qualify at the NCM level: 557 or thirty percent. (Source: *Ibid.*, p. 24.)

   Despite this corruption of the original experiment in creating unilingual work units, it is still possible to get a rough idea of how such units would function in the government at large by examining the military more closely.

   For example, consider the job prospects for unilingual francophones. Because some of the units are highly vertically integrated, it is possible for a non-commissioned member of the armed forces to rise to the highest non-commissioned rank (chief warrant officer) without ever learning a word of English. Particularly good advancement opportunities exist in the infantry, armoured division, the artillery, the medical corps and the service battalions. However, it is much more difficult for francophones to build in areas like engineering where technical documents are usually in English only. In these fields, second-language skills for francophones are a must above the rank of sergeant.

   For pilots, the situation is more restrictive yet. Combat and transport pilots must expect to be pressed into service on foreign missions, where the language of the air is universally English.
89 New Brunswick's previous Public Service language rules, which were very similar to the federal model, had been the source of considerable dissatisfaction among public servants and were among the primary causes of the rise of the anti-bilingual Confederation of Regions Party (CoR), which

became the opposition party following the 1991 provincial election. In response to this rising tide of dissatisfaction, the provincial government instituted a new language policy in August 1988.

Unfortunately, New Brunswick's brilliantly conceived approach to language is largely subverted by the fact that the provincial Board of Management and its political masters have insisted on retaining linguistic staffing quotas for the provincial Public Service as a whole. The retention of these quotas means that even after the target teams have been fully established in 1993, the Board of Management will continue to maintain a regime under which twenty-five percent of all posts will be designated "Bilingual Essential," twelve percent "French Essential," and so on. At best, this intrusion from the system of individual post-designations will be an annoyance. At worst, it may render the whole experiment meaningless, by destroying the flexibility of the target teams. In the worst-case scenario, all that would have been changed by the target team approach would be a decentralization of control over the choice of which individual posts to assign to each linguistic designation. This does not destroy the validity of the target team approach, but it means that New Brunswick's results must be examined with caution, and any failings it encounters in practice must be studied to determine if they are the result of the retention of individual post designations or of the new system. Source: New Brunswick Board of Management, *Implementation of the Official Languages Policy: Report*, mimeograph, February 1990.

90 The size of each individual target team and the language skill qualifications needed by each team are established on the basis of seven criteria: 1) the geographical clientele—does the team serve a French or English region? 2) the specific clientele served—for example, target teams serving tourists may perform special linguistic functions not needed to service other clients in the same geographical area; 3) the mandate and organization of the departmental agency or institution in question; 4) the nature of the service provided. How important is it that the language in which the services are provided be top quality? High levels of language skill are needed in such areas as health care, court services, and tax assessments, but not in many other areas; 5) the level of specialization of tasks performed; 6) the number of employees in each office and team. The smaller the team, the less flexible the linguistic designation of each post; 7) the physical location of a team.

This list is taken from New Brunswick Board of Management, *Implementation of the Official Languages Policy*, February 1990, pp. 6-7.

91 Professional Institute of the Public Service of Canada, "PIPSC Calls for a 'Common Sense' Approach to Language in the Public Service." Press release, December 8, 1992, p. 2.

9. LANGUAGE AND EDUCATION

1 A typical incident of flag-burning is described in a Canadian Press story, "French, English Students Scuffle." *Globe and Mail*, March 15, 1990, p. A5.

2 For the extent of Ottawa's involvement in the court challenges process, see Ian Ross Brodie, *Interest Groups and the Charter of Rights*, pp. 91-93. The federal government achieved considerable early success with this strategy. By the end of 1985, 21 out of 22 cases relating to Section 23 had resulted in an extension of minority education rights. See F.L. Morton, "The Political Impact of the Canadian Charter of Rights and Freedoms." *Canadian Journal of Political Science*, Vol. 20, No. 1, March 1987, p. 46.

3 Commissioner of Official Languages, *Annual Report*, 1991. Ottawa: 1992, Minister of Supply and Services, p. 174.

4 A Concordia University survey conducted in early 1993 among Westmount residents found that sixty-six percent favoured mandatory French immersion. Unsigned article, "Westmounters Want Mandatory Immersion," Montreal *Downtowner*, April 7, 1993, p. 1.

5 Even at the CEGEP level, English immersion is not offered openly. Robert Mazerolle writes that it is offered at Collège Brébeuf, for example, in the following manner: "The structure in vogue usually involves students taking upgrade courses while simultaneously struggling along in core courses." Mazerolle's comments are quoted in *The Globe and Mail*'s "Middle Kingdom" section, October 25, 1993, p. A13.

6 It is not possible to make an exact calculation of the dollars channelled into French immersion each year by various levels of government, because of the lack of any central book-keeping. However, some idea of the total cost can be gathered from the fact that New Brunswick, with 18,000 of Canada's 295,000 French-immersion students, claims the *additional* cost of this program to the province (not

counting normal per-student education costs) is in excess of $6.5 million. Sources: Commissioner of Official Languages, *Annual Report 1991*, pp. 172-174; Department of the Secretary of State of Canada and New Brunswick Ministry of Intergovernmental Affairs, *1990-91 Appendices (to the Canada-New Brunswick Agreement on Official Languages in Education)*, Ottawa: mimeograph, p. 16.

One curious result of the total victory of asymmetrical bilingualism in Canadian education is that it may, in the end, benefit anglophones more than francophones by swelling the numbers of anglophones qualified for inclusion in the bilingual elite that has exclusive access to all the best publicly-controlled jobs in the country. In the long run, therefore, it is to be wondered whether this unity policy will not undo another unity incentive of equal or greater importance, destroying the government's ability to overstaff the country's subsidized bureaucrat-gentry class with bilingual francophones.

7   Georges Mathews, *Quiet Resolution*, p. 112.
8   Robert Grace, *The Irish in Quebec*. Quebec City: Institut Québécois de recherche sur la culture, 1993, p. 128.
9   Dion, "Explaining Quebec Nationalism," p. 42.
10 Ibid.
11 Bill 58, introduced May 15, 1986, under the name *An Act Respecting the Eligibility of Certain Children for Instruction in English*.
12 Philip Authier, "It's not our Intention to Ease Bill 101 for Anglo Schools: Pagé." The *Gazette*, Montreal, June 15, 1991, p. A3.
13 Wardhaugh, *Language and Nationhood*, p. 245.
14 The dispute was followed closely in the weekly newspaper *The Native People*, published in Edmonton. See especially the issues of September 2, 1977, September 9, 1977, and September 30, 1977.
15 *Gazette Officielle du Québec*, Part 2. July 11, 1984, Vol. 116, No 29, p. 2675.
16 Ryan's words caused quite a stir. See Mordecai Richler's comments on them in *Oh Canada! Oh Quebec!*, pp. 53-54.
17 B&B Commission, *Report*, Vol. 2, pp. 61-62
18 Leclerc, *Langue et Société*, p. 185. My translation. Italics are in the original.
19 Richler, *Oh Canada! Oh Quebec!* p. 28.
20 Scowen, now a prominent minority-rights activist, writes: "A recent minister of education, Claude Ryan, who speaks excellent English himself, has expressed serious reservations about teaching this second language to French children. He says, 'English is the language of North America. We've long understood that premature exposure to English might not be comparable with the best development of the child.' This approach has astonishing consequences. For instance, the average earnings of a bilingual worker in Quebec are higher than those of someone who speaks only French or English. Incredibly, some claim that this proves discrimination against the unilingual French person and that the government has a responsibility to correct the situation. It is difficult to imagine another place in the developed world where such an attitude to the knowledge of two languages could exist." Reed Scowen, *A Different Vision*, p. 93.
21 Richler, *Oh Canada! Oh Quebec!*, p. 54.
22 B&B Commission, *Report*, Vol. 2, p. 129.
23 See, for example, Peggy Berkowitz, "Protestant school ignores Quebec ban on English." Ottawa *Citizen*, March 18, 1989, p. 3, which describes the illegal teaching of English in a French Protestant school in Val D'Or.
24 Gary Caldwell, "Anglo-Quebec: Demographic Realities and Options for the Future." Richard Bourhis (ed.), *Conflict and Language Planning in Quebec*. Avon, England: Multilingual Matters, 1984, p. 210.
25 The findings of the Parent Report on this issue are summerized in Alison D'Anglejan, "Language Planning in Quebec: An Historical Overview and Future Trends." Richard Bourhis (ed.), *Conflict and Language Planning in Quebec*, pp. 33-34.
26 Porter, *The Vertical Mosaic*, pp. 188-191.
27 Joy, *Languages in Conflict*, p. 42.
28 See Alison D'Anglejan, "Language and Planning in Quebec." Bourhis (ed.), *Conflict and Language Planning in Quebec*, p. 34.
29 In 1987, thirty-five percent of all students in French-language Montreal schools were of non-French-Québécois origin. See Marc Levine, *The Reconquest of Montreal*, p. 142.

30 Ibid., p. 101.
31 Chambers Report, p. 5.
32 Sources: Michel Paillé, "La charte de la langue française et l'école: Bilan et orientations démographiques." Conseil de la langue française (ed.), *L'état de la langue française au Québec: Bilan et Perspective*, Vol. 4. Quebec City: mimeograph, September 1983, p. 26; figures supplied by the Direction Générale de l'enseignement collégial, Ministère de L'Enseignement supérieur et de la Science, Quebec City, in response to a request for information, August 24, 1993. Departmental reference no. 93-71.
33 For reasons that I do not entirely understand, bilingual people seem to feel most comfortable socializing with each other in the language in which they first spoke together. For example, my wife, who is Chinese, always speaks English to one of her Chinese friends whom she met years ago at university, because she first socialized with her in English. With other Chinese friends whom she first met in Chinese-language environments, she uses Chinese. It is possible that a similar phenomenon is at work in Quebec's schools.
34 This phenomenon gets very little coverage in either the English-language or French-language media in Quebec. One article giving a specific example (the Ecole Saint-Bruno in Chateauguay) is Jean-Paul Proulx, "Une 'école anglaise' dispense son enseignement en français." *Le Devoir*, March 3, 1988.
35 Christopher Manfredi, *Judicial Power and the Charter*. Toronto: McClelland and Stewart, 1993, pp. 178-179.
36 See Ontario Court of Appeals, *Reference re. Education Act of Ontario and Minority Language Education Rights*, June 26, 1984, p. 32.
37 Bill 3, passed by the Lévesque government in 1984, would have abolished the Protestant/Catholic division of Quebec's school boards and replaced it with a purely English/French division. The bill was appealed by the Quebec Association of Protestant School Boards and struck down within a year.
38 Louise Perkins. Letter to the editor, Sarnia *Observer*, October 10, 1991.
39 Joncas is quoted in Jennifer Lewington, "Poor Marks Push Francophones to Seek Separate School Boards." *Globe and Mail*, February 19, 1992, p. A3.
40 D'Iberville Fortier, comments made before the Standing Joint Committee of Parliament on Official Languages. See the Committee's *Minutes* for November 6, 1991, p. 1:27.
41 See Statistics Canada, *Home Language and Mother Tongue: The Nation* (1991 Census), pp. 10, 11, 55.
42 As measured by home language, 1991 Census. Statistics Canada, *Home Language and Mother Tongue: The Nation*, pp. 55-61.
43 Outside the counties of eastern and north-eastern Ontario and northern New Brunswick that contain sizable francophone populations, there are only 198,000 francophones (as measured by home language) in all of English Canada. By contrast, there are 364,000 persons in these nine provinces who speak Chinese at home, and 171,000 who speak Italian. Sources: Statistics Canada, *Home Language and Mother Tongue: The Nation* (1991 Census); special run of home language data by county from the 1991 census, prepared by Statistics Canada.
44 See George Koch, "Double Standard." *Alberta Report*, February 19, 1990, p. 18.
45 This report is quoted in Vallée and Dufour, "The Bilingual Belt," p. 36.
46 See the text of the decision, especially pp. 351-352.
47 J.C. Charron, Letter to the editor, *Midland Free Press*, May 2, 1990.
48 Ken MacQueen, "Playground Dispute." Ottawa *Citizen*, June 4, 1990.
49 See, for example, the tabular presentation of French-language minority rights on a province-by-province basis (circa 1978) in Fédération des francophones hors Québec, *The Heirs of Lord Durham*, p. 46. For a more legally exact review, see the province-by-province review of education rights on pp. 15-16 of *Re-Education Act (Ont) and Minority Language Rights*. Judgment of Ontario Court of Appeal, June 26, 1984.
50 Fédération des francophones hors Québec, *The Heirs of Lord Durham*, p. 48.
51 The literature on the voucher-based choice system is vast. A good starting point, and source of much of the information cited here, is Joseph and Diane Bast, (eds.), *Rebuilding America's Schools: Vouchers, Credits and Privatization*. Chicago: Heartland Institute, 1992.
52 Sources: *Statistics Canada, Home Language and Mother Tongue: The Nation*. Table 4: "Population by Home Language and Sex, Showing Age Groups, for Canada, Provinces and Territories, 1991—20% Sample Data." To obtain an estimated number of school-age children (age 6-16), I added together the total numbers in the 5-9 and 10-14 age groups, and forty percent of the total numbers in the

FOOTNOTES 291

15-19 age group. Also included are half of all children in these age groups who are recorded as having English and French as multiple mother tongues.
53 These figures are derived from the 1990-91 appendices to the Official Languages in Education agreements signed between Ottawa and each of the provinces and territories. See the fuller discussion in Chapter 10.
54 See Janet Beales, "Survey of Educational Vouchers and Their Budgetary Impact on California," *Policy Insight No. 144*. San Francisco: Reason Foundation, August 1992.
55 Marc Levine, *The Reconquest of Montreal*, p. 64. See also pp. 61, 70-71, 83, 93-96, 101, 138-143.
56 Quoted in Levine, p. 95.
57 *Ibid.*, p. 83.
58 Quebec Department of Education, Task Force on English Education, *Report to the Minister of Education of Quebec* ("Chambers Report"), January 1992, p. 2.
59 The following organizations are cited as having intervened in support of a negative decision: Ontario Public Schools Trustees, Metropolitan Toronto School Board, Ontario English Catholic Teachers' Association, Ontario Secondary School Teachers' Association, Ontario Separate School Trustees' Association, Metropolitan Separate School Board. The following organizations are cited as having intervened in favour of a positive decision: Association des enseignants franco-ontariens, Association française des conseils scolaires de l'Ontario, Conseil francophone de planification scolaire d'Ottawa-Carleton. See Ontario Court of Appeal, *Re Education Act* (Ont) and Minority Language Rights, p. 7.
60 Unsigned article, "French Schooling Rejected by Parent.," *Globe and Mail*, September 5, 1985.

10. THE DOLLARS AND SENSE OF OFFICIAL BILINGUALISM

1 Commissioner of Official Languages, *Annual Report*, 1975, p. 19.
2 Victor Goldbloom, Commissioner of Official Languages. Speech delivered to the Downtown Edmonton Rotary Club, January 30, 1992. The Commissioner's speech writer seems to have made a typographical error, since $654,000,000 / 26,000,000 = $25 per Canadian per annum. The $25 is the annual per-capita cost figure cited in publications of the Commissioner. See, for example, *Some Basic Facts*, Ottawa, 1991, p. 23.
3 Ronald Leitch, (President of the Alliance for the Preservation of English in Canada). Speech delivered to the Northeast Edmonton Rotary Club, April 24, 1992, mimeograph.
4 David Alexander, Letter to the editor, Gananoque *Reporter*, May 24, 1989, p. 5.
5 These figures will be explained later on in the chapter. The $299,076,265 that I have calculated as the total provincial cost of complying with federal language programs consists entirely of provincial expenditures of minority official language education and second-language education. I have subtracted Ottawa's contribution from shared-cost programs, as described in the 1990-91 appendices to the Canada-provincial agreements on education.
6 Commissioner of Official Languages, *Annual Report*, 1991, p. 70.
7 Commissioner of Official Languages, *Annual Report*, 1975, p. 2.
8 Maurice Heroux, *The Office of the Commissioner of Official Languages: A Twenty-Year Chronicle, From 1970 to mid 1989*. Ottawa: Commissioner of Official Languages, 1989, p. 46. This pattern is standard in government of Canada publications. See also (for example) Table 24, "Official Languages Program Costs Within Federal Institutions, 1983-84 to 1991-92" in President of the Treasury Board, *Official Languages in Federal Institutions: Annual Report 1991-92*, February 1993. This table lists each year's costs in constant 1981 dollars, even though the table starts in 1983!
9 Commissioner of Official Languages, *Some Basic Facts*, p. 24.
10 Daniel Latouche, "Betrayal and Indignation on the Canadian Trail: A Reply from Quebec," in Philip Resnick, *Letters to a Québécois Friend*, p. 109.
11 Many observers have commented on the provincial government's underfunding of McGill University. See, for example, William Watson, "Separation and the English of Quebec." John McCallum (ed.), *Survival: Official Language Rights in Canada*. Toronto: C.D. Howe Institute, 1992, p. 116.
12 Dr. Winnifred Potter of Montreal has conducted research on behalf of the Equality Party, which appears to confirm that the Quebec government has adopted a similar practice with regard to federal funding intended for the province's English-language education system. Nor is Quebec the only province to engage in this sort of redirection. As early as 1973, the Commissioner of Official Languages stated in his annual report that he had received fifteen complaints from six provinces

about misallocations of federal funds intended for minority-language education. See the Commissioner's *Annual Report*, 1972-1973, pp. 492-500.

13 The *Annual Report* of the Commissioner of Official Languages divides up total federal expenses considerably differently than I do. He assigns a cost of $331,395,000 to "Internal" costs, by which he means all costs other than transfers of money and than the costs associated with his own office. In order to make his estimate comparable with my own, I have excluded from his total the costs associated with serving the public. It appears that $53,066,000 ought to be subtracted from his total. This figure represents the costs associated with language training and bilingual bonuses for public servants who use their second-language skills to serve the public. Sixty-five percent of all public servants in bilingual-imperative posts are involved in serving the public, so sixty-five percent of the expenditures associated with these two expenses have been subtracted from the Commissioner's $331,395,000 total. Sources: Commissioner of Official Languages, *Annual Report*, 1991, pp. 32, 170; Standing Joint Committee of Parliament on Official Languages, *Minutes*, February 12, 1985, p. 2:21.

14 The cost estimate for translations is one of the most accurate in the Commissioner's *Annual Report*. It is listed as "Secretary of State: Official Languages Service." See p. 170 in the 1991 *Annual Report*.

15 The dollar figure for salary costs of public servants attending language training during working hours was arrived at by multiplying the total number of man-hours of language training in 1990 (1,395,696 hours) by the percentage of these hours that take place at government expense during regular working hours (sixty percent). This figure was multiplied by $20, which I assumed to be the average hourly compensation of public servants who are on language training (the actual figure is almost certainly higher). Sources: Public Service Commission, *Staffing Support Information*, Ottawa, 1990, p. 86. (total man-hours); testimony of Myer Belkin, Director, Policy Division, Treasury Board Secretariat before the Standing Joint Committee of Parliament on Official Languages. See the Committee's minutes for February 12, 1985, p. 2:25 (percentage of training that takes place on government time).

16 To calculate this figure, I have assumed that all exams require 2.5 hours of employee time. This is based on the fact that there are three types of exam, and most employees must sit for all three of them before receiving a complete second-language-ability designation. Written exams and comprehension exams require one hour each, and oral interaction exams require 30-45 minutes. To be conservative, I have not taken into account preparation time or travel time to exam sites, which might or might not be considered paid time, depending on the individual circumstances of the public servant in question. I have assumed that each public servant receives $20 per hour in compensation (pay and other benefits), and multiplied the total by the minimum number of people likely to have taken the exams: 7,658, since this is the number of persons that the Public Service Commission reports as being on language training. See Public Service Commission, *Annual Report 1991: Statistics*, p. 73. Information on the time use of language examinations was provided over the telephone by sources at the Public Service Commission.

17 Donald Savoie, *The Politics of Public Spending in Canada*. Toronto: University of Toronto Press, 1990, p. 228.

18 To see how these costs have been applied to American affirmative action regulations, see Peter Brimelow and Leslie Spencer, "When Quotas Replace Merit, Everybody Suffers." *Forbes*, February 15, 1993, p. 90.

19 Auditor General, Report to the House of Commons: Fiscal Year Ended 31 March 1983. Ottawa: Minister of Supply and Services, 1983, p. 195.

20 The correspondence regarding this complaint is as follows: Letter from Denis Mercier (office of the Commissioner of Official Languages) to Raymonde Gour-Tanguay (Official Languages Division, Department of Energy, Mines and Resources), July 29, 1986; letter from Raymonde Gour-Tanguay to Dennis Orchard (Director General, Communications Division, Department of Energy, Mines and Resources, August 5, 1986); letter from Dennis Orchard to Raymonde Gour-Tanguay, August 12, 1986; letter from Raymonde Gour-Tanguay to Denis Mercier, August 14, 1986. Commissioner of Official Languages' file no. AD3430-3. All quotes are my translations from the French. Italics are mine.

21 The correspondence regarding this complaint is as follows: Letter from Raymonde Gour-Tanguay to L.D. Smith (Assistant Director, Property Planning and Management Division), August 27, 1986; letter from L.D. Smith to Raymonde Gour-Tanguay, September 8, 1986. File no. 6360-01/41. Quotation is from Gour-Tanguay's letter.

FOOTNOTES

22 Treasury Board of Canada, *Chairing Meetings: How to Make Your Meetings a Success in Both Official Languages*. Ottawa: Communications Division, Treasury Board of Canada, January 1988. This manual, which at first appears to be simply a helpful guide, is given semi-official status as a regulatory document by Department of Finance and Treasury Board of Canada joint circular no. 1988-36 (P). See, in particular, Appendix II in the guide, which states the rules in such a form that extensive translation facilities clearly cannot be avoided.

23 Public Service Commission, *Staffing Support Information*. Ottawa: mimeograph, April 1990, pp. 80-81. Italics are mine. The document is one of four which together comprise the Public Service Commission's *Staffing Manual*.

24 Letter from Richard Gauvin to 'Ken,' May 8, 1992. No file number indicated on the letter.

25 Public Service Commission of Canada, *Annual Report: Statistics, 1991*. The relevant tables are on pp. 18-66. As well, periodic reports are issued by the PSC and the Treasury Board, which report on very detailed investigations into the state of official languages hiring and promotion in each region of the country. See, for example, Public Service Commission of Canada and Treasury Board of Canada Secretariat, *Participation of Official Language Minorities in the Federal Public Service in New Brunswick, Northern and Eastern Ontario, and the Bilingual Regions of Quebec*. Ottawa: mimeograph, February 1983; Commissioner of Official Languages, *Report Submitted to the Governor in Council (Anglophone Participation in the Federal Public Service in Quebec)*. Ottawa: mimeograph, January 1987; Commissioner of Official Languages, *Special Report to Parliament Pursuant to Section 67 of the Official Languages Act, on the Tabling of Draft Regulations and in Particular of Regulations on Communications with and Services to the Public*. Ottawa: mimeograph, October 1990.

26 Ten years later, the Francobank affair was still being brought up as an example of systemic discrimination by opponents of official bilingualism. Ron Leitch, for example, mentions it in his April 24, 1992 speech in Edmonton.

27 Sources used for this table which are not cited in the preceding text are:
   - Auditor General, Report to the House of Commons: Fiscal Year Ended 31 March 1985. Ottawa: Minister of Supply and Services, 1985. (The Public Service Commission does not break down its regulatory activities by function, so this report gives a more accurate estimate than is available from the PSC itself. The report states that in 1985, the PSC spent $6 million on "Management Category Programs," $40 million on "Non-management Category Staffing Programs," $2.3 million on audits and $4.3 million on appeals and investigations. I have asumed that ten percent of this amount, or $5.6 million, was directed towards official languages programs);
   - Official Languages Branch, Treasury Board, *Official Languages Program Costs 1991-1992*. Ottawa: mimeograph, 1993, annex 1, p. 3. (This document lists the cost of official language units within each department, which are totalled and presented in published reports as the entire internal cost of Public Service bilingualism. In fact, this is merely the direct cost of enforcing official languages policy within each department, as the instruction sheet to the departmental auditors responsible for working out these costs makes clear:
      > This item should include expenditures incurred for the *administration of the Official Languages Program*, including activities such as general administration, planning evaluation, policy development, maintenance of OLIS [Official Languages Information System] and other information systems, language testing, coordination of language training and translation.... This section should indicate *only person-years and dollars allocated to the Official Languages unit*.

      It is quite clear that the totals included in this document do not include the direct enforcement costs of the three guardian agencies (Commissioner of Official Languages, Treasury Board Secretariat and Public Service Commission), since only the PSC records any expenses at all in this document, and this total ($199,000) is so small that one has to assume it is the salary cost for exclusively internal monitoring of bilingualism within the PSC itself);
   - Commissioner of Official Languages, *Annual Report*, 1991, pp. 161-163. (These pages provide a breakdown of the activities of each of the branches of the Office of the Commissioner of Official Languages.)

28 "Bilingualism in the Private Sector," in *Language and Society*, Spring, 1991.

29 *Ibid*.

30 The total costs of these programs are listed in Department of Finance, *Public Accounts 1992*, Ottawa: Minister of Supply and Services, 1992, Vol. 2, Part 1, p. 4.15.

31 There is a detailed breakdown of expenditures under this category in *Ibid*. Vol. 2, Part 2, pp. 7.11-7.14. However, this breakdown is by end-user only. It is impossible to tell how, for example, the Conseil scolaire Gerald Ferguson, in Tracadie, New Brunswick, spent the $429,552 awarded it under this program. Some of the money might have gone to language training, or perhaps not.
32 *Ibid.*, Vol. 2, Part 1, pp. 6.13, 7.26.
33 Sources used for this table which are not cited in the preceding text are:
    - Department of Finance, *Public Accounts 1992*, Vol. 2, Part 1, p. 16.10 (grant to Commission of International Jurists and grant to *Institut international de droit d'expression française*);
    - *Ibid.*, Vol. 2, Part 1, p. 28.4 ("payments to Crown Corporations in Accordance with the *Official Languages Act*");
    - Commissioner of Official Languages, *Annual Report*, 1991, pp. 21-22. See also Secretary of State, *Annual Report on Official Languages*, 1991-92, pp. 15, 19 (Program for the Integration of Both Official Languages in the Administration of Justice).
34 Establishing the cost to the federal government cannot be done by direct means, since budgets are not kept for advertising in the minority press. The total of $5.05 million was established by (1) taking the number of lines of federal government advertising in typical issues of *L'Express* (Toronto) and *Le Soleil de Colombie* (Vancouver) and averaging them, then assuming that this average is applicable to all minority newspapers; (2) multiplying the number of lines by the per-line advertising cost for each newspaper (excluding the Montreal *Gazette* and Ottawa's *Le Droit*); (3) multiplying this total, in the case of each newspaper, by the number of issues; (4) adding these totals together. Sources for circulation figures and per line ad rates: Quebec Community Newspaper Association, 'Rate Sheet No. 11,' Ste-Anne-de-Bellevue, Quebec, January 1993; Association de la presse francophone hors Québec, Opérations publicitaires et services de communications, '1993 Rate Card,' Ottawa, 1993. *The Gazette*, *The Suburban*, The Montreal *Monitor*, the Montreal *Downtowner* and *Le Droit* were not counted because they are large-circulation papers with sufficient readership that ads placed in them cannot be regarded as mere subsidies.
35 A typical policy statement in favour of this practice is found in the recommendations of the Standing Joint Committee of Parliament on Official Languages, regarding regulations to be adopted under the 1988 *Official Languages Act*. The Committee argues that:
    > Weekly and monthly minority language newspapers are very important to the vitality of minority language communities that cannot support a local daily newspaper. Their economic survival may depend to a significant degree on a fair distribution of federal commercial advertising expenditures between majority language dailies and themselves.

    (See the Committee's minutes for May 2, 1991, p. 32:5.)

    As a result of the committee's ongoing efforts, many federal departments have now signed promises to place advertisements in the recommended manner. For example, the Department of Communications has issued the following policy statement:
    > The Department does not very often place advertising in the press. When it does so, it ensures that the advertising is placed in newspapers of both official languages. When there is no minority official-language newspaper, the Department publishes its notices in the local newspaper in both official languages.

    (See Department of Communications and Treasury Board, *Letter of Understanding on Official Languages Between the Department of Communications and the Treasury Board*, Ottawa: mimeograph, June 19, 1989, p. 5.)
36 Quoted in Fédération des Francophones hors Québec, *The Heirs of Lord Durham*, pp. 61-62.
37 *L'Express*, Toronto, Vol. 10, No. 2, January 22-28, 1985.
38 See the pamphlet "Your CBC," published by CBC Head Office, January 1992. CBC stereo radio offers considerably less thorough coverage. Only seventy percent of anglophones and seventy-six percent of francophones have access to this service in their own language.
39 The CBC's French-language radio network has ten stations and eighty broadcasters outside Quebec (it has six stations and seventy-two rebroadcasters in Quebec). The English radio network, including both AM and FM stereo services, has three stations and forty broadcasters in Quebec (it has forty stations and 348 rebroadcasters outside of Quebec). The English television network, excluding *Newsworld*, has one station, one affiliated station, and forty rebroadcasters in Quebec. (It has nine stations, twenty-one affiliated stations, and 394 rebroadcasters outside Quebec.) Source: Canadian

Broadcasting Corporation, Communication Services, pamphlet series "Stations and Rebroadcasters," March 1992.
40 This is manifestly not true for the CBC's programming budget. Nearly all of the Corporation's budget for French-language programming is spent in Quebec, and nearly all the budget for English-language programming is spent elsewhere.
41 See Canadian Broadcasting Corporation, *Annual Report 1991-1992*, p. 25. The total annual cost of "distribution activities" was $157,372,000 in the reported year. Arguably, some of this budget could be classified not as a minority service at all, but as an educational tool designed, in the words of the CBC's first general manager, to:

> make the whole of Canada bilingual, to make available to the Canadian citizen of the future, the culture, literature and thought of both parent languages. . . . Broadcasting will work through entertainment, through the schools, through all agents of adult education, to encourage a better mutual understanding, and to spread a desire among all Canadians to speak the two parent languages.

(Gladstone Murray is quoted in Neil Morrison, "Canadian Broadcasting and 'Les Deux Nations.'" Richard Lochead (ed.), *Beyond the Printed Word: The Evolution of Canada's Broadcast News Heritage*, Volume I: Canadian Broadcasting. Kingston, Ontario: Quarry Press, 1991, p. 243.)

If his words are true, it may mean that it is unfair to regard the French-language retransmission facilities in St. John's, Newfoundland or the English facilities at Alma in Quebec's solidly French Lac St-Jean region as being extravagant expenses made solely to benefit microscopic minorities. On the other hand, to judge by the level of cultural understanding and bilingualism in these regions, it has been a pretty dismal failure at this secondary task as well.

Other costs are difficult to calculate. For example, the Canadian Broadcast Corporation devotes $647 million annually to English language services and $402 million to French-language services. (See Canadian Broadcasting Corporation, *Annual Report 1991-1992*, June 30, 1992, p. 25. Figures are for fiscal year 1991 and do not include distribution costs, which are not broken down by language or region.) Much of this expense would be eliminated if the CBC broadcasted in one language only. But it is unimaginable that there would not be French-language radio or television broadcasting in Quebec without the CBC. So in a sense much of the cost of running the CBC in both languages can be attributed to its occupation of a market that would otherwise be occupied by private French-language broadcasters. The real cost of official language policy at the CBC is probably much lower: the cost of retransmitting and of producing local programming in French deep inside the English Canadian heartland, or in English inside the French-Canadian heartland, where private enterprise would not do so.

42 Sources for all information:
- Secretary of State, "Community Radio." An insert from an untitled folder containing program initiatives of the Department of the Secretary of State. Ottawa: no publisher indicated, no date (probably 1990);
- Tom Sloan, "On the Same Wavelength," *Language and Society*, Fall 1993, pp. 4-6.

43 Grant Purves, *Official Bilingualism in Canada*, p. 8
44 The federal government's share of subsidies to La châine was planned to end in 1991. See David Pugliese, "TV Ontario to keep its French network," Ottawa *Citizen*, August 19, 1990, p. A12.
45 The rebroadcast points outside Quebec that had been assigned to TV5 as of December 31, 1990 are listed in *Francophonies*, Vol. 5, No. 1, February 1991, p. 6.
46 "TV Ontario broadcasts two network signals: TVO—English, with French-language programming on Sundays noon to signoff; and *La châine*—French, with English-language programming on Sundays noon to signoff." See *TV Ontario Signal*, Vol. 10, No. 8, April 1, 1992, p. 2.
47 In response to a letter from my research assistant on this question, Daniel Giasson of the Department of Communications wrote, "We have . . . been informed by program officials that the department does not have information on the market value of band widths."
48 Some indication of the cost can be ascertained from the fact that there is a lobby group, l'Alliance des radios communautaires du Canada, which offers, exclusively to French-language radio broadcasters located outside Quebec, services in the process of seeking permits from the CRTC. The organization, which also offers a variety of other start-up services to hors-Québec French broadcasters, has twenty-three member stations, including two in the Northwest Territories and one in Newfoundland.

49 Hubert Guindon, "The Modernization of Quebec and the Legitimacy of the Canadian State." *Canadian Review of Sociology and Anthropology*, Vol. 15, No. 2, 1978, p. 232.
50 *Ibid.*
51 Source: L'Alliance des radios communautaires du Canada, untitled information packet, no date (received by mail from the organization, June 1993).
52 Sources used for this table which are not cited in the preceding text are: Secretary of State, *Official Languages, Annual Report 1991-1992*, p.16 (subsidy to community radio); Department of Finance, *Public Accounts of Canada 1992*, Vol. 2, Part 1, p. 4.16 (subsidy to TV 5).
53 For additional information on these lawsuits, see Commissioner of Official Languages, *Annual Report*, 1991, pp. 64-65, 162.
54 Source used for this table which is not cited in the preceding text:
    • Commissioner of Official Languages, *Annual Report*, 1991, pp. 161-163. (These pages provide a breakdown of the activities of each of the branches of the Office of the Commissioner of Official Languages.)
55 Secretary of State, *Annual Report 1989-90*, p. 10.
56 Commissioner of Official Languages, *Annual Report*, 1991, p. 170.
57 *1990-91 Appendices: New Brunswick*. Ottawa: mimeograph. p. 2.
58 *1990-91 Appendices: Quebec*. Ottawa: mimeograph.
59 *Ibid.*, p. 11.
60 *Ibid.*, p. 12.
61 I have assumed that the teaching of English as a second language would be mandatory in French schools in New Brunswick even in the absence of federally-sponsored official bilingualism. Therefore, I have subtracted the $2.3 million that the New Brunswick government assigns to this category. See *1990-91 Appendices: New Brunswick*, p. 5.
62 I have assumed that the teaching of French as a second language would be mandatory in English schools in New Brunswick even in the absence of federally-sponsored official bilingualism. The only French second-language education expense in New Brunswick which can be regarded as genuinely additional to the expenses that would be incurred under such a system is the $6.5 million for extra classrooms to accommodate French immersion classes. See *Ibid.*, p. 16.
63 In the 1990-91 appendices to the Canada-New Brunswick agreement on official languages in education, the provincial government provides a proof of additional expenditures which includes many costs that seem likely to have been made even in the absence of official bilingualism. In consequence, I have rejected the province's estimate in favour of an item-by-item examination of the expenditures. The only expenditures that seem to me to be genuinely attributable to the policy of official bilingualism are:
    • $12,812,514 for the delivery of certain technical courses in French at three community colleges;
    • $2,207,933 for French-language nurses' diploma training;
    • $476,316 for the Memramcook Institute, which provides continuing education courses to adults in French.
    See *Ibid.*, p. 13.
64 I have assumed that the teaching of English as a second language would be mandatory in French schools in Quebec even in the absence of federally-sponsored Official Bilingualism. Therefore, I have subtracted the $232.7 million that the Quebec government assigns to this category. See *1990-91 Appendices: Quebec*, p. 12.
65 I have assumed that the teaching of French as a second language would be mandatory in English schools in Quebec even in the absence of federally-sponsored Official Bilingualism. This seems to accord with the view of the Quebec government, which assigns this category no costs at all. See *Ibid.*
66 The Quebec government maintains that this figure is $203 million. From this figure I have subtracted the $98.9 million that is claimed as extra expenses relating to running universities in both English and French, and three-quarters of the $41.6 million that the province claims it could save by forcing all students into larger classes with a higher student/teacher ratio, if there were a single French-language system across the province. See *1990-91 Appendices: Quebec*, pp. 7-11.
67 About ten percent of the English-language students in Ontario live in regions of the province where French is a useful job skill, and therefore would probably be part of the educational program even in the absence of any federal measures in favour of FSL classes. For this reason, I have subtracted

FOOTNOTES 297

about ten percent from the $138 million that the Ontario government sets as the additional cost of FSL education. See *1990-91 Appendices: Ontario*, pp. 20, 25, 29, 33.
68 The Ontario government maintains that this figure is $169,654,055. From this figure I have subtracted the following items, which do not seem to be expenses additional to those which would be incurred if French education were available only to persons residing in eastern and north-eastern Ontario:
   • three-quarters of all grant money paid to French-language school boards based on eligible sum (as per *General Legislative Grants*, 141/90), since this portion would presumably have been incurred in heavily francophone areas where French-language education predates federal bilingualism laws. (75% of $29,312,904 = $21,984,678);
   • three-quarters of all grant money paid to French-language instructional units (as per *General Legislative Grants*, 141/90), since this portion would presumably have been incurred in heavily francophone areas where French-language education predates federal bilingualism laws. (75% of $18,888,633 = $14,166,474);
   • costs associated with supplementary programs and administrative expenditures in the Ministry of Education ($3,188,870);
   • regional offices in Ottawa, Sudbury and North Bay ($3,015,456);
   • an annual conference on francophone education ($24,450);
   • costs associated with the province's Curriculum Policy Development Branch ($1,498,626);
   • costs associated with special education for disabled francophone students ($2,737,600);
   • costs associated with assessment and evaluation of schools to see if they conform with Ontario curriculum guidelines ($1,006,600);
   • costs associated with an independent learning centre ($4,323,578);
   • costs associated with professional development for teachers in the French-language system ($216,780);
   • costs incurred in researching assessment and evaluation instruments ($14,979);
   • half the costs associated with additional expenses at Ontario's French-language and bilingual colleges and universities, on the assumption that such expenses would be incurred somewhere in the Canadian university system—probably in Quebec—-if French-language university instruction were not available in Ontario, but that they would, to a large extent, be incurred at larger, more cost-effective schools (50% of $39,978,947 = $19,989,473).
   See *Ibid.*, pp. 6-14.
69 Pierre Arbour, *Québec Inc. et la tentation du dirigisme*. Montreal: L'étincelle editeur, 1993, p. 162.
70 Figures vary considerably from year to year, due to the vagaries of the equalization payment system. The precise percentage for any given year can be established by consulting the federal Department of Finance's records of provincial revenue shortfalls subject to equalization and comparing these numbers to the actual entitlements awarded in that year.
71 See Department of Finance, *Public Accounts 1992*, Vol. 2, Part 1, p. 6.13.
72 Source information regarding "cultural infrastructure": *Ibid.*, Vol. 2, Part 1, p. 4.15, Vol. 2, Part 2, p. 7.8. See also Vol. 2, Part 1, p. 4.16, where it is noted that an additional $12,971,003 was transferred as a "contribution to cultural infrastructure projects in Quebec and Alberta." No further details (even to the extent of a Quebec-Alberta breakdown) are provided. It is entirely possible (although not certain) that some of this money as well finds its way into language-related spending, since some of the money given to other provinces under the "cultural infrastructure" umbrella unquestionably is used in this manner. See, for example, the $308,679 awarded to P.E.I. for use by the *Association des musées acadiens, inc.*, of Mascouche (*Ibid.*, Vol. 2, Part 2, p. 7.8).
73 This amount is a very rough estimate. See my comments in the text above.
74 Department of Finance, *Public Accounts 1992*, Vol. 2, Part 2, pp. 7.92, 7.94.
75 A more complete list of publications is provided in Commissioner of Official Languages, *Annual Report*, 1991, p. 161.
76 See Richard Goreham, *Language Rights and the Court Challenges Program: A Review of its Accomplishments and Impact of its Abolition*. Ottawa: Commissioner of Official Languages, 1993.
77 Celeste McGovern, "Pre-election Pandering to Gays and Feminists." *Alberta Report*, September 13, 1993, p. 9.

78 Source used for this table which is not cited in the preceding text:
    • Commissioner of Official Languages, *Annual Report*, 1991, pp. 161-163. (These pages provide a breakdown of the activities of each of the branches of the Office of the Commissioner of Official Languages).
79 William Niskanen, "The Total Cost of Regulation?" *Regulation*, Summer 1991, p. 25.

CONCLUSION

1 George Grant, *Lament for a Nation: The Defeat of Canadian Nationalism*. Ottawa: Carleton University Press, 1989, p. 76.
2 Hubert Guindon, "The Modernization of Quebec and the Legitimacy of the Canadian State." *Canadian Review of Sociology and Anthropology*, Vol. 15, No. 2, 1978, p. 233.

APPENDIX

1 Milton and Rose Friedman, *Tyranny of the Status Quo*. New York: Avon, 1984, p. 75.
2 President of the Treasury Board, *Official Languages in Federal Institutions: Annual Report 1991-1992*. Ottawa: February 1993, p. 55.
3 Jean Delisle, "Serving Official Bilingualism for Half a Century," in *Language and Society*, Winter 1985, p. 4.
4 Auditor General, *Report to the House of Commons: Fiscal Year Ended 31 March 1991*. Ottawa: Minister of Supply and Services, 1991, pp. 489-490.
5 *Ibid.*, pp. 489-491.
6 Department of National Defence and Treasury Board Secretariat, *Letter of Understanding*, p. 41.
7 For example, recommendation 14, from Volume 3A of the commission's report, reads: "We recommend that the practice, current in many government departments, of translating as a matter of routine all letters and documents written in French cease immediately."
8 One Treasury Board document describes "work instrument" as follows:
    Work instruments include documents such as manuals, circulars, texts, and so on that are required by public servants to perform their duties. These are to be available in both languages only according to the following criteria: the document must be necessary to serve the public or have direct impact on the health and safety of individuals; the document must have a long term utilization requirement; and it must have a wide distribution requirement.
    Treasury Board, *Language Reform in Federal Institutions*, p. 32.
9 Diane Francis, "Megabucks Lost in the Translation," *Financial Post*, March 13, 1991, p. 3.
10 Roch-André Leblanc, "Does it Really Cost 100 Million Dollars to Translate Maintenance Manuals for the Frigates?" *Language and Society*, p. 30.
11 Ronald Leitch, Speech to the Northeast Edmonton Rotary, April 24, 1992. Leitch seems to be the first observer of Canadian language policy to have noted this kind of inconsistency.
12 Minutes of the Standing Joint Committee for Official Languages, December 12, 1989, p. 7:16. According to the Auditor-General's 1991 Report, the average page of translated material contains 300 words. Each word costs 41.6 cents to translate.
13 DND *Letter of Understanding*, p. 41.
14 Ministerial Committee on Official Languages in the Department of National Defence and the Canadian Armed Forces, *Report*, Ottawa, 1992, mimeograph, p. 9.
15 *Ibid.*, p. 13.
16 *Ibid.*, p. 27.
17 Auditor General's Report, 1991, p. 483.
18 It is possible that this is because many nominally bilingual occupants of bilingually-designated posts are not confident of their second language skills. Evidence for this is provided by a passage from Treasury Board Circular 1981-29, p. 38: "Recent studies on the use of translation services indicate that many requests for translations into French were for short administrative texts (less than two pages) written by bilingual incumbents of bilingual positions. This situation clearly indicates that writing capacities in the two official languages are underused."
19 Treasury Board Circular 1981-29, p. 33.

Notes for Figures

1. LANGUAGE AND JUSTICE
1.1 Sources: Canada. Treasury Board. *Impact of Proposed Demographic Rules in Census Metropolitan Areas and Census Subdivisions in the Federal Electoral Districts.* Ottawa: Mimeograph, 1991; Statistics Canada (1991 Census), *Home Language and Mother Tongue: The Nation.*
1.2 Sources: Statistics Canada (1991 Census), *Home Language and Mother Tongue: The Nation*, pp. 12, 13, 28; Statistics Canada (1991 Census), *Knowledge of Languages: The Nation*, pp. 35, 44, 45, 54, 55; K. D. McRae, *Conflict and Compromise: Switzerland*, pp. 55-56.
1.3 Sources: Royal Commission on Bilingualism and Biculturalism, *Report.* Vol. 1, p. 81; Statistics Canada (1991 Census), *Knowledge of Languages: The Nation*, p. 8.

2. LINGUISTIC INTOLERANCE AND DEMOGRAPHIC DECLINE
2.1 Source: Ronald Rudin, *The Forgotten Quebecers: A History of English-Speaking Quebec.* Quebec City: Institut Québécois de recherche sur la culture, 1985, p. 153.
2.2 Sources: Ronald Rudin, *The Forgotten Quebecers: A History of English-Speaking Quebec.* Quebec City: Institut Québécois de recherche sur la culture, 1985, p. 153; Richard Joy, *Languages in Conflict.* Ottawa: self-published, 1967, p. 28; Lionel Albert, William Shaw, *Partition: The Price of Quebec's Independence.* Montreal: Thornhill, 1980, p. 95.

5. ASSIMILATION AND THE FAILURE OF FEDERAL ACTION
5.1 Source: Statistics Canada, (1991 Census of Canada). *Knowledge of Languages: The Nation.* Ottawa: Minister of Industry, Science and Technology, 1992.
5.2 Source: Statistics Canada, (1991 Census of Canada). *Knowledge of Languages: The Nation.* Ottawa: Minister of Industry, Science and Technology, 1992.
5.3 Source: Statistics Canada, (1991 Census of Canada). *Knowledge of Languages: The Nation.* Ottawa: Minister of Industry, Science and Technology, 1992.
5.4 Source: Census of Canada, Various years, 1921 - 1991.
5.5 Sources: Richard Joy, *Languages in Conflict.* Ottawa: self-published, 1967, p. 28; Statistics Canada, Special tabulation of home language data by county for regions of Ontario and Quebec.
5.6 Source: Commissioner of Official Languages, *Annual Report 1991.* Ottawa: Minister of Supply and Services, 1992, pp. 176-177. Figures for Alberta are unavailable for 1970-71, so I have also excluded them for 1991-92. (2,788 students attended French-language classes in Alberta in 1991-92).

6. SPEAKING IN TONGUES
6.1 Sources: Statistics Canada (1991 Census), *Home Language and Mother Tongue: The Nation*, pp. 10, 220, 250; Statistics Canada (1991 Census), *Knowledge of Languages: The Nation*, p. 8.
6.2 Source: Canada. Treasury Board. *Impact of Proposed Demographic Rules in Census Metropolitan Areas and Census Subdivisions in the Federal Electoral Districts.* Ottawa: Mimeograph, 1991.
6.3 Sources: Canada. Treasury Board. *Impact of Proposed Demographic Rules in Census Metropolitan Areas and Census Subdivisions in the Federal Electoral Districts.* Ottawa: Mimeograph, 1991; Statistics Canada, *Population and dwelling Characteristics—Census Divisions and Subdivisions: Manitoba.* Ottawa: Minister of Supply and Services, 1987; Statistics Canada, *Population and Dwelling Characteristics—Census Divisions and Subdivisions: New Brunswick.* Ottawa: Minister of Supply and Services, 1987; Statistics Canada, *Population and Dwelling Characteristics—Census Divisions and Subdivisions: Nova Scotia.* Ottawa: Minister of Supply and Services, 1987; Statistics Canada, *Population and Dwelling*

Characteristics—Census Divisions and Subdivisions: Ontario. Ottawa: Minister of Supply and Services, 1987; Statistics Canada, *Population and Dwelling Characteristics—Census Divisions and Subdivisions: Quebec.* Ottawa: Minister of Supply and Services, 1987; Statistics Canada, *Profile of Census Tracts in Montreal: Part A.* Ottawa: Minister of Industry, Science and Technology, 1993; Statistics Canada, *Profile of Census Tracts in Ottawa: Part A.* Ottawa: Minister of Industry, Science and Technology, 1993; Statistics Canada, *Profile of Census Tracts in Winnipeg: Part A.* Ottawa: Minister of Industry, Science and Technology, 1993.

8. LORD OF THE FILES

8.1 Sources: Professional Institute of the Public Service of Canada. *Survey of Official Languages: Final Report.* Ottawa: Mimeograph, 1991, pp. 84-88; Statistics Canada. *Knowledge of Languages: The Nation.* Ottawa: Ministry of Industry, Science and Technology, 1992.

8.2 Source: Letter from Treasury Board of Canada, June 17, 1993, in response to a request for information under the *Access to Information Act.* Treasury Board file no. 135-9394-0010.

8.3 Source: Royal Commission on Bilingualism and Biculturalism. *Report.* Vol. 3A. Ottawa: Queen's Printer, 1969, p. 266.

9. LANGUAGE AND EDUCATION

9.1 Sources: Michel Paillé, "La Charte de la langue française et l'école: bilan et orientations démographiques," *L'état de la langue française au Québec.* Quebec City: Conseil de la langue française, 1983, p. 26; Government du Québec, Ministère de l'Enseignement Supérieur et du la Science, Direction Générale de l'enseignement collégial, *Systeme d'information réseau collegial par type de formation, famille de programmes, annee du programme d'etudes et sexe.* Quebec City: mimeograph, 1993.

10. THE DOLLARS AND SENSE OF BILINGUALISM

10.1 Source: Maurice Heroux, *The Office of the Commissioner of Official Languages: A Twenty-Year Chronicle, From 1970 to mid 1989.* Ottawa: Commissioner of Official Languages, 1989, p. 46.

10.2 Sources: Commissioner of Official Languages. *Some Basic Facts.* Office of the Commissioner of Official Languages, June 1991, p. 24; Commissioner of Official Languages, *Annual Report.* Various years, 1977-1992.

10.3- Sources: All notes are incorporated into regular footnotes for Chapter 10.
10.9

10.10 Sources: Commissioner of Official Languages. *Annual Report.* Various years, 1977-1992; Secretary of State, Education, Support Programmes Branch, *Discription and Financial Summary of Federal-Provincial Programs for the Official Languages in Education 1970-1971 to 1982-83.* Ottawa: Mimeograph, 1983, p. 36; Leslie A. Pal, *Interests of State: The Politics of Language, Multiculturalism and Feminism in Canada.* Montreal and Kingston: McGill-Queen's University Press, 1993, p. 156; Pierre Arbour, *Québec Inc. et la tentation du dirigisme.* Montreal: L'Etincelle éditeur, 1993.

10.11 Sources: Table 10.10; Canada, Department of Finance, *Public Accounts of Canada.* Various years, 1971-1992. Ottawa: Minister of Supply and Services.

10.12 Source: Table 10.11.

Bibliography

Newspaper/Magazine Articles, Speeches and Transcripts
Alexander, David. Letter to the Editor. *The Reporter*. Gananoque: May 24, 1989, p. 5.
APEC Newsletter. Various issues. Toronto: 1980-1993.
Arpin, Claude. "Newspaper Reflects Diminishing Anglo Numbers." *The Gazette*. Montreal: April 7, 1993, p. A4.
Aubry, Jack. "Numbers Game." *The Citizen*. Ottawa: March 23, 1991. p. B4.
Beaulne, François. "Letter to an English Quebecer." *The Gazette*. Montreal: October 15, 1991.
Berkowitz, Peggy. "Protestant School Ignores Quebec Ban on English." *The Citizen*. Ottawa: March 18, 1989, p. 3.
Bonin, Bernard. "Pendant que d'autres pays étouffent, le Québec fait face à une croissance trop lente." *Le Devoir*. Montreal: September 27, 1974, p. A5.
Brimelow, Peter and Spencer, Leslie. "When Quotas Replace Merit, Everybody Suffers." *Forbes*. New York: February 15, 1993.
Brooks, Janet Rae. "Quebec's Abandoned Confreres." *The Globe and Mail*. Toronto: June 20, 1992, p. D2.
Brunet, Robin. "A Choice at Any Cost." *Alberta Report*. Edmonton: October 7, 1991, pp. 40-41.
Bunner, Paul and Day, Philip. "Halting Bilingualism's Creep." *Alberta Report*. Edmonton: February 22, 1988, p. 13.
Caldwell, Gary. "Anglo-Quebec on the Verge of its History." *Language and Society*. Ottawa: Autumn 1982, p. 5.
Camp, Dalton. "The Plot to Kill Canada." *Saturday Night*. Toronto: June 1991, pp. 12-19, 60-61.
Canadian Press. "French, English Students Scuffle." *The Globe and Mail*. Toronto: March 15, 1990, p. A5.
_____. "Teed-off Residents Sink Bilingual Golf Course Idea." *The Gazette*. Montreal, March 2, 1989, p. A2.
Charron, J.C. Letter to the editor. *Midland Free Press*. May 2, 1990.
Chronicle-Telegraph. Quebec City, April 22, 1992.
Creusot, André. "New Regulations Under Scrutiny." *Language and Society*. Ottawa: Spring 1991, p. 29.
Delisle, Jean. "Serving Official Bilingualism for Half a Century." *Language and Society*. Ottawa: Winter 1985.
Duhaime, Colette. "Privatized Airports: Will They Concern Themselves with Language?" *Language and Society*. Ottawa: Spring 1991.
_____. "Petro-Canada Should Continue to be Subject to the Official Languages Act." *Language and Society*. Ottawa: Spring 1991, p. 31.

Francis, Diane. "Magabucks lost in the translation." *The Financial Post*. Toronto: March 13, 1991.
Garfinkel, Perry. "Madawaska: Down East with a French Accent." *National Geographic*. Washington, D.C.: September, 1980, p. 380.
Galt, George. "Can't Live With Them, Can't Live Without Them." *Saturday Night*. Toronto: June 1991, p. 11.
Goldbloom, Victor. *Speech to the Downtown Rotary Club of Edmonton*. Ottawa: Mimeograph. January 30, 1992.
_____. *Speech to the Chamber of Commerce, Laval, Quebec*. Ottawa: Mimeograph. May 28, 1992.
Guinan, Dorothy. "The Chronicle Telegraph: Quebec City's English Newspaper." *Language and Society*. Ottawa: Fall 1991, p. 32.
Gwyn, Sandra. "Speaking the Unspeakable, Bilingually." *Saturday Night*. Toronto: July-August 1976.
Hébert, Chantal. "Une le épidémie de 'Bilinguité' payante pour les fonctionnaires." *Le Devoir*. Montreal: May 6, 1992, p. A-3.
Henripin, Jacques. "Faut-il tenter d'accroitre la fecondité au Quebec?" *Bulletin de l'association de Démographes au Québec*. Montreal: November 1974, p. 92.
Hill, Bert. "Francophones Groups Want Own Voice." *The Citizen*. Ottawa: January 29, 1992, p. C6.
Immen, Wallace. "Francophones Given Edge in Federal Science Hiring." *The Globe and Mail*. Toronto: March 7, 1981, p. 12.
Jenkinson, Michael. "Ottawa Moves Towards Deregulating Metric Sizes." *Alberta Report*. Edmonton: April 5, 1993, p. 20-21.
Kennedy, Mark. "What Price Bilingualism? Estimates Vary So Widely, There's No Bottom Line." *Citizen*. Ottawa: March 23, 1991, p. B5.
Koch, George. "Double Standard." *Alberta Report*. Edmonton: February 19, 1990, p. 18.
_____. "Come Fly With Fortier." *Alberta Report*. Edmonton: November 5, 1990, p. 18.
Leblanc, Roch-André. "Does it really cost $100 million dollars to translate maintenance manuals for the frigates?" *Language and Society*. Ottawa: Winter 1991.
Leclerc, Jacques. *Langue et Société*. Laval, Quebec: Mondia Editeurs, 1986.
Le Cours, Rudy. "Bourassa: créer des districts bilingues en étendant la loi 101." *Le Devoir*. Montreal: November 29, 1986, p. A2.
Le Soleil de Colombie. Vancouver: September 25, 1992.
Lewington, Jennifer. "Poor Marks Push Francophones to Seek Separate School Boards." *The Globe and Mail*. Toronto: February 19, 1992, p. A3.
L'Express. Toronto. Vol. 10, No. 2, Week of January 22-28, 1985.
MacGregor, Roy. "Commissioner 13 Reports." *The Citizen*. Ottawa: June 20, 1991, p. B1.
MacQueen, Ken. "Playground Dispute." *The Citizen*. Ottawa: June 4, 1990.
Matas, Robert. "Store Owners Forced to Say Au Revoir." *The Globe and Mail*. Toronto: May 7, 1991, p. A5.
Morton, F.L. "The Language Conflict is About Power, Not Poetry." *Alberta Report*. Edmonton: May 15, 1989, p. 16.
The Native People. Edmonton: Issues of September 2, 1977, September 9, 1977, and September 30, 1977.
Nichols, Marjorie. "The Language of Privatization." *Language and Society*. Ottawa: Winter 1987, pp. 5-6.

O'Keefe, Michael. "Inside the Federal Public Service: Languages at Work." *Language and Society*. Ottawa: Summer 1991, p. 25.
Paris, Erna. "Guilt, Anxiety, and Bilingualism in the Civil Service." *Saturday Night*. Toronto. March 1972, p. 18.
Perkins, Louise. Letter to the editor. *The Observer*. Sarnia: October 10, 1991.
Picard, André. "Crees Vow to Seize Land if Quebec Separates." *The Globe and Mail*. Toronto: July 31, 1991, p. A2.
Priest, Gordon. "Aboriginal Languages in Canada." *Language and Society*. Ottawa: Winter 1985, pp. 16-17.
Proulx, Jean-Paul. "Une 'école anglaise' dispense son enseignement en français." *Le Devoir*. Montreal: March 3, 1988.
Pugliese, David. "Union Urges Bilingual Cuts." *The Citizen*. Ottawa: December 9, 1992, p. A6.
Richler, Mordecai. "Gros Mac Attack." *New York Times Magazine*. New York: July 18, 1993, p. 10.
Richler, Mordecai. "Language Problems." *The Atlantic*. Boston: June 1983, pp. 10-24.
Robertson, Gordon. "Principle and the Art of the Possible." *Language and Society*. Ottawa: Summer 1983, p. 13.
Robinson, Jennifer. "Who Speaks for the Anglos?" *The Gazette*. Montreal: August 6, 1988, p. B1.
Robinson, Svend. Letter to Tony Kondaks. June 1, 1989.
Scott, Sarah. "Scrap Bilingual Cereals: Jeanniot." *The Gazette*. Montreal: April 26, 1991, p. A2.
Shulman, Morton. "Bilingual Clerks? Baloney." *The Sun*. Toronto: May 30, 1982, p. 22.
Sloan, Tom. "On the Same Wavelength." *Language and Society*. Ottawa: Fall 1993.
Smith, Doug. "Nationalism: The Modern Janus." (Transcript). *Ideas*. Ottawa: Canadian Broadcasting Corporation, ID 9291. May, 1993.
Thérien, Marc. "Progress in Official Languages at the Federal Level." *Language and Society*. Ottawa: Summer 1989.
Tombs, George. "Franco-Americans Grapple with Assimilation." Montreal *Gazette*, August 13, 1988, p. B5.
Trudeau, Pierre. "Trudeau Speaks Out." *Maclean's*. Toronto: September 28, 1992.
TV Ontario Signal. Vol. 10, No. 8, April 1, 1992, p. 2.
Unsigned article. "Bilingualism in the Private and Voluntary Sector." *Language and Society*. Ottawa: Spring 1991.
Vanagas, Steve. "Redefining Merit." *British Columbia Report*. Vancouver: July 12, 1993, p. 10.
_____. "Ford of Canada Won't Import Capri." *Automotive News*. November 27, 1989.
_____. "French Schooling Rejected by Parents." *Globe and Mail*. Toronto: September 5, 1985.
_____. "Hints of More Francization Ring Business Alarm Bells." *Financial Post*. Toronto: May 7, 1983.
_____. "It's Not Our Aim To Ease Bill 101 for Anglo Schools." *The Gazette*. Montreal: June 15, 1991, pp. A3-A4.
_____. "Three Out of Four Canadians Want Their Children to be Bilingual." *The Gazette*. Montreal: March 26, 1991.
_____. "Westmounters Want Mandatory Immersion." *The Downtowner*. Montreal: April 7, 1993, p. 1.

Unsigned Editorial. "Thanks, But No Thanks, Maz." *The Journal*. Edmonton: March 12, 1993.
Watson, William. "How Would Getty's Bilingualism Work?" *Financial Post*. Toronto: January 16, 1992.
Webster, Norman. "Danger Ahead! Time to Wake Up: Spicer Is Trying to Save Canada's Bilingualism." *The Gazette*. Montreal: July 6, 1991.
Whyte, Kenneth. "Prime Beef." *Saturday Night*. Toronto: October 1991, pp. 70-71, 89-91.

Books and Scholarly Articles
Akow, Marisa. "The Unofficial Official Languages Act." Commissioner of Official Languages. *You Put it in Words*. Ottawa: Minister of Supply and Services, 1986.
Albert, Lionel and William Shaw. *Partition: The Price of Quebec Independence*. Montreal: Thornhill, 1980.
Allaire, Yvan and Roger Miller. *Canadian Business Response to the Legislation on Francization in the Workplace*. Montreal: C.D. Howe Institute, 1980.
Andrew, J.V. *Bilingual Today, French Tomorrow*. Richmond Hill: BMG Publishing, 1977.
Arbour, Pierre. *Québec Inc. et la tentation du dirigisme*. Montreal: L'étincelle éditeur, 1993.
Bast, Joseph and Diane (eds.). *Rebuilding America's Schools: Vouchers, Credits and Privatization*. Chicago: Heartland Institute, 1992.
Bastarache, Michel. "Bilingualism and the Judicial System." Bastarache, Michel (ed.) *Language Rights in Canada*. Montreal: Les éditions Yvan Blais, 1987.
Beales, Janet. *Survey of Educational Vouchers and Their Budgetary Impact on California*. Policy Insight No. 144. San Francisco: Reason Foundation, August 1992.
Beattie, Christopher. *Minority Men in a Majority Setting: Francophones in the Canadian Public Services*. Ottawa: Carleton University Press, 1975.
Bernard, André (ed.). "L'abstentionnisme des électeurs de langue anglaise du Québec." *Le Processus Electoral au Quebec: Les Elections Provinciales de 1970 et 1973*. Montreal: Éditions Hurtubise HMH, 1976.
Bibby, Reginald. *Mosaic Madness: The Poverty and Potential of Life in Canada*. Toronto: Stoddart, 1990.
Bissonette, Lise. "School Restructuration on the Island of Montreal: A Missed Opportunity for the Anglophones." Gary Caldwell and Eric Waddell (eds.) *The English of Quebec: From Majority to Minority Status*. Quebec City: Institut québécois de recherche sur la culture, 1982.
Black, Conrad. *Duplessis*. Toronto: McClelland and Stewart, 1977.
Boissevain, Jeremy. *The Italians of Montreal: Social Adjustment in a Plural Society*. Background Study No. 7 for the Royal Commission on Bilingualism and Biculturalism. Ottawa: Information Canada, 1970.
Borins, Sanford. *The Language of the Skies: The Bilingual Air Traffic Control Conflict in Canada*. Kingston and Montreal: McGill-Queen's University Press, The Institute of Public Administration of Canada, 1983.
Braën, André. "Bilingualism and Legislation." Michel Bastarache (ed.) *Language Rights in Canada*. Montreal: Les éditions Yvon Blais, 1987.
Braid, Don and Sydney Sharp. *Breakup: Why the West Feels Left Out of Canada*. Toronto: Key Porter, 1990.
Brimelow, Peter. *The Patriot Game: Canada and the Canadian Question Revisited*. Stanford: Hoover Institution Press, 1986.
Breton, Raymond. "Institutional Completeness of Ethnic Communities and the Personal Relations of Immigrants." *American Journal of Sociology*, Vol. 70, 1964.

Breton, Raymond and Gail Grant. *La langue de travail au Québec: Synthèse de la recherche sur la rencontre de deux langues.* Montreal: Institute for Research on Public Policy, 1981.
Buckley, Kenneth. "Population and Migration." M.C. Urquhart (ed.), *Historical Statistics of Canada.* Toronto: MacMillan, 1965.
Buckner, P.A. "Rebellions of 1837." *The Canadian Encyclopedia.* Vol. 3. Edmonton: Hurtig Publishers, 1988.
Caldwell, Gary. "Anglo-Quebec: Demographic Realities and Options for the Future." Richard Bourhis (ed.) *Conflict and Language Planning in Quebec.* Avon, England: Multilingual Matters, 1984.
──────────────. "People and Society." Gary Caldwell and Eric Waddell (eds.) *The English of Quebec: From Majority to Minority Status.* Quebec City: Institut québécois de recherche sur la culture, 1982.
Cartwright, Donald. "Accommodation Among the Anglophone Minority in Quebec to Official Language Policy: A Shift in Traditional Patterns of Language Contact." *Journal of Multilingual and Multicultural Development.* Vol. 8, nos. 1 and 2, 1987.
──────────────. *Official-Language Populations in Canada: Patterns and Contacts.* Occasional Paper No. 16, The Institute for Research on Public Policy, July 1980.
Castonguay, Charles. "Pour une politique des districts bilingues au Québec." *The Journal of Canadian Studies.* August 1976.
──────────────. "Why Hide the Facts? The Federalist Approach to the Language Crisis in Canada." *Canadian Public Policy.* Vol. 5, no. 1, Winter 1979, p. 6.
Charbonneau, Hubert and Robert Maheu. *Les aspects démographiques de la question linguistique.* Synthèse réalisée pour le compte de la Commission d'enquête sur la situation de la langue française et sur les droits lingusitiques au Québec. Quebec City: Editeur officiel du Québec, 1973.
Connors, K., N. Ménard, R. Singh. "Testing Linguistic and Functional Competence in Immersion Programs." Michel Paradis (ed.) *Aspects of Bilingualism.* Hornbeam Press, 1978.
Cook, Ramsay. *Canada and the French-Canadian Question.* Toronto: MacMillan, 1967.
Coté, Marcel. "Language and Public Policy." *Survival: Official Language Rights in Canada.* Toronto: C.D. Howe Institute, 1992.
Courchene, Thomas. "Avenues of Adjustment: The Transfer Payment System and Regional Disparities." *Canadian Confederation at the Crossroads.* Vancouver: Fraser Institute, 1978.
Creighton, Donald. *The Empire of the St. Lawrence.* Toronto: Macmillan of Canada, 1956.
Dallaire, Louise and Réjean Lachapelle. *Demolinguistic Profiles: A National Synopsis.* Ottawa: Promotion of Official Languages Branch, Department of the Secretary of State of Canada, 1990.
D'Anglejan, Alison. "Language Planning in Quebec: An Historical Overview and Future Trends." Richard Bourhis (ed.) *Conflict and Language Planning in Quebec.* Avon, England: Multilingual Matters, 1984.
Didier, Emmanuel. "Private Law of Language." Michel Bastarache (ed.) *Language Rights in Canada.* Montreal: Les éditions Yvon Blais, 1987.
Dion, Stéphane. "Explaining Quebec Nationalism." R. Kent Weaver (ed.) *The Collapse of Canada?* Washington: The Brookings Institute, 1992.
Doern, Russell. *The Battle Over Bilingualism: The Manitoba Language Question 1983-85.* Winnipeg: Cambridge Publishers, 1985.
Drolet, Jean-Yves. *Etude des conditions faites aux étudiants anglophones dans des régions du Québec*

ou la population Canadienne-anglaise est peu nombreuse. A working paper prepared for the Royal Commission on Bilingualism and Biculturalism. Ottawa: Mimeograph, 1969.

Dufour, Christian. *A Canadian Challenge: Le Defi Québécois*. Lantzville, British Columbia and Halifax: Oolichan Books and the Institute for Research on Public Policy, 1990.

Dyck, Rand. *Provincial Politics in Canada: Second Edition*. Scarborough: Prentice-Hall Canada Inc., 1991.

Eagles, D. Monroe, James Bickerton, Alain-G Gagnon and Patrick Smith. *The Almanac of Canadian Politics*. Peterborough, Ontario: Broadview Press, 1991.

The Economist Book of Vital World Statistics. London: The Economist Books, 1990.

Epps, Bernard. *The Outlaw of Megantic*. Toronto: McClelland and Stewart, 1973.

Fédération des francophones hors Québec. *The Heirs of Lord Durham: Manifesto of a Vanishing People*. Ottawa: Fédération des Francophones hors Québec, 1978.

Fidler, Richard, ed. *Canada, Adieu: Quebec Debates Its Future*. Lantzville, British Columbia and Halifax: Oolichan Books and the Institute for Public Policy, 1991.

Friedman, Milton and Rose. *Tyranny of the Status Quo*. New York: Avon, 1984.

Foucher, Pierre. "The Right to Receive Public Services in Both Official Languages." Michel Bastarache (ed.). *Language Rights in Canada*. Montreal: Les éditions Yvon Blais, 1987.

George, M.V. *Internal Migration in Canada: Demographic Analyses*. Ottawa: Dominion Bureau of Statistics, 1970.

Gill, Robert. "Federal, Provincial, and Local Language Legislation in Manitoba and the Franco-Manitobans." *American Review of Canadian Studies*. Vol. 12, no. 1, Spring 1982.

_____. "Language Policy in Saskatchewan, Alberta and British Columbia and the Future of French in the West." *American Review of Canadian Studies*. Vol. 12, no. 1, Spring 1982.

_____. "Federal and Provincial Language Policy in Ontario and the Future of the Franco-Ontarians." *American Review of Canadian Studies*. Vol. 13, no. 1, Spring 1983.

Goreham, Richard. *Language Rights and the Court Challenges Program: A Review of its Accomplishments and Impact of its Abolition*. Ottawa: Commissioner of Official Languages, 1993.

Grace, Robert. *The Irish in Quebec*. Quebec City: Institut québécois de recherche sur sur la culture, 1993.

Green, Leslie and Réaume, Denise. "Bilingualism, Territorialism, and Linguistic Justice." *The Newsletter of the Network on the Constitution*. Vol. 1, no. 3, July 1991.

Green, Thomas Hill. "The Senses of Freedom." John Rodman (ed.) *The Political Theory of T.H. Green: Selected Writings*. New York: Appleton-Century-Crofts, 1964.

Guindon, Hubert. "The Modernization of Quebec and the Legitimacy of the Canadian State." *Canadian Review of Sociology and Anthropology*. Vol. 15, no. 2, 1978.

Gwyn, Richard. *The Northern Magus*. Markham, Ontario: Paperjacks, 1980.

Hamelin, Jean and Yves Roby. "L'Evolution économique et sociale du Québec." *Recherches Sociographique*. Vol. 10, 1969.

Hamon, Edouard. *Les Canadiens-Français de la Nouvelle-Angleterre*. Quebec City: Editions N.S. Hardy, 1891.

Henripin, Jacques. "Faut-il tenter d'accroitre la fecondité au Quebec?" *Bulletin de l'association de Démographes au Québec*. Montreal: November 1974.

Heroux, Maurice. *The Office of the Commissioner of Official Languages: A Twenty-Year Chronicle, From 1970 to mid 1989*. Ottawa: Commissioner of Official Languages, 1989.

Horton, Donald. *André Laurendeau: French Canadian Nationalist 1912-1968*. Toronto: Oxford University Press, 1992.

Jacobs, Jane. *The Question of Separatism: Quebec and the Struggle over Sovereignty*. Toronto: Random House, 1980.
Joy, Richard. *Canada's Official Language Minorities*. Montreal: C.D. Howe Institute, 1978.
_____. *Canada's Official Languages: The Progress of Bilingualism*. Toronto: University of Toronto Press, 1992.
_____. *Languages in Conflict*. Toronto: McClelland and Stewart Limited, 1972.
Kalbach, Warren. "Population." *The Canadian Encyclopedia*. Vol. 3. Edmonton: Hurtig Publishers, 1988.
Kernaghan, Kenneth. "Representative Bureaucracy: The Canadian Perspective." *Canadian Public Policy*. Vol. 21, 1978.
Lachapelle, Réjean. *Immigration and the Ethnolinguistic Character of Canada and Quebec*. Study no. 15 for the Language Studies Program of Statistics Canada, 1988.
_____. "Changes in Fertility among Canada's Linguistic Groups." *Canadian Social Trends*. Autumn 1988.
Laponce, J.A. *Languages and Their Territories*. Toronto: University of Toronto Press, 1987.
_____. "The City Centre as Conflictual Space in the Bilingual City: The Case of Montreal." Jean Gottman (ed.), *Center and Periphery: Spatial Variation in Politics*. Beverly Hills: Sage Publications, 1980.
Laporte, Pierre. "Status Language Planning in Quebec: An Historical Overview and Future Trends." Richard Bourhis (ed.) *Conflict and Language Planning in Quebec*. Clevedon, England: Multilingual Matters, 1984.
Lapierre, Laurier. *Federal Intervention Under Section 93 of the BNA Act*. Report submitted to the Royal Commission on Bilingualism and Biculturalism. Ottawa: Mimeograph, May 1966.
Latouche, Daniel. "Betrayal and Indignation on the Canadian Trail: A Reply from Quebec." Philip Resnick. *Letters to a Québécois Friend*. Montreal and Kingston: McGill-Queen's University Press, 1990.
Lavoie, Yolande. "Les mouvements migratoires des canadiens entre leurs pays et les Etats-Unis au XIXé et au XXé siecles: étude quantative." *La population du Québec: études retrospectives*. Boréal Express, Montreal, 1973.
Laxer, James and Laxer, Robert. *The Liberal Ideal of Canada: Pierre Trudeau and the Question of Canadian Survival*. Toronto: Lorimer, 1977.
LeBlanc, Robert. "The Francophone 'Conquest' of New England: Geopolitical Conceptions and Imperial Ambition of French-Canadian Nationalists in the Nineteenth Century." *American Review of Canadian Studies*. 1985, Vol. 15, no. 3.
Lengyel, Catherine and Dominic Watson. *La situation de la langue française en Colombie-Britannique*. Quebec City: Editeur officiel du Québec, 1983.
Levine, Marc V. *The Reconquest of Montreal: Language Policy and Social Change in a Bilingual City*. Philadelphia: Temple University Press, 1990.
Lieberson, S. *Linguistic and Ethnic Segregation in Montreal*. Unpublished Report No. 7 for the Royal Commission on Bilingualism and Biculturalism. Ottawa: Mimeograph, 1967.
Lisée, Jean-François. *In the Eye of the Eagle*. Toronto: 1990, Harper and Collins.
Little, J.I. "Watching the Frontier Disappear: The English-speaking Reaction to French-Canadian Colonization in the Eastern Townships, 1844-90." *Journal of Canadian Studies*. Winter 1980-81.
Mackey, William. "La mortalité des langues et le bilingualisme des peuples." *Anthropologie et Sociétés*. 1983, Vol. 7, no. 3.
MacNaughton, Katherine F.C. *The Development of the Theory and Practice of Education in New Brunswick 1784-1900*. Fredericton, New Brunswick: University of New Brunswick, 1947.

Manfredi, Christopher. *Judicial Power and the Charter.* Toronto: McClelland and Stewart, 1993.
Mathews, Georges. *Quiet Resolution: Quebec's Challenge to Canada.* Toronto: Summerhill, 1990.
_____. *Le choc démographique.* Montreal: Boréal Express, 1984.
McLeod Arnopoulos, Sheila and Dominique Clift. *The English Fact in Quebec.* Montreal: McGill-Queen's University Press, 1980.
McRae, Kenneth D. *Conflict and Compromise in Multilingual Societies Vol. 1:* Switzerland. Waterloo: Wilfrid Laurier University Press. 1983.
_____. *Conflict and Compromise in Multilingual Societies Vol. 2:* Belgium. Waterloo: Wilfrid Laurier University Press. 1986.
_____. "Bilingual Language Districts in Finland and Canada: Adventures in the Transplanting of an Institution." *Canadian Public Policy.* Vol. 4, no. 3, Summer 1978.
McRoberts, Kenneth and Dale Posgate. *Quebec: Social Change and Political Crisis.* Toronto: McClelland and Stewart, 1980.
Mentzel, Peter. "Nationalism." *Humane Studies Review.* Vol. 8, no. 1. Spring 1993.
Migué, Jean-Luc. *Nationalistic Policies in Canada: An Economic Approach.* C.D. Howe Institute.
Miller, R. and I. McKinnon. *Corporate Recruitment Practices,* Montreal: Alliance Quebec, 1982.
Miller, Roger. "The Response of Business Firms." Richard Bourhis (ed.), *Conflict and Language Planning in Quebec.* Avon, England: Multilingual Matters, 1984.
Miller, J.R. "'As a Politician He is a Great Enigma': The Social and Political Ideas of D'Alton McCarthy." *Canadian Historical Review.* Vol. 58, no. 4, 1977.
Millett, David. "The Social Context of Bilingualism in Eastern Ontario." *American Review of Canadian Studies.* Vol. 13, no. 1. Spring 1983.
Milne, David. *The Canadian Constitution: From Patriation to Meech Lake.* Toronto: Lorimer, 1989.
Monière, Denis. *Ideologies in Quebec: The Historical Development.* Toronto: University of Toronto Press, 1981.
Morrison, Neil. "Canadian Broadcasting and 'Les Deux Nations.'" Richard Lochead, (ed.). *Beyond the Printed Word: The Evolution of Canada's Broadcast News Heritage.* Volume I: Canadian Broadcasting. Kingston, Ontario: Quarry Press, 1991.
Morton, F.L. "The Political Impact of the Canadian Charter of Rights and Freedoms." *Canadian Journal of Political Science.* Vol. 20, No. 1, March 1987.
Neatby, H. Blair. *Laurier and a Liberal Quebec.* Ottawa: The Carleton Library, 1973.
_____. "Mackenzie King and French Canada." *Journal of Canadian Studies.* Vol. 11, no.1, February 1976.
Niskanen, William. "The Total Cost of Regulation?" *Regulation.* Washington D.C.:Summer 1991.
Ouellet, Fernand. "Lower Canada." *The Canadian Encyclopaedia,* Vol. 2. Edmonton: Hurtig Publishers, 1988.
Paillé, Michel. "La charte de la langue française et l'école: Bilan et orientations démographiques." Conseil de la langue française (ed.) *L'état de la langue française au Québec: Bilan et Perspective.* Vol. 4. Quebec City: Mimeograph, September 1983.
Pal, Leslie. *Interests of State: The Politics of Language, Multiculturalism and Feminism.* Montreal and Kingston: McGill-Queen's University Press, 1993.
Pelletier, Gérard. "1968: Language Policy and the Mood in Quebec." Axworthy, Thomas and Pierre Trudeau (eds.) *Toward a Just Society: The Trudeau Years.* Toronto: Viking, 1990.

Pinard, Maurice and Richard Hamilton. "The Independence Issue and the Polarization of the Electorate: The 1973 Quebec Election." *Canadian Journal of Political Science*. Vol. 10, no. 2, June 1977.

_____. "The Parti Québécois Comes to Power: An Analysis of the 1976 Election." *Canadian Journal of Political Science*. Vol. 11, no. 4, December 1978.

Porter, John. *The Vertical Mosaic*. Toronto: University of Toronto Press, 1965.

Purves, Grant. *Official Bilingualism in Canada*. Current Issue Review 86-11E. Library of Parliament Research Branch. Ottawa: November 17, 1990.

Radwanski, George. *Trudeau*. Toronto: MacMillan, 1978.

Reid, Scott. *Canada Remapped: How the Partition of Quebec Will Reshape the Nation*. Vancouver: Arsenal Pulp Press, 1992.

Richards, John. "The Case for an Explicit Division of Powers Over Language." John McCallum, Series Editor. *Survival: Official Language Rights in Canada*. Toronto: C.D. Howe Institute, 1992.

Richler, Mordecai. *Oh Canada! Oh Quebec!: Requiem for a Divided Country*. Toronto: Penguin Books, 1992.

Robichaud, Jacques. "Le bilinguisme dans l'administration fédérale du Canada (1969-1982)." *Les cahiers de Droit*. March 1983.

Rudin, Ronald. *The Forgotten Quebecers: A History of English-Speaking Quebec 1759-1980*. Quebec City: Institut québécois de recherche sur sur la culture, 1985.

Savoie, Donald. *The Politics of Public Spending in Canada*. Toronto: University of Toronto Press, 1990.

Sawatsky, John. *Mulroney: The Politics of Ambition*. Toronto: McClelland and Stewart, 1991.

Schull, Jonathan. *Laurier, The First Canadian*. Toronto: Macmillan, 1965.

Scowen, Reed. *A Different Vision: The English in Quebec in the 1990s*. Don Mills: Maxwell Macmillan Canada, 1991.

Sowell, Thomas. *Ethnic America*, New York: Basic Books, 1981.

Steele, Catherine. *Can Bilingualism Work?* Fredericton: New Ireland Press, 1990.

Steele, G.G.E. "Bilingualism in the Canadian Public Service." An address to the National Conference, Civil Service Federation Convention. *Civil Service Review*. Ottawa: Vol. 38, no. 3, August 25, 1965.

Stevenson, Garth. *Unfulfilled Union: Canadian Federalism and National Unity*. Toronto: Gage Publishing Ltd., 1982.

Stigler, George. "The Development of Utility Theory." George Stigler, *Essays in the History of Economics*. Chicago: University of Chicago Press, 1965.

Symons, T.J.B. "Ontario's Quiet Revolution." Burns, R.M. (ed.) *One Country or Two?* Montreal: McGill-Queens, 1971.

Tetley, William. "The English and Language Legislation: A Personal History." Gary Caldwell and Eric Waddell, (eds.) *The English of Quebec: From Majority to Minority Status*. Quebec City: Institut québécois de recherche sur la culture, 1982.

Thomas, Paul. "The Administrative Machine in Canada." Paul Fox and Graham White. *Politics: Canada*. Seventh edition. Toronto: McGraw-Hill Ryerson, 1991.

Thorburn, Hugh. *Politics in New Brunswick*. Toronto: University of Toronto Press, 1961.

Trudeau, Pierre. *Federalism and the French Canadians*. Toronto: Macmillan, 1968.

Trudeau, Pierre. Testimony at preliminary hearing, Royal Commission on Bilingualism and Biculturalism. November 7, 1963. Typed transcript of the hearing. National Archives of Canada, Record Group 33: Royal Commissions. Series 80: Royal Commission on Bilingualism and Biculturalism, Volume 110.

Vaillancourt, François. "English and Anglophones in Quebec: An Economic Perspective." *Survival: Official Language Rights in Canada*. Montreal: C.D. Howe Institute, 1992.
Van Loon, Richard J. and Michael S. Whittington. *The Canadian Political System: Environment, Structure and Process*. 3rd Edition. Toronto: McGraw-Hill Ryerson, 1981.
Veltman, Calvin. "Ethnic Assimilation in Quebec: A Statistical Analysis." *American Journal of Canadian Studies*. Autumn 1975, p. 128.
_____. *L'Avenir du Français aux Etats-Unis*. Quebec City: Conseil de la langue française, 1987.
Wakatsuki, Yasuo. "Japanese Emigration to the United States, 1866-1924." *Perspectives on American History*. Vol. 12, 1979.
Waddell, Eric. "Language, Community and National Identity: Some Reflections on French-English Relations in Canada." Alain-G. Gagnon and James Bickerton, *Canadian Politics: An Introduction to the Discipline*. Peterborough: Broadview Press, 1990.
Wade, Mason. *The French Canadians: 1760-1967*. Toronto: Macmillan, 1968.
_____. "The French Parish and *Survivance* in Nineteenth-Century New England." *The Catholic Historical Review*. Vol. 36, July 1950.
Wardhaugh, Ronald. *Language and Nationhood: The Canadian Experience*. Vancouver: New Star Books, 1983.
Watson, William. "Separation and the English of Quebec." John McCallum, Series Editor, *Survival: Official Language Rights in Canada*. Toronto: C.D. Howe Institute, 1992.
Whitaker, Reginald. "Quebec's Use of the Notwithstanding Clause was Right." Paul Fox and Graham White (eds.). *Politics: Canada*. Seventh Edition. Toronto: McGraw-Hill Ryerson, 1991.
Wilson, V. Seymour. "Language Policy." G. Bruce Doern and V. Seymour Wilson (eds.) *Issues in Canadian Public Policy*. Toronto: Macmillan of Canada, 1974.
Wilson, V. Seymour and Willard Mullins. "Representative Bureaucracy: Linguistic/Ethnic Aspects in Canadian Public Policy." *Canadian Public Administration*, Vol. 21, 1978.
Woolfson, Peter. "Language in Quebec: Legal and Societal Issues." *The American Review of Canadian Studies*. 1983, Vol. 13, no. 2.

Documents

Association de la presse francophone hors Québec, Opérations publicitaires et services de communications, *1993 Rate Card*. Ottawa: 1993.
Bouthillier, Guy. "La bataille pour le français continue et seul un Québec souverain nous permettra de la gagner." Press release issued by Mouvement Québec français, June 2, 1992.
Canada. *A National Understanding: The Official Languages of Canada*. Ottawa: Minister of Supply and Services, 1977.
_____. Auditor General. Report to the House of Commons: Fiscal Year Ended 31 March 1983. Ottawa: Minister of Supply and Services, 1983.
_____. _____. Report to the House of Commons: Fiscal Year Ended 31 March 1985. Ottawa: Minister of Supply and Services, 1985.
_____. Bas-Canada. Chambre d'assemblée. *Les 92 résolutions proposées à la chambre par Bédard*. February 21, 1834. Original document. National Library of Canada. Catalogue no. FC2921.B3.Fol.
_____. Bilingual Districts Advisory Board. *Recommendations of the Bilingual Districts Advisory Board*, Ottawa: Information Canada, March 1971.
_____. _____. *Report*. Ottawa: Information Canada, 1975.

BIBLIOGRAPHY   311

_____. Canada Post Corporation. Media Relations Branch. Mimeographed lists of bilingual post office locations as of December 1992, compiled for internal use by Canada Post. No document title.

_____. Canadian Broadcasting Corporation. *Your CBC*. CBC Head Office, January 1992.

_____. _____. Communication Services. Pamphlet Series, *Stations and Rebroadcasters*, March 1992.

_____. Citizen's Forum on Canada's Future. *Report to the People and Government of Canada*. Ottawa: Minister of Supply and Services, 1991.

_____. Coast Guard. *Memorandum of Understanding on Official Languages Between the Commissioner of the Coast Guard and the Deputy Minister*. Transport Canada. Ottawa: October, 1991.

_____. Commissioner of Official Languages. *Annual Report*. Census of Canada. Various Years, 1971-1991. Ottawa: Minister of Supply and Services.

_____. _____. *Official Languages: Some Basic Facts*. Office of the Commissioner of Official Languages, June 1991.

_____. _____. *Special Report to Parliament Pursuant to Section 67 of the Official Languages Act, on the Tabling of Draft Regulations and in Particular of Regulations on Communications With and Services to the Public*. Ottawa: Mimeograph, October 23, 1990.

_____. _____. *Report Submitted to the Governor in Council (Anglophone Participation in the Federal Public Service in Quebec)*. Ottawa: Mimeograph, January, 1987.

_____. Department of Communications and Treasury Board. *Letter of Understanding on Official Languages Between the Department of Communications and the Treasury Board*, Ottawa: Mimeograph, June 19, 1989.

_____. *Canada Gazette*. "Regulations on Communications with and Services to the Public." Part II, Vol 126, No. 1. January 1, 1992.

_____. Department of Finance. *Public Accounts of Canada*. Various years, 1971-1992. Ottawa: Minister of Supply and Services.

_____. _____. Federal-Provincial Relations Division. *The Equalization Program: Nature and purpose of program, explanation of how payments are calculated, special program characteristics, use of program outputs to calculate indices of fiscal capacity and historical summary of program entitlements, 1957-58 to 1992-93*. Ottawa: Mimeograph, November 1992, p. 17.

_____. _____ and Treasury Board. *Circular 1989-38*(P). Ottawa: Mimeograph, 1989.

_____. Dominion Bureau of Statistics. Census of Canada. Various years, 1871-1971. Ottawa: Queen's Printer.

_____. Dominion Bureau of Statistics. *Statistical Yearbook of Canada* and *Canada Yearbook*. Various years, 1871-1971. Ottawa: Government Printing Bureau, Queen's Printer.

_____. House of Commons Debates, 1890. Comments of D'Alton McCarthy.

_____. _____, April 6, 1966. Comments of Lester Pearson.

_____. _____, November 21, 1975. Comments of René Matte.

_____. _____, July 6, 1988. Comments of Raymond Garneau.

_____. *Impact of Official Languages Regulations on the Federal Electoral Districts*. Section "A". Ottawa: Mimeograph, 1992.

_____.Department of National Defence and Treasury Board Secretariat, Official

Languages Branch. *Letter of Understanding on Official Languages Between National Defence and the Treasury Board*. Ottawa: June 10, 1991.

_____. Public Service Commission. *Annual Report*. Various years, 1979-92. Ottawa: Minister of Supply and Services.

_____. _____. *1991 Annual Report: Statistics*. Ottawa: Minister of Supply and Services, 1992.

_____. _____. *Brief to the Legislative Committee on Bill C-72 on the Status and Use of the Official Languages of Canada*. Ottawa: Mimeograph, April 19, 1988.

_____. _____. *Staffing Support Information*. Ottawa: Mimeograph, April 1990.

_____. _____ and Treasury Board Secretariat. Circular 1975-111. Ottawa: Mimeograph, September 25, 1975.

_____. _____ and _____. Circular 1977-46. Ottawa: Mimeograph, September 1977.

_____. _____ and _____. Circular 1982-6. Ottawa: Mimeograph, January 29, 1982.

_____. _____ and _____. *Participation of Official Language Minorities in the Federal Public Service in New Brunswick, Northern and Eastern Ontario, and the Bilingual Regions of Quebec*. Ottawa: Mimeograph, February 1983.

_____. Royal Commission on Bilingualism and Biculturalism. *Report*. Ottawa: Queen's Printer, 1967-1971. Six volumes.

_____.Royal Commission on Government Organization (Glasscoe Commission) *Report*. Vol. I. Ottawa: Queen's Printer, 1962.

_____. Secretary of State. *Annual Report 1989-90*, p. 10.

_____. _____. "Community Radio." Ottawa: no publisher indicated, no date (probably 1990).

_____. _____. *Official Languages, Annual Report*. Various Years, 1971-1991. Ottawa: Minister of Supply and Services.

_____. _____. *Descriptive and Financial Summary of Federal-Provincial Programmes for the Official Languages in Education 1970-1971 to 1982-1983*. Ottawa: Mimeograph, November 1983.

_____. _____. *Descriptive and Financial Summary of Federal-Provincial Programmes for the Official Languages in Education 1983-1984 to 1987-1988*. Ottawa: Mimeograph, November 1989.

_____. _____ and various provincial ministries of intergovernmental affairs and education, *1990-91 Appendices to the Federal-Provincial/Territorial Agreements on Official Languages in Education*. Ottawa: Mimeograph, 1991.

_____. Standing Joint Committee of Parliament for Official Languages. Committee *Minutes*. February 12, 1985; February 10, 1987; December 12, 1989; December 13, 1990, May 2, 1991; June 11, 1991; and November 6, 1991.

_____. Dominion Bureau of Statistics/Statistics Canada. Various years 1881-1991. Ottawa: Queen's Printer/Ministry of Supply and Services.

_____. _____. (1971 Census of Canada). *Population and Housing Characteristics by Census Tracts: Montreal*. Ottawa: Minister of Industry, Trade and Commerce, October 1974, Catalogue No. 95-733 (CT-3B).

_____. _____. (1981 Census of Canada). *Languages, Ethnic Origin, Religion, Place of Birth, Schooling: Quebec*. Ottawa: Minister of Supply and Services, April 1984, Catalogue No. 93-929.

———. ———. (1986 Census of Canada). *Language Rate Transfer Dimensions*. Ottawa: Minister of Supply and Services, 1989.

———. ———. (1991 Census of Canada). *Home Language and Mother Tongue: The Nation*. Ottawa: Minister of Industry, Sciences and Technology, 1993.

———. ———. (1991 Census of Canada). *Population by Home Language, for Census Metropolitan Areas 1991*, Table 3, *Home Language and Mother Tongue—The Nation*. Ottawa: Minister of Industry, Sciences and Technology, 1993.

———. ———. (1991 Census of Canada). *Population Estimates by First Official Language Spoken, 1991*. Catalogue no. 94-320. Ottawa: Minister of Industry, Sciences and Technology, 1993.

———. ———. (1991 Census of Canada). Special tabulation of home language data for selected counties in New Brunswick, Ontario and Quebec.

———. ———. *The Daily*. September 15, 1992. Catalogue no. 11-001E.

———. ———. *The Daily*. January 12, 1993. Catalogue no. 11-001E.

———. Treasury Board. *Chairing Meetings: How to Make Your Meetings a Success in Both Official Languages*. Ottawa: Communications Division, Treasury Board of Canada, January 1988.

———. ———. Circular 1970-95. Ottawa: Mimeograph, September 14, 1970.

———. ———. Circular 1971-21. Ottawa: Mimeograph, March 9, 1971.

———. ———. Circular 1973-88. Ottawa: Mimeograph, June 30, 1973.

———. ———. *Good Morning . . . Bonjour*. Ottawa: Communications Division, Treasury Board, 1988.

———. ———. *Impact of Official Languages Regulations on the Federal Electoral Districts*. Ottawa: Mimeograph, 1992.

———. ———. *Language Reform in Federal Institutions*. Ottawa: 1979, Mimeograph.

———. ———. Letter dated June 2, 1993 in response to a request made under the *Access to Information Act*. Treasury Board file no: 135-9394-0010.

———. ———. Letter dated June 17, 1993 in response to a request for information under the *Access to Information Act*. Treasury Board File No: 135-9394-0014.

———. ———. *Official Languages Annual Report, 1990-1991*. Ottawa: Minister of Supply and Services, 1991.

———. ———. Official Languages Branch. *Anglophones and Francophones in the Scientific and Professional Categories of the Public Service of Canada*. Ottawa: Mimeograph, December 1991.

———. ———. ———. *Information session for the Preparation of Letters of Understanding on Official Languages*, Ottawa: Mimeograph, 1989.

———. ———. ———. *Regulations on Services to the Public: a Description of the Treasury Board Secretariat's Preferred Approach*. Ottawa: Mimeograph, October 2, 1987.

———. ———. ———. *Official Languages Program Costs 1991-1992*. Ottawa: Mimeograph, 1993.

———. ———. ———. *The Use of Both Official Languages in the Bilingual Regions of the Federal Public Service*. Ottawa: Treasury Board, 1980.

_____._____._____. *Official Languages in the Public Service of Canada: A Statement of Selected Policy Changes.* Ottawa: Mimeograph, December 1991.

_____._____._____. *Official Languages in Federal Institutions: Annual Report 1990-91*, Ottawa: Communications and Coordination Directorate, Treasury Board of Canada, 1991.

_____._____._____. *Why So Many Rules?* Mimeographed document included in a package of materials sent to all Members of Parliament. November 8, 1990.

_____._____. "Revised Policies." Ottawa: Mimeograph, 1977.

_____._____. *Survey on the Use of Both Official Languages.* Ottawa: Mimeograph, 1987.

_____._____ and Department of National Defence. *Letter of Understanding on Official Language between Department of National Defence and the Treasury Board.* Ottawa: Mimeograph, June 10, 1991.

_____. Task Force on National Unity. *A Future Together: Observations and Recommendations.* Ottawa: Minister of Supply and Services, January 1979.

Federation of Canadian Municipalities. *At Your Service . . . in Both Official Languages: A Guide to the Delivery of Municipal Services in English and French.* Ottawa: Federation of Canadian Municipalities, 1987.

Francophonies. Vol. 5, No. 1, February, 1991, p. 6.

L'Alliance des radios communautaires du Canada, untitled information packet. Ottawa: Undated, probably 1992 or 1993.

New Brunswick. *Implementation of the Official Languages Policy: Report.* Fredericton, New Brunswick: New Brunswick Board of Management, February, 1990.

Ontario. Ministry of Citizenship, *Mother Tongue Atlas of Metropolitan Toronto. Vol. 3.* Toronto: 1990.

Professional Institute of the Public Service of Canada. *PIPSC Calls for a 'Common Sense' Approach to Language in the Public Service.* Ottawa: Press release, December 8, 1992.

_____. *Survey of Official Languages: Final Report.* Ottawa: Mimeograph, 1991.

Québec Conseil de la langue française, *Indicateurs de la situation linguistique au Québec.* Quebec City: Conseil de la langue française, April 1991.

_____. Department of Education, Task Force on English Education, *Report to the Minister of Education of Quebec.* ("Chambers Report"). Quebec City: Mimeograph, January 1992.

_____. Directeur-général des élections du Québec. *Rapport des résultats officials du scrutin: Référendum du 20 mai 1980.* Quebec City: Editeur officiel du Québec, 1980.

_____._____. *Rapport des résultats officiels du scrutin du 13 avril 1981.* Quebec City: Editeur officiel du Québec, 1981.

_____._____. *Rapport des résultats officiels du scrutin de 25 septembre 1989.* Quebec City: Editeur officiel du Québec, 1990.

_____. Ministère des Finances, *Comptes publiques 1991-1992.* Quebec City: Ministère des finances, December 1992.

_____. Commission of Inquiry on the Position of the French Language and on Language Rights in Quebec. (Gendron Commission). *Report.* Quebec City, 1972.

Quebec Community Newspaper Association, *Rate Sheet #11.* Ste-Anne-de-Bellevue, Quebec: January 1993.

Index

1837 rebellion 45

Acadia 48, 50, 120-121
Acadian 122
Acadians 51-52, 68
Access to Information Act 129, 231
'Aibodeni' 89
Air Canada 157-159, 161, 168, 240
Akow, Marisa 132
Alberta 32, 79, 110, 117
Alberta Act 203
Allaire, Yvan 83
Alliance for the Preservation of English in Canada 222
Alliance Quebec 153, 227
American Revolution 110
An Act to Amend the Education Department Act 59
An Act to Promote the French Language in Quebec 59
Anceaux, J.C. 89
Arbour, Pierre 244
Argenteuil 87
Arnopoulos, Sheila McLeod 40
Assemblée Nationale 77
assimilation 84, 104
asymmetrical bilingualism 16-17, 27, 35-37, 64-65, 78-79, 133
Auditor-General 255
Austrian Empire 97
Aylmer 105

B&B Commission 27, 33-34, 131-132, 135, 147, 179-180, 182-183, 194-197, 206, 256, 258
Baffin Island 128
Bagotville 257
Bastarache, Michel 141
Belgium 24
Bennett, R.B. 73, 130
Bertrand, Jean-Jacques 59

bilingual districts 131-132, 135-136, 146-148
Bilingual Districts Advisory Board 133-135, 152
'bilingual-essential' 176
'bilingual regions' 106
Bill 101 56, 58-61, 70-71, 75, 77, 94, 99, 114, 116, 152, 154, 165-167, 200, 203-207, 211, 243
Bill 178 71-72
Bill 22 60, 69-70, 75, 207
Bill 63 59
Bill 85 59
Bill 86 207
Bill C-72 78, 187
Bloc Québécois 35
Boissevian, Jeremy 93
Book Publishing Industry Development Program 235
Borden, Robert 73
Borins, Sanford 192
Bouchard, Lucien 35
Bourassa, Robert 32, 69, 71, 75, 77, 79, 81, 133, 152, 202, 206
Braid, Don 32
Breton, Raymond 121
Brimelow, Peter 28, 63, 157
Britain 40, 96
British Columbia 91, 129, 141, 143, 171, 201, 219, 237
British North America Act 51
Brittany 97
Broderick, Ann 117
Buckner, Philip 46
'Bucks for Babies' 61
Butler, Edith 33

Caisse de dépot et placement 244
Caldwell, Gary 59
Calgary 108, 128, 144, 156, 213
Calgary *Herald* 32

California 216
Campbell, Kim 245
Canada Council 235-236
Canada Film Development Corporation 235-236
Canada Post 139, 145, 157, 178, 237
Canadian Armed Forces 195
Canadian Bill of Rights 140
Canadian Broadcasting Corporation 116, 157, 166, 237-239
Canadian Charter of Rights and Freedoms 64, 71, 129, 135, 211, 224
Canadian National Railways 160, 168
Canadian Radio-Television and Telecommunications Commission 237-239
Canadian Union of Postal Workers 139
Cape Breton Island 108
Cape Spear 168
Caraquet 52
Caraquet riots 199
Cartier, Georges-Etienne 72
Castonguay, Charles 130, 142
Catholics 50-52
Cauceseau, Nicolae 86
CEGEP 209
Center for the Study of American Business 229, 240
Charest, Jean 117
Charlottetown Accord 65, 70, 214
Charter of Rights and Freedoms 76, 138, 141, 152, 200, 207, 214, 241
Charter of the French Language 60
Cheticamp 219
Chrétien, Jean 185
Chronicle-Telegraph 118, 160
Clift, Dominique 40, 74
Cloutier, Sylvain 139
College d'enseignement général et professionel 208
Commission de surveillance et des enquêtes 61
Commission of Inquiry on the Position of the French Language 208
Commissioner of Federal Judicial Affairs 235-236
Commissioner of Official Languages 64, 66, 102-103, 158, 176, 194, 212, 222-224, 226, 228, 231, 233-234, 240, 245-246
Common Schools Act 51, 199
Communications, Department of 239
Compton County 117
Conquest, the 41
Constitutional Act of 1791 43
Consumer and Corporate Affairs, Department of 162, 165
Consumer Packaging and Labelling Act 161, 163-165, 240
'contact regions' 106
Cook, Ramsay 32
Corporation des enseignants du Québec 218
Courchene, Thomas 167
Court Challenges Program 246
Criminal Code 141

Danish 92
Delisle, Jean 255
Depression, the 121
Didier, Emmanuel 155
Dion, Léon 191
Dion, Stéphane 36, 57, 203
direct costs 230
Director General of Official Languages 233
'Distinct Society' 58
Drury, Bud 185
Dufour, Christian 64
Duplessis, Maurice 32, 69, 73

Eastern Townships 43, 49-50, 53, 101, 113, 202, 216
Elliott, Grace 117
Employment and Immigration, Department of 236
Energy, Mines and Resources, Department of 231
Equality Party 37, 71
Esquimalt 214
Ethier-Blais, Jean 33

Fallon, Michael Francis 53
Fédération des francophones hors Québec 65, 138, 214
Ferguson, Howard 55

Finland 92, 131-132, 147-148, 152
First World War 97
Fortier, D'Iberville 212
Fox, James 257
France 96-97
Francis, Diane 256-257
Franco-Americans 121
Franco-Ontarians 68, 201
Fredericton 157
French Language Services Act 79
Friedman, Milton 254-255
Frobisher Bay 128
Frost, Stanley 218

Gaelic 95
Galt, George 31
Garneau, Raymond 138
Gaspé Peninsula 87-88, 95, 101, 216
Gauthier, Jean-Robert 178
Gellner, Ernest 19
German Empire 97
Glasscoe Report on Government Organization 188
Gloucester county 98
Goldbloom, Victor 102, 222, 226
Gravelbourg 84
Green, Leslie 31
Grisons 95
Guindon, Hubert 104, 239
Gulf of St. Lawrence 107
Gwyn, Sandra 184-185

Halifax 153, 159
Hamon, Edouard 48, 120
Hawkesbury 107
heartland 103-109, 113-114, 116, 118, 120-122, 126
Henripin, Jacques 61
HMCS Algonquin 195
HMCS Skeena 195
Hockin, Horatio 37
Home schooling 217
Hopper, William 158
House of Commons 74
Hull 91
Hungary 97
Huntingdon 113
Hutterites 90

Iceland 92
indirect costs 230
Irish Free State 95

James Bay Agreement 204
Japan 111
Jeanniot, Pierre 161
Jolicoeur, Gérard 111
Joncas, Laurent 212
Joy, Richard 47, 91, 96, 100, 152
justice 17-18, 20

Kernaghan, Kenneth 170
King Victor Emmanuel 48
King, Mackenzie 73, 82, 119
Klondike 168
Kondaks, Tony 37

l'Alliance des radios communautaires du Canada 239
L'Evangeline 32
L'Express 238
La châine 239
La Liberté et le Patriote 117
Lac St-Jean 140
Lachute Watchman 118
Lang, Andrew 102
language 18
Language and Society 160, 255-256
language frontier 22
Language rights 21
Lapointe, Ernest 73
Laponce, Jean 18, 85, 88, 92, 97, 189
Latin 89, 93
Latouche, Daniel 227
Laurendeau, André 33
Laurier, Wilfrid 47, 56
Lavoie, Daniel 33
Le Canadien 43
Le Droit 53
Le Progrès 118
Leclerc, Jacques 19, 35, 86, 92, 97, 205
Leitch, Ron 222
Lesage, Jean 182
'Letters of Understanding' 178
Lévesque, René 61, 76, 78, 152, 184
Levine, Marc 218
Library of Parliament 157

Lower Canada 42, 47, 53
Lower Canada rebellion 46

MacGregor, Roy 161
Mackenzie, William Lyon 46
Madawaska county 98, 114
Madawaska Valley 122
Mahé decision 213
Maillardville 91
Maillet, Antonine 33
Maine 106, 120, 122
Malaysia 230
Manitoba 26, 55-56, 68, 72, 78, 92, 109-113, 133, 142, 201, 214
Manitoba Act 55
Martin, Margaret 157
Massachusetts 48
Mathews, Georges 33, 71, 80, 202
McCarthy, D'Alton 55
McConnell, J.W. 69
McGill University 87, 227, 242
McLeod-Arnopoulos, Sheila 74
Meech Lake Accord 58, 65, 78, 80-81, 214
Mentzel, Peter 96
micro-vouchers 217
Midland 213
Miller, Roger 166
Milwaukee 215
Montreal 26, 42, 45, 48, 59-60, 71, 74, 87, 93, 101, 105, 107, 113-114, 116-119, 122-123, 131, 142-143, 148-149, 165, 191, 202, 210, 216, 218-219, 235
Montreal *Gazette* 102, 113, 166
Morrisson, Robert N. 195
Morton, F.L. 20
Mullins, Willard 171
Mulroney, Brian 64, 78, 81-82, 126, 141

Nanaimo 94
National Capital Region 185
National Civil Service Federation 188
National Defence, Department of 232, 256-257
negative obligation 20-21
negative rights 20

Neilson, John 44
Neilson-Papineau coalition 44
Nepean 94
Network on the Constitution 31
New Brunswick 32, 50-51, 67-68, 72, 79, 98, 101, 106-108, 110, 112-114, 120, 122-123, 133-134, 141-143, 156, 171, 193-194, 196, 199, 203, 213-214, 216, 241, 243
New England 48, 119-122
New Guinea 89
New Hampshire 48, 120
New York City 215
New York *Commercial Advertiser* 119
New York State 114, 165
Newfoundland 107, 111, 133, 140, 201, 219, 239
Niagara Falls 90
Nichols, Marjorie 158
Noce, Vincent Della 188
Northwest Territories 55, 204, 236, 239
Northwest Territories Act 32, 55
Norweigan 92
Nova Scotia 92, 110-111, 114, 237

Occitan 87
Office de la langue française 59
Official Bilingualism 33, 100, 161
Official Languages Act 60, 75, 78, 100-102, 110, 122-123, 129, 132, 135-136, 140-142, 147, 158, 160, 182, 187, 195, 235
Official Languages Information System 234
Old Slavonic 89
Ontario 48, 52-56, 68, 72, 79, 98, 101, 106-110, 122, 142-143, 191, 193-194, 213-214, 216, 223, 243
Ontario Court of Appeals 219
opportunity costs 230
Orange Lodge 53
Orleans 105
Ottawa 94, 105, 114, 148-149, 191-192
Ottawa River 108
Ottoman Empire 97

'padlock law' 73

'polarization' 100
Pagé, Michel 204
Papal States 48
Papineau, Jacques 62
Papineau, Louis-Joseph 44
Parent Commission on Education 208
Parent Report 208
Parizeau, Jacques 77, 206
Parti Canadien 44
Parti Québécois 60, 70-71, 75, 77, 133, 167, 186, 202
Patriotes 46
Peace River 108
Pearson, Lester 33-34, 174, 180-182
Pearson, Richard 165
Pelletier, Gérard 184
Péquistes 191
Personality 24
personality principle 16, 22, 26
Pessamessa, Péire 87
Petro-Canada 157-158
Pointe-Claire 165
Poland 97
polarization 102
Pontiac County 106, 113
positive obligation 20-21
positive rights 20
potential demand 136
Prince Edward Island 26, 50-51, 88, 110-111, 203
Professional Institute of Public Service of Canada 175, 197
Promotion of Official Languages 235
Public Schools Act 51
Public Service 169-171, 174-184, 186-192, 194-198, 200, 227-234, 245
Public Service Commission 174, 180, 186, 188, 232-234
Public Service Employment Act 180-181

Quebec City 42, 45, 48, 113-114, 118-119, 128, 137, 141, 144, 155, 160, 216
'Quebec Clause' 207
Québécois 32, 58-59, 65, 69, 72, 75, 102, 107, 134, 148, 170, 191, 198-199, 239

Queen's Printer 74
Quiet Revolution 32, 42, 57-58, 69

Réaume, Denise 31
Red Enseign 74
Reform Party 78
Regina v. Allain 142
Regina v. Belleau 142
Regional Municipality of Ottawa-Carleton 212
Regulation 17 53, 55, 57, 68, 73, 98, 200
Report of the Royal Commission on Bilingualism and Biculturalism 89
Revenge of the Cradles, the 42, 46
Revenue Canada 144
Rhode Island 120
Richler, Mordecai 144-145, 206
Riel, Louis 73
Robertson, Gordon 190
Robin and Company, Charles 95
Robinson, Svend 37
Romania 86
Romansch 95
Roosevelt, Franklin 119
Roy, Gabrielle 33, 119
Royal 22nd Regiment 195
Royal Canadian Mounted Police 241
Royal Commission on Bilingualism and Biculturalism 27, 30, 93, 103, 130, 153, 192, 258
Russian Empire 97
Ryan, Claude 205

Saguenay 129
Saguenay-Lac St Jean 239
Salmo 165
Saskatchewan 32, 109, 114, 117, 119, 133, 139-140
Sault Ste. Marie 213
Sauvé, Jeanne 119
Savoie, Donald 229
Schreyer, Edward 56
Scotti, Ciro Paul 71
Scowen, Reed 71, 206
Second World War 98
Secretariat permanent des peuples francophones 32

Secretary of State, Department of 235, 237, 241
Section 23 211-212, 214
Sellar, Robert 113
'Settlement Languages Program' 236
Sharpe, Sydney 32
Sherbrooke 48-49, 91
Shulman, Morton 156
Sifton, Clifford 203
Singapore 26, 230
South Africa 25-26
Sovereignty-Association 58, 69, 167
Sowell, Thomas 86
Spicer, Keith 28, 66, 78, 194, 224, 226
St-Laurent, Louis 73, 117
St-Leonard 59
Standing Joint Committee on Official Languages 139, 158, 178, 245, 257
Supply and Services, Department of 256
Supreme Court of Canada 246
Swedish 92
Switzerland 24, 26, 230

Taché, E.P. 63
tanstead 49
Tardivel, Jules-Paul 49
territorial bilingualism 16, 27, 33, 146
territorial principle 22
territorialism 15, 27, 30, 32
territoriality 24
Toronto 84, 117, 128, 134, 137, 144-145, 150-152, 168, 213, 237, 239
Toronto International Airport 156-157
'transition zones' 106
Translation Bureau 255-256, 258-259
Transport Canada 157
Transportation, Department of 157

Treasury Board 136, 178-179, 183-185, 187, 224, 231-234, 255-257, 259
Trudeau, Pierre 26, 28-30, 33, 58, 63-64, 72, 74-76, 78-79, 82, 100, 117, 130, 132-133, 135-136, 146, 154, 167, 182-184, 250
Tupper, Charles 72
TV Ontario 238
TV5 238

Union Bill 44
Union Nationale 60, 69
United States 49, 120, 220
Unity Party 71
Upper Canada 47

Vancouver 108, 144, 150-152, 159, 213
Vawn 139
Vermont 114, 165, 215
VIA Rail 240
Victoria 157
vouchers 215-217, 219-221

Wakatsuki, Yasuo 111
Wales 97
Welland 90
Whitaker, Reginald 36
Wilson, Seymour 171
Windsor 110
Winnipeg 78, 148, 158

Yapen 89
Yugoslavia 97
Yukon 142, 236

Zurich 26